Women and American Television

AN ENCYCLOPEDIA

Women and American Television

AN ENCYCLOPEDIA

DENISE LOWE

ABC-CLIO

Santa Barbara, California
Denver, Colorado
Oxford, England

Library of Congress Cataloging-in-Publication Data

Lowe, Denise.
    Women and American television : an encyclopedia / Denise Lowe.
        p. cm.
    Includes bibliographical references and index.
    ISBN 0-87436-970-3
    1. Women on television. 2. Women in television broadcasting—United
    States—Encyclopedias. 3. Television serials—United States—Encyclopedias.
    I. Title.

PN1992.8.W65 L69 1999
791.45'75'08209073—dc21   99-050178

05 04 03 02 01 00 99   10 9 8 7 6 5 4 3 2 1 (cloth)

ABC-CLIO, Inc.
130 Cremona Drive, P.O. Box 1911
Santa Barbara, California 93116-1911

This book is printed on acid-free paper ∞.

Manufactured in the United States of America

Contents

Sidebar Articles

Appendixes

Preface

I am an avowed feminist, even in the decade that some nonfeminists have tried to attach all manner of negative connotations to the term. I simply recognize that women are treated differently than men in all aspects of life and seldom to their benefit.

One of the ways people are "educated" to accept this inequity is through the elements of popular culture. Films, television, advertising, books, magazines—all are agents of indoctrination. In my graduate work, I investigated the means by which covert messages are transmitted within the portrayal of female characters on television, specifically single career women.

While I was gathering my research I was struck by the lack of information about women who worked in television. Men of less repute were readily covered, but women who made real contributions were left out of so-called comprehensive references.

So while one can find volumes written about "Uncle Miltie" (Milton Berle) and Sid Caesar, there has been little written about Gertrude Berg, Chloe Aaron, and Mildred Freed Alberg. Each of these women left a lasting impression on the medium. Arguably, more of an impact than Berle and Caesar, yet most people have never heard of any of them.

As I began researching this book, I was appalled that women's professional organizations that should keep archives on previous members and notable accomplishments did not. Since I started this volume, I am happy to say that several organizations have announced that they are starting archives, but I am afraid that much information is probably lost forever.

When faced with determining the scope and criteria for this book, I, as a rabid historian, wanted to include everything that minutely pertained to women and television to make up for the previous lack of information and validation. But my editor patiently explained to me, several times, that this was not a multivolume work and that I had to *choose* the most important information to include.

So although I am sure that people and events have been left out—mostly due to inadequate reference material—I have tried to include individuals who were trendsetters or groundbreakers or cultural icons. So although Farrah Fawcett and Loni Anderson did not make a lasting impact on the medium, while they were popular, they *were* the medium to many viewers.

As for other topics in the book, I have included every series that featured a female character in a lead role that lasted at least six months. While this includes a host of seemingly insignificant programs, for some of which only a brief description could be written, television is perpetually building upon earlier series. This season's new hit might well have been inspired by a series the creator watched and enjoyed as a young person.

In addition, if a series was controversial, groundbreaking, or vastly popular—with or without a prominent female character—it was included. Sadly, several series that had excellent potential simply did not get a chance to prove themselves because excellence must be instant in the fast-paced world of television ratings.

Finally, I included important events and developments that had a lasting impact on the medium. These include governmental rulings, advances in equipment, and new technologies.

And television being television, things change so quickly that what might be the latest information today is old news tomorrow. For all the things that have changed since the book went to press, I apologize and hope that the reader appreciates that updates had to stop as the "presses rolled."

As for the people who have helped me in this undertaking—I want to thank my mother and my sister for putting up with me constantly dragging research with me on all my visits, and I can now say that all my early television viewing was just advance "research."

I want to thank my graduate advisors—Leila Zenderland and Pam Steinle—for encouraging my academic and literary efforts even when I wasn't sure I could survive the "ordeal." They were always available as sounding boards and cheerleaders.

I especially want to thank the reference librarians at the main branch of Anaheim Library. When I was unable to find some information, they always had another idea to try and often found just what I needed.

I want to thank ABC-CLIO and Todd Hallman for giving me the opportunity to write this book. I also want to thank Martin Manning for his suggestions and evaluations of ideas.

A

Aaron, Chloe (1938–)

After the Public Broadcasting Act was approved, the Corporation for Public Broadcasting was created to distribute and manage the federal funds. Because the corporation could not operate as a network, the Public Broadcasting Service (PBS) was formed to develop programs for national distribution.

In 1976, a time when women were not generally considered for executive positions in television, Chloe Aaron was named senior vice-president for programming at PBS. She was the first woman to attain the level of vice-president with PBS, and the highest-ranking woman in the television industry. A quarter of a century later, men continue to dominate the executive tier of television, and Aaron's achievement continues to be a high point in women's involvement in executive television. Aaron was responsible for choosing which programs PBS offered to public television stations throughout the country, thereby influencing millions of viewers. She approved every program seen in prime time during her tenure.

Her route to television was anything but direct. Originally, her goal was to become a drama critic, but after graduating from Occidental College with a bachelor's degree in English, she worked briefly as a researcher at Huntington Library in San Marino, California. She soon decided to pursue a master's degree in American literary cultural history at George Washington University, but interrupted her studies to travel with her new husband to his foreign-service posting in Ecuador for two years.

During that time, she helped create and managed a bilingual theater. Returning to Washington, D.C., she wrote her thesis to complete her degree, and accepted an editorial position with the *National Banking Review.*

By the end of the 1960s, Aaron had become a full-time freelance journalist with articles appearing in such publications as the *Washington Post, Washington Star,* and *New York Magazine.* As television was a hot topic during that period, she wrote more articles dealing with television than with drama. An article on the possibility of public television becoming a forum for quality films and entertainment resulted in Aaron becoming a consultant to the National Endowment for the Arts.

She developed the National Endowment Public Media Program, which funded film, television, and radio projects. She was offered the job of implementing and directing the program, and this work led to the position with PBS.

Aaron developed a plan at PBS called Common Carriage, which required stations to broadcast selected PBS programs at the same time. PBS promoted these programs in national publications, resulting in larger viewing audiences. This plan had a tremendous impact on the number of people aware of and viewing PBS offerings.

ACTION FOR CHILDREN'S TELEVISION

In 1968, Action for Children's Television (ACT) was founded by Peggy Charren and a group of people concerned with the extensive commercial product tie-ins and poor quality of children's programming. The group petitioned networks and took legal action to force improvement in programs produced for children.

After being pretty much ignored by the three major networks, ACT lobbied the Federal Communications Commission (FCC), the federal entity that regulates the television industry. Reacting to citizens' complaints, in 1971 the FCC created a permanent unit focusing on the issues of children's television.

After continued efforts by ACT, in 1973 the National Association of Broadcasters issued guidelines that prohibited host-selling of products and limited commercial time during children's programs. Unfortunately, most of the pro-ACT decisions were made by bodies unable to enforce the rulings, and broadcast cooperation continues to be voluntary.

In July 1992, ACT was dissolved.

See also Charren, Peggy; Educational Programming.

ACTION/ADVENTURE GENRE

The action/adventure genre, which got its start with *Martin Kane, Private Eye* (1949–1954) and *The Plainclothesman* (1949–1954), has been predominantly occupied by men throughout the history of television. From 1958 through the 1960s, a formula was used, beginning with *77 Sunset Strip* (1958–1964), a drama featuring two former government agents turned private detectives.

This program and its imitators relegated women to window dressing, as reflected in the formula used by the imitators: "two parts private eye, one part cutie pie." *77 Sunset Strip* had beautiful switchboard operator Suzanne (Jacqueline Beer, 1958–1963) and later, secretary Hannah (Joan Staley, 1963–1964). *Hawaiian Eye* (1959–1963) featured perky photographer/singer Cricket (Connie Stevens), *Bourbon Street Beat* (1959–1960) had gorgeous secretary Melody (Arlene Howell), and *Surfside Six* (1960–1962) boasted nightclub entertainer Cha-Cha (Margarita Sierra). As late as the mid-1970s, the two private eyes on *Switch* (1975–1978) had receptionist/assistant Maggie (Sharon Gless).

Of course, a few exceptions to this formula could be found. *Honey West* (1965–1966) was a no-nonsense female private eye (Anne Francis) who inherited a detective agency from her father, and Mrs. Emma Peel (Diana Rigg) of *The Avengers* (1966–1969) was sophisticated as well as brilliant and lethal. In *The Girl from U.N.C.L.E.* (1967–1968), a spinoff of the cult hit *The Man from U.N.C.L.E.*, April Dancer (Stefanie Powers) was the able and creative female agent who fought the agents of the evil conspiracy T.H.R.U.S.H. A few years later, *Get Christie Love* (1974–1975), featuring *Laugh-In* alumna

Teresa Graves in the title role, was panned by many because Detective Love was too forceful and independent (thereby unfeminine).

On successful shows, women were generally casted to be saved and/or to look good. On the first incarnation of *Mission: Impossible* (1966–1973), Cinnamon Carter (Barbara Bain) was usually a glamorous decoy and/or bait. Although *Charlie's Angels* (1976–1981) allowed the Angels to be central to the action, any illusion of power was nullified by their dress, or often lack thereof, and the ever-present male authorities—Charlie and, to a lesser degree, Bosley.

However, 1976 brought the premiere of a female-centered show in which the woman was active yet feminine, if not completely human. In *The Bionic Woman* (1976–1978), Jamie Somers (Lindsay Wagner) actively fought criminals and spies, aided by the superiority of her bionic body parts. During this same period (1976–1981), *Wonder Woman* (Lynda Carter) fought Nazis in the 1940s and, in a shift to modern times, terrorists and other criminal types. An Amazon warrior-princess who was sent by her mother, the queen, to protect mankind, Wonder Woman was equal to any challenge and routinely bested the criminals who wanted to control the world. By virtue of better-than-human personas, both these women were given a leeway that mortal women would not have been granted.

Also seen during the same general period, Ernesta (Helen Hayes) and Gwen (Mildred Natwick) Snoop, septuagenarian mystery writers, used their fiction crime experience to solve real crimes that baffled the police on *The Snoop*

(continued on next page)

(continued from previous page)

Sisters (1973–1974). Several years later, *The Feather and Father Gang* (1977) featured Toni "Feather" Danton (Stefanie Powers) as an attorney who, with her father, Harry (Harold Gould), a former con man, and his "associates," used disguises and elaborate stings to con the con artists.

The *Hart to Hart* (1979–1984) movie series offered a sophisticated mystery-solving couple—a formula that proved successful in such films as *The Thin Man*. This version had freelance author-photographer Jennifer Hart (Stefanie Powers) and her millionaire husband, Jonathan (Robert Wagner).

Another popular series featuring an amateur detective was *Murder, She Wrote* (1984–1997) in which mystery writer Jessica Fletcher (Angela Lansbury) was forever finding dead bodies or thrust into mysterious circumstances. Although well into her golden years, Jessica worked through the often convoluted plots one step ahead of the authorities. When the series went off the air, the popular character returned in several made-for-TV movies.

In one of NBC's *Thrillogy* series, *The Pretender* (1996–), Miss Parker (Andrea Parker) is in charge of capturing the elusive Jarod (Michael T. Weiss), the genius who escaped from the think tank run by her father. More recently, on *Charmed* (1998–) the three Halliwell sisters use their magical powers to thwart evildoers who cross their paths.

Interestingly, one exception to the not-too-active female portrayal favored by television networks is animated women. Animated (thereby unreal) women have always been allowed to be forceful and self-directed. *She-Ra* (premiered 1985) was an action hero in her own right, and Lady Jaye of the third incarnation of *G.I. Joes* (premiered 1985) was very much her own person, willing *and* able to fight the evil COBRA forces. More recently, on the live-action cartoon series, two of the Power Rangers are girls and Princess Deidre is one of the Mystic Knights of Tir Na Nog. Even in these cartoons, it is made very clear that all these characters are special, and therefore exceptions.

See also Animated Women; *The Avengers; Beauty and the Beast; The Bionic Woman; Charlie's Angels; Charmed; Get Christie Love; The Girl from U.N.C.L.E.; Hart to Hart; Honey West; Murder, She Wrote; The Snoop Sisters; Xena, Warrior Princess; Wonder Woman.*

Adato, Perry Miller (1935–)

Perry Miller Adato received a Director's Guild of America (DGA) award for her 1977 PBS documentary *Georgia O'Keeffe*, becoming the first woman to do so. She later won DGA awards for her features on Carl Sandburg (*Echoes and Silences*, 1982) and Eugene O'Neill (*Eugene O'Neill: A Glory of Ghosts*, 1986).

She began her career as organizer and director of the Film Advertising Center in New York City, and then became a film consultant and researcher for CBS in New York City. Eventually, she became producer and director of cultural documentaries for the national production division of WNET in New York City.

Born in Yonkers, New York, Adato attended Marshalov School for Drama as well as the New School for Social Research, both in New York City. In 1984 she received an honorary doctorate (L.H.D.) from Illinois Wesleyan University.

Alberg, Mildred Freed (1921–)

Mildred Freed Alberg was the producer responsible for bringing quality programs to network television with the creation of a series that became known as *The Hallmark Hall of Fame.*

Alberg was born in Montreal, Quebec. Unable to attend college because of family financial difficulties, in 1939 she went to New York City and parlayed a job as typist into a position on a ghost-writing team. During World War II, she wrote public service announcements and radio dramatizations. After the war, she worked for the newly formed relief organization, CARE, and was promoted to director of information in 1947. To raise awareness of the organization and the need for humanitarian aid, she produced dramatic vignettes based on CARE case histories.

In 1950, Alberg began her campaign to bring classic, high-quality drama to television. On 26 April 1953, NBC broadcast the first dramatization of what would become *The Hallmark Hall of Fame* with a two-hour presentation of *Hamlet,* starring Maurice Evans, the renowned British Shakespearean actor and later Samantha Stevens's father on *Bewitched* (1964– 1972). In that one evening, more people saw *Hamlet* than during all the years since its creation.

Alberg remained executive producer of *The Hallmark Hall of Fame* until 1959, when her production company, Milberg, began producing *Our American Heritage* specials showcasing pivotal events in the lives of famous Americans such as Thomas Jefferson, Ulysses S. Grant, and Andrew Carnegie. The series, which continued until 1961, received an Emmy and was named "outstanding educational program of 1959."

After several years of working in the theater and on films, Alberg returned to television in the early 1970s to produce archeologically enhanced biblical narratives (*Jacob and Joseph* in 1974 and *The Story of David* in 1976). During the same period, she produced her first documentary for PBS, *The Royal Archives of Elba,* which explored a "library" of 17,000 stone fragments and tablets discovered in the early 1970s.

Alberg retired from television production in the early 1980s, but her work speaks of a quality possible, yet rarely seen, on television.

See also *Hallmark Hall of Fame.*

Alice (1976–1985)

Alice starred Linda Lavin as a widowed mother waitressing in Mel's Diner while trying to attain her dream of becoming a country singer. Based on the 1975 hit movie, *Alice Doesn't Live Here Anymore,* the series was hailed as a realistic depiction of the life of a blue-collar working woman. As often happens with television, Lavin became closely associated with her character, and she joined the campaign to achieve rights for working women. In 1977 she received the Grass Roots Award from the National Commission on Working Women for her realistic depiction of the character Alice Hyatt.

In addition to Mel (Vic Tayback), the diner's owner, the original cast also included outspoken Flo (Polly Holliday) and naive Vera (Beth Howland) as the diner's other waitresses. The series dealt mostly with interpersonal issues in typical sitcom fashion, but it also demonstrated a group of women who were supportive and caring of one another, even though very different temperamentally.

In 1980, Flo left for her own series and Belle was introduced. Played by Diane Ladd (who had played Flo in the movie), the character was Flo with a different accent. In 1981, Belle was replaced by Jolene (Celia Weston) to retain the female triumvirate.

In the final episode, Mel sold the diner and gave each of the waitresses a $5,000 bonus. The windfall enabled Alice to move to Nashville with her band, Jolene to open a beauty shop, and Vera, who had married during the 1983 season and was now pregnant, to become a full-time mother.

See also Careers for Women on Television.

All in the Family (1971–1983)

Based on the British series *Till Death Do Us Part, All in the Family* was the first of Norman Lear's reality programs that would change the look of the sitcom world from one of happy equilibrium to a less than perfect world. The popular series focused on the lives of the Bunker family, headed by bigoted, uneducated Archie (Carroll O'Connor), who had no problem expressing his prejudices. He was often held in check—and upstaged—by his wife, Edith (Jean Stapleton). Archie often called her Dingbat, but Edith's naive utterances often reflected her own style of wisdom.

Their childlike daughter, Gloria (Sally Struthers), was married to graduate student Michael Stivic (Rob Reiner). Not only was he a liberal, he was a "Polack," called Meathead by his disgusted father-in-law. Much of the program's humor revolved around verbal confrontations between Archie and Meathead.

By 1980 the original premise of the show had changed. The Stivic family (with baby Joey) had moved to California and Edith had died. The action now centered exclusively around the bar that Archie purchased during the 1978–1979 season and the regulars who stopped in.

Unlike most series, *All in the Family*–cum–*Archie's Place* remained a hit, weathering all the cast changes and focal shifts. Now available on video, the series lives on as an example of early reality TV.

Allen, Debbie (1950–)

After appearing in such Broadway plays as *Purlie* (1972), *Raisin* (1973), and *Ain't Misbehavin'* (1978), Debbie Allen turned to television and appeared in varied programs such as *Roots: The Next Generations* (1979), episodes of *The Love Boat* (1977–1986), and *The Cosby Show* (1984–1992). In 1986, Allen returned to Broadway and appeared in a revival of *Sweet Charity*, for which she received a Tony nomination.

She is perhaps best known as producer, choreographer, and star of *Fame* (network, 1982–1983; original episode syndication, 1983–1987), a series dealing with the lives of students and faculty at the famous High School for the Performing Arts in New York City. She played dance instructor Lydia Grant, a role she reprised from the movie on which the series was based, and for which she won two Emmys.

In 1988, after a disappointing first season, Allen was asked to produce and direct the *Cosby* spinoff *A Different World* (1987–1993). As a 1971 graduate of prestigious Howard University in Washington, D.C., she had firsthand experience of life at a black college. Under her direction, the series explored social problems within the nonthreatening environment of a sitcom.

While working on *A Different World*, Allen directed the pilot for *Fresh Prince of Bel Air* (1990–1996) and did the choreography for five Academy Awards broadcasts (1991–1995). She directed the TV musical *Polly*, an all-black revival of the Pollyanna story, and its sequel, *Polly: One More Time.* In 1995 she appeared in the sitcom *In the House* as a single mom, Jackie Warren. This formerly wealthy woman rented a house from a football player, Marion (LL Cool J), who eventually became her children's nanny while recovering from an injury that had him sidelined.

In addition to directing episodes of the *Jamie Foxx Show* (1996–) and *Between Brothers* (1997–1998), some of her most recent projects include codirecting Steven Spielberg's film *Amistad* (1997), which deals with a mutiny in 1839 by Africans aboard a slave ship. She also produced two *Amistad*-related documentaries, *Cinque: Freedom Fighter* for A&E, and *Ships of Slaves: The Middle Passage,* for the History Channel.

Allen directed and choreographed *Brothers of the Night,* which opened in April 1998 at the Kennedy Center in Washington, D.C. She appeared as Harriet Tubman in the play *Harriet's Return* (1998), and produced and directed *One Day,* a musical special commemorating Dr. Martin Luther King, for Black History Month for the Disney Channel.

See also Black Female Roles.

Allen, Gracie (1906–1964)

Born Gracie Ethel Cecile Rosalie into a vaudevillian family, Gracie Allen had years of performing experience before she met and created an act with George Burns. Her first stage appearance was at age six, and she performed solo or with her sisters until 1922, when she joined Burns, whom she married in 1926. Allen was originally the straight man for Burns, but the couple soon realized that she got laughs no matter what she said. They reorganized the act and became hits—first in vaudeville, then on radio and in films, and eventually on television.

Her breathless, irrational, oxymoronic ramblings were a type of verbalized screwball comedy. She took statements literally and responded, seemingly, with whatever came into her mind. The character she created was enchantingly offbeat, and her illogical statements always seemed to have a whimsical logic. Both Allen and the character she portrayed were so popular that in 1939 she was the first actress to have a movie named for her, *The Gracie Allen Murder Case.*

The *George Burns and Gracie Allen Show* (1950–1958) premiered on CBS in the fall of 1950. Set in the Burnses' home, Burns acted as both on-screen narrator/observer and Allen's straight man in situations that oc-curred because Gracie misunderstood an event or conversation. The show was still extremely popular when it ended because of Allen's ill health. She died in 1964, and is one of the few women inducted into the Academy of Television Arts and Sciences' Hall of Fame.

Allison, Fran (1924–1989)

The on-stage human component of the popular children's show *Kukla, Fran & Ollie* (1952–1957, 1969–1971, 1975), Fran Allison was a singer and radio actress before joining Burr Tillstrom's two puppets in 1947. She re-mained with the show until it went off the air in its final incarnation in 1975. Allison was perfectly at ease conversing with the perpetually worried Kukla or the carefree dragon Ollie, or any of the other Kuklapolitan Play-ers (Fletcher Rabbit, Beulah Witch, Col. Crackie, Mercedes, Cecil Bill, or Mme. Ophelia Oglepuss). The show focused on everyday experiences but also offered songs and full-dress plays and operettas.

Concurrently with her work on *Kukla, Fran & Ollie*, Allison appeared on the *Breakfast Club* (1954–1955), a staple on radio for 35 years that failed in its television effort. Allison appeared as Aunt Fanny, a gossipy character who dressed in an exaggerated rural style.

After the demise of *Kukla, Fran & Ollie*, Allison appeared in commer-cials and on quiz shows. In the early 1980s she hosted her own senior-citizen talk show in Los Angeles.

See also *Kukla, Fran & Ollie*.

All's Fair (1976–1977)

The series dealt with the May-December romance between freelance pho-tographer Charlotte "Charley" Drake (Bernadette Peters) and political col-umnist Richard Barrington (Richard Crenna). The comedy revolved around the problems stereotypically associated with this type of relationship (Richard was 49 and Charley was 23) and the differences in opinions on government and just about everything else between liberal Charley and conservative Richard.

The Washington, D.C., setting provided ample issues for the couple to disagree about, but love always won by the end of the episode. Eventually,

Richard became a special assistant to President Carter. One poignant episode dealt with how the couple would handle Charley becoming pregnant, but in typical sitcom fashion the dilemma solved itself when Charley fell, causing her to miscarry.

Ally McBeal (1997–)

Unlike previous legal series, this program focuses on the real, surreal, and imaginary professional and personal events in the life of a young female attorney, Ally McBeal (Calista Flockhart, in her first television role). Premiering on Fox's fall 1997 schedule, the offbeat comedy with its occasional doses of drama quickly became one of the season's hits. The series, written by David E. Kelley, garnered critical acclaim, three Golden Globes (best comedy and best actress for Flockhart in 1997 and best comedy in 1998), and several popularity-driven awards.

Calista Flockhart with the cast of Ally McBeal *at the 1999 Screen Actors Guild Awards telecast.* Ally McBeal *won this award for Outstanding Performance by an Ensemble in a Comedy Series. (Corbis/AFP)*

Ally is portrayed as legally talented, but quirky and basically insecure. After being sexually harassed by a colleague, she quits the firm and joins a law firm run by a legally inept, ethically malleable, and often morally destitute classmate, Richard Fish (Greg Germann). Unbeknownst to her, however, her childhood sweetheart, college lover, and motivation for attending law school, Billy (Gil Bellows), has already agreed to work for the firm. While Ally is still reeling from coming face-to-face with her love-that-got-away and the fact that he had married in the interim, Billy's wife, Georgia (Courtney Thorne-Smith), also joins the firm.

On a weekly basis the audience is privy to Ally's thoughts and fantasies, as well as the overt action dealing with the interpersonal dynamics among characters as well as the more obvious legal cases taken by the firm. Ally's rich inner life is depicted by computer-generated effects that add quirkiness to the show. One of the most popular effects of the first season was the "dancing baby" (a manifestation of Ally's ticking biological clock), which had its own site on the World Wide Web.

In a TV first, on 27 April 1998, an uncharacteristically serious episode dealt with a client facing a murder charge. Since none of the firm's attorneys was qualified to handle it, attorneys were brought in from across town to assist them with the trial. The assisting attorneys were the grimly realistic lawyers from David E. Kelley's ABC series *The Practice* (1997–). The story that began on *Ally McBeal* concluded that same night on *The Practice* during the next hour on ABC.

At the beginning of the 1998–1999 season, two new characters were added to the quirky legal firm: Nelle Porter (Portia de Rossi) and Ling Woo (Lucy Liu). Nell is a talented if sometimes too somber attorney brought into the firm by Richard as a "rainmaker." Ling, a client brought in by Nell, was initially extremely unpopular with everyone in the office except Fish, who began dating her. After the attorneys learned that she had edited a law review and possessed a good legal mind, Ling was invited to join the firm, over the objections of Ally and Georgia.

Although not an actress, singer-songwriter Vonda Shepard is seen and/or heard weekly when she supplies background vocals and performs during the scenes that take place in the bar downstairs from the office. The series' theme is a song that Shepard, called "Ally McBeal's muse" by some, wrote in 1992 entitled "Searchin' My Soul," and she released an *Ally McBeal* soundtrack in May 1998.

See also Careers for Women on Television.

Amanda (1949–)

The first network daytime series hosted by a black woman, this early offering on the Dumont network featured actress Amanda Randolph singing both hymns and more modern songs. The 15-minute program appeared on WABD before moving to Dumont.

See also Black Female Roles, Variety Programs.

Amanpour, Christiane (1959–)

Christiane Amanpour is perhaps the most highly visible news correspondent today. Unlike many of her sister reporters, Amanpour elected to remain "in the trenches" and report by satellite from many of the hottest news spots in the world—Northern Ireland, Yugoslavia, Croatia, Bosnia-Herzegovina, South Africa, Afghanistan, Pakistan, Iran, Israel, and Somalia.

TV screen shot of CNN journalist Christiane Amanpour during a 1998 interview with Iranian president Mohammad Khatami. (Reuters/CNN/Archive Photos)

While working as a reporter for *60 Minutes* in 1983, Amanpour also worked for Cable Network News (CNN). In 1993, Amanpour was awarded a Peabody for her "balanced and courageous coverage of world crises for a global audience." In 1998, she parlayed her experience into a reported $2 million contract to continue working as a foreign correspondent for CNN as well as being a special contributor for *60 Minutes.*

Amanpour was raised in London after her family fled Iran when Khomeini seized power. She attended the University of Rhode Island and settled in Paris when not on assignment.

See also News.

Anderson, Gillian

See *The X-Files*

Anderson, Loni (1945–)

Loni Anderson played Jennifer Marlowe on *WKRP in Cincinnati* (1978–1982), the efficient receptionist–office manager. Although her role was mostly sexy window dressing, the character was depicted as intelligent rather than as a typical sexy screwball or dumb blonde. An ensemble program, the series was very popular, if rather mundane. Its major selling point was Anderson, who became one of the sex symbols of the late 1970s; her posters were seen everywhere.

Anderson's popularity led to many guest appearances and a few made-for-TV movies, most notably one on the life of Jayne Mansfield, the sex symbol from the 1950s. Anderson married Burt Reynolds and became fodder for the tabloids. After their much-publicized divorce, she briefly returned to series television as ambitious administrator Casey MacAfee on *Nurses* (1991–1994) during its final season.

Angel (1960–1961)

Angel (Annie Farge) was a French immigrant newly married to John Smith (Marshall Thompson). The series' humor derived from Angel's attempt to adjust to the American way of life and her frequent misunderstandings of everyday situations and the English language.

Angie (1979–1980)

Highly popular in its first season, this series was a standardized Cinderella story of a waitress, Angie Falco (Donna Pescow), from a blue-collar Italian family. She met and married a blue-blooded doctor, Brad Benson (Robert Hayes). Predictably, the humor centered on adjustments to married life and interfering in-laws.

Created by Garry Marshall and originally titled *After Once upon a Time,* the series exhausted the humor of poor-girl-marries-well by the end of the first season. Changes were made in the second season in hopes of saving the series, but as often happens, the change in format brought an end to the show.

The series was the first sitcom for Donna Pescow, who later appeared in the syndicated comedy *Out of This World* (1987–1991) as the mother, Donna Garland, of a teenage daughter, Evie (Maureen Flannigan), whose father was from another planet. Being part alien, Evie was endowed with certain supernatural powers such as stopping time and materializing objects at will.

ANIMATED WOMEN

Animated women were originally restricted to early-morning or afternoon children's cartoons. Female characters generally were included only as damsels-in-distress to be saved or to draw young girls to otherwise boy-centered series. Examples include Betty and Veronica in the various incarnations of the popular comic book *Archie,* as well as long-suffering Nell in *Dudley Do-Right* and Olive Oyl in *Popeye.* Females were subtly shown their place, as with Sue Richards of *The Fantastic Four.* Although married to Reed Richards (Mr. Fantastic), she was still called "Invisible GIRL."

Of course, not all cartoon females appeared as stereotyped characters. Wonder Woman and Spiderwoman were independent women and active crime-fighters. Sabrina, a teenage witch, solved problems as well as caused trouble. Perhaps the most positive female characterization was that of Velma in the various versions of *Scooby-Doo.* She was the brains and problem-solver of the group, and although the other female in the group, Daphne, was more window dressing, both were important to the story plots.

Another action-oriented female was incredibly wealthy Goldie Gold of *Goldie Gold and Action Jack* (1981–1982). Although she was the publisher of the *Gold Street Journal,* her real interest was investigating unusual occurrences and embarking on exciting adventures accompanied by reporter/bodyguard Jack Travis and her labrador, Nugget. *(continued on next page)*

(continued from previous page)

Perhaps the most powerful female cartoon character was *She-Ra, Princess of Power* (1985–1986). The show was a spinoff of *He-Man*, as she was actually Adam's twin sister, Adora, except when her magic sword transformed her into She-Ra to battle with the evil forces of Hordak. She fought her own battles and outwitted the villains bent on taking over her planet, Eternia.

One of the few women to join the ranks of *G.I. Joes* (premiered 1985), Lady Jaye was a member of an antiterrorist group that battled the forces of COBRA. Brave and resourceful, she was a competent opponent for the evil COBRA commander's forces.

In September 1997, a short-lived, female-centered cartoon, produced in France, was introduced on Saturday mornings: *The Legend of Calamity Jane*. With typical creative license, the series focuses on historical figure Martha Jane Cannary and her fictionalized exploits in the Old West. Unlike the real Calamity Jane, the cartoon character was beautiful, virginal, and devoted herself to helping people. Again, unlike the real Calamity, who was an expert shot, the cartoon Calamity uses a bullwhip and was committed to the Comanche Indian tribe who (in the cartoon) raised her.

PRIME-TIME CARTOONS

The first cartoon to hit prime time was the 1959 introduction of *Rocky and Bullwinkle* (later *The Bullwinkle Show*), with one of its chief villains being the Russian femme fatale Natasha Fataly. She was not a successful spy, but often appeared more intelligent than her partner, Boris Badenov.

The Flintstones (1960–1966), a stone-age version of *The Honeymooners*, premiered the next year. Central to this consumer goods–laden environment was the idealized 1950s wife in the characters of Wilma Flintstone and neighbor, Betty Rubble.

Following the popularity of *The Flintstones*, *The Jetsons* (1962–1963) was introduced, again featuring the ideal mom of the future, Jane Jetson. Jane efficiently and lovingly cared for her family, expressing few if any interests beyond her family's well-being.

Prime-time cartoons faded from the screen until the introduction of that blatantly dysfunctional family, *The Simpsons*, in 1989. The show deals with the seemingly idyllic, but deeply flawed, town of Springfield and the always unlucky Simpson family who lives there. Throughout the chaos, the mother, Marge, plays peacemaker and faces every trauma with the admonition "Just smile."

Two other females who challenged prime time were Aeon Flux and Daria Morgendorffer. Originally part of MTV's *Liquid Television, Aeon Flux* (1995–1996) was a science-fictionish program that featured the fashionable, if androgynous, Aeon. *Daria*, also on MTV, is a spinoff of the moronic series *Beavis and Butthead*, and premiered as its own program in 1997. Daria is an intelligent 16-year-old girl who can't find her niche in her family or the larger world. Her parents are overwhelmed by their oldest daughter and life in general, and her younger sister, Quinn, is the stereotypical dumb-blonde-in-training.

ANTHOLOGY HOSTESSES

Dramatic anthologies were extremely popular in the early years of television. In 1951, 16 nonepisodic programs of classic or original plays aired weekly. These anthologies marked the height of the golden age of drama on television that ruled the medium's first decade.

These anthologies, many of which were named for corporate sponsors (*Philco Playhouse, U.S. Steel Hour,* and *General Electric Theatre*), brought many female movie stars to the fledgling enterprise. The networks hoped to attract viewers by using established, recognizable names as hostesses (and often uncredited producers) of these 30-minute dramas.

Loretta Young hosted one of the longest-running anthology series and brought a refinement to television as she floated on-screen in beautiful evening gowns to introduce, and often star in, the evening's presentation on *The Loretta Young Show* (1953–1961). These plays were all uplifting and expressed prosocial views, each ending with Young reading a poem or passage from the Bible to restate the play's message.

Lesser-known anthologies hosted by women included *The Barbara Stanwyck Show* (1960–1961), featuring serious dramas in which Stanwyck starred (all but four). Another popular anthology hostess was Jane Wyman, who hosted *The Fireside Theatre* (later renamed *The Jane Wyman Show*) from 1955 to 1958 and starred in many of the plays. June Allyson hosted *The Dupont Show with June Allyson* (1959–1961) and occasionally starred in the plays in the series that reflected contemporary American life. Although the series did not achieve the critical success of other anthologies, fine dramas were produced, proving the appropriateness of film to the new medium.

Anthologies lost popularity as television became more widely broadcast. Originally viewed in more culturally aware urban areas, television soon reached a larger audience, and some feel that quality was sacrificed for wider mass appeal. When anthologies stopped bringing potential consumers to the sponsors, they were replaced by programs that could. The tradition of quality dramatic presentations is continued by the programs *Hallmark Hall of Fame, Mobil Masterpiece Theatre,* and *Mystery!*

See also Young, Loretta.

The Ann Sothern Show (1958–1961)

This television series is one of many in which a woman's ability is not recognized as powerful in its own right, but must be subverted in the role of helpmate to a man. Not surprisingly, it showed the competence of a woman in a situation comedy, which allowed the audience to laugh at the woman rather than feel threatened by her.

After working as assistant manager of the Bartley House Hotel in New York, Katy O'Connor (Ann Sothern) was passed over for the position of manager when her boss was transferred to California and replaced by James Devery (Don Porter) as the new manager. The humor derived from the problems inherent in running a big-city hotel.

See also Careers for Women on Television.

Annie Oakley (1953–1956)

The television series *Annie Oakley* was loosely based on the historical figure. Pigtailed Annie (Gail Davis) was a crack shot ready to confront any bad man near Diablo, where she lived with her younger brother, Tagg (Jimmy Hawkins). Her partner in fighting, and platonic suitor, was Deputy Lofty Craig (Brad Johnson).

This series was one of the few within the Western genre that allowed a woman to be forceful and self-sufficient. Most women in Western series were either window dressing or dependent on men for protection.

See also Davis, Gail.

Any Day Now (1998–)

Using the advertising trailer "two different lives, one incredible friendship," *Any Day Now* follows the friendship of Mary Elizabeth O'Brian, known as M.E. (Annie Potts), and Rene Jackson (Lorraine Toussaint), who grew up together in Alabama in the 1960s. Even though their skins were of different colors, their friendship withstood the hate and prejudice around them until they came to an irreconcilable difference and went their separate ways.

In 1998, Rene returns to her hometown and the two women rebuild their friendship. M.E. is now married with children, and Rene is a successful lawyer. The series includes flashbacks to the young M.E. (Mae Middleton) and Rene (Shari Dyon Perry).

Anything but Love (1989–1992)

A typical opposites-attract comedy, *Anything but Love* featured the calm and cheerful Hannah Miller (Jamie Lee Curtis), who dreamed of being a writer, and the neurotic, disorganized investigative reporter Marty Gold (Richard Lewis). The humor derived from the development of their relationship and mutual understanding as they worked across from each other at *Chicago Weekly* magazine. Adding to the mix was the usual assortment of slightly strange friends and coworkers always found in urban-based sitcoms.

By the second season, Hannah and Marty decided that they were in love. Sadly, as is often the case, the chemistry between the two characters was better and sharper before they became romantically involved.

Applegate, Jody (1963–)

As the new anchor on MSNBC, coanchor of *Weekend Today,* and frequent stand-in anchor on *The Today Show* (1952–), Jody Applegate is being groomed by NBC to become a major news presence of the future. Applegate's affiliation with MSNBC points to a well-rooted future with a network that has a track record of promoting female anchors.

After graduating from New York University, Applegate did some acting and commercial work. She worked briefly for a radio station before moving to C-SPAN as reporter and anchor. She briefly appeared on a now-defunct health series at NBC, *Dr. Dean,* before moving to San Francisco for a traffic-reporting job at KRON-TV.

Her big break came as anchor of *Good Morning Arizona* out of KTVK in Phoenix. With the success of this series, Applegate was called up to *Weekend Today.*

See also News.

The Autobiography of Miss Jane Pittman (1974)

The Autobiography of Miss Jane Pittman, based on the novel by Ernest Gaines, is one of the programs the television industry points to with pride when trying to justify some of their lesser offerings. Starring Cicely Tyson as Jane Pittman, the two-hour drama traced Pittman's life from slavery to old age during the civil rights movement of the 1960s. The poignant movie ends with a powerful statement as the now-ancient woman drinks from a water fountain marked "For Whites Only."

The movie was a critical success and attracted a large viewing audience. It won nine Emmy awards, including outstanding special, best actress (Tyson), actress of the year (Tyson), best direction of a special, and best writing adaptation for a drama.

See also Tyson, Cicely.

ASIAN WOMEN

Television is purported to be a medium of the white middle class, so the characters portrayed are predominantly white—and, most often, male. Ethnic minorities, especially females, were virtually nonexistent until recently. Asian women in long-running or leading roles are still extremely rare.

One of the first Asian women to appear in a recurring role on a popular series was Miyoshi Umeki, who played Mrs. Livingston on *The Courtship of Eddie's Father* (1969–1972). Her character, the philosophical housekeeper, was always deferential to "Mr. Eddie's father," yet she was also Eddie's nurturing surrogate mother.

The next major series with an Asian female character was *All-American Girl* (1994–1995), which featured an almost exclusively Asian cast. It starred stand-up comic Margaret Cho as Margaret Kim, the nontraditional young Korean-American whose likes and ideas clashed with her mother's (Jodi Long) traditional hopes and dreams for her daughter. The scene-stealer was the hip grandmother (Amy Hill), who generally sided with her granddaughter.

In 1996, HBO premiered *Arli$$* which featured Sandra Oh as Rita, the ambitious executive assistant to an amoral sports agent, Arliss

Michaels (Robert Wuhl). Rita is willing to do whatever is necessary to accomplish her goal and become successful.

The 1997 season introduced a few new Asian-American characters in supporting roles on established series. Kelly Hu, a former Miss Teen USA, was cast as task-oriented Detective Michelle Chan on *Nash Bridges* (1996–). Amy Hill joined the cast of *Naked Truth* (1995–1998) as a Korean-American photographer, and Lauren Tom was added to the cast of *Grace under Fire* (1993–1997).

The 1998 season brought new Asian characters to television. Ling Woo (Lucy Liu) joined the cast of *Ally McBeal* (1997–) as the difficult client turned coworker when she revealed that she passed the bar exam but never bothered to practice. Kelly Hu moved to the new CBS series *Martial Law* (1998–) as Grace Chen, a Hong Kong police officer and martial arts expert assigned to work in Los Angeles.

Lesser-known or nonrecurring roles exist for Asian women, but Asians of both sexes are grossly underrepresented on television. Unfortunately, until advertisers view Asians as a viable purchasing group, the possibility of consistent visibility is scant.

The Avengers (1965–1969)

The Avengers was probably the most popular televisual British import in a decade of British-mania. Produced for five years in Britain before it premiered in the United States, the series focused on the suave, unflappable secret agent John Steed (Patrick Macnee) and his various female partners. His original partner (not seen in the United States) was Cathy Gale (Honor Blackman, who played Pussy Galore in the James Bond movie *Goldfin-*

Diana Rigg practices judo with her fighting coach while preparing for her role as Emma Peel on the television series The Avengers, *1965. (Corbis/Bettmann)*

ger), but his partner when the series began its American run was Mrs. Emma Peel (Diana Rigg), the cool, extremely competent "talented amateur" who joined Steed in his battle with the always bizarre forces of evil.

The chemistry between the two characters, while not explicitly sexual, brought an added edge to the series. Steed was the very proper British gentleman, and Mrs. Peel caught the attention of young viewers as a perfect, if unattainable, role model for females during the fledgling years of the twentieth century's second wave of feminism. Beyond being beautiful, Mrs. Peel was elegant, independent, and intellectually brilliant. She was as comfortable reading a treatise on higher mathematics as reading a road map. She was an expert at cipher, spoke many languages, and was a black belt in karate.

In a decade when American young people couldn't get enough of anything British, Mrs. Peel made leather jumpsuits and jackboots look elegant and stylish. She could take care of herself in almost any situation, never losing her "proper British" calm, and often saved Steed from the clutches of evildoers.

Sadly for the series fans, on 20 March 1968, Mrs. Peel left the series after her husband, long thought dead, returned. She was replaced by Tara King (Linda Thorson), but the magic was gone and the series slowly faded into sporadic syndicated reruns.

After a long hiatus from television, Diana Rigg, the most popular of Steed's partners, returned as the host of PBS's *Mystery!* series and made occasional appearances in quality productions such as the 1997 remake of *Rebecca* for *Mobil Masterpiece Theatre*.

See also Action/Adventure Genre.

B

Babes (1990–1991)

This series was unusual as all three of the stars were extremely overweight. The episodes revolved around the three Gilbert sisters in Manhattan— Darlene (Susan Peretz), the eldest, was a divorced dog groomer; Charlene (Wendie Jo Sperber) was an outgoing makeup artist; and Marlene (Lesley Boone) was the trusting and naive baby sister. In the beginning, weight and the logistics of three large individuals living in a studio apartment were the source of the jokes, but eventually humor came from their social and work lives. This series and its innovative cast appeared on the fledgling Fox network during the period when the network was trying to find its "voice."

Babylon 5 (1994–1999)

Set on a space station beginning in the year 2258, this series featured two female central characters: Commander Susan Ivanova (Caludia Christian) was the second in command of the military forces who controlled the station, while Delenn (Mira Furlan) was the Minbari ambassador who emerged from her hibernation cocoon as a new species and eventually fell in love with the station's military commander, John Sheridan (Bruce Boxleitner).

Bacall, Lauren (1924–)

Lauren Bacall, a native New Yorker, enrolled in the American Academy of Dramatic Arts when she was 15. She was accorded immediate star status after appearing in her first movie, *To Have or Have Not* (1944), and starred in several other Bogart films (*The Big Sleep,* 1946; *Dark Passage,* 1947; *Key Largo,* 1948). Bacall also appeared with Bogart in his only television appearance: a re-creation of his film role in *The Petrified Forest* on *Producer's Showcase* in 1955.

Bacall appeared in dramatic presentations on *Ford Star Jubilee* and *Dupont Show of the Month* as well as episodic television and specials, but the majority of her post-Bogart work has been on Broadway or in films.

In addition to her feature films, Bacall starred in several TV movies, beginning with *Perfect Gentlemen* in 1978. Her most recent television appearances include the remake of *Dinner at Eight* (1989), *A Little Piece of Sunshine* (1990), *The Portrait* (1993), and *From the Mixed-Up Files of Mrs. Basil E. Frankweiler* (1995). She has also done the voice-over on many commercials for products, the most recent of which was for Fancy Feast cat food. She has written two autobiographies, *Myself* (1978) and *Lauren Bacall Now* (1994).

Ball, Lucille (1911–1989)

One of the most recognized faces in the world belongs to a woman known to millions simply as Lucy. Lucille Ball went from waitress and salesgirl to model to Goldwyn Girl to radio clown to unlikely leading lady in a groundbreaking sitcom that is still seen in regular syndicated reruns more than 40 years after the series ended. Beyond being a television legend, she was the first woman president of a major Hollywood studio—a studio she cofounded.

Ball left home at 15 to study drama in New York City with such acting powerhouses as Bette Davis. While waiting for her big break, she modeled under the name Diane Belmont until she was virtually bedridden for three years by rheumatoid arthritis. After a near-miraculous recovery, she returned to New York and became the Chesterfield Girl for the cigarette company's advertising campaign. This exposure brought her to the attention of Hollywood, and she headed west to try her luck with the movies.

During her early years in Hollywood, she had a successful B-grade movie career, and even appeared in a few films that were considered A-grade, such as *Stage Door* (1937) and *The Big Street* (1942). Also during this

BACKLASH

A period during the 1980s when religious fundamentalists and conservative right-wingers systematically challenged women and the gains of the Second Wave feminist movement. Women were blamed for society's ills and were "shown" that all personal problems stemmed from independence and "excessive" involvement in their careers.

The media contended that highly educated and, generally, independent women would probably never find a man according to a Harvard-Yale study that was later proved to be flawed and erroneous. Other social institutions as well as the media endeavored to point women back to the home and family as their true calling and greatest reward.

During this period women were virtually removed from the televisual environment by a proliferation of male-buddy shows such as *The A-Team* (1983–1987), *Miami Vice* (1984–1989), *Tour of Duty* (1987–1990), *Jake and the Fatman* (1987–1992), and *Wise Guy* (1987–1990), where women were generally limited to portrayals of victims or sex objects.

While there were a few strong female characters such as Officer Lucy Bates (*Hill Street Blues,* 1981–1987) and Detectives Chris Cagney and Mary Beth Lacy (*Cagney and Lacey,* 1982–1988), for the most part women were relegated to traditional sitcom fare or the overblown characterizations of the rich and wanna-be-rich on nighttime soap operas such as *Dallas* (1978–1991) and *Dynasty* (1981–1989), to mention only two of the more popular series. Even "women as mothers" lessened as all-male households took over child care (*My Two Dads,* 1987–1990, and *Full House,* 1987–1995).

While it was politically correct for female characters to have a "career," few were ever shown *doing* anything related to the profession. Elyse Keaton (*Family Ties,* 1982–1989) was an architect, while Claire Huxtable (*The Cosby Show,* 1984–1992) was an attorney, but they, like their many televisual peers, never seemed to leave the house and were always available to their husband and children. And, in 1988, there was an unprecedented "baby boom" among previously independent women on such programs as *Night Court* (1984–1992), *Designing Women* (1986–1993), *L.A. Law* (1986–1994), *Beauty and the Beast* (1987–1990), and *thirtysomething* (1987–1991). The ticking of female characters' biological "clocks" became the focus of episodes and motherhood was happily embraced by all. Even Murphy Brown, one of television's most independent of characters, became pregnant.

And, while the main thrust of the backlash has become more covert, the messages are still being transmitted and mouthed by female characters that women would be more happy and find "true" fulfillment in home and family. Repeatedly, programs "show" that careers are just dull substitutes for love, which is what every woman truly desires and will give up everything to attain. The downside or "price" that women must pay to have careers are routinely shown more often than the corresponding side for men's careers.

All these messages are subtle and pervasive, and only time will tell whether they have a lasting impact on the female view of careers and other life options.

Lucille Ball and Desi Arnaz from the successful series I Love Lucy *wash dishes on their five-acre ranch where they also raise cattle and dabble in farming, 1952. (Corbis/Bettmann)*

period, she married Cuban bandleader Desi Arnaz, but their careers necessitated long periods of separation.

In 1947, *My Favorite Husband* premiered on radio. The lead character, Liz Cooper, was an early version of the persona that would become Lucy Ricardo. The series' popularity brought with it acknowledgment of Ball as a comic, which led to several lead roles in comic films such as *Fuller Brush Girl* (1950), *Sorrowful Jones* (1949), and *Fancy Pants* (1950), the latter two with Bob Hope.

In a bid to save her marriage, which was faltering due to lengthy separations (and Arnaz's roving eye), Ball and Arnaz proposed a situation comedy for the fledgling medium of television. At first, CBS balked at having Arnaz play Ball's husband, but after the couple staged a successful music and comedy road show, the network approved the premise and work on the series began.

In 1950, Ball and Arnaz formed Desilu Productions to produce a pilot for CBS. After finding a sponsor, Phillip Morris, and fine-tuning the concept, the series went into production. It was ground-breaking in many areas: the first series to be produced on the West Coast, the first to be filmed by an innovative three-camera technique developed by Arnaz, and the first filmed before a live audience. By using film (another Arnaz idea), the show was guaranteed immortality by a never-before-possible innovation: the rerun.

I Love Lucy premiered on 15 October 1951 and became a part of popular cultural history. By the end of the first season, the series was the number one hit on television. Life in the United States paused on Monday nights so that viewers could watch Lucy's antics. In the second season, the birth of Little Ricky drew approximately 71 percent of television viewers, or more than 44 million people.

The phenomenal success of *I Love Lucy* also brought success to Desilu Studios, which began producing other series for television such as *Our Miss Brooks* (Eve Arden), *Private Secretary* (Ann Sothern), *Make Room for Daddy* (Danny Thomas), and *The Untouchables* (Robert Stack). However, after six seasons and with two children to raise, Ball decided to cut back on her work schedule. From 1957 to 1960, only occasional Lucy-Desi comedy specials appeared, and although the business partnership flourished, the marriage, for all intents and purposes, was over. Ball and Arnaz divorced in 1960.

After the divorce, Ball made her stage debut in *Wildcats*, in which she played a wildcatter in the early 1900s, and did feature films. In 1962, *The Lucy Show* premiered. About the same time, Arnaz sold his Desilu stock to Ball and she became president of the largest film and television production studio in the world. However, the studio was financially troubled, and since Ball was interested in selling out, she began a program to get it back on track. She had advisers, but the final approval on projects and scripts was hers. Under her leadership, Desilu produced such classic programs as *Star Trek* and *Mission Impossible*. In 1967 she sold Desilu for $17 million (net $10 million), and production of *The Lucy Show* ceased.

Ball immediately formed her own production company, Lucille Ball Productions, and produced a new series, *Here's Lucy* (1968–1974), starring Ball and her real-life children, Lucy Arnaz and Desi Arnaz Jr. In addition to her own series, her production company made television movies and programs for the expanding cable networks. After the end of *Here's Lucy,* Ball made occasional guest appearances and television specials and appeared in the filmed musical *Mame* in 1974.

In 1985, Ball became the first woman inducted into the Television Academy of Arts and Sciences' Hall of Fame. That same year, she made a radical shift from her usual roles and appeared in the TV drama *Stone Pillow,* about a homeless woman's attempt to adjust to a normal life. In 1986, Ball's final series attempt failed when *Life with Lucy* ran only a few episodes.

Ball died on 26 April 1989. In June 1989 she was posthumously awarded the Television Academy's Governor's Award—the only woman to receive this honor. She has been honored by many groups and organizations, including the Kennedy Center for the Arts, and specials and retrospectives have been done on her work.

She remains an icon and television legend who has brought laughter to audiences around the world and is still watched by millions on a daily basis.

See also *Here's Lucy, I Love Lucy, The Lucy Show.*

Bankhead, Tallulah (1903–1968)

Remembered mostly for her trademark deep voice so often parodied by comics, Tallulah Bankhead was also an accomplished actress and a renowned beauty in her youth. She was born into a powerful political family in Alabama, the daughter of Congressman William Bankhead, who served one term (1936–1940) as Speaker of the House. After attending convent schools and winning a magazine beauty contest, at 15 Bankhead went to New York to become an actress. She appeared in a number of unremarkable plays and silent films, among them *Squab Farm* (1918), *30 a Week* (1918), and *When Men Betray* (1918). Although she received some recognition as a member of the formidable Algonquin Roundtable (made up of the best wits and critics of the time), she soon realized that the American public was not ready for her.

Bankhead immigrated to England, and became known as much, if not more, for her clever witticisms and unconventional behavior than for her acting. After achieving fame in England, she returned to New York and won the New York Drama Critics' Award in 1939 for her portrayal of Regina in Lillian Hellman's play *Little Foxes.* In 1942 she again received the award for her role in *The Skin of Our Teeth*, and in 1944 she received the New York Film Critics' Award for her appearance in Alfred Hitchcock's *Lifeboat*, perhaps her best dramatic role.

After these successes, her appearances grew fewer as she became dependent on drugs and alcohol. Her autobiography, *Tallulah, My Autobiography*, was published in 1952, and she appeared sporadically in televised dramatic anthologies from 1954 to 1962. One of her last television roles was as the Black Widow in two episodes of the cult favorite *Batman* in 1967.

She died in New York on 12 December 1968.

Barrett, Rona (1934–)

In the tradition of such early Hollywood gossip columnists as Louella Parsons and Hedda Hopper, Rona Barrett contributed two-minute gossip reports to various broadcasts until 1969, when she acquired her own short-lived syndicated series. In 1976 she became a regular contributor on ABC's *Good Morning America* and had a prime-time special, *Rona Barrett Looks at the Oscars*. In 1981 she had a two-month magazine-style series, *Television Inside and Out*, a combination of gossip, information, and opinions.

Barrett appears sporadically on television, and is perhaps best remembered as never facing the camera squarely but always speaking in profile, showing only the left side of her face.

Barrymore, Ethel (1879–1959)

Born into the first family of theater, Ethel Barrymore made her stage debut at age 14 in *The Rivals*. Her first starring role was in 1901 (at age 22) in *Captain Jinks of the Horse Marines*. She opened the Ethel Barrymore Theatre in New York in 1928, and her career spanned everything from tragedy to lighthearted comedy. She was acknowledged as one of the "first ladies of Broadway."

During the 1950s, she appeared on several of television's dramatic anthology series, including *Hollywood Opening Night* ("Mysterious Ways"), *G.E. Theatre* ("Prosper's Old Mother"), and *Playhouse 90* ("Eloise"). She also hosted a non-network series, *Ethel Barrymore Theatre*, in 1956, and appeared in two of the productions: "The Daughters of Mars" and "General Delivery."

She wrote her autobiography, *Memories*, in 1955.

Baywatch (1989–)

Critics find it difficult to determine why this series is so popular, but considering that its major audience consists of preteens and teens, the series' environment and beautiful cast might be sufficient to ensure its longevity. Generally seen as being more exposé and exploitation of svelte bodies than a realistic portrayal of Los Angeles County lifeguards, the show is often called "Babe Watch."

The plots are soap operaish, and a tremendous emphasis is placed on interpersonal relationships. Although the show is often cited for exploitation of its female characters by both dress (or lack thereof) and camera angles, the male characters are also put on review, if to a slightly less explicit degree. As if its popularity had not ensured it a place in the archives of popular culture, several of its stars have become poster favorites, most notably Pamela Anderson (C. J. Parker) and Jasmine Bleeth (Caroline Holden).

Baywatch Nights (1995–1997)

After the phenomenal success of *Baywatch*, the franchise created *Baywatch Nights*, a spinoff with Mitch Buchannon (David Hasselhoff) as a private detective, although one of the unsolved mysteries of this series is how being a lifeguard qualified him to be a detective. During the first season, which dealt with normal criminal activities, he was assisted by ex-cop Garner Ellerby (Greg Alan Williams), photographer Griff Walker (Eddie Cibran), and former New York–based private detective Ryan McBride (Angie Harmon), with club owner Donna Marco (Donna D'Errico) lending little more than scenic enhancement.

In the second season, Ellerby was replaced by Diamont Teague (Dorian Gregory), and the series began to focus on paranormal or science fiction/fantasy topics, possibly to attract the viewers that made *The X-Files* a megahit. Unfortunately, the writing and acting were not on a par with *The X-Files*, and the series did not return for a third season.

Although *Nights*, like *Baywatch*, was mundane and often predictable, the character of Ryan McBride is worth closer examination. Like many female characters who do not conform to traditional role expectations, she was given a name that is generally given to males. She was also overaccomplished; not only was she an experienced private investigator, she also had a brilliant scientific mind. She easily understood the most convoluted experiments encountered on *Nights,* and could use any type of advanced laboratory equipment with ease.

Yet, for all her expertise, she was not nurturing enough to keep fish alive in the office aquarium. As often happens with female characters, to be successful in male-dominated arenas the character must be flawed in traditionally female areas. This either/or dichotomy is prevalent in both dramatic and comedy series.

Beauty and the Beast (1987–1990)

Based loosely on the fairy tale, *Beauty and the Beast* is the story of Assistant District Attorney Catherine Chandler (Linda Hamilton) and the poetic and soulful beast-man, Vincent (Ron Perlman). After saving Catherine from an assault in Central Park in which she was left for dead, Vincent removed her to the underground world in which he lived with others beneath New York City.

Despite their differences, Catherine and the lion-faced Vincent fell in love and developed a psychic bond, which allowed him to know when she was in danger— which was often, as her tenacity led her into many dangerous situations. The second-season cliffhanger resulted in Catherine becoming pregnant with Vincent's child, and the third season opened with Catherine being kidnapped by the evil criminal mastermind Gabriel, who attempted to control Vincent through his unborn child. After giving birth to a baby boy, Catherine was killed by lethal injection, and the remainder of the season revolved around Vincent's quest to rescue his son. In the series finale, Vincent saved his son,

Linda Hamilton and Ron Perlman pose in character for their series Beauty and the Beast. *(Fotos International/Archive Photos)*

whom he named Jacob after his adopted father and the leader of the tunnel society, and they returned to the underground society. Fittingly, Gabriel was killed with Catherine's gun.

Beauty and the Beast had a loyal following, and when it was revealed that CBS was considering canceling the show, a tremendous outcry ensued. Ron Perlman capitalized on Vincent's popularity and made a successful recording of poems as read by "Vincent" (*Beauty and the Beast of Love and Hope*). Other *Beauty and the Beast* products also proved very popular. However, Linda Hamilton wanted to return to films after the second season, and without "Beauty," the magic of the show was lost. Since its demise, the show has attained a true cult following.

See also Action/Adventure Genre.

Beavers, Louise (1902–1962)

Louise Beavers was one of the first black women to appear in a recurring role on television. Although born in Cleveland, she was raised in Los Angeles and began making movies in 1927. Her breakthrough was the 1934 film *Imitation of Life,* in which she gave a forceful portrayal as Aunt Delilah, but in general, she was relegated to cheerful "mammy" roles that did not allow her to show her talent.

In 1952 she replaced Ethel Waters as the star of *Beulah* until the series ended in 1953. She made several guest appearances on such programs as *Stage Door, Playhouse 90,* and *The Wonderful World of Disney.*

See also *Beulah,* Black Female Roles.

Berg, Gertrude (1899–1966)

In an industry in which men receive much of the publicity and praise, Gertrude Berg was a prolific writer, producer, and firm-minded businesswoman who created an entertainment empire centered around television's favorite Jewish mother.

Berg was born 3 October 1899 in New York City to theater owner Jacob Edelstein and his wife, Diana. She began writing skits as a teenager and, although she never graduated from high school, she took playwriting and acting courses at Columbia University.

Prior to the Depression, she married and had two children. After her husband lost his job, she supported the family by reading copy in Yiddish on the radio and writing scripts that often didn't sell. Finally, *The Rise of the Goldbergs* sold, and she was asked to play the lead character, Molly Goldberg, as well as write the scripts. The show premiered on NBC radio in 1929. The humor derived from exaggerated circumstances and the characters—mostly Molly's mangled English, which became known as "Mollypropisms" or "Goldbergisms." At the height of the show's popularity, she made $7,500 a week, becoming the highest-paid woman in radio.

Berg took her characters on a national stage tour in 1934, but returned to radio in 1935 with a new series for NBC—*House of Glass*—starring as Sophie, the cook at a Catskills resort. The show lasted less than a year because the audience could not relate to Berg as someone other than Molly Goldberg.

The Goldbergs returned to radio in early 1938, and ran on both NBC and CBS until 1945. Berg not only wrote all the scripts (in longhand) but produced, directed, and cast the series. She was a perfectionist and demanded authenticity in all areas of the program down to the sound effects—if the script called for breaking eggs, she broke eggs during the broadcast.

In January 1949, *The Goldbergs* moved to television, and for most of its run was in the top five shows, attracting an average audience of 40 million viewers. In 1950, Berg won the first Emmy awarded for best actress in a continuing performance.

Tragedy hit the Goldberg world when the name of Philip Loeb, who played father Jake Goldberg, appeared in *Red Channels*, the book purporting to contain names of entertainers with Communist ties. Although under extreme pressure, Berg refused to fire him for as long as possible; when she was finally forced to let him go, she personally paid his salary for more than two years. (After years of persecution, in 1955 Loeb killed himself, a victim of this country's second indefensible witch-hunt.)

Following the Loeb incident, *The Goldbergs* went off the air from mid-1951 to 1952, when it returned and ran until October 1954, first on NBC and then briefly on Dumont. It was resurrected again from 1955 to 1956 with syndicated first-run episodes.

In 1961, Berg returned to television after two years of appearing in the highly successful Broadway play *A Majority of One,* for which she won a Tony for Best Actress. The series *Mrs. G Goes to College* (later *The Ger-trude Berg Show*) cast her basically as Molly Goldberg as a widow going to college after her husband had died. For whatever reason, Berg's ethnic humor had lost its audience and the series barely lasted a year.

She wrote her autobiography in 1963, entitled *Molly & Me,* and was preparing for the production of another Broadway play when she suddenly died of a heart attack.

Berger, Lisa (1965–)

As executive vice-president of creative affairs at Fox Television Studios, Lisa Berger is in charge of the development of new programs for distribution to Fox channels. Before moving to Fox Television, Berger worked for MTV for 12 years in programming, eventually being named vice-president of original programming.

Bergman, Ingrid (1915–1982)

Orphaned young, Ingrid Bergman attended the Royal Theatre of Dramatic Arts in Stockholm before being cast in her first American film, the 1939 remake of the Swedish film *Intermezzo.* She made many other film classics, including *Casablanca* (1943) and *Murder on the Orient Express* (1974). She won two Best Actress Oscars, for *Gaslight* (1944) and *Anastasia* (1956).

She won a Tony for her portrayal of Joan of Arc in *Joan of Lorraine* (1946) before appearing in some of the dramatic anthology series: "The Turn of the Screw" on *Ford Star Time* (1959) and "The Human Voice" (1967) on *ABC Stage '67.* In addition, she hosted the PBS series *Childhood* in 1977. Bergman's final appearance was in the critically acclaimed television miniseries *A Woman Called Golda,* for which she won an Emmy for Outstanding Actress in 1982. She died of cancer later that same year. Her autobiography, *Ingrid Bergman: My Story,* was published in 1972.

Betty Hutton Show (1959–1960)

This short-lived series was a slightly irregular rags-to-riches story. Goldie Appleby (Betty Hutton) was a heart-of-gold showgirl turned manicurist who inherited a wealthy client's estate and was made guardian of three teenagers. Predictably, the laughs concerned the adjustments made by all to their new living arrangements.

Beulah (1950–1953)

Termed "television's favorite black maid," Beulah worked for an inept white family, the Hendersons, whom she constantly rescued with her famous line "Somebody bawl fo' Beulah?" The managing-maid persona was re-created in the series *Hazel* in 1961.

Beulah originated as a supporting character on radio's *Fibber McGee and Molly* in 1944, but Beulah soon had her own program, which in turn was brought to television in 1950. The character was first played by Ethel Waters, but she was replaced in 1952 by Louise Beavers (Hattie McDaniel was first choice, but illness prevented her from remaining with the series for more than a few episodes). The series was still very popular when Beavers left in 1953.

Beulah was only a stereotypical role of a faithful, managing mammy-cum-maid, but it was one of the first television vehicles for black performers. Also appearing on the series were Butterfly McQueen (1950–1952), and Ruby Dandridge (1952–1953) as Beulah's best friend, Oriole.

See also Beavers, Louise; Black Female Roles; Dandridge, Ruby; Waters, Ethel.

Bewitched (1964–1972)

Samantha (Elizabeth Montgomery) was an attractive witch who married a mortal named Darrin Stephens (Dick York, 1965–1969; Dick Sargent, 1969–1972), who did not want her to use her magical powers. To placate her husband, Sam tried to be a normal housewife, but something always happened that made it necessary for her to use witchcraft.

Often that something was interference by her mother, Endora (Agnes Moorehead), who strongly disapproved of Sam's marriage and husband, whom she never called by his correct name. Sam's warlock father, Maurice (Maurice Evans), was outwardly less disapproving, but he too felt that she was wasting herself and her powers on her mortal husband. Other relatives included Aunt Clara (Marion Lorne), who was sweet but forgetfully inept at spells; Uncle Arthur (Paul Lynde), who loved practical jokes as long as they were done to someone else; and Cousin Serena (also played by Montgomery), who often worked with Endora to cause trouble in Sam's marriage.

Darrin worked for an advertising firm, and his boss, Larry (David White), was often confused by the goings-on with Darrin's "family." Generally, the strange events around the Stephens's household were explained as advertising campaign demonstrations.

In 1966 the Stephens's first child was born. Tabitha (Erin and Diane Murphy) was, like her mother, a witch. Occasional problems occurred when Tabitha, who did not fully understand why she and her mother could not use their witchcraft, would cast spells—generally at Grandmama's instigation. In 1969 a second child, Adam (David and Greg Lawrence), was born and he, like his father, was mortal.

The show ranked as the most popular half-hour series to appear on ABC until 1977, and continues to appear in syndication throughout the world. It received 22 Emmy nominations (five for Montgomery as Best Actress in a Comedy Series) and won three Emmys. In 1966, Alice Pearce, who appeared occasionally as the Stephens's confused neighbor, Gladys Kravitz, posthumously won Best Actress in a Supporting Role in a Comedy, and in 1968, Marion Lorne posthumously won the same award. Also in 1966, William Asher received the Emmy for Outstanding Directorial Achievement in Comedy.

Several years after *Bewitched* ended, ABC tried to recapture the magic with a new series entitled *Tabitha* (1977–1978). In this series, Tabitha (Lisa Hartman) was grown-up and, like her mother, trying not to use her powers while she worked as a production assistant on *The Paul Thurston Show*. Also working at the television station was Tabitha's brother Adam (David Ankrum).

The Bionic Woman (1976–1978)

This series, a spinoff of *The Six Million Dollar Man* (1974–1978), centered around a tennis pro, Jaime Sommers (Lindsay Wagner), who had once been engaged to Major Steve Austin (Lee Majors). When she was critically injured in a skydiving accident, she was reconstructed using bionics—both legs, an arm, and an ear were replaced. After recovering from surgery, she was enlisted as an agent by Austin's agency, the Office of Scientific Information (OSI). Her cover story when she was not on assignment was that she was a teacher at an army post near Ojai, California.

See also Action/Adventure Genre.

Black, Carole (1945–)

In 1994, Black became the first woman to head a commercial television station in the nation's second largest market-city as president and general manager of KNBC, the NBC affiliate in Los Angeles. In February 1999, Black moved to Lifetime as president and CEO. Prior to moving to network television, she oversaw the worldwide marketing program of Disney Home Video and led that division moved into first place in sales nationally to become the leading profit-maker for Walt Disney Studios. She was also responsible for the development of the Disney Afternoon, bringing that franchise into the forefront of daytime broadcast television.

As general manager of KNBC, Black increased coverage and sponsorship of neighborhood events and established KNBC as a highly visible local entity. She also expanded the station's community outreach, and increased the station's news broadcasts. Under her leadership, 1997 was the most profitable in the station's 47-year history.

After graduating from Ohio State University with a bachelor's degree in English literature, Black worked for Procter & Gamble in brand management. She soon moved to Disney Company as senior vice-president for television and vice-president of worldwide marketing of home video.

BLACK FEMALE ROLES

With the advent of cable channels, an alternative exists to network programming, especially Black Entertainment Television (BET), but network depiction of the black experience has always been controversial. Black women are usually portrayed within the family unit or as the proverbial black matriarch. Although black actors and creative personnel are becoming more influential and prominent, critics still charge that not enough roles portray the diverse black experience with dignity and accuracy.

Two of the most recent black series—*The Hughleys* (1998–) and *The PJ's* (1999), center around the male; women appear in both series, but their roles are secondary and supportive. However, three current sitcoms are more female-oriented, and are generally cited as having positive images. *Moesha* (1995–) features singer/actress Brandy (Norwood) as a young girl facing the challenges of growing up in the 1990s. *Sister, Sister* (1994–1999) was about twins (Tia and Tamara Mowry) separated at birth who find each other 14 years later and the humorous pitfalls of trying to blend two very different households. *For Your Love* (1998–1999) was about two friends living the good life in suburbia and the rocky course of love and friendship.

(continued on next page)

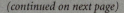

(continued from previous page)

While most network dramas feature at least one black character in ensemble casts, none stars a black actor. A new drama on Lifetime, *Any Day Now* (1998–), features a prominent black actor in the character of Renee Jackson (Lorraine Toussaint). When she returns to her hometown, she and her childhood friend Mary Elizabeth O'Brien (Annie Potts) reestablish their friendship; together they face the challenges of their different lives and the racial tension that still exists in their town. The series is cited for its sensitivity in handling the dynamics of a long-standing friendship between two diverse characters—a black lawyer and a white housewife.

Still, even with the success of the black comedy, a successful black-oriented drama does not exist. Some critics claim that this failure is because mainstream America would not be comfortable with a black person in a position of power without the cushion of laughter. For better or worse, the history of black television is predominantly one of comedy.

COMEDY AND VARIETY

One of the first series to feature a black performer was *Beulah* (1950–1953), which featured the portly, managing black maid and her often inept employers. The star, Ethel Waters, became the first black actor to be nominated for an Emmy—in 1962 for her guest appearance on *Route 66* (1960–1964). When Waters left the series in 1952, Louise Beavers took over the role for the final year.

Later, when *Amos 'n Andy* (1951–1953) premiered with an all-black cast, civil rights groups protested the stereotypical portrayals. Interestingly, criticism of inaccurate depictions or stereotypical characterizations generally revolved around male characters being crude or buffoonish, with little or nothing said about the way female characters were portrayed.

During the same period, the first black woman to host a 15-minute variety program on Dumont (1950) was musician Hazel Scott. Although Amanda Randolph first appeared in the short-lived Dumont domestic comedy *The Laytons* (1948), she is best remembered as Louise, the maid, on *The Danny Thomas Show* (1953–1964). Her sister Lillian, who had been in the *Amos 'n Andy* cast, appeared as domestic Birdie Lee on *The Great Gildersleeve* (1955–1956) and later appeared as Bill Cosby's mother on *The Bill Cosby Show* (1969–1970).

As the nation went into a decade of conservatism and conformity, few blacks appeared on television in any capacity other than as domestics. However, Sammy Davis Jr. (Best Specialty Act) and Harry Belafonte (Best Male Singer and Best Specialty Act) were nominated for Emmy Awards in 1955, and the play *Green Pastures*, with an all-black cast, aired in 1957.

With the civil rights movement gaining momentum in the 1960s, more black characters appeared on television. Ruby Dandridge played the accustomed black role of housekeeper as Delilah on *Father of the Bride* (1961–1962). The first prominent black character to appear on television in a nondomestic role was Diahann Carroll as the widowed mother in *Julia* (1968–1971). However, both black and white critics during that period charged that the series did not reflect black experience. Nevertheless, in the first season, Carroll became the first black female to be nominated for an Emmy in the comedy category.

(continued on next page)

(continued from previous page)

During this same period, Chelsea Brown (1968–1969) and Teresa Graves (1969–1970) joined the cast of the popular *Rowan and Martin's Laugh-In* (1968–1973). ABC briefly aired an all-black version of Neil Simon's hit play and movie *Barefoot in the Park* (1970–1971), and several female actors appeared in supporting roles on established series such as *The Bill Cosby Show* and *Sanford and Son* (1972–1977).

The CBS sitcom *Good Times* (1974–1979) was a spinoff of the popular Norman Lear series *Maude* (1972–1978), which featured Maude's outspoken maid Florida Evans and her family in the housing projects on the south side of Chicago. That same year, *That's My Mama* (1974–1975) premiered with Teresa Merritt as "Mama" Curtis, who wanted nothing more than for her son to get married, and interfered in his life accordingly. A year later, *The Jeffersons* (1975–1985) premiered and introduced one of the most identifiable black female characters— Louise "Weezie" Jefferson (Isabel Sanford). In 1981, Sanford became the first black to win an Emmy for Best Actress in a Comedy.

In these comedies and others during those and succeeding years, the female characters were part of a family unit (*Family Matters*, 1989–1992; *Parent'Hood*, 1995–1998) or a surrogate family unit (*What's Happening*, 1976–1979; *A Different World*, 1987–1993; *Out All Night*, 1992–1993).

DRAMA

Cicely Tyson got her start on television in 1963 on *East Side/West Side* as secretary Jane Foster. Although praised for its realism, the series lasted only one year. During this same period, Diana Sands, Ruby Dee, and Eartha Kitt received Emmy nominations for their television guest appearances.

In 1966, Nichelle Nichols appeared on the bridge of the vessel that would become the most successful science fiction franchise in history— the USS *Enterprise.* As Communications Officer Uhura on *Star Trek* (1966–1969), Nichols appeared in all *Star Trek* movies and continues to have a positive impact on viewers as a competent, efficient woman in extreme situations in syndicated reruns 30 years after the initial five-year mission.

A few years later, Gail Fisher appeared as Peggy Fair, secretary-cum-assistant to detective Joe Mannix on *Mannix* (1968–1975). She became the first black woman to win an Emmy as Supporting Actress in the drama category in 1970, and was nominated three more times (1971, 1972, 1973).

Denise Nicholas portrayed a concerned school counselor in the comedy-drama *Room 222* (1969–1974), about an integrated high school in a large city. The detective series *Get Christie Love* (1974–1975), starring Teresa Graves, entered the record books on several fronts. It was the first weekly detective series to feature a black actor in the starring role, and it was the first drama to feature a black woman as the central character.

With the introduction of the miniseries, black female actors received further recognition and avenues to demonstrate their talents. Cicely Tyson excelled in her portrayal of Miss Jane Pittman (*The Autobiography of Miss Jane Pittman*, 1974), for which she won Emmys in two categories—Best Lead Actress in a Drama and Actress of the Year. She also appeared in *A*

(continued on page 41)

Gail Fisher and Mike Connors set out to find an over-the-hill prizefighter wanted for murder on Mannix, 1970. Fisher won an Emmy for Best Supporting Actress for her role on the show. (Photofest)

(continued from page 39)

Woman Called Moses, and she later starred with Melissa Gilbert in the legal drama *Sweet Justice* (1994–1995) as idealistic lawyer Carrie Grace Battle, for which she received an Emmy nomination in 1994.

Later that decade, both *Roots* series (1977, 1979) brought many excellent black actors to the attention of television viewers. The list of stars includes Cicely Tyson (Binta), Madge Sinclair (Bell), Ruby Dee (Queen Haley), Olivia Cole (Mathilda), Lynn Moody (Irene Harvey), Leslie Uggams (Kizzy), Maya Angelou (Nyo Boto), Debbi Morgan (Elizabeth Harvey), Irene Cara (Bertha Palmer Haley), Lillian Randolph (Sister Sara), and Debbie Allen (Nan Branch Haley). Olivia Cole won an Emmy for Outstanding Single Performance by a Supporting Actress for her role as Mathilda in 1977.

The 1980s was the decade when Alfre Woodard came into her own. In addition to appearing in the drama *St. Elsewhere* (1982–1988) as Dr. Roxanne Turner, in the comedy *Sara* (1985) as Rozalyn Dupree, and in the detective drama *Tucker's Witch* (1982–1983) as Marcia Fulbright, she won two Emmys for guest appearances on other series. Her first Emmy was for her 1983 performance on *Hill Street Blues* (1981–1987), and the second was for her 1986 appearance on *L.A. Law* (1986–1994). In 1997, she again won an Emmy for Outstanding Actress in a Miniseries or Special for her performance in *Miss Evers' Boys.*

Madge Sinclair appeared as Nurse Ernestine Shoop in *Trapper John, M.D.* (1979–1986), and was nominated for three Emmys for Best Supporting Actress in a Drama. She had earlier been nominated for her role as Bell in *Roots* (1977). Also in the 1980s, Debbie Allen was a multiple Emmy nominee (1983, 1984, 1985) for her performance as dance instructor Lydia Grant in *Fame* (1982–1987).

Brewster Place (1990) starred Oprah Winfrey as Mattie Michael and was based on the popular 1989 television movie *The Women of Brewster Place,* itself based on the novel by Gloria Naylor. Lasting only three months, the series dealt with the lives of the people living in the neighborhood of Brewster Place.

One of the most popular series in recent times is *Touched by an Angel* (1994–), which stars Roma Downey as Tess and Della Reese as her boss, Monica—guardian angels sent to Earth to help troubled souls.

See also Allen, Debbie; *The Autobiography of Miss Jane Pittman;* Beavers, Louise; *Beulah;* Bowser, Yvette Lee; Carroll, Diahann; Dandridge, Ruby; Dee, Ruby; dePasse, Suzanne; *Get Christie Love; Touched by an Angel;* Waters, Ethel; *The Whoopi Goldberg Show;* Winfrey, Oprah.

BLACKLIST

One of the most inexcusable episodes in American history happened when the country, out of fear and prejudice, allowed the lives of many people to be ruined after their names appeared on a list of persons *suspected* of Communist sympathies. Whether or not the allegation was true did not matter. If a person's name appeared on the list, that person was virtually unemployable.

The epitome in blacklist publications appeared three days before the outbreak of the Korean War in the form of a 213-page paperback entitled *Red Channels*, listing 151 names, 130 organizations, and 17 publications that were too liberal for the ultraconservative editors who compiled the book. Approximately 300 people were eventually blacklisted and an additional 100 or so were graylisted; many never regained their careers, and some died as a result of the persecution.

One of the more insidious arms of the blacklist monster was a newsletter entitled "Counterattack," which regularly published career and working information on supposed Communists and their sympathizers. Readers were urged to contact the advertisers and backers of productions these "suspects" worked on and voice their disapproval by pledging to stop purchasing their products. Once put in a bad light, companies paid a $24 annual subscription fee to the publishers of "Counterattack" to keep abreast of whom not to employ, and thereby rehabilitate their image.

The infamous hearings ended in 1954, but the power of the blacklist continued in some cases into the 1960s. Many of those affected were writers such as Connie Lee Bennett, who was credited on 24 productions until 1953 and then disappeared from the industry; Marguerite Roberts with 20 credits prior to 1951, then nothing until 1962; and Louise Rousseau with 16 credits prior to 1949, then nothing. Of the actresses affected, Angela Clarke had 17 credits prior to 1954, then nothing until 1962; Karen Morley had 44 credits prior to 1951, then nothing in the following years; and Gale Sondergaard had 39 credits and a Best Supporting Actress Oscar prior to 1949, then nothing until 1969.

See also Grant, Lee; McCarthyism.

Bloodworth-Thomason, Linda (1948–)

Best known in recent years as a presidential friend, Linda Bloodworth-Thomason sold scripts to some of the most successful sitcoms on television, including *M*A*S*H* and *Rhoda,* before becoming a producer. With her husband, Harry, she formed Mozark Productions and specialized in series set in the South.

Their first offering was *Filthy Rich* (1982–1983), which parodied the successful prime-time soap opera *Dallas* (1978–1991). Next came *Designing Women* (1986–1993), which focused on four women working at Sugar-bakers, an interior design business in Atlanta, Georgia. Their next series was *Evening Shade* (1991–1994), centered in the small town of Evening Shade, Arkansas, with its sometimes eccentric inhabitants.

They also created *Hearts Afire* (1992–1995), set in Washington, D.C., in the office of an aging southern senator, and the relationship (and eventual marriage) of his legislative assistant (John Ritter) and his press secretary (Markie Post). In 1995 they offered *Woman of the House,* which had brash, outspoken Suzanne Sugarbaker (Delta Burke, as her character from *Designing Women*) taking over her husband's seat in the House of Representatives after his death.

In 1990, Mozark Productions made history when it signed a contract with CBS to produce five series over an eight-year period for approximately $45 million, which at that time was the biggest deal ever made with an independent production company.

See also *Designing Women.*

Bolen, Lin (1941–)

Lin Bolen became the first woman to head a network's daytime (10 A.M.– 4 P.M.) programming in 1972 when she was hired by the NBC affiliate in Los Angeles. Soon she transferred to New York City to assume the job on a national scale, becoming the highest-ranking woman at any of the networks.

In less than three years under her direction, NBC's daytime programming became first in the ratings. Bolen is responsible for expanding soap operas to an hour from the original 30-minute format, and increasing the prizes awarded on game shows. In 1976 she left the network to form her own production company.

Born in Benton, Illinois, in 1941, Bolen studied advertising at City College in New York before beginning her career by producing commercials.

Bondy, Kim (1965–)

Kim Bondy is executive producer of *NBC News at Sunrise*—one of the few female producers of a network news program, and news director of *Today.* Prior to her 1998 assignments she was broadcast producer for NBC's *Nightly News,* where she monitored breaking stories, reporters, and assignments to ensure current, comprehensive coverage at broadcast time.

Bondy changed her career plans from law to broadcasting after graduating from the University of New Orleans (1988) and beginning an internship at WDSU-TV. She became news director at CITN-TV in Grand Cayman in 1993 and moved to WCAU, an NBC-owned station, as managing editor in 1995.

Bowser, Yvette Lee (1965–)

The first black woman to produce a hit prime-time series (*Living Single,* 1992–1998), Yvette Lee Bowser was raised in Southern California and graduated from Stanford with degrees in political science and psychology. She began her television career as a writer on *A Different World* (1987–1993), and eventually became a producer on that series. She also worked as a producer on *Hangin' with Mr. Cooper* (1992–1997) before creating and producing *Living Single,* which was a reflection of her life as a single woman. In 1998 she premiered a new series, *For Your Love,* which chronicled the phases of a woman's life, in this case the time after a woman marries. The series focused on two best friends living the American dream in suburbia with the husbands of their dreams and the everyday problems and challenges of life in the 1990s.

Bowser's own production company, Sister Lee Productions, is dedicated to the realistic portrayal of today's black woman.

See also Black Female Roles.

Bridget Loves Bernie (1972–1973)

Based loosely on *Abie's Irish Rose,* an extremely popular Broadway play from the 1920s, *Bridget Loves Bernie* was one of the many ethnic comedies that appeared on network television in the 1970s. The show centered on the married lives of wealthy Catholic schoolteacher Bridget Theresa Mary Coleen Fitzgerald (Meredith Baxter) and Jewish cab driver–cum–writer Bernie Steinberg (David Birney). Predictably, the adjustments of the couple to their new status and their respective in-laws were the focus of the humor.

Even though the show drew consistently high ratings, the series was canceled after one season. Many believe that protests from religious groups who objected to the series' position on mixed-religion marriages was the motivation for the network's pulling of the show.

Broadside (1964–1965)

Created by Edward J. Montagne, who also created *McHale's Navy* (1962–1966), *Broadside* was women's turn to show that war was fun during a period of promilitary programming on television. In this series, Navy WAVEs were sent to Ranakai Island in the South Pacific during World War II to "man" the motor pool. Situations centered around the expected disruption caused by a group of females amid thousands of males, and actions taken by the base commander to get the WAVEs transferred off his once peaceful island. The series allowed women to be successful in a nontraditional profession, but this was negated by the fact that their jobs were played for laughs.

Brothers, Dr. Joyce (1928–)

Joyce Brothers made her television debut as a quiz show contestant when she was a graduate student at Columbia University. She won the top prize on both *The $64,000 Question* (1956) and *The $64,000 Challenge* (1957) in the category of boxing. She parlayed her celebrity into a cohosting job on NBC's *Sports Showcase* (1956), as well as numerous guest appearances on both radio and television.

She became a perennial guest on programs ranging from sitcoms to news specials. She also had several of her own syndicated series, including *Dr. Joyce Brothers* (1958–1963), *Consult Dr. Brothers* (1960–1966), *Ask Dr. Brothers* (1965–1975), *Living Easy with Dr. Joyce Brothers* (1972–1975), and *The Dr. Joyce Brothers Program* (1985). With her guest appearances as well as on her own programs, Dr. Brothers brought acceptance to issues not discussed on television, including psychological illness and sexuality. She has also written many books, among them *The Successful Woman* (1989), and *Widowed* (1992), prompted by her own grieving process following the death of her husband in 1989.

Brown, Hilary (1946–)

Hilary Brown, born in Canada, became one of the first female foreign correspondents for ABC in 1973 after working several years as a freelance reporter/stringer in the Middle East. Brown was first based in ABC's London bureau, then sent to the Paris bureau headquarters.

BUDDY CHARACTERS

A concept using male characters (*I Spy*, 1965–1968; *The Wild, Wild West*, 1965–1970; *Starsky and Hutch*, 1975–1979; *Miami Vice*, 1984–1989; *Jake and the Fat Man*, 1987–1992) who are dependent on one another for protection and/or support through the challenges and dangers they face. The device is seldom used with females even though, traditionally, females form deeper bonds in same-sex relationships.

On the few series that conform, to some degree, to the female buddy format, the bonds are generally more supportive than protective, except when the characters are involved in law enforcement. Some examples of female buddy programs include *I Love Lucy* (1951–1961), *Laverne and Shirley* (1976–1983), *Charlie's Angels* (1976–1981), *Cagney and Lacey* (1982–1988), and *The Golden Girls* (1985–1992).

See also *Cagney and Lacey, Charlie's Angels, The Golden Girls, I Love Lucy, Laverne and Shirley.*

Becoming dissatisfied with doing the investigative work in researching a story only to have male reporters appear on the air using her facts, in 1977 she moved to NBC. For two years, NBC posted her to Tel Aviv, where she was given her own airtime to report her stories. During this time she and her husband (British correspondent John Bierman) had a son, Jonathan. In 1980, after ten years as a foreign correspondent, NBC transferred her back to the United States and assigned her, without preparation or contacts, to the Pentagon. After a disappointing and frustrating year, she moved back to ABC News and was assigned to the New York bureau.

This was the feminist backlash period in the United States, and male reporters got the best assignments regardless of experience or ability. After being refused an assignment to Rome at the last minute, Brown returned with her family to Canada to anchor *The News Hour* on CBC in Toronto.

Burke, Karey (1966–)

Born in Southern California and a magna cum laude and Phi Beta Kappa alumna of UCLA, Karey Burke was only 30 when she was named one of the four prime-time programming vice-presidents at NBC Entertainment in 1996 after eight years with the network. As senior vice-president of prime-time series, she leads the group responsible for various current comedy and drama series and oversees the development of proposed series. Hits under her supervision include *Friends* (1994–), *Mad about You* (1992–1999), *Caroline in the City* (1995–1999), *3rd Rock from the Sun* (1996–), and *Homicide: Life on the Street* (1993–1999).

Burke began her entertainment career in 1988 as an assistant in the comedy development division in NBC, then moved into drama development. In 1991, Burke changed networks and assumed the position of director of development at ABC. After two years she returned to NBC as director of comedy development, and in 1994 was named director of prime-time series.

Burnett, Carol (1933–)

Born in San Antonio to alcoholic parents, Carol Burnett was raised by her maternal grandmother. Her early years were tumultuous, with her grandmother the only security she knew. Eventually her sometimes-fragmented family moved to California with the vague goal of getting Burnett's mother work in films. Although her mother never entered show business, the family lived on the fringes of Hollywood and knew many people loosely connected to the film world. After graduating from high school, Burnett scraped together the tuition to enter UCLA, where she studied acting. During the summers, she performed in Northern California with the Stumptown Players, a group of UCLA graduates and theater arts students.

Convinced that her future lay in musical comedy, she left school during her senior year, thanks to a $1,000 loan from a man whose name she has never revealed, and went to New York. She lived in the famed Rehearsal Club, a residence for young women pursuing theatrical careers made famous in the film *Stage Door*.

After becoming discouraged by the practice of "no agent–no audition" and "no work–no agent," she approached Eddie Foy Jr. for help. He set up an appointment with his agent, which came to nothing, but the agent jokingly suggested that Burnett increase her visibility by putting on her own show. As the months went by without any long-term work, Burnett and a group from the Rehearsal Club decided to stage a show that would allow each woman to showcase her talent. During this planning period, Burnett received word that her father had died after a long battle with alcoholism and tuberculosis.

Carol Burnett performing as one of her most famous characters, a charwoman, on her show in 1972. (Corbis/Bettmann)

With financial assistance from the women on the club's board of directors, the show premiered in March 1955. Invitations went out to agents, critics, reporters, actors, actresses, and anyone who might be able to assist the struggling performers break into show business. To the surprise of the performers, many famous people attended the revue. The gamble paid off when the revue was well received and agents began calling.

After signing with the William Morris Agency, Burnett began getting semisteady work in industrial shows and summer stock, and an occasional television job on such programs as the *Colgate Comedy Hour.* Of all types of work, Burnett said that she liked television the least since "you couldn't see the audience." Interestingly, on her own series, Burnett would often "bring up the lights" and talk with the audience.

However, after the initial flurry of small jobs, Burnett's career once again stalled. On the advice of an agent friend, Burnett worked up an audition act to further distinguish her from other hopefuls. Soon she had a short-term regular job on Paul Winchell's children's show on NBC. During the first show, on 17 December 1955, she made her signature gesture, pulling her ear to say "hi" to her grandmother—a signal she continues to this day. After the first show, she married her longtime boyfriend from UCLA, Don Saroyan.

Not long after her run on the Paul Winchell show, she was cast on the Buddy Hackett sitcom *Stanley* (1956–1957) for 13 weeks as Hackett's girlfriend, Celia. After the series ended, she once more did summer stock, but this time as lead comedienne.

The following fall, she made her first appearance on *The Garry Moore Show* (1958–1967). Moore liked her so much that he issued an open invitation for her to appear on his show any time she had new material. Her work on the Moore show got her booked on *The Ed Sullivan Show* (1949–1971). She also performed at the Blue Angel, a popular cabaret in Manhattan that featured young talent.

During this period, she and writer Ken Welch wrote a song entitled "I Made a Fool of Myself over John Foster Dulles," then U.S. secretary of state. The parody was an instant hit with audiences, and she was booked on *The Jack Paar Show.* In one week, she made two appearances on the Paar show and one on Ed Sullivan's show. Unfortunately, as is often the case in show business, after the fame came more unemployment.

About this time, she also took responsibility for her younger sister, Christine, who was running wild in Los Angeles. To ensure a proper environment for her sister, Burnett and her husband took out a loan to send Christine to an all-girls' school in New Jersey. Shortly after bringing her sister east, Burnett's mother died, leaving her grandmother alone in Los Angeles.

Burnett was working on a fairly regular basis on television shows such as the audience-participation quiz show *Pantomime Quiz* (1950–1963) when she was called in as a last-minute replacement for a flu-stricken Martha Raye on a prime-time variety show hosted by Garry Moore; she received rave reviews. She then starred in a George Abbott musical, *Once upon a Mattress,* based on the fairy tale "The Princess and the Pea." It premiered off-Broadway in May 1959, then moved to Broadway, where it played for more than a year.

While still appearing in the play, Burnett was asked to be a regular on Garry Moore's Tuesday night variety show. Sadly, just as she'd found a measure of professional success, her marriage ended.

Burnett appeared on the Moore show for almost three years, and she met the man she would later marry: Joe Hamilton, who produced the show. She appeared briefly on *The Entertainers* (1964–1965) before signing a million-dollar contract with CBS to do a series of specials over a 10-year period and her own comedy-variety series, *The Carol Burnett Show* (1967–1979). With a core of regular cast members that included Harvey Korman, Lyle Waggoner, Vicki Lawrence, and Tim Conway, the series was so highly rated and critically successful that from 1967 to 1975, Burnett held the title "Queen of Television Comedy."

Burnett's versatility as a performer (she could sing, dance, act, mime, and clown) was the most obvious reason for the show's success. Articles of the period liken her style of comedy to that of the physical comedy of Lucille Ball and her predecessors. After 11 years, Burnett ended the series with a two-hour finale of "finest" performances and new sketches.

When a popular sketch from her show developed into its own series, *Mama's Family* (1983–1985), Burnett reprised her role as the foul-mouthed Eunice Higgins. However, when the series left NBC and began production in syndication, continuing until 1990, Burnett left also.

Burnett returned to star in weekly television in 1990 when she hosted a comedy anthology entitled *Carol & Company* (1990–1991). Each week a half-hour playlet featured someone in a bizarre but funny situation, such as the woman applying for a loan at the bank her son is in the process of robbing, and the former asylum inmate trying to remain calm and sane while faced with red tape at the Department of Motor Vehicles.

In 1991, Burnett once more tried a weekly comedy variety series, again titled *The Carol Burnett Show,* which lasted only one season. Not until the 1996 season did Burnett return to television, when she became Helen Hunt's occasionally seen mother on *Mad about You* (1992–1999), a role for which she won an Emmy for Best Guest Star on a comedy series in 1997.

Carol Burnett was inducted into the Academy of Television Arts and Sciences Hall of Fame in 1985, the second woman to be so honored. In addition, she is the president of her own production company, Kolola Productions.

See also Variety Programs.

The Burning Bed (1984)

In this two-hour, fact-based social drama, Farrah Fawcett (formerly a model and one of *Charlie's Angels*) played a battered wife accused of killing her husband after years of physical and mental abuse. The subsequent trial was one of the first to use the victim defense as a legal justification, and Fawcett's character was ultimately acquitted.

Critics and viewers were surprised by Fawcett's thought-provoking and powerful portrayal in her first nonglamorous role. The movie, one of the highest rated ever (a 36.2 rating and 52-percent viewing share), raised awareness and interest in the issue of spousal abuse and the needs of battered women.

See also *Charlie's Angels;* Fawcett, Farrah.

C

CA-TV

Community Antenna Television (CA-TV) was the earliest form of cable TV. In 1948, CA-TV was established in remote parts of Pennsylvania and Oregon to bring television signals into areas where normal reception was either nonexistent or limited by distance or terrain. By the 1960s, independent and urban network stations had been brought into rural areas, further increasing these stations' audience base.

Cagney and Lacey (1982–1988)

Cagney and Lacey was one of several drama series from the 1980s to be included in what critics called "the second Golden Age of television." Considered a quality show by critics, the series was one of the last female buddy shows. It had a small but loyal viewership that made for a precarious existence of cancellations and rebirths.

The idea was conceived by the writing team of Barbara Corday and Barbara Avedon in the early 1970s, but could not find financial backing until 1981. After the made-for-television movie garnered a respectable ratings share, CBS put it on its fall 1982 schedule.

The series dealt primarily with the personal and, secondarily, professional lives of two female detectives in New York City. Mary Beth Lacey (Tyne Daly) was married with children and had an often out-of-work husband. Her partner, Chris Cagney (Meg Foster for a few episodes,

53

CABLE TV

With the current proliferation of cable channels, it's hard for young people to envision a world with only three major networks and a handful of independent stations. Basically an outgrowth of CA-TV, cable stations were brought under FCC jurisdiction in 1966. They brought programming to the same areas that CA-TV had served, and the first offerings were mainly uncut movies and sporting events without commercial interruption. Although cable was not taken as a serious threat initially, the networks voiced concerns that cable would corner the movie market.

One of the first widely offered stations was Home Box Office (HBO), established in 1972 as a subsidiary of Time-Warner; it became a driving force in the acceptance and expansion of the cable network. The new industry boomed in the late 1970s, and was given a real boost when the government removed the favored status enjoyed by the three major networks.

Today there is a channel for almost any interest. CNN offers continuous news coverage. MTV, VH1, and TNN offer music. The Learning Channel, Discovery Channel, and History Channel offer historical and educational programs. A&E and Bravo offer cultural as well as educational programming. The Sci-Fi Channel specializes in science fiction programs, while the Cooking Channel airs cooking programs 24 hours a day. Comedy Central can make you laugh day or night, and Nickelodeon offers entertainment suitable for youngsters and serves as a haven for former series' reruns. And the list goes on.

then Sharon Gless for the remainder of the series), was single, ambitious, and unlucky romantically.

In addition to being partners, Cagney and Lacey were good friends who faced criminals, chauvinistic coworkers, and life's uncertainties together. A true reality show, not all criminals were brought to justice and not all problems were solved in the requisite hour.

The story lines concerned many controversial topics including drug and alcohol addiction, date rape, abortion, breast cancer, and child abuse. Within the lives of the protagonists, these topics were scripted with a frankness that educated the viewing audience and highlighted many of the concerns of the women's movement during a period of televisual backlash that tended to negate or trivialize women's advances and concerns.

Praised for the show's realistic depiction of working women and the problems they faced, Cagney and Lacey were shown as active protagonists mentally and physically able to solve their own cases, rather than as women in distress, as in many previous series. Although Gless replaced Foster to add more femininity to the character, the series never fell into the "jiggle" exploitation trap in which some programs became mired.

Tyne Daly as Detective Mary Beth Lacey and Sharon Gless as Detective Christine Cagney in the police drama series Cagney and Lacey *(American Stock/Archive Photos)*

The series won two Emmys for Best Drama Series (1984–1985, 1985–1986). Daly won Best Actress four times (1983, 1984, 1985, 1988) and Gless won twice (1986, 1987). Both Gless and Daly were among *Ms.* magazine's Women of the Year in 1987.

In addition, the series received an award for best program from the National Commission on Working Women in 1985, and the Humanities Award in 1986. Also in 1986, the series was listed among the "Class of '86 Honor Roll" in *Channels,* honoring "the highest standards in the media."

See also Careers for Women on Television, Detective/Police Drama Series.

Cara Williams Show (1964–1965)

This series featured a married couple who pretended to be single so they could continue to work at Fenwick Diversified Industries, which had a policy against hiring married couples. Frank Bridges (Frank Aletter) was an efficiency expert and Cara Wilton (Williams) was a secretary with such a complex filing system that no one else could find anything in her files—making her indispensable to her often-frustrated boss, Mr. Burkhardt (Paul Reed). Situations and comedy revolved around the couple's attempts to keep their marriage a secret.

Caroline in the City (1996–1999)

Caroline (Lea Thompson), a successful syndicated cartoonist, was not as successful in her personal life. A nineties mix of chutzpah, insecurity, and naïveté, she struggled to navigate the social minefields of life. Caroline was the star of the series, but the show was very much an ensemble program of quirky, though supportive, friends.

Caroline's assistant, Richard (Malcomb Gets), got paid extra to listen to her personal problems, and her best friend, Annie (Amy Pietz), was constantly on hand to give often-questionable advice. Rounding out the ensemble were Del (Eric Lutes) and Charlie (Andy Lauer).

During the first season, the hint of a Caroline-Richard romance was strong, but Richard married a woman he met on vacation. Midway through the 1997–1998 season, the indication that Caroline and Richard still had deep feelings for one another was introduced, with the added complication that Richard was married. The fianl season brought the Caroline-Richard relationship back to the fore, with Richard once more single, and the couple exploring their feelings for one another.

CAREERS FOR WOMEN ON TELEVISION

In the early years of television, most women did not work outside the home. The limited cultural view of a woman's proper place was reflected in the television world, and most female characters answered the highest calling a woman could aspire to—they were wives and mothers. Even when the family lifestyle would have benefited from another income had the woman worked, such as working-class wife Alice Kramden (Audrey Meadows) on *The Honeymooners* (1955–1956), the wife remained in the home.

Of course, some female characters had not yet found husbands, so they were allowed to work—but only until they found Mr. Right. These wanna-be-wives, who were always white, were relegated to socially approved jobs such as secretary, receptionist, or teacher, and their primary focus was to find a husband.

MAIDS AND HOUSEKEEPERS

In the early years of television, no "acceptability" stigma was attached to black female characters working, but they were relegated to maid or housekeeper roles. Always calm amid the chaos of their employers' lives, managing maids became a mainstay in the early televisual world. One of the first was *Beulah* (Ethel Waters; then Louise Beavers, 1950–1953), followed by Louise (Amanda Randolph) on *The Danny Thomas Show* (1953–1964). Later maids included Birdie (Lillian Randolph) on *The Great Gildersleeve* (1955–1956), Delilah (Ruby Dandridge) on *Father of the Bride* (1961–1962), Florence (Marla Gibbs) on *The Jeffersons* (1975–1985), and Florida (Esther Rolle) on *Maude* for the first four seasons (1972–1976) before she got her own series.

TEACHERS

One of the allowable jobs open to single female characters in the early days was that of teacher, which has traditionally been viewed as a premarriage job for women. One of the first successful television teachers was Connie Brooks (Eve Arden) of *Our Miss Brooks* (1952–1956), a woman as dedicated to marrying Mr. Boynton (Robert Rockwell) as to teaching.

Although *Mr. Novak* (1963–1965) was quite popular, it focused on a male teacher, with little attention given to his female coworkers. However, *Room 222* (1969–1974) had not only a dedicated male teacher, but also a school counselor, Liz McIntyre (Denise Nicholas), and an idealist young female teacher, Alice Johnson (Karen Valentine), working together in an integrated city high school.

The most recent school-based series was the short-lived *Dangerous Minds* (1996), which featured an ex-Marine, Louanne Johnson (Annie Potts), turned teacher to troubled inner-city youths. Based on a popular movie, the series did not last an entire season.

SECRETARIES

Another job that was acceptable for female characters to hold while waiting for a husband was that of secretary. One of the first secretaries on television was Susie McNamera (Ann Sothern) of *Private Secretary* (1953–1955). She established the character of efficient-if-meddling secretary that appeared often in sitcoms. Another early secretary was Charmaine "Shultzy" Schultz (Ann B. Davis), who worked for a fashion photographer on *The Bob Cummings Show*

(continued on next page)

(continued from previous page)

(1955–1959). She portrayed another early stock television character—the secretary in love with her boss. Years later, secretaries were represented on *The Bob Newhart Show* (1972–1978) by Carol Kester (Marcia Wallace), who could efficiently run a three-doctor office but was more interested in her romantic life, or lack thereof.

Perhaps the most readily remembered secretary on television is Jane Hathaway (Nancy Kulp) of *The Beverly Hillbillies* (1962–1971). An intelligent, efficient woman, Jane was brought to near incoherence by the intellectually challenged Jethro Bodine (Max Baer Jr.).

Another secretary from the early television period was Della Street (Barbara Hale), the invaluable secretary-assistant to the epitome of legal jurisprudence, *Perry Mason* (1957–1966). A more recent example of legal secretary is Elaine (Jane Krakowski), who is efficient but more interested in minding others' business than her own, from the ensemble series *Ally McBeal* (1997–).

COOKS AND WAITRESSES

Two other acceptable, if menial, jobs allowed female characters were as cook or waitress. On *Alice* (1976–1985), Alice (Linda Lavin), Flo (Polly Holliday), Vera (Beth Howland), and later Belle (Diane Ladd) and Jolene (Celia Weston) all worked at Mel's Diner. Veronica Rooney (Anne Meara) worked as a cook on *Archie Bunker's Place* (1979–1982).

For a much more upscale establishment, *It's a Living* (1980–1982, 1985–1989) featured a posh Los Angeles eatery called At the Top and the women who worked there: Lois (Susan Sullivan), Dot (Gail Edwards), Vicki (Wendy Schaal), Cassie (Ann Julian), Jan (Barrie Youngfellow), Amy (Crystal Bernard), and Ginger (Sheryl Lee Ralph). Another restaurant-centered series was *Love & War* (1992–1995), in which restaurateur Wally Porter (Susan Dey) worked with housewife turned waitress Nadine Berkus (Joanna Gleason) to make the Blue Shamrock the new "in" spot in New York. When Wally left, gourmet chef Dana (Annie Potts) took over the transformation of the Shamrock.

JOURNALISTS

The first female character to work in print journalism was Lois Lane (Phyllis Coates, then Noel Neill) on the original *Superman* series (1951–1957). In the later incarnation, *Lois & Clark—The New Adventures of Superman* (1993–1996), Lois Lane (Teri Hatcher) was a career-obsessed, competitive reporter who, while still enamored of Superman, was capable and intelligent—except when it came to figuring out Superman's real identity.

Another early character to work in the field of writing, although not as a journalist, was Sally Rogers (Rose Marie) on *The Dick Van Dyke Show* (1961–1966). Portrayed as a successful comedy writer, the character was based on either Lucille Kallen or Selma Diamond (depending on your source), both successful television writers from the early days of television.

One of the best-remembered female characters to work in the field of journalism was Mary Richards from *The Mary Tyler Moore Show* (1970–1977). Although she had the title of associate producer of the evening news, Mary was a jill-of-all-trades who most often did what appeared to be clerical work.

The next female character to work in journalism was Billie Newman McCovey (Linda Kelsey) as an idealist newspaper reporter on *Lou*

(continued on next page)

(continued from previous page)

Grant (1977–1982). Then, in 1988 the most successful and at times controversial of journalists was introduced: Murphy Brown (Candice Bergen, 1988–1998). Murphy was the high-profile coanchor of a fictitious network newsmagazine, *FYI*, who for ten years showed the viewing audience the joys and price one pays for tremendous success.

Journalism once more became a popular field of employment for characters on other series in the 1990s. Hannah Miller (Jamie Lee Curtis) struggled to become a successful magazine writer on *Anything but Love* (1989–1992), Khadijah James (Queen Latifah) edited *Flavor* magazine on *Living Single* (1993–1997), *Caroline in the City* (1995–1999) focused on the life of a cartoonist, the main character (Brooke Shields) in *Suddenly Susan* (1996–) writes for *The Gate* in San Francisco, and Nora Wilde (Tea Leoni) worked as a reluctant paparazzi on *Naked Truth* (1995–1997).

LAW ENFORCEMENT

Whether public or private, women came to the television career of law enforcement later than men. On the series by the same name (1965–1966), Honey West (Anne Francis), a private investigator, was one of the first female characters to be depicted as other than window dressing and as competent as a man. This series was followed closely by a British import, *The Avengers* (1966–1968), in which Mrs. Emma Peel (Diana Rigg) worked with secret agent John Steed (Patrick Macnee).

Soon after the end of *The Avengers* came *The Mod Squad* (1968–1973), in which Julie Barnes (Peggy Lipton) and two young men working for the police department infiltrated youth organizations to find the adults who took advantage

of disenfranchised youth. Julie was most often used as a decoy or window dressing, and was always in need of saving by her male partners. Another series that premiered the same year and whose female lead filled a role much like Julie Barnes featured Sergeant Pepper Anderson (Angie Dickinson) as *Police Woman* (1974–1978). Yet another series from the same year featured a female detective, Christie Love (Teresa Graves), who was seen by many as too independent—a trait that resulted in the early cancellation of *Get Christie Love* (1974–1975).

The next major series featured three former police officers working as private investigators for an unseen employer. *Charlie's Angels* (1976–1981) featured female operatives who were beautiful but also capable and resourceful. Although the series had several threesomes over its years on television, no group matched the original casting of Sabrina Duncan (Kate Jackson), Jill Munroe (Farrah Fawcett-Majors), and Kelly Garrett (Jaclyn Smith).

When the next female-centered police series appeared, *Cagney and Lacey* (1982–1988), the two main characters were allowed to be on their own and never in need of saving by male colleagues. Chris Cagney (Meg Foster, then Sharon Gless) and Mary Beth Lacey (Tyne Daly) were true equals to their male counterparts. On another successful police drama of that time, *Hill Street Blues* (1981–1987), another female officer, Lucy Bates (Betty Thomas), was depicted as able and competent.

These competent depictions led the way for later portrayals of women who were professionals, for all their troubled private lives. *Under Suspicion* (1994–1995) featured Rose "Phil" Phil-

(continued on next page)

(continued from previous page)

lips as the only female homicide detective in a precinct in Portland, Oregon. Later, on *N.Y.P.D. Blue* (1993–), Detective Diane Russell (Kim Delaney) earned her place in the precinct through grit, determination, and a willingness to face her own demons as much as through her relationship with Bobby Simone (Jimmy Smits).

MEDICINE

Medical series have been popular over the years on television, but early shows focused on doctors who were always male, with little attention given to females, who were either patients or nurses. This imbalance changed with series such as *St. Elsewhere* (1982–1988), *Chicago Hope* (1994–), and *ER* (1994–), where female characters are doctors as often as nurses.

Although on *Nurses* (1991–1994) all the characters were overworked nurses except for Dr. Riskin (Florence Stanley) during the first season, *Dr. Quinn, Medicine Woman* (1993–1998) focused on Michaela "Mike" Quinn, who moved from Boston to Colorado to practice medicine in the 1860s. Still within the medical sphere, a short-lived series on WB, *Rescue 77* (1999), followed the lives of three EMTs in Los Angeles—one of whom was a woman.

LAW

The first series to feature a female lawyer was *Willy* (1954–1955), in which Willa Dodger (June Havoc) first opened her practice in her hometown in New Hampshire, then moved to New York to provide legal counsel to an entertainment organization. This series did not focus on her legal career, but rather her personal relationships. The next female-centered legal series was *The Jean Arthur Show* (1966), which focused on a fortyish widow, Patricia Marshall (Arthur),

who happened to be the best defense attorney in town but who had a habit of getting too involved in her clients' lives.

Later series did not focus on female lawyers, but many nevertheless included them. *Hill Street Blues* (1981–1987) featured dedicated Assistant DA Joyce Davenport (Veronica Hamel), *NYPD Blue* (1993–) had Assistant DA Sylvia Costas (Sharon Lawrence), *The Client* (1995) highlighted attorney Reggie Love (JoBeth Williams) as the recovering alcoholic trying to regain custody of her own children while protecting children through her family-law practice, *L.A. Law* (1986–1994) had as many female attorneys as male (albeit the females were much more interested in their personal lives than their professional ones), *Civil Wars* (1991–1993) included Sydney Guilford (Mariel Hemingway) as a divorce lawyer and a partner in the firm, *Reasonable Doubts* (1991–1993) featured Assistant DA Tess Kaufman (Marlee Matlin), and *Sweet Justice* (1994–1995) had both civil rights lawyer Carrie Grace Battle (Cicely Tyson) and idealist Wall Street transplant Kate Delacroy (Melissa Gilbert) to fight for the underdog.

A fair share of female attorneys made their presence known on comedies. *Night Court* (1984–1992) had Public Defender Christine Sullivan (Markie Post), and *Living Single* (1993–1997) had Maxine Shaw (Erika Alexander) as a divorce lawyer. *Sara* (1988) featured idealist lawyer Sara McKenna (Geena Davis), and the short-lived *Foley Square* (1985–1986) featured two of three assistant DAs who were female: Alex Harrigan (Margaret Colin) and Molly Dobbs (Cathy Silvers).

Ally McBeal (1997–), one of the more popular of recent legal series, focuses on the profes-

(continued on next page)

(continued from previous page)

sional, personal, and fantasy life of a young Harvard-educated lawyer (Calista Flockhart), and her friends and coworkers—most of whom work in some legal capacity.

See also *Alice; Ally McBeal; The Avengers; Beulah; Cagney and Lacey; Caroline in the City; Charlie's Angels; Dr. Quinn, Medicine Woman; Get Christie Love; Hill Street Blues; Honey West; The Jean Arthur Show; The Mary Tyler Moore Show; Mod Squad; Murphy Brown; Nurses; Our Miss Brooks; Police Woman; Private Secretary;* Rolle, Esther; *Sara* (1985); *Sweet Justice; Under Suspicion; Willy.*

Carroll, Diahann (1935–)

Born Carol Diann Johnson in New York City, Diahann Carroll began her career as a model and went on to star in the first television series to feature a black female lead in a nondomestic role. In 1954 she appeared in *House of Flowers* and in nightclubs until starring in 1962 in *No Strings,* a play written especially for her and for which she won a Tony for Best Actress.

Her series, *Julia* (1968–1971), was about a widowed nurse raising her son alone after her husband was killed in Vietnam. This series was one of the first programs to be fully integrated, but was viewed by some blacks as conformist, and the character of Julia was seen as more white than black.

After the end of her series, Carroll rarely appeared on television. She had a four-week summer-replacement variety show in 1976, but

Diahann Carroll and Harry Belafonte sing together on her musical special she starred in that aired in 1971. (Corbis/Bettmann)

her most notable performance was in 1974 with her sensitive portrayal in *Claudine,* for which she won an Oscar nomination. She also appeared in Maya Angelou's *Sister, Sister,* in which she played the resentful older sister.

From 1984 to 1987 she appeared on *Dynasty* as Dominique Devereaux, the self-proclaimed "black bitch" who was Blake Carrington's illegitimate half sister. She is one of the few performers to be nominated for an Oscar, Emmy, Grammy, and Tony.

See also Black Female Roles.

Carsey, Marcy (1945–)

Marcy Carsey is co-owner and executive producer of one of the most successful independent production companies in television, Carsey-Werner. She was inducted into the Television Hall of Fame in 1995, along with her partner, Tom Werner. In 1998 her company began planning a new basic cable channel, Oxygen, geared toward women.

Responsible for some of the biggest hits in recent years, Carsey-Werner employs the management concept of allowing creative people the freedom to create. They find a star, develop a concept, hire the personnel to make it happen and maintain quality control with script reviews. This concept generally works well, but it can be troublesome with stars such as Roseanne and Brett Butler, two of the company's more difficult recent stars.

Born in South Weymouth, Maine, Carsey entered the entertainment business as a tour guide at NBC's headquarters in Rockefeller Center. She later became a production assistant/gofer for *The Tonight Show*. After leaving NBC, she briefly worked for an advertising agency before moving to California and becoming a freelance story analyst and editor.

In 1974 she was hired by ABC as an executive in the comedy programming department. By 1976 she was vice-president in charge of prime-time comedy development, and in 1979 she was named vice-president of comedy and variety programs. While working with ABC, she met her partner-to-be, Tom Werner.

In 1980 she left her position as vice-president of prime-time series to start Carsey Productions. In 1981, Werner joined her, and the name changed to Carsey-Werner Company.

Their first series was *Oh, Madeline* (1983–1984), which they adapted from a British program, *Pig in the Middle*. Their next series, *The Cosby Show* (1984–1992), was a tremen-

Marcy Carsey pictured at the thirty-sixth annual Publicists Guild awards luncheon. Carsey shared the 1999 Motion Picture Showmanship Award with Werner. (Reuters/Rose Prouser/Archive Photos)

dous hit, and established the company. From *The Cosby Show* the company spun off *A Different World* (1987–1993), followed the next year by *Roseanne* (1988–1997).

Not all of their series have been hits, but at the start of the 1996–1997 television season, Carsey-Werner had seven sitcoms on the three major networks: *Roseanne* (1988–1997), *Grace under Fire* (1993–1998), *3rd Rock from the Sun* (1996–), *Cybill* (1995–1998), *Men Behaving Badly* (1995–1997), *Cosby* (1996–), and *Townies* (1996).

See also *Cybill, Grace under Fire, Roseanne.*

Charlie's Angels (1976–1981)

One of Aaron Spelling's first successful series, *Charlie's Angels* featured women as lead characters, but sometimes appeared to be written to titillate men with excessive doses of "T&A" and, too often, more emphasis on revealing outfits than plots. The interchangeable team of model-perfect detectives took their orders from an unseen, super-rich boss named Charlie, who called the operatives "angels."

The original angels included cool Sabrina Duncan (Kate Jackson), the unofficial leader of the group; athletic, lion-maned Jill Munroe (Farrah Fawcett); and glamorous and intelligent Kelly Garrett (Jaclyn Smith). With the popularity of the series, Farrah Fawcett had phenomenal success marketing several cheesecake posters.

Heady from her success, Fawcett left the series after one year for film stardom, and her character was replaced by Kris Munroe (Cheryl Ladd), supposedly Jill's younger sister. When Jackson left after three years, her character was replaced by police brat Tiffany Welles (Shelley Hack), who was replaced the next year by street-smart Julie Rogers (Tanya Roberts).

Although the creators were committed to keeping the hair-color mix consistent, they were never able to duplicate the original chemistry that made the series a hit. The three original stars went on to make names for themselves with other projects, while their replacements disappeared into obscurity.

Fawcett never achieved stardom on the big screen, but she appeared in some highly acclaimed made-for-television movies, most notably *The Burning Bed* (1984), which was ranked number 25 on the "Most Watched Movies on Television" compiled by Nielsen Media Research (1993). Jackson starred in the comedy-adventure series *Scarecrow and Mrs. King* (1983–

1987) and numerous television movies. Smith appeared in many television movies, such as *Rage of Angels* (1983), *Sentimental Journey* (1984), and *Windmills of the Gods* (1988), as well as becoming a spokesperson for many consumer products and creating her own sportswear clothing line.

Charmed (1998–)

This series is a combination cop show and sci-fi fest. The Halliwell sisters—Prue (Shannen Doherty), Piper (Holly Marie Combs), and Phoebe (Alyssa Milano)—learn after their grandmother's death that they are witches and that each has inherited a power. Prue can move objects with her mind, Piper can stop time, and Phoebe receives glimpses of the future.

Together they make a formidable team to fight the evil forces (warlocks, demons, etc.) who want to take their powers away from them and cause general havoc among humans. Armed with a magic recipe book that the sisters found in the attic of their grandmother's San Francisco home, the trio use their powers to protect the unsuspecting and the weak. Because they are most powerful together ("the power of three"), they decide to share their grandmother's house, which results in comic moments and female bonding.

Charren, Peggy (1928–)

In 1968, Peggy Charren founded Action for Children's Television (ACT), a grass-roots organization devoted to improving children's programming. ACT and its founder are credited with accomplishing more to improve children's television than any other organization or person.

Charren received a degree in English from Connecticut College in 1949. After graduation, for a brief period she was head of the film department at WPIX-TV in New York City, which was her only association with the television industry until the formation of ACT.

After several successful business ventures, Charren became a member of the Creative Arts Council in Newton, Massachusetts, in 1966. In 1968, after becoming a stay-at-home parent, Charren became concerned with the lack of quality and the extreme commercialization of children's programs. What began as a group of concerned friends discussing television became a national advocacy organization.

For the organization's first four years, Charren served as chair and then, in 1972, became president, known for her forceful, dedicated leadership. While fighting Capitol Hill and broadcasters to ensure better children's programming, Charren wrote several books on television: *Changing Channels: Living (Sensibly) with Television* (1983), *The TV-Smart Book for Kids,* and *Television, Children, and the Constitutional Bicentennial* (both in 1986).

Amid personal and organizational criticism, Charren remained committed to her goal of improving and reforming programming for children. She received the Trustees Award from the National Academy of Television Arts and Sciences, and in 1992 received a Peabody for her lifetime achievements. In January 1992, ACT was dissolved. Charren was named visiting scholar at Harvard University in 1993 and continues to be a vocal advocate for improved children's programming.

See also Action for Children's Television; Mandated Educational Programming.

Chase, Sylvia (1938–)

One of the early woman journalists on television news, Sylvia Chase appeared on ABC's *20/20* (1978–1986) and on CBS as a news correspondent. She moved to San Francisco in 1989 to anchor the local evening news on KRON-TV. In addition, she reports, anchors, and produces investigative documentaries and news specials. After graduating from UCLA in 1961, she became active in state politics until 1969, when she became a reporter for KNX-TV in Los Angeles. She moved to CBS in 1971, then to ABC seven years later. Chase has won numerous awards throughout her career, including four Emmys (1978, 1908, 1986, and 1987); the Headliners award (1979, 1983, and 1994); the Golden Eagle award (1994, 1995, and 1996); and a Peabody in 1989.

Cheers (1982–1993)

Cheers was a highly rated and critically acclaimed series often touted for its intelligent writing and superior cast. It dominated its night, and was consistently rated as one of the top shows in the Nielsen's. The show won many Emmys and made several of its stars household names.

However, the female characters were traditional sitcom roles. Class-conscious, out-of-touch, quasi-intellectual Diane Chambers (Shelley Long, 1982–1987) was replaced by vulnerable, neurotic career woman Rebecca Howe (Kirstie Alley, 1987–1993). Another member of the "family" was acerbic psychiatrist Dr. Lilith Sternin (Bebe Neuwirth, 1986–1993). Through the entire run of the series, sarcastic, sharp-witted Carla Tortelli Lebac (Rhea Perlman) was a waitress at the bar.

The series took place in a Boston bar called Cheers, originally owned by a shiftless former baseball player, Sam Malone (Ted Danson). Although he was rather dense and self-centered, both Diane and Rebecca fell in love with him, if only briefly. The basis of each female character was her relationship to one of the male characters.

Because of their male-based characterization, none of the female characters was role-model material. In addition, their personality flaws were exaggerated to the point of neurosis, much more so than the male characters of the series.

Cher (1948–)

Cher (Cherilyn Sarkisian La Piere) began her show business career as the singing partner of her then-husband Sonny Bono, as the hippy duo Sonny & Cher during the 1960s.

Born in El Centro, California, Cher participated in plays and musicals prior to being discovered by Bono, who was then a record producer for Phil Spector. Their first song, *I Got You Babe,* was a number-one hit in 1965. They continued a successful recording career into the mid-1970s, and had their own hit variety series, *The Sonny and Cher Comedy Hour* (1971–1974), with much of the show's popularity owing to Cher's wry wit and outlandish wardrobe.

After the two divorced in 1974, Cher had her own series, *Cher* (1975–1976). It was moderately popular, but did not receive the ratings the previous joint effort had gotten. In 1977, Sonny and Cher reconciled (professionally) for a revamped *Sonny and Cher Show* (1976–1977). It, too, did not regain the popularity of the first series, probably because one of the most popular aspects of the original was Cher's put-downs of Sonny, which after the divorce just weren't as humorous.

Cher turned her attention to an acting career. She appeared on Broadway in *Come Back to the Five and Dime, Jimmy Dean, Jimmy Dean* and in such films as *Good Times* and *Charity.* Her first hit film was *Silkwood* (1983), for which she received an Oscar nomination as Best Supporting Actress. She appeared in *Mask* in 1985, and in 1988 won the Best Actress Oscar for her role in the offbeat romantic comedy *Moonstruck.* She had other critical successes in such popular films as *Mermaids* (1990) before turning her attention to directing (*If These Walls Could Talk,* 1997) and producing (*Oak Ridge,* 1998). In 1999, she made a nationwide concert tour and appeared in the film *Tea with Mussolini.*

See also Variety Programs.

Child, Julia (1912–)

Julia Child had one of the first television series devoted to the art of cooking. Born Julia McWilliams in Pasadena, she graduated from Smith College in 1934, no small feat when only 5 percent of the female population attended college, and fewer still graduated; most opted to marry before attaining their degrees. She joined the Office of Strategic Services when World War II broke out and was sent to Ceylon, where her interest in food preparation began. Child married in 1946, and when her husband was posted to Paris in 1948, she was able to attend the Cordon Bleu cooking school.

In 1951 she and two of her former classmates opened their own school, L'Ecole des Trois Gourmandes. To acquaint the American public with French cooking, in 1961 they published *Mastering the Art of French Cooking,* hailed as possibly the best book on the subject. The Childs settled in Massachusetts that same year, and in 1962 she was asked to prepare a pilot for a possible series on cooking.

In 1963, *The French Chef* premiered on Public Broadcasting Service (PBS) stations. Child took the mystery out of gourmet cooking, and her wit and enthusiasm drew viewers to the program. She showed every step of the food preparation and did not shy away from letting viewers see occasional mishaps. Child tried to empower her viewers to try new things, while some of the chefs and purveyors of domesticity who followed her seemed to want their viewers to feel inadequate.

The program won a Peabody in 1965, and Child won an Emmy in 1966, the first person from public television to do so. In 1968 a cookbook based on the series was published, entitled *The French Chef Cookbook.* As her series continued, Child wrote several other cookbooks, including *From Julia Child's Kitchen* (1975) and *Julia Child and Company* (1978), based on her series that dealt with more Americanized cooking.

China Beach (1988–1991)

China Beach, a drama that emphasized the relationships among characters with occasional graphic depictions of war, was called a masterpiece by many critics. One of the series included in the so-called second golden age of television, the series's locale was an evacuation hospital and USO Center near DaNang during the Vietnam War. The events were seen primarily through the eyes of Nurse Colleen McMurphy (Dana Delaney), the focus of this fundamentally antiwar series.

The Vietnam War was the backdrop, but the experiences and interactions of the predominantly female cast were the real focus of the episodes. Even though the series was slanted to attract female viewers, some sexualization of the female characters occurred via story lines, camera angles, and revealing clothing, considered de rigueur to maintain appeal for male viewers.

Although McMurphy was clearly the focal point, several other female characters were seen regularly. Another pivotal character was K. C. Koloski (Marg Helgenberger), a prostitute and heroin addict whose rocky relationship with McMurphy was a dominant subtext throughout. During the series, K. C. became pregnant, and her daughter was delivered by McMurphy on a Saigon street. Eventually, K. C. decided to give up her child; later flash-forward episodes included the teenage Karen, who was raised by series regular Boonie Lanier (Brian Wimmer) and his family. Before the series ended, K. C. and Karen met in a flash-forward episode in which several cast members visited the Vietnam Memorial in 1988.

Another important yet short-lived character was Cherry White (Nan Woods), a young Red Cross volunteer who came to Vietnam to find her brother, listed as missing in action. Through her search, the series went into the dark underbelly of a country at war. Before she was killed, during the series's depiction of the 1968 Tet Offensive, she found her brother. He had become a drug addict.

The flash-forward episodes during the final season were a departure from other series, and allowed the writers to bring the characters home and show how they adjusted to life after the war. Through these future views, the audience was shown that of all the characters, McMurphy was the one who was unable to come to terms with a normal life. She remained lost and unsettled, too caught up in memories that refused to fade.

The series won many awards, including a Golden Globe for Best Drama, a Peabody, and two Writers Guild Awards. In addition, the series received many awards from women's organizations such as Alliance of Women Veterans and the National Commission on Working Women. Dana Delaney won two Emmys as Outstanding Lead Actress in a Drama Series.

Christy (1994–1995)

Shown intermittently during its one season on CBS, *Christy* was the story of a young woman who left her comfortable home in 1912 to journey to Appalachia to teach at a mission school in the poor community of Cutter Gap. Based on the novel by Catherine Marshall, the stories were nostalgic and uplifting as Christy worked to bring a better life to the town's impoverished population.

Chubbuck, Chris (1944–1974)

Chris Chubbuck was the host of *Seacoast Digest,* a morning program seen on WXLT-TV in Sarasota, Florida. On 15 July 1974, just minutes after the start of the program, Chubbuck put a gun to her head and committed suicide on camera.

Before pulling out her gun, Chubbuck reportedly said, "In keeping with Channel 40's policy of bringing you the latest in blood and guts in living color, you're going to see another first—an attempt at suicide." Sadly, this policy, sometimes tagged "if it bleeds, it leads," is still endorsed by many stations.

Chung, Connie (1948–)

Connie Chung, one of the most recognizable women to work in network news, was the subject of a bidding war between NBC and CBS in 1989. She eventually signed with CBS for an estimated salary of $1 million a year and substitute anchor rights for NBC's *Nightly News with Tom Brokaw,* as well as anchor duties on the Sunday edition of *Evening News.* Although more recently she cut back her schedule to "take an aggressive approach to having a baby," she continues to do at least six news specials a year.

Chung began her career in television journalism as a secretary at WTTG in Washington, D.C., but moved into news writing, then became an on-air reporter. She joined CBS News as a Washington correspondent in 1971, later moving to the CBS affiliate in Los Angeles, the number-two market in the country, to anchor the three evening news broadcasts (4:30, 6:00, and 11:00 P.M.).

In 1983 she moved to NBC News as a correspondent and anchor for the Saturday edition of *Nightly News, News at Sunrise,* and the short-lived newsmagazine *1986.* When she returned to CBS in 1989, she briefly had a series called *Saturday Night with Connie Chung* (1989–1990), which featured news stories and dramatic reenactments of elements of the news stories. For its final months the program was retitled *Face to Face with Connie Chung,* focusing on both celebrity and noncelebrity interviews.

See also News.

Cigarette Ad Ban (1971)

In 1967 attorney John Banzhaf argued before the Federal Communications Commission that broadcasters should include health warnings after every cigarette commercial in fulfillment of the Fairness Doctrine. As a result of his campaign, health agencies began to air antismoking Public Service Announcements (PSA), eventually resulting in a congressional ban on cigarette advertising on television after 1970.

This ban caused a sharp decrease in television advertising revenues, which broadcasters scrambled to replace, and brought about an increase in lower-budget programming. At the same time, the effectiveness of the antismoking PSAs caused less mainstream citizen groups to request free airtime to discuss their "public service" issue.

See also Commercials, Fairness Doctrine.

City Hospital (1951–1953)

City Hospital was originally seen on Saturday afternoons from November 1951 to April 1952, then biweekly in prime time from March 1952 (overlapping the afternoon showing) until October 1953. Generally a standard "life and trials of medical personnel" drama, this series stands out for being one of the first to include a female doctor.

Dr. Kate Morrow (Ann Burr) was one of the two major regularly appearing characters. In the role of medical professional, the character was at odds with the prevailing expectations of society, in which a woman's place was in the home raising children, working only to further her *husband's* career.

Coca, Imogene (1908–)

Imogene Coca, best known as Sid Caesar's costar on *Your Show of Shows* (1950–1954), came from a show-business family—her mother once worked for Houdini and her father was a musical conductor. She began her career as a song-and-dance performer, appearing in 1948 on *Buzzy Wuzzy,* which lasted only four weeks, and then partnered with Caesar on *Admiral Broadway Revue* in 1949.

Your Show of Shows featured rapid-paced zaniness alternating with comedy sketches and variety routines. Caesar was certainly the star of the show, but without Coca the show would not have worked so well nor been so popular. She was the stabilizing force of the series with her physical, often nonverbal nuttiness, which perfectly offset Caesar's outlandish excesses. For her work on the series, Coca won an Emmy for Best Actress in 1951.

After *Your Show of Shows* ended, she had her own series, *The Imogene Coca Show* (1954–1955), but it never found an audience or a format. In 1958, she and Caesar reunited for a short-lived variety program called *Sid Caesar Invites You.* She also made guest appearances on such diverse programs as *The U.S. Steel Hour* (1953–1963), *The Jane Wyman/Fireside Theatre* (1949–1958), *Playhouse 90* (1956–1960), *Love American Style* (1969–1974), *Bewitched* (1964–1972), and *Fantasy Island* (1978–1984).

In 1963 she starred in a situation comedy called *Grindl,* in which she played an extremely competent employee of Foster's Temporary Agency, having a different employer and new job each week. In 1966 she costarred in another short-lived sitcom, *It's about Time,* as Shad, a stone-age cave dweller turned reluctant twentieth-century transplant.

Cohen, Betty (1956–)

As president of the Cartoon Network and Turner Learning, Betty Cohen has been instrumental in establishing the Cartoon Network as one of Time Warner's most successful and powerful divisions. She is also moving the network into the consumer market by offering products tied to network series.

After graduating Phi Beta Kappa from Stanford University, Cohen began as a writer-producer for Cable Health Network and Lifetime Television before moving to on-air promotions for Nickelodeon and Nick-at-Nite. In 1988 she went to TNT, becoming senior vice-president and general manager of TNT and executive vice-president of the Cartoon Network. In this position she oversaw the development and expansion of both companies in the domestic and international markets.

In addition to her other responsibilities, Cohen is on the board of governors for the American Center for Children's Television.

COLOR TV

CBS and RCA competed for the first approved method to transmit television images in color. CBS's method was called spinning disk, and RCA's method was dot sequential. Although CBS was the first to perfect and broadcast a color picture in 1951, RCA's method was the one approved by the FCC in 1953 after RCA and the National Television System Committee worked to standardize color transmission, which at first was seldom the same color at any given moment of transmission.

The idea was welcomed by consumers, but the first sets were prohibitively expensive, costing more than $1,000 in the early 1950s. In 1954 only 1 percent of homes with televisions had color sets. As with other technologies, as more color sets were produced, costs came down and more programs were broadcast in color. By 1977 more than 75 percent of homes had color sets, and in the 1990s, color sets are found in virtually every home.

COMMERCIALS

Commercials are the driving force of television. In fact, television exists to bring a target audience of potential consumers to advertisers. Advertisers today buy time on shows that appeal to the demographic they wish to reach, but originally advertisers sponsored—and thereby controlled—entire shows. In 1945, for example, Esso gasoline completely supported WNBT-NBC in New York.

In 1986 the average viewer was subjected to an estimated 24,000 commercials each year. Television advertising is *big* business; it is a $40-billion-a-year industry in which advertisements that appear during the Super Bowl are hyped almost as much as the game.

The first commercial appeared to a limited audience in 1941. It was for Bulova watches, and cost $9. Understandably, early commercials were primitive. They were either simple animated spots (Lucky Strikes' dancing cigarettes) or featured human spokespersons (Texaco's singing Men of Texaco or Betty Furness representing Westinghouse). Years later, one of the first special-effects commercials featured people floating into rental cars as the announcer intoned, "Hertz puts *you* in the driver's seat."

As early as 1952, people were aware of the potential importance and influence of television advertising. That year the National Association

(continued on next page)

(continued from previous page)

of Radio and Television Broadcasters endorsed the Television Code, nearly half of which concerned the already $288-million yearly advertising industry. As an indication of advertising's persuasiveness, in 1952 Elsie the Cow (Borden's animated spokes-animal) topped recognition polls over both actor Van Johnson and U.S. Senator Robert Taft.

Television advertising often impacts more than buying patterns. In 1970, Coca Cola produced a commercial that resulted in a hit record and was later voted one of the best commercials of all time. It showed an ethnically mixed group of young people on a hillside, holding hands and singing "I'd like to teach the world to sing. . . ." The noncommercial version of the song sold over a million copies.

On 2 January 1971, the congressional ban on cigarette advertising on television went into effect, eliminating over $220 million in advertising revenues. Such well-known and award-winning commercials as the Lucky Strike dancing cigarettes and the ultramacho Marlboro Man (employed to shift the target audience from the original women to men) passed into historical archives.

The early 1970s were watershed years for television-regulation activism. The Action for Children's Television (ACT), a group concerned with excessive advertising during children's programs, was formed. In 1972 their efforts resulted in a reduction in the commercial time allowed per hour and eliminated tie-ins to consumer products within the programs. Still, even with the extra attention paid to advertising targeted to children, most advertising during children's programming is for unhealthy food items such as sweetened cereals, cookies, candy, and carbonated drinks.

In 1977, *Advertising Age* estimated that television advertising for that year made up more than 20 percent of all advertising in the United States. Advertising costs continued to rise until in 1983, 30 seconds on the 2 1/2-hour series finale of the popular sitcom *M*A*S*H* (1972–1983) sold for $450,000. During the 1984 Super Bowl, Apple spent nearly $1 million to produce and broadcast the Orwellian commercial called "1984."

The advent of cable was touted by some as commercial-free television, but except for premium channels, all cable channels include advertising. By 1993 over 98 percent of all U.S. households had at least one television set, so commercials are a pervasive and important component of every viewer's day.

See also Consumerism.

CONSUMERISM

Consumerism is the mainstay of the American economy. Billions of dollars are spent each year to entice consumers to buy particular products. On television, more than 30 percent of viewing time is devoted to advertising, so a viewer who watches four hours of television a day is exposed, potentially, to over 100 commercials on a daily basis. It is not unusual to hear young children singing advertising jingles almost before they can walk.

After World War II, American society eagerly embraced the consumer ideology propagated by industry and the government to bring the country more fully out of the slump of the Depression. To sell their products, advertisers created an entire lifestyle that depended on a person's consumption style. Social reality became a matter of comparing possessions. A person's worth was determined by how much was owned—even if the requisite "things" caused tremendous credit debt.

To promote the level of consumption necessary to generate the profits wanted by industry, the products themselves are not advertised so much as the style of life attainable from the product's use. The viewer is informed of a problem or lack, then shown how the advertiser's product will solve it.

According to the world created by advertisers, all problems can be solved easily just by purchasing the correct product. Unfortunately, in a television-consuming culture, this offers people a false sense of security, an unrealistic problem-solving paradigm, and even worse, a false reality and view of the world.

See also Commercials.

Cooney, Joan Ganz (1930–)

After receiving a degree in education, Joan Ganz Cooney worked as a reporter for the *Arizona Republic* in 1953, and then in the Information Department at RCA. Soon she moved to NBC, where she wrote soap opera summaries, and later publicity for *U.S. Steel Hour* (1955–1962), a dramatic anthology.

In 1962, Cooney shifted direction when she joined WNDT, an educational station in New York, as a documentary producer. She produced several socially conscious documentaries, including *A Chance at the Beginning,* about the Head Start program, and *Poverty, Antipoverty and the Poor,* a three-hour program that won a local Emmy in 1966.

While still producing documentaries, she was hired by the Carnegie Corporation to conduct a study on the possible use of television for preschool education. As a result of her findings and suggestions, Cooney began to campaign for funding, and in 1968 founded Children's Television Workshop.

The first educational series she created was the award-winning *Sesame Street,* which premiered in November 1969. The show focused on teaching the alphabet, numbers, and basic reasoning via fast-paced animated segments, comedy, music, and the cuddly Muppets. With the success of *Sesame Street,* Cooney soon offered other programs geared to aiding children learn in an environment of fun. Her creations include *The Electric Co.* (1971–) for older children (7–10) needing help to learn to read; *3–2–1 Contact* (1980–), a science program aimed at still older children (8–12); *Where in the World Is Carmen Sandiego?* (1980–), a geography program; *Square One TV* (1987–), a math series for children learning more involved math concepts (8–12); and in 1992, *Ghost Writer,* a mystery reading series.

Joan Ganz Cooney poses with Sesame Street *stuffed animals, 1985. (Corbis/Owen Franken)*

Cooney has won many awards for her work in children's education. In 1986 she was inducted into *Working Woman* magazine's "Working Woman's Hall of Fame," and in 1990 she was honored with an Emmy for Lifetime Achievement and inducted into the Academy of Television Arts and Sciences' Hall of Fame.

In 1990, Cooney resigned as CEO of the Children's Television Workshop to chair the executive committee and oversee the workshop's creative planning.

See also Action for Children's Television, Mandated Educational Programming.

Corday, Barbara (1944–)

Barbara Corday was the first woman to head a major production studio's television division when she served as president of Columbia Pictures Television from 1984 to 1987. In addition, as a talented writer and producer, she and her writing partner, Barbara Avedon, created the female-buddy cop show, *Cagney and Lacey* (1982–1988).

Her first job in show business was as a publicist, but her goal was to be a writer. In the early 1970s, while she was working with the organization Another Mother for Peace, she met and started her collaboration with Avedon. In 1979, Corday became director of comedy development for ABC, while continuing to develop ideas with Avedon. A year later, she was made a vice-president at ABC.

Even though she has held several executive positions, Corday is best known for her work on *Cagney and Lacey,* a concept that took nearly 13 years to appear on the screen—first as a television movie, then as a series. She maintains that the series was successful because it went into the characters' lives more than previous shows had done.

Corday, Betty (1920–1987)

Betty Corday, one of the creators of the long-running daytime drama *Days of Our Lives* (1965–), began her soap career by producing radio dramas such as *Young Dr. Malone* and *Pepper Young's Family.*

In the early 1960s she assisted her husband, Ted, and Irna Phillips in developing the concept for *Days of Our Lives.* Eventually, she and Ted formed Corday Productions to produce the series. After Ted died in 1966, she became the executive producer until 1985, when she retired; her son took over the show's leadership. She continued to work on scripts for the show until her death in 1987.

In 1995, Betty and Ted Corday were posthumously awarded a Lifetime Achievement Award for "extraordinary contributions to daytime television."

Corporation for Public Broadcasting (1968)

Established by the Public Broadcasting Act of 1967, the Corporation for Public Broadcasting (CPB) is a nonprofit corporation that administers the federal funds allocated to it and promotes the development of quality programming. Although supposedly nonpolitical, all five-year appointments to the ten-person board are made by the president with the advice and approval of Congress.

Political infighting has almost eliminated the corporation's original power. Currently, CPB controls the programming, but local stations dictate PBS's program choices by indicating which ones they are willing to televise. This leaves a minuscule amount, approximately 16 percent, of the budget in CPB's control.

Couric, Katie (1957–)

Katie Couric is the extremely popular girl-next-door cohost of *Today* (1952–) on NBC. Couric won the admiration of many by the professionalism she exhibited on-air after she lost her husband, Jay Monahan, to cancer early in 1998. Later that year she signed a $28 million contract to continue her hosting duties through 2002.

Couric's first job in journalism after graduating with honors from the University of Virginia in 1979 was as a desk assistant with ABC's Washington, D.C., news bureau. When CNN began broadcasting, she moved to the cable network as an assignment assistant. She worked as a producer for CNN's Atlanta bureau before moving into reporting, first in Miami, and then in Washington, D.C.

In 1989 she was NBC's deputy correspondent covering the Pentagon, then a general correspondent before becoming a coanchor on *Today* in 1991.

Craft, Christine (1944–)

Christine Craft is the former anchorwoman for KMBC-TV in Kansas City, Missouri, who won a $500,000 award in a sex discrimination suit in 1983 against her station and Metromedia. She was fired because viewers supposedly found her "too informal in dress and manner, too opinionated and lacking warmth and comfort" and "not being deferential enough to men." An appeals court judge overturned the decision, saying that the station was justified in firing her for reasons other than job performance.

Craft started as a weather girl in Salinas, California, then moved to KPIX in San Francisco. When asked to appear in a bathing suit to do a weather report, she appeared in a turn-of-the-century bathing costume that covered her from neck to ankles. When she moved to CBS to work on *Women in Sports,* the network bleached her hair and supplied her with a makeup regime, indicating that appearance was the most important aspect of her job.

In 1979 she became a general-assignment reporter and coanchor of the 11 P.M. news at KEYT-TV. A year later, Craft accepted KMBC's offer to anchor their nightly news broadcast. When ratings didn't increase, the management demoted her from the anchor position because (by her recollection) she was "too old, too unattractive and not deferential enough to men."

She brought suit for "sexual discrimination in an advisory capacity," in addition to charging a violation of the Equal Pay Act (she received $35,000 as anchor while her male counterpart made $52,000) and fraud because KMBC had specified, at her insistence, that they were hiring her for her journalistic abilities, not her looks—and then fired her because of her appearance and manner.

Craft won twice before a jury (she also received a $325,000 award on her fraud suit), but both decisions were overturned by male judges. When the cases went before the U.S. Supreme Court, only Sandra Day O'Connor was willing to hear the case; O'Connor's male colleagues felt no legal basis existed.

Craft hoped that her case would enable women to remain before the cameras as they grew older, but women in the news field continue to feel more pressure in the area of physical appearance than their male counterparts. The scenario was used in a 1998 episode of *Ally McBeal* (1997–), in which Ally defended a female anchor (Kate Jackson) who had been fired, not because of her journalistic credentials, but because male viewers didn't find her attractive enough "to want to sleep with her."

Craft occasionally hosted a radio talk show in Sacramento in the late 1990s while attending McGeorge School of Law. In 1988, she published *Too Old, Too Ugly, and Not Deferential to Men,* a book about her experiences.

Crist, Judith (1922–)

Judith Crist, *TV Guide*'s movie critic for many years, received her undergraduate degree from Hunter College in 1941 and a master's in journalism from Columbia University in 1945. During World War II, she worked as a teacher, then became a reporter and columnist on the *New York Herald Tribune* (1945–1960), and later, the on-air film critic for the *Today Show* (1963–1973). Although she continued contributing to other publications, Crist joined *TV Guide* in 1965 and often saw as many as 400 films a year.

She was an instructor and lecturer in journalism at Hunter College (1947), Sarah Lawrence College (1958), and Columbia Graduate School (1959–1962), in addition to writing several books including *The Private Eye, the Cowboy & the Very Naked Girl* (1968), *Judith Crist's TV Guide to the Movies* (1974), and *Take 22: Moviemakers on Moviemaking* (1984).

Crist has received many awards throughout her career, such as the New York Newspaper Guild "Page One" Award (1955), George Polk Award (1961), and New York Newspaper Women's Club Award (1955, 1959, 1963, 1965, 1967), as well as academic honors and awards from Hunter College and Columbia University.

Cybill (1995–1997)

This series, starring Cybill Shepherd in the title role, focused on the trials and tribulations of a forty-something, twice-married actress whose life often resembled a soap opera.

Obviously no longer the nubile ingenue, the character Cybill was often relegated to appearing in strange commercials and unbelievably hackneyed roles instead of the better roles she would like to attract. She was aided and led astray by her best friend, Maryann (Christine Baranski), a cynical, hard-drinking divorcée who lived to make her ex-husband, Dr. Dick, regret the day he was born.

Cybill's older daughter, Rachel (Dedee Pfeiffer), had made her a grandmother, while her younger daughter, Zoey (Alicia Witt), brought new meaning to the term *angst*. Also, occasionally seen were Cybill's first ex-husband, Jeff (Tom Wopat), a usually out-of-work stuntman, and her second ex-husband, Ira (Alan Rosenberg), a neurotic novelist.

D

Dandridge, Ruby (1900–1987)

Although she always played dowdy, mammy-type characters, Ruby Dandridge, with her trademark high-pitched voice, was a popular black supporting actress from the 1930s to 1950s. As was true of many black women, she was relegated mainly to maid or housekeeper roles, so her range of talent was rarely seen.

She played several such roles on radio. She was Geranium on *The Judy Canova Show* in 1943; Raindrop on *The Gene Autry Show* in 1944; Oriole on *Beulah,* both on radio and on television in its final year (1953); and Delilah on *Father of the Bride* (1961–1962). In each role, Dandridge played the dutiful black maid in a predominantly white cast, except on *Beulah,* where several black actors appeared.

See also Black Female Roles.

Daniels, Susanne (1955–)

Susanne Daniels was named president of programming at the WB Network in December 1998 after serving as vice-president of programming since 1995. She helped develop the youth-oriented hits *Buffy: The Vampire Slayer* (1996–), *Dawson's Creek* (1997–), *Felicity* (1998–), and *Charmed* (1998–).

After receiving a bachelor's degree in English from Harvard, Daniels worked as an assistant on NBC's *Saturday Night Live* before moving to ABC, where she worked as a director in diverse genres from docudrama to variety programming. She then moved to Fox as director of comedy development, and eventually to the WB Network as part of the network launch team in 1993.

Dark Shadows (1966–1971)

Technically a soap opera, *Dark Shadows* stands alone because of its bizarre plots and strange assortment of characters, who generally had multiple incarnations. Tremendously popular with younger viewers, the series was shown late in the afternoon, thus allowing them to get home from school in time to watch. Its gothic overtones created a mystique that set it apart from the traditional soap opera fare, and it became the first, never to be equaled, "horror" opera.

From the beginning, the series had an eerie atmosphere as Victoria Winters (Alexandre Moltke) arrived in the gloomy town of Collinsport,

Michael McGuire appears as the Head of Judah Zachery with Grayson Hall as Dr. Julia Hoffman and Nancy Barrett as Leticia Faye in a Dark Shadows *plot line that sent characters back in time to the 1800s. (Archive Photos)*

Maine, to become governess to young David Collins (David Henesy). While waiting for a ride to Collinswood Manor, Vickie was befriended by Maggie Evans (Kathryn Leigh Scott), a waitress at the town's cafe, who warned her of strange happenings at the manor. Upon arriving at the appropriately dark and forbidding house, Vickie was introduced to the Collins family— David; his father, Roger (Louis Edmonds); his aunt, Elizabeth (Joan Bennett); and his cousin, Carolyn (Nancy Barrett).

For the next few months, series events unfolded in regular soap opera style with a gothic twist. Victoria was kidnapped when she learned that the caretaker had killed a man, only to be saved when her kidnapper had a heart attack after seeing the ghost of Josette DuPres (also played by Scott), an ancestor of the Collins clan. Then the ghost of David's mother, Laura (Diana Millay), tried to get David to commit suicide so that he could join her in the afterlife. Elizabeth Collins was being blackmailed into marriage with Jason McGuire (Dennis Patrick), who looked just like her husband, Paul, who had died under mysterious circumstances.

On 14 April 1967, all these lesser plots paled to insignificance when Barnabas Collins (Jonathan Fried) was introduced to viewers after lackey Willie Loomis (John Karlen) released him from his crypt. Barnabas had been imprisoned in his crypt because, although charming and urbane, he was also a vampire. His first act upon his release was to kidnap Maggie who, as mentioned earlier, looked just like his wife, Josette DuPres, whom he had lost when an evil witch, Angelique (Lara Parker), put a hex on her.

Maggie's escape and subsequent stay at Windcliffe Sanitarium brought Dr. Julia Hoffman (Grayson Hall) to investigate her wild claims. She became intrigued with Barnabas, and began experiments to turn him into a mortal again. Her quest continued for the remainder of the series.

Not surprisingly, Victoria soon went insane from flashback dreams and unexplained happenings, and Maggie became governess. Then, Angelique returned in the guise of Roger's new wife, Cassandra. Added into this mix of characters was a werewolf, Chris Jennings (David Briscoe), whose twin brother, Tom, was a vampire. Chris and sister Amy (Denise Nickerson) summoned werewolf Quentin Collins (David Selby) from 1897, and his character became almost as popular as that of his cousin Barnabas.

The series released several of its songs, and "Quentin's Theme" became popular enough to place on Billboard's Top 20. The song enjoyed a resurgence of popularity after Romanian gymnast Nadia Comaneci used it in her gold medal–winning performance at the 1976 Olympics, and it was renamed "Nadia's Theme."

The series frequently had story lines that went back in time, or the characters went to a parallel time that showed how things would be if a character had made a different choice at a crucial point in her/his life. Most cast members appeared as several characters throughout the series, generally playing ancestors or descendants of their original characters.

When the series was canceled in 1971, viewers were so upset with the ambiguity of the ending that head writer Sam Hall wrote an article explaining how he would have resolved the stories. To most viewers' satisfaction, both Quentin and Barnabas would have been cured, and Barnabas would have married Julia before leaving Collinsport.

While still in production, *Dark Shadows* spawned two feature films—*House of Dark Shadows* (1970) and *Night of Dark Shadows* (1971). After cancellation the series immediately went into syndication and was shown throughout the 1970s and 1980s. In 1989 *Dark Shadows'* 1,245 episodes went into video release. The series was purchased in 1992 by the Sci-Fi Channel and shown daily on that network beginning in September of that year. The concept was retooled in 1991, but it was soon canceled because it lacked the impact of the original.

Davis, Bette (1908–1989)

Bette Davis was born Ruth Elizabeth Davis in Lowell, Massachusetts, and by the time she was age five, she was reading Balzac. She shortened her name in honor of one of her favorite characters from his writings, La Cousine Bette.

She attended John Murray Anderson School of Theatre before making her Broadway debut in 1929 in *Broken Dreams,* a domestic comedy. She received critical attention in a 1932 film, *The Man Who Played God,* but became a popular hit with her role in *Of Human Bondage* (1934). She won an Oscar as Best Actress for her roles in *Dangerous* (1935) and *Jezebel* (1937). The story goes that she nicknamed the statuette "Oscar" after her then-husband, Harmon Oscar Nelson, a New York musician.

She perfected the role of forceful yet troubled independent woman in films such as *Dark Victory* (1939) and *All about Eve* (1950). She was one of the highest-paid actresses during the war years, but the postwar return-to-femininity attitude made it difficult for her to find satisfactory roles since she played independent women.

As film roles became scarce, Davis turned to television, appearing in several 1950s drama anthologies, including *Ford Theatre* (1949–1957),

Schlitz Playhouse of Stars (1951–1959), *Studio 57* (1954–1955), and *20th Century Fox Hour* (1955–1957). She also appeared on a variety of episodic series such as *Wagon Train* (1957–1965), *The June Allyson Show* (1959–1961), *The Virginian* (1962–1971), *Perry Mason* (1957–1966), *Gunsmoke* (1955–1964, 1967–1971), *It Takes a Thief* (1968–1970), and most recently, *Hotel* (1983–1988).

She also appeared in many made-for-television movies, including *Madame Sin* (1972), *Judge and Jake Wyler* (1972), *Scream Pretty Peggy* (1973), *Family Reunion* (1981), *A Piano for Mrs. Cimino* (1982), *Little Gloria, Happy at Last* (1982), and *Murder with Mirrors* (1985). She won an Emmy in 1979 for her performance in *Strangers: The Story of a Mother and Daughter,* which many critics called her best performance in 30 years.

She also received a Lifetime Achievement Award from the Film Institute in 1977, and was posthumously honored at the Kennedy Center for the Arts. She was further immortalized by a Kim Carnes song entitled "Bette Davis Eyes" (1981).

Davis, Gail (1926–1997)

The actress who played Annie Oakley on television was born Billy Jeanne Grayson in Little Rock, Arkansas. She was discovered by Gene Autry while she was attending the University of Texas at Austin.

Autry featured her in many of his movies and nearly 30 episodes of his own series, and eventually created the series *Annie Oakley* (1953–1956) for her. The character was made for her, because she was actually a trick shot and excellent rider who had performed in Autry's traveling rodeo. In addition to *The Gene Autry Show* (1950–1956), she appeared as similar characters on *The Lone Ranger* (1949–1957), *The Cisco Kid* (1950–1956), *The Range Rider* (1951–1952), and *Death Valley Days* (1952–1972) before her own series started.

After her series ended, Davis managed other celebrities. In 1994 she received the Golden Boot award in recognition of her work in Westerns.

See also *Annie Oakley.*

Davis, Pyper (1965–)

As president of fit-tv, Pyper Davis is in charge of its 1999 relaunch with expanded cable access to 10 million homes. The network combines fitness, health, and lifestyle information geared to the female viewer with such programs as *Fit Resort & Spa, Fit It In,* and *Fit on Location.*

A Princeton graduate, Davis began her career in entertainment with Rupert Murdoch's News Corporation in 1992. Later, as senior vice-president, she worked on the launch of the Fox Sports Network.

The Days and Nights of Molly Dodd (1987–1991)

This series, from which the term *dramedy* was coined, followed the life of Molly Dodd (Blair Brown), who was trying to reestablish her life after her divorce from her irresponsible, saxophone-playing husband, Fred (William Converse-Roberts). Not trained for anything specific, she regularly changed her rather low-level jobs and was surrounded by eccentric friends and neighbors. Being only sporadically employed, she spent a lot of time evaluating her life and the people in it—often in fantasy sequences, in which she sometimes talked her problems through with a person from her past.

Although seldom remembered by viewers, Molly Dodd was the first unmarried television character to have a baby on her own; she and the baby's father, a black detective named Nathaniel Hawthorne (Richard Lawson), finally decided to get married, but Nathaniel died of an allergic reaction to MSG.

The birth of her daughter Emily caused little notice in 1991. Yet in 1992, the fact that unmarried Murphy Brown was having a baby became a political issue during the presidential campaign.

Death of a Princess (1980)

This docudrama was based on a real incident that occurred in 1977. Princess Mish-al (or Misha'), the 19-year-old unmarried granddaughter of Amir Muhammad ibn abdul Aziz, the oldest surviving son of King Ibn Saud, was put to death for having an affair with a commoner. When it was announced that the program would air, it created a small international incident because the Saudi ruling family, who controlled most of their country's oil reserves, brought tremendous pressure to ban its showing.

The program related the circumstances of the princess's murder, which was supposedly the prescribed penalty for a woman taken in adultery in the *shari'a*, the law of Islam. However, the male members of the Saudi ruling family were well known for their affairs with Western commoners and excessive lifestyles that went unpunished and uncurtailed.

The program did not sensationalize the incident, but it drew the attention of viewers to the great inequity in how women were treated in Islamic countries. In the furor that resulted from the program, many felt the princess had been used as a sacrifice to show that the ruling family, unpopular with their subjects because of their excesses, would still uphold Islamic law.

Also revealed in the subsequent publicity concerning the incident was the fact that the *shari'a* calls for a trial (no evidence of this happening), and the need for four witnesses to testify to the act before the accused could be condemned. Additionally, no provision in the law called for her lover's decapitation.

The program galvanized many women's organizations to pay closer attention to the plight of Islamic women in a culture that allows men to do anything to a woman with impunity.

Suzanne Taleb, the Egyptian actress who portrayed the princess, was only on-screen for eight minutes, yet she was blacklisted and harassed in her homeland to such a degree that she eventually moved to London.

December Bride (1954–1961)

Lily Ruskin (Spring Byington) was a vivacious widow who lived with her daughter, Ruth (Frances Rafferty), and son-in-law, Matt Henshaw (Dean Miller), who were constantly playing Cupid. The show's charm was a direct result of the irrepressible wit of the character Lily and Byington's captivating presence. The most positive aspect of the show was the portrayal of an older woman as vital and self-sufficient.

Prior to moving into television, Byington was nominated for Best Supporting Actress as Jean Arthur in *You Can't Take It with You* (1938).

See also Older Women on Television.

Dee, Ruby (1924–)

Ruby Dee became the first black woman in a recurring role in a prime-time soap opera when she appeared as Alma Miles during the last season of the series *Peyton Place* (1964–1969). Prior to that role, Dee had appeared as a guest on such series as *East Side/West Side* (1963–1964); *The Great Adventure* (1963–1964), in which she portrayed Harriet Tubman; *The Fugitive* (1963–1967); and *The Nurses* (1962–1965), for which she received an Emmy nomination.

She appeared in *Roots: The Next Generation* (1979) as Queen Haley, *Gore Vidal's Lincoln* (1987), and a PBS series, *With Ossie and Ruby*, in which she appeared with her husband, Ossie Davis. In 1999 she and Davis wrote a book, *With Ossie and Ruby,* discussing their 50-year marriage and their commitment to eliminating racism and oppression.

Dee began her career performing with the American Negro Theatre in the mid-1940s and made her Broadway debut in *Anna Lucasta* (1946). She made her first film in 1950, *No Way Out,* and many consider her finest performance to be *Raisin in the Sun* (1961). Recent films include *Do the Right Thing* (1989) and *Jungle Fever* (1991).

See also Black Female Roles.

Dekoven, Lindy (1954–)

Lindy Dekoven, executive vice-president at NBC Entertainment for miniseries and television motion pictures, received her bachelor's degree in elementary education from the University of Arizona before becoming an independent producer. She worked for Walt Disney Television as director of network development before moving to the Landsburg Company as vice-president of creative affairs. In 1991 she was named vice-president for movies and miniseries at Lorimar.

In 1993, Dekoven moved to NBC; as executive vice-president, she controls a $200–$300 million annual budget and has moved the network toward covering more controversial topics, such as the Emmy-winning *Serving in Silence: The Margarethe Cammermeyer Story* (1995), *Pandora's Clock* (1996), and extravaganza miniseries such as *Asteroid* (1996), Homer's *The Odyssey* (1997), *Merlin* (1998), and *Crime and Punishment* (1998).

dePasse, Suzanne (1958–)

Suzanne dePasse began her career as an assistant to Motown president Barry Gordy, then worked as a producer before she was named president of Motown Productions—the first black woman to head a major entertainment corporation. She worked on several specials showcasing Motown artists before she broadened her focus to miniseries and episodic programs. She was instrumental in the production of the miniseries *Lonesome Dove,* which received the highest rating of any miniseries in the five years prior to 1989 and was awarded seven Emmys.

Through her own production company, dePasse Entertainment, she continues to work on a broad range of productions, emphasizing the realistic depiction of the black experience. In the 1998–1999 season she had two returning sitcoms on WB: *Sister, Sister* (1994–1999) and *Smart Guy* (1997–1999).

See also Black Female Roles.

Designing Women (1986–1993)

Created by Linda Bloodworth-Thomason (who also wrote every script for the first two seasons), *Designing Women* concerned a group of women in Atlanta operating an interior decorating business with the personal, rather than professional, lives of the women being the focal point. The series could arguably be called the first series "about nothing," since conversational interactions of the characters were emphasized, and most scenes took place in the living room turned office.

In this pseudo-workplace, the episodes stressed sisterhood and the supportive, almost familial relationships among the characters. Like previous series that focused on working women, the characters were seldom seen actually working, giving an illusion of friends gathering to discuss their lives. Because of the homelike ambience of their "office," even when they were at work they were safely "in the home."

The cast originally consisted of outspoken widow Julia Sugarbaker (Dixie Carter), who had the good taste, connections, and drive to propel the business to success. Her younger sister, Suzanne (Delta Burke), a former beauty queen, relied on her physical appearance to get by while collecting alimony from three ex-husbands; as a silent partner, she demonstrated no interest in the business. MaryJo Shively (Annie Potts) was a recently divorced mother of two attempting to rebuild her life, and Charlene Frazier (Jean Smart) was the often naively trusting office manager who, although lacking a formal education or sophistication, was often the voice of common sense. The only male character in this tableau was Anthony Bouvier (Meshach Taylor), the firm's delivery man.

The humor was based on the repartee of the four women. Within the conversational format, the series dealt with social issues including sexism, sex education and AIDS awareness, violence against women, and pornography. The character of Julia was often used to express profeminist sentiments or to motivate the other characters to action. In almost direct contrast to Julia's character, a socially conscious woman of the 1980s, was the depiction of Suzanne, who because of her self-centered view of life often made remarks that were sexist, racist, or classist, enabling the other characters to counter with more liberal statements.

This very popular series was touted by some feminists for its handling of female issues, but it was known more for its feminine appeal than its feminist sentiments; even though the female characters were romantically involved with men, the primary focus was always the relationships among the women.

When Burke left the show in 1991, she was replaced by a Sugarbaker cousin, Allison (Julia Duffy), a pushy, overbearing woman. She in turn was replaced after a year by wealthy eccentric B. J. Poteet (Judith Ivey), who became part-owner of the business. Smart also left the show in 1991, and her character's sister, Carlene (Jan Hooks), joined the group.

See also Bloodworth-Thomason, Linda.

DETECTIVE/POLICE DRAMA SERIES

The detective/police genre is closely related to the action/adventure format. Many early action/adventure series focused on law enforcement, and these early programs rarely featured women as other than secretaries or victims.

The 1960s brought the viewing audience some female characters who were active and central to series. Honey West (Anne Francis on *Honey West,* 1965–1966) was a competent as well as beautiful private eye, Mrs. Emma Peel (Diana Rigg on *The Avengers,* 1966–1968) was a "talented amateur" who partnered Agent John Steed in his cases, and Christie Love (Teresa Graves on *Get Christie Love,* 1974–1975) was an independent, competent police detective.

However, women were generally cast in roles to lessen the possibility of the series being charged with sexual discrimination by the growing number of feminist television critics. In many series, female police officers were often little more than window dressing, decoys, or potential damsels-in-distress for the male characters to save.

The successful series *Ironside* (1967–1975), in which Raymond Burr portrayed former chief of detectives Robert T. Ironside, had two female policewomen during the years it appeared. Officer Eve Whitfield (Barbara Anderson, 1967–1971) and Officer Fran Belding (Elizabeth Baur, 1971–1975) were less equal on the streets during the action than in the office during the planning.

In 1968, in an effort to lessen anxiety for adult television viewers about the growing youth movement, *Mod Squad* (1968–1973) premiered with a group of probationers—two male and one female (Peggy Lipton)—acting as semicops who infiltrated the youth movement to catch the adults who were corrupting and misleading the young people. A year after *Mod Squad* ended, *Police Woman* (1974–1978) featured Sergeant Pepper Anderson (Angie Dickinson). Although she was able to defend herself when necessary, she was more often the bait that brought the criminals to her male partners, who did most of the arresting and fighting.

(continued on next page)

(continued from previous page)

With the premiere of *Cagney and Lacey* (1982–1988), the two central female characters portrayed police detectives actively involved in their cases who definitely did not need to be rescued by their male counterparts. Mary Beth Lacey (Tyne Daly) was a wife and mother, and partner Chris Cagney (Meg Foster for the first episodes, then Sharon Gless for the remainder of the series) was attractive and single, which enabled the writers to explore both married and single life in relation to friendships and career. Yet, even with this popular series, the network mantra was "Beware of being unfeminine." After this series went off the air in 1988, not until *Under Suspicion* (1994–1995) did a woman once again appear in a female-centered police drama.

Other series have featured female officers among ensemble casts. *Hill Street Blues* (1981–1987) had Officer (later Sergeant) Lucy Bates (Betty Thomas) as a recurring character who was as active and competent as any of the male characters. She grappled with personal as well as professional problems like her male counterparts, but she was a fully functioning member of the force. *Hunter* (1984–1991), although focusing on male detective Rick Hunter (Fred Dryer), also featured his partner, Detective DeeDee McCall (Stepfanie Kramer).

More recently, series such as *NYPD Blue* (1993–) have female characters who are depicted primarily in their relationships to the male characters. Officer Janice Licalsi (Amy Brenneman, 1993–1994) was Detective John Kelly's "almost" love interest, Assistant DA Sylvia Costas (Sharon Lawrence, 1993–) was Detective Andy Sipowicz's girlfriend turned wife, Administrative Assistant Donna Abandando (Gail O'Grady, 1994–1996) was involved in an on-again/off-again relationship with Detective Greg Medavoy, and Detective Diane Russell (1996–) was the love interest, then wife, of Detective Bobby Simone (Jimmy Smits, 1994–1999). Although involved in the action and evolution of the story lines, these women are first and foremost significant others to the male characters.

A recent series that departed slightly from the norm of women as other-centered and cast a woman as an active central character in a police drama was the noirish *Under Suspicion* (1994–1995). Loosely inspired by the British series *Prime Suspect*, the American version had Detective Rose "Phil" Phillips (Karen Sillas) as the only female officer in an all-male precinct. Often working alone, Phil fought crime in the streets and the sexist attitudes of her coworkers as she grappled with issues in her personal life.

See also Action/Adventure Genre, *The Avengers, Cagney and Lacey, Get Christie Love, Hill Street Blues, Honey West, Mod Squad, Police Woman, Under Suspicion.*

Dewhurst, Colleen (1926–1991)

Born in Canada, Colleen Dewhurst was renowned for her performances in several Eugene O'Neill plays. She also appeared in several films, beginning with *A Nun's Story* (1959). Perhaps her most impressive role was that of Diane Keaton's mother in *Annie Hall* (1977).

Dewhurst was also very active in television. She appeared in several of the dramatic anthologies of the 1950s, including *U.S. Steel Hour* (1953–1963) and *DuPont Show of the Week* (1961–1964). She guest-starred on such diverse series as *Ben Casey* (1961–1966), *The FBI* (1965–1974), *The Big Valley* (1965–1969), *The Love Boat* (1977–1986), and *The New Twilight Zone* (1985–1987).

In addition, she appeared in several made-for-TV movies such as *Silent Victory: The Kitty O'Neill Story* (1979), *Guyana Tragedy* (1980), *Between Two Women* (1986), and *Sword of Gideon* (1986). Her list of specials is equally impressive: *The Crucible* (1967), *The Story of Jacob and Joseph* (1974), *Three Women Alone* (1974), and *Tennessee Williams' South* (1987).

Although she played many roles on television, she is probably best remembered as Murphy Brown's tart-tongued mother, Avery Brown, a role that earned her two Emmy awards. After Dewhurst's death, *Murphy Brown* aired an episode revolving around the death of Avery Brown.

See also *Murphy Brown*.

Dharma and Greg (1997–)

Dharma Finkelstein (Jenna Elfman), the free-spirited daughter of hippie parents (Mimi Kennedy and Alan Rachins), was raised and home-schooled in Marin County. She married preppy lawyer Greg Montgomery (Thomas Gibson) on their first date, and although Dharma's parents accepted this turn of events, Greg's wealthy parents (Susan Sullivan and Mitchell Ryan) were appalled by their new in-laws (Dharma's parents never bothered to get married) and their casual behavior.

This battle of cultures makes up many of the episodes. Like several previous sitcom characters, Dharma has a naive wisdom that often shows up her materialistic in-laws, and her spontaneity helps her husband relax and enjoy the simple things that his stuffy upbringing never allowed him to experience.

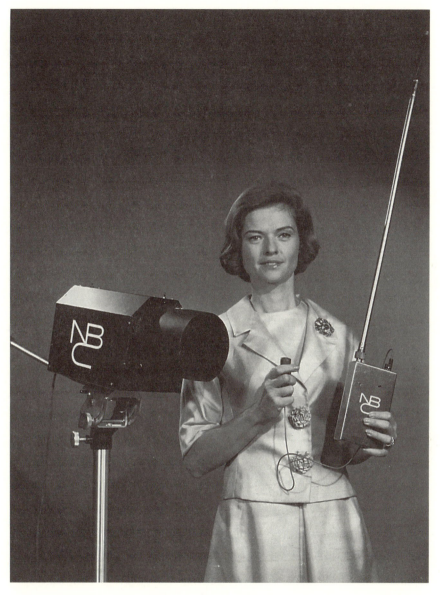

NBC correspondent Nancy Dickerson poses with "black beam sound" equipment, 1964. (Photofest)

Dickerson, Nancy (1927–1997)

One of the first women to receive national attention as a journalist, Nancy Dickerson worked as a teacher before getting a job with the Senate Foreign Relations Committee. She was the first woman to author a major committee report.

In 1954 she joined the CBS production staff as associate producer of the political series *Face the Nation* (1954–), where journalists question public figures on current issues. In 1960 she became the first female correspondent for CBS and the first woman in the anchor booth at the Democratic National Convention that year.

In 1963, Dickerson moved to NBC to get more airtime and was given her own daily news show, *Nancy Dickerson with the News,* a five-minute afternoon headline recap that was the first to feature a female anchor. She covered the White House for NBC throughout the turbulent 1960s and was featured on another daily newscast, *Inside Washington.*

In 1970 she formed her own production company, specializing in news documentaries, and won a Peabody Award in 1982 for her retrospective on Watergate. She continued to be active in journalism until 1996.

See also News.

Dinsdale, Shirley (1927–1999)

In 1949, Shirley Dinsdale won an Emmy award as "outstanding television personality," becoming the first person to receive television's highest award. Dinsdale and her pigtailed, freckled-faced puppet, Judy Splinters, had a 15-minute children's program that appeared on KTLA (Los Angeles) five days a week.

Dinsdale was only 15 when she began her show business career and trained with renowned ventriloquist Edgar Bergen. At 17, she had her own radio show, eventually going on to television. She was also the summer replacement for *Kukla, Fran & Ollie* in 1949.

After winning the Emmy, Dinsdale hosted children's shows in both New York and Chicago before retiring in 1973. She died of cancer in 1999.

Dr. Quinn, Medicine Woman (1993–1998)

As the series opened, Dr. Michaela "Mike" Quinn (Jane Seymour) moved from Boston to Colorado Springs, Colorado, in the 1860s to practice medicine. She quickly won over the skeptical townspeople, bringing her liberal ideas of equality and fairness to the traditionally minded populace in story lines that allowed her to express her before-her-time views.

Interestingly, the character had the potential to be a watershed in the depiction of independent women, but the threat of her independence was immediately curtailed by her assumption of the role of surrogate mother.

Upon arriving in town, Dr. Mike was befriended by the owner of the town boardinghouse, Charlotte Cooper, who had three children. As Charlotte lay dying of a rattlesnake bite, she asked Dr. Mike to adopt her children.

Another early supporter of her efforts was a mountain man, Byron Sully (Joe Lando). As she gained the respect and affection of the townspeople, she also won Sully's love, and the two married during the 1994–1995 season. During the next season, they had a baby (coinciding with the actual birth of Jane Seymour's twins).

Doerfer Plan

The Doerfer Plan was a 1960 agreement between the Federal Communications Commission (FCC) and the three major networks that required each network to air noncompeting weekly public-affairs programs during prime time in partial reparation for the quiz show scandals. Although the plan called for "collusion" by the networks to ensure that the programs would not air against one another, the Justice Department allowed this violation of antitrust laws because the action was for a "worthy purpose." Local news and social documentaries became a popular means of complying with this ruling.

Doris Day Show (1968–1973)

The *Doris Day Show* had many incarnations in its attempt to reflect the changing social times. The series began as a traditional story of a widow, Doris Martin (Day), and her two sons moving back to the family ranch, and the humor derived from their adjustments to country living.

In a supposed reaction to the new emphasis on independent career-minded women, the second season showed Doris Martin commuting to San Francisco for a secretarial job with *Today's World* magazine. This format change brought the show into the Nielsen's Top Ten. For some reason, during the third season the family moved to San Francisco, living above an Italian restaurant while Doris Martin began writing articles in addition to her secretarial duties.

In a slightly bizarre twist, the fourth and final season found Doris Martin suddenly single with no children (reflecting a complete cast change) and working as a staff writer, bringing the series in line with the urban career-woman format popularized by *The Mary Tyler Moore Show* (1970–1977). The elimination of her family occurred without explanation (being from the pre-*Dynasty*-shower-dream-sequence days) and continued as the series focus until its cancellation.

Although Day has been called film's "Queen of Modern Romantic Comedy," her series is remembered as perhaps holding the record for format changes: four in five years.

The Dottie Mack Show

See Variety Series

Duke, Patty (1946–)

Although Patty Duke won a special Oscar at the age of 16 for her portrayal of Helen Keller in *The Miracle Worker* (1962), the majority of her work has been for television. Prior to appearing in *The Miracle Worker,* Duke played roles on the daytime soap operas *The Brighter Day* (1954–1962) and *Kitty Fogle* (1958), as well as many of the dramatic anthologies that were popular during the early years of television. She even appeared on *The $64,000 Challenge* and won over $8,000.

After receiving her Oscar, Duke had her own successful sitcom, *The Patty Duke Show* (1963–1966), in which she played two identical cousins, Patty and Cathy Lane, coming of age in Brooklyn Heights, New York. This light family comedy was extremely popular with teenagers, not only because the lead was a teenager herself, but also because popular singing stars such as Chad and Jeremy, Frankie Avalon, and Bobby Vinton made guest appearances.

In addition to making guest appearances on episodic series, Duke has appeared in many made-for-TV movies such as *My Sweet Charlie* (1970), *If Tomorrow Comes* (1971), *Look What's Happened to Rosemary's Baby* (1976), *A Time to Triumph* (1986), *Fatal Judgment* (1988), and *Amityville: The Evil Escapes* (1989), as well as miniseries such as *Captains & Kings* (1976) and *George Washington* (1984).

Unfortunately, Duke has not been able to find a successful series since *The Patty Duke Show,* although she has made three attempts. In the short-lived sitcom *Hail to the Chief* (1985), she portrayed the first female American president, Julia Mansfield, in a series created by Susan Harris and written in serial fashion with ongoing, if absurd, story lines. In another short-lived sitcom attempt, *Karen's Song* (1987), Duke portrayed Karen Mathews, a newly promoted book editor who fell in love with a man 12 years her junior.

In a departure from her previous sitcom forays, Duke moved to drama in *Amazing Grace* (1995), a series with the dubious distinction of being the lowest-rated NBC program for the season, yet the show received much critical acclaim. In this series, which lasted only one month, Duke portrayed Hannah Miller, a former nurse turned drug addict who had gotten clean and became a preacher and crusader for the downtrodden.

Although her recent attempts into series television have all been unsuccessful, Duke is still widely respected for her acting, and she continues to be successful in movies and miniseries. Some of her more recent roles include the dedicated teacher of an autistic boy in *Cries from the Heart* (1994), Miss Sook Faulk in the remake of Truman Capote's *A Christmas Memory* (1997), and the mother whose son disappeared in *When He Didn't Come Home* (1998).

Duvall, Shelley (1949–)

Originally a screen actress known for her offbeat natural style of acting in such films as *3 Women* (1977), *The Shining* (1980), and *Popeye* (1980), Shelley Duvall moved into producing in the 1980s, concentrating on high-quality children's entertainment. One of her most notable productions was *Faerie Tale Theatre* (1982–1987) for Showtime; it adapted classic children's fairy tales and is still regularly rerun on the Disney Channel. Other successful projects included *Shelley Duvall's Tall Tales and Legends* (1985–1988), which adapted stories from American folklore for viewing by children, and *Shelley Duvall's Bedtime Stories*.

Some view her success in interpreting and enlarging the characters in *The Little Mermaid* (Pam Dawber as the mermaid), *Beauty and the Beast* (Susan Sarandon as Beauty), and *Aladdin and His Wonderful Lamp* (Valerie Bertinelli as Aladdin's girlfriend) with live actors as the impetus that moved Disney Studios back to full-length animated movies. Duvall continues to produce children's programming through her two production companies, Think Entertainment and Platypus Productions.

E

Earth 2 (1994–1995)

This science-fiction soap opera possibly holds the record for the number of times it was preempted: 11 times in 33 weeks. Not surprisingly (although it had many things going for it, including being produced by Steven Spielberg's Amblin Entertainment), the series never found an audience—mostly because the audience could never find the series.

Earth 2 was set 200 years into the future; pollution had made Earth virtually uninhabitable, forcing most people to live on space stations, but the artificial environments caused children to become ill with severe immune deficiencies. Scientist Devon Adair (Debrah Farentino), whose son Ulysses (Joey Zimmerman) suffered from the disease and was confined to a life-support suit, led a group of adventurers to an Earthlike planet to establish a colony, New Pacifica, where it was hoped that the healthful environment would cure the children.

Unfortunately, the main ship was sabotaged and the escape vehicles all landed at different locations on the planet. Devon's group landed on the wrong side of the planet, and most of their equipment was destroyed in the crash. The episodes focused on their efforts to reach the other side of the planet, the dangers they encountered, and the process of becoming a cohesive group.

The series presented several strong female characters—in fact, in many ways the women were stronger than the male characters. Devon was a competent, decisive leader, yet also a tender and loving mother to Ulysses. The group's physician was Dr. Julia Heller (Jessica Steen), literally bred to be a doctor. At the beginning of the series, she was more emotionless automaton than person. Eventually, she was exposed as a spy for the unethical authorities, but meanwhile waged an internal battle of loyalties as she bonded with the other group members and grappled with her emerging humanness. The final lead female character was Bess Martin (Rebecca Gayheart), the wife of the ineffectual government official, Morgan (John Gegenhuber). Her character was outwardly the traditionally supportive and caring wife despite Morgan's many faults, but her own strength of character and stamina showed in stark contrast to her weak husband.

Dr. Francis Horowitz, from the popular Ding Dong School, *speaks with children at the New Memphis Public Library in Tennessee, 4 May 1955. (Photofest)*

EDUCATIONAL PROGRAMMING

From television's inception, series have educated as well as entertained children, teaching a combination of prosocial behavior, learning fundamentals, and even religious basics.

One of the first educational programs for preschoolers was *Ding Dong School* (1952–1956), in which Miss Frances (Dr. Frances Horwich of the education department of Roosevelt College in Chicago) instructed children prior to the advent of "cartoon babysitters." Billed as "the nursery school of the air," the show got its name from the opening sequence, in which a bell was used to call "school" into session. Dr. Horwich died in 1997.

During this same period, *Happy's Party* (1952–1953), hosted by Ida Mae Maber, was broadcast from Pittsburgh on the Dumont network. The series featured a puppet named Happy who tried to expose young viewers to culturally accepted educational and social values.

Another early educational series was *Romper Room*, created by Nancy and Bert Claster. *Romper Room* premiered in Baltimore in 1953 with host Miss Nancy seeing the young viewers through her Magic Mirror. For 11 years Miss Nancy taught manners (with Do Bee and Don't Bee) and led interactive learning activities. The format was widely syndicated and adapted to local markets, using local children and a resident "teacher." The final *Romper Room* went off the air in 1994, although Claster Productions continues to distribute children's programming. Nancy Claster also died in 1997.

Shari Lewis used her puppets to teach prosocial behavior in several children's programs over the years. One of her most popular puppets was the shy Lamb Chop, a cuddly talking lamb. Along with Charlie Horse and Hush Puppy, Lamb Chop and the young viewers "learned" the behaviors and attitudes of "good" children.

However, in 1969 all previous educational efforts paled in comparison to *Sesame Street*. Developed by Joan Ganz Cooney and the Children's Television Workshop, the show is set on a city street populated by a variety of humans and puppets created by the late Jim Henson. Through a fast-paced combination of animation, puppets, songs, and skits, the program teaches letters, numbers, and language.

In 1975, NBC premiered *Vegetable Soup* (1975–1976), through which children were exposed to other cultures in order to appreciate diversity. The "other scope" segment featured profiles of successful minority professionals, while "Real People" was an ethnically diverse soap opera spoof. Long John Spoilsport (James Earl Jones) modeled behaviors that viewers should not copy in "Adventures in Saniland," and the "Woody the Spoon" cartoon featured the voice of Bette Midler reciting recipes for dishes from different cultures.

A few long-running, male-centered children's programs have also aired. *Howdy Doody* premiered in 1947, and for 13 years (and 2,343 shows) entertained children with the typical happenings in the circus town Doodyville. Starring Bob Smith as Buffalo Bob with Howdy Doody, the freckle-faced puppet, each program had an in-studio audience of children sitting in bleachers called the Peanut Gallery.

Captain Kangaroo premiered in 1955 and starred Bob Keeshan (formerly Clarabell the

(continued on next page)

(continued from previous page)

clown on Howdy Doody) as the gentle, soft-spoken captain. The show stressed prosocial values, morality, and religion. In 1981, CBS began a series of time-slot changes that resulted in the series going off the air in 1984.

Mister Rogers' Neighborhood, which premiered in 1968, stars Fred Rogers, a Presbyterian minister from Pittsburgh. Aided by puppets, songs, and guest characters, Mr. Rogers gently teaches children how to handle such difficulties of life as anger, death, and divorce, and promotes prosocial values. Mister Rogers also presents career segments that often feature women explaining their jobs, thereby acting as positive role models for young female viewers.

Beginning in 1972, ABC featured *Schoolhouse Rock,* five-minute animated spots that exposed young viewers to such educational subjects as the parts of grammar (*Grammar Rock*), simple mathematics (*Multiplication Rock*), and American history (*American Rock*). ABC periodically presents *Afterschool Specials* (1972–), a series of quality productions geared to an 8- to 14-year-old audience; they feature children in pivotal roles resolving problems through their own actions or realization. Topics covered in the past have ranged from divorce, family, and relationships to physical handicaps, health issues such as AIDS, early pregnancy, and physical abuse.

Many cable networks are devoted almost exclusively to educational programming for all ages. The most consistently educational and informative are the Discovery Channel, the Learning Channel, and the History Channel.

Eleanor and Franklin (1976)

This two-part miniseries was the first of three segments to focus on the lives and relationship of Eleanor and Franklin Roosevelt. The first installment, shown on *ABC Theatre,* was a four-hour adaptation of Joseph P. Lash's book *Eleanor and Franklin.* The special proved so popular that another was presented, highlighting the White House years (1977), followed by a final segment based on another Lash book, *Eleanor: The Years Alone* (1978).

Jane Alexander portrayed Eleanor, and Franklin was portrayed by Ed Herrmann. The first two installments won Emmys as Outstanding Special.

Elizabeth R (1973)

An excellent BBC import that traced the life of Queen Elizabeth I from her early teens (15) to her death. The six-part miniseries was broadcast on PBS and starred Glenda Jackson in a tour de force as the Virgin Queen.

Ellen (1994–1998)

One of the many series focusing on thirty-something angst, *Ellen* was originally entitled *These Friends of Mine*. After the first season, the concept was retooled and the series called simply *Ellen* after the star, former stand-up comic Ellen DeGeneres.

The series revolved around Ellen Morgan, an insecure bookstore manager turned owner and her group of slightly neurotic friends. The series was one of a long list of sitcoms about "nothing" in an attempt to imitate the Nielsen topper, *Seinfeld*.

The series's high point, in publicity but not plot, was the controversy over Ellen DeGeneres's sexual orientation and the "coming out" of character Ellen Morgan. After a prolonged period of debate and threatened boycotts, Ellen Morgan revealed that she was a lesbian in a tastefully done, humorous episode at the end of the 1996–1997 season, called the "Puppy" episode. Subsequent episodes acknowledged the character's sexuality, and a steady girlfriend was created for Ellen Morgan, which brought protests from a variety of citizen groups as well as the network, even with assurrances by DeGeneres to "go slowly" with the lesbian story line.

Ellen won a Peabody in 1998 for the hour-long "Puppy" episode as a "landmark moment in televison history."

See also Lesbians on Television.

Ellerbee, Linda (1944–)

In her career as a broadcast journalist, Linda Ellerbee has worked for NBC, ABC, and CNN. She briefly attended Vanderbilt University, then worked in radio before joining the Associated Press for a short time in 1972. Her first job in broadcast journalism was with KHOU-TV, the CBS affiliate in Houston, replacing Jessica Savitch. By mid-1973, she had moved to WCBS-TV in New York City.

In 1975, Ellerbee moved to NBC. In 1977 she received her own news show, *Now*, which she roundly denounced as a "disaster," and coanchored *NBC News Weekend* (1978–1980). She moved to *Nightly News* as a reporter (1980–1982), and in 1982 cowrote and coanchored an experimental news program for NBC called *NBC News Overnight*. Although the series lasted only 18 months, it was called "possibly the best written and most intelligent news program ever."

Ellerbee coanchored *Summer Sunday* (1984), an information and interview series, and contributed regularly to *Today* with her Friday report, *T.G.I.F.* She even appeared as herself in an episode of *Murphy Brown,* in which she and the fictional journalist Murphy reminisced about their early careers.

She entered a new realm of television in 1987 when she formed her own production company, Lucky Duck Productions, to produce television specials. One of her company's most notable projects was the production of *The American Heritage Television Specials* for PBS in association with *American Heritage* magazine. She won a Peabody for *It's Only Television* (1992).

She moved into print journalism in 1988 when she began writing a newspaper column for Hearst's King Features Syndicate. She is the author of two autobiographical books—*And So It Goes* (1987) and *Move On! Adventures in the Real World* (1991).

One of her most recent and acclaimed efforts was hosting the HBO documentary *Addiction,* a study of people with substance-abuse problems and the effects on their lives. Her frank, no-holds-barred commentary won praise from critics and her peers in the television industry.

Ellerbee continues to work in television as a commentator on CNN (1989–) and as the host of *Nick News* (1992–), a newsmagazine geared to younger viewers about the important issues within society.

Emerson, Faye (1918–1983)

Faye Emerson was one of the several early television celebrities known as "personalities," who could draw large audiences to anything in which they appeared. Most early personalities were women, possibly because rapport was so necessary to draw audiences to the new medium. During the early 1950s, Emerson was touted as the unofficial "first lady of television."

Born in Elizabeth, Louisiana, Faye Margaret Emerson was an only child whose family moved often as she was growing up. Although she first wanted to be a writer, she soon learned that she had a dramatic flair.

After a year at San Diego State College, she tried unsuccessfully to break into acting in New York. With no prospects for parts in the East, she returned to San Diego and joined the San Diego Players. She was briefly married, and while her husband was serving in the Navy during World War II, she was offered a contract with Warner Brothers Studios. She made a

Undated still from the television series the Faye Emerson Show. *(Photofest)*

succession of "B" movies, generally playing the good-girl-gone-bad, until she dyed her hair blonde, after which she began receiving slightly better roles.

Undoubtedly bringing her more notoriety than her film career, Emerson married Elliott Roosevelt, the second son of Franklin and Eleanor Roosevelt, in 1944. She quit acting in 1946 and began a career as presidential in-law and publicity magnet. In 1949 she began appearing regularly on the radio program *My Silent Partner,* and did occasional theater work.

Because of her social connections, good looks, and charm, Emerson was a natural choice to add class to television's mass programming. Her television career truly began in October 1949 with her 15-minute talk show, *The Faye Emerson Show* (CBS). Although originally a local New York program, by March 1950 it was shown nationally and was an unexpected hit despite its 11 P.M. time slot.

During the same period, she also appeared on NBC on *Fifteen with Faye*. Both shows were an opportunity for Emerson to tell her viewing friends about her week and allow her guests (generally authors, actors, or actresses) to discuss their latest projects. She was the first individual to host two programs on two different networks at the same time.

Her popularity during this time was immense; she was the most recognizable woman on television. In addition to her own programs, she frequently guested on other shows either as herself or as an actress in live productions.

The source of her popularity was not simply because she had a pretty face or wore plunging necklines (which her moralistic critics often decried). On *Who Said That?*, a show that queried panelists on quotations and events from the news, she had the highest average accuracy of any panel member, many of whom were newsmen or radio announcers. She was intelligent, sharp-witted, and charmingly unaffected.

After receiving a quickie Mexican divorce from Roosevelt, Emerson announced on her 8 November 1950 show that she was engaged to bandleader Skitch Henderson, becoming the first person to announce an engagement on television.

She briefly hosted *Faye Emerson's Wonderful Town* (1951–1952), one of the most expensive series ever produced. Emerson traveled to various towns to profile local civic leaders and visit noteworthy sites. When that series ended, she and her husband had a show, *Faye and Skitch* (1953–1954). She then became a regular panelist on *I've Got a Secret* (1952–1967, 1976) until 1958. Her final television venture was as a panelist on the quiz show *Masquerade* (1952–1960) from 1958 to 1960.

She left show business for good in 1963 and moved to Europe. She lived on Majorca until her death in 1993.

Emme (1963–)

Emme, the first plus-size (14–16) supermodel, hosts *Fashion Emergency* (1997–) on E! cable network. Through the makeovers on the program and her book *True Beauty: Positive Attitudes and Practical Tips from the World's Leading Plus-Size Model*, Emme tries to make fashion fun and accessible to everyone. She believes that while Kate Moss might "represent the ideal, I represent the reality," since 60 percent of the female population wears a size 12 or larger.

Emme, who is 5 feet 11 inches and weighs approximately 180 pounds, was born in New York City and raised in Saudi Arabia. She began her television career as a reporter and weatherperson in Flagstaff, Arizona, after attending Syracuse University on an athletic (rowing) scholarship. She was named *Glamour* magazine's Woman of the Year in 1997.

English, Diane (1948–)

Diane English created and wrote one of the most influential sitcoms in recent years: *Murphy Brown* (1988–1998). With her husband and partner Joel Shukovsky, she operates a successful independent production studio.

Born in Buffalo, New York, English graduated from Buffalo State College and taught high school for a year. After moving to New York City, she was an associate director at the TV lab at WNET-TV in addition to working as a TV critic for *Vogue* magazine (1977–1980).

In 1980 she adapted *The Lathe of Heaven,* by Ursula Le Guin, as the first feature-length movie to be presented on PBS, and won a Writer's Guild nomination. After this success, she wrote original scripts for both established series and original movies such as *My Life as a Man* (1984) and *Classified Love* (1986).

The first series that English created and wrote was *Foley Square* (1985–1986), about Alexandra "Alex" Harrigan (Margaret Colin), an assistant district attorney in New York City whose successful career was played off against her ticking biological clock. It ran only 14 episodes, but it established the pattern for English's later characters: successful career women with internal conflicts and male confidants.

Her next series was *My Sister Sam* (1986–1988), which focused on photographer Samantha "Sam" Russell (Pam Dawber) who, just as her career mushroomed, took responsibility for her younger sister, Patti (Rebecca Schaeffer). As in her previous series, Sam had a male best friend, and the stories alternated between professional issues and Sam's attempt to balance her role as sister with her role as parent.

Her next offering, *Murphy Brown* (1988–1998), struck gold. With Candice Bergen starring as Murphy, the driven and dedicated journalist and coanchor of a fictional television newsmagazine, *FYI,* the series had far-reaching influences on the way career women were portrayed on television. Far from perfect (she was a recovering alcoholic and former chain-smoker), Murphy was nonetheless a role model for modern women and young girls. English won an Emmy for writing the pilot episode.

After a dispute with Warner Bros. over control of the series, English left *Murphy Brown* and worked on other series. However, for the series' final year, she returned to write and produce episodes, and even made a cameo appearance in the final episode.

During the years away from *Murphy Brown*, she created and produced other series. Her next series was *Love & War* (1992–1995), which starred Jay Thomas as a cynical newspaper columnist and Susan Dey, then Annie Potts, as his love interest. In 1995 she created a series for Robert Pastorelli (Eldin from *Murphy Brown*) entitled *Double Rush*, which cast him as a former rock-and-roll musician who now owned a bicycle messenger/delivery service in Manhattan with very eccentric employees.

Throughout her career, English won many awards, including a Golden Globe in 1989. She won the Writer's Guild Award for Outstanding Writing on a Comedy Series twice (1990, 1992), the Genie Award (1990) from the Women in Radio and TV, and a Peabody in 1991.

See also *Murphy Brown*.

Ethel and Albert (1953–1956)

This series concerned the everyday occurrences in the lives of a middle-aged couple, Ethel (Peggy Lynch) and Albert Arbuckle (Alan Bunce), who lived in the quiet community of Sandy Harbor. The episodes involved such mundane things as uncooperative household appliances and ruined dinners.

Lynch created the series, which had been a hit on radio in the 1940s before moving to television in 1953.

Evans, Dale (1912–)

Remembered by baby boomers as Mrs. "King of the Cowboys," Dale Evans starred with her husband Roy Rogers in their long-running series *The Roy Rogers Show* (1951–1957). Evans played light ingenue-type roles in movies before being cast with Rogers in *The Cowboy and the Señorita* (1944) and meeting her partner-for-life. Other films followed in quick succession: *Lights of Old Santa Fe* (1944), *Don't Fence Me In* (1945), *Along the Navajo Trail* (1945), and *Roll on Texas Moon* (1946). They were married in 1947.

Evans wrote the words to their popular series' theme song, *Happy Trails to You*, and often joked with her husband during interviews that his horse, Trigger, got better billing than she did. After the end of *The Roy*

Rogers Show, they had a short-lived variety series (where she finally got billing), *The Roy Rogers and Dale Evans Show* (1962).

When this series ended, they retired from public life to raise their family, and eventually built a memorabilia museum in Victorville, California. Both deeply religious, they became evangelists and speakers before religious groups as well as writers of inspirational books.

In 1987 they taped a series of reminiscences as introductions to a retrospective of their movies on cable TV. Rogers died in 1998.

Eve Arden Show (1957–1958)

This short-lived series concerned the life and trials of Liza Hammond (Eve Arden), a widowed novelist and lecturer, and her 12-year-old twin daughters Jenny (Gail Stone) and Mary (Karen Greene). Liza received parenting assistance and advice from her mother, Nora (Frances Bavier). The sitcom was based on Emily Kimbrough's autobiography.

F

Fairness Doctrine

This regulation requires broadcasters to devote a "reasonable" amount of broadcast time to the discussion and exploration of controversial issues of importance to the public, and requires that opposing views be given equal time. Although everyone endorses the concept of fairness, few agree on how to achieve it in actual practice, causing the concept to be hotly debated on a regular basis.

Originating in the ideals set forth in the Radio Act of 1927 (operating in the public interest) and the Communications Act of 1934 ("public interest" requires fair competition of opposing views), the concept was formally articulated in the FCC's Editorializing Report of 1949. In 1959, Congress codified the doctrine in the Communications Act by amending section 315 to reflect the fairness requirement.

Through the years, the doctrine was challenged—in some cases all the way to the U.S. Supreme Court—as an infringement on journalistic freedom relative to the First Amendment. However, it stood until the deregulatory climate of the Reagan era brought a repeal of the doctrine under FCC chairman and Reaganite Dennis Patrick. Patrick's action was eventually overturned by an appeals court, but not before the doctrine had been greatly weakened.

Today the ideal remains in theory, if not always in action. Still, many people fear that without the doctrine and the control it exerts, broadcasters might abuse their gatekeeper position relative to the flow of news and events.

FAMILIES TV-STYLE

Although political debate in the 1990s revealed that "family" has no single definition or structure, throughout the decades television series have presented the accepted example for the times. By presenting one structure as preferred, other structures seemed somehow less legitimate.

The very early years of television showed families with wise mothers, hardworking fathers, and inquisitive but well-behaved children. Mostly ethnic comedies, these series were mother-focused, such as *The Goldbergs* (1949–1954), in which Molly Goldberg offered wisdom through "mollyisms" in a supposedly realistic depiction of family life. Another mother-centered series, *Mama* (1949–1956), although set at the turn of the century, modeled the postwar family ideal.

Comedies such as these continued into the 1950s, and the father-centered family was introduced. Series such as *Ozzie and Harriet* (1952–1964), *Father Knows Best* (1954–1963), and *Leave It to Beaver* (1957–1963) featured patient, involved fathers and nurturing, supportive mothers. Another popular series of this period, *The Donna Reed Show* (1958–1966), centered more on the mother character, but featured a father who was never too busy for his children.

While the fathers worked and the children went to school, the mother remained at home surrounded by appliances and other labor-saving devices. Although isolated from the larger world, the mother happily made her home a haven of security and calm for her family. The televisual suburbs were populated by well-mannered families enjoying the good life as a reward for the father's hard work and the mother's thrift and homemaking expertise.

Television in the 1960s reflected a nationwide increase in divorce rates by showing single-parent homes, although generally through the death of a spouse rather than the desolation of a marriage. Although not a common occurrence in the real world at that time, motherless families in which a man was the sole or surrogate parent appeared, including such popular series as *My Three Sons* (1960–1972), *The Andy Griffith Show* (1960–1968), *Family Affair* (1966–1971), *The Courtship of Eddie's Father* (1969–1972), and *Mayberry R.F.D.* (1968–1971).

Lucille Ball, the quintessential 1950s screwball wife, was now a widow with two children in two unrelated series, *The Lucy Show* (1962–1968) and *Here's Lucy* (1968–1974), the latter of which had the distinction of featuring Ball's two real-life children. Less popular series that featured mothers as the sole parent included *The Ghost & Mrs. Muir* (1968–1970), *The Doris Day Show* (1969–1973), and *The Debbie Reynolds Show* (1969–1970).

Intact families were somewhat rare during this decade, except for series that had begun in the previous decade, and stepfamilies had an extremely popular representative in *The Brady Bunch* (1969–1974). For some critics and historians, this series represents an entire generation: those in Gen X.

Intact families returned in a big way during the 1970s in three popular series, all of which were set in previous decades. *The Waltons* (1972–1981) was set in the Depression era, and *Little House on the Prairie* (1974–1983) was set in the 1800s. Both series featured large families with wise fathers and loving mothers, for whom family meant everything. *(continued on next page)*

(continued from previous page)

Perhaps the most popular of the three series, *Happy Days* (1974–1984) was set in the prosperous postwar "good ol' days" of the 1950s. The central family, the Cunninghams, was composed of the wise and understanding father, the supportive and nurturing mother, and three children (although the oldest was away at college).

Of course, single-parent households were also well represented during the 1970s, but with the exception of *Nanny and the Professor* (1970–1971), all new families were female-headed. *The Partridge Family* (1970–1974) had a mother who was so "cool" that she formed a rock band with her children. Shirley Jones (the mother) and David Cassidy (the eldest son) had several real hits on record charts as "The Partridge Family," including "I Think I Love You," which sold over four million copies.

Once the divorce rate reached double digits and divorce was no longer a disgrace, television was willing to depict divorced women as well as widows. The longest-running, mother-headed household was that of Ann Romano (Bonnie Franklin) in *One Day at a Time* (1975–1984). One of the first women to be single through divorce rather than death of a spouse, she and her two daughters moved to her hometown to start life over.

Two other series of the period featured the more standard widows. *Phyllis* (1975–1977) was a spinoff of the megahit *Mary Tyler Moore Show* (1970–1977) and featured former landlady Phyllis Lindstrom (Cloris Leachman), who had moved to San Francisco to create a new life for herself and her daughter after the death of her never-seen husband, Lars. *Alice* (1976–1985) featured the lives of a recent widow with dreams of becoming a country singer and her son as they adapted to life alone.

The 1980s featured intact families in a big way. The most popular series of that time was *The Cosby Show* (1984–1992), which showed the Huxtable family—firm but loving parents with well-adjusted and generally well-behaved children. This series was one of the most popular in television history, ranking as number one in the ratings from 1985 to 1988.

Other intact television families included *Family Ties* (1982–1989), about a couple who were former flower children but were now the establishment, albeit with liberal views. They had spawned a son who was conservative to the core, as well as three other "normal" children. A few years later, *Growing Pains* (1985–1992) introduced an updated 1950s-father-as-all-wise series that featured a psychiatrist father who worked out of his home in order to take care of the kids so his wife could return to work, eventually as a TV reporter.

Of course, single-headed families were also in evidence. *Kate and Allie* (1984–1989) were two divorced mothers raising their children alone while trying to establish lives of their own. Perhaps the most unusually premised single-mother series was *Scarecrow and Mrs. King* (1983–1987), which had a mother working as a secret agent when not mothering her two sons.

During the 1980s, several series were introduced that had nonfamily members in the role of all-wise father figures. The first male role-reversal series was *Charles in Charge* (1984–1985, 1987–1990), which featured a male college student who worked as governess-housekeeper in exchange for room and board. *Who's the Boss* (1985–1992) was another role-reversal comedy in which the man worked as housekeeper to the

(continued on next page)

(continued from previous page)

woman executive and "mothered" the children. Finally, in a series based on the 1940s movies starring Clifton Webb, *Mr. Belvedere* (1985–1990) was a British housekeeper-cook who looked after the Owens family and dispensed sage advice.

During that same decade, the first antifamily series premiered. One of the first series on the new Fox network, *Married . . . with Children* (1987–1997) chronicled the lives of the dysfunctional Bundy family with frank language and less-than-subtle innuendo. When *Roseanne* (1988–1998) premiered, it continued the dysfunctional-family trend with the story of the Connors, a working-class family who could seldom say anything nice to one another.

As the 1990s neared, a new batch of family series premiered. Although some female-headed households were featured, such as *Grace under Fire* (1993–1997), *Phenom* (1993–1994), and *Sabrina, the Teenage Witch* (1997–), the more successful series featured male-headed households. One of the most popular was *Full House* (1987–1995), which had a widower raising his three children with the help of his best friend and his brother-in-law. Another father-headed series was *Blossom* (1991–1995), in which a divorced father had custody of his three offspring.

Stepfamilies were represented by *Step-by-Step* (1991–1997), but for the most part families were once more intact. The series *7th Heaven* (1998–) became a hit by featuring a nondysfunctional family—a minister and his wife who raise their seven children with humor, patience, and a heavy dose of common sense. *Promised Land* (1996–), a spinoff of *Touched by an Angel,* focuses on a family's search for good in the people they encounter. *Dinosaurs* (1991–1993) featured an audio-animatronic family who parodied the family life they portrayed as well as the consumerism that marks American culture.

Television reflects, to a degree, the diversity that exists in the United States as to what constitutes a family. Of course, television depictions are of the more accepted forms of family, and many family-centered shows are sitcoms, which means that situations are played for laughs, negating any opportunity for different forms of family in other than humorous guise.

Family Hour

A concept forcefully encouraged by FCC chairman Richard C. Wiley and adopted by the television industry in 1975, the "family hour" designated the first two hours of prime time (7–9 P.M.). During this period, only programs suitable for all age groups were broadcast, which meant that violence and sexual innuendos had to be minimized.

Judge Warren J. Ferguson ruled in 1976 that Wiley's actions had violated the networks' First Amendment rights, thereby opening the door for more liberal program scheduling. By 1977 most networks had abandoned the guidelines. Although it is generally considered a passé concept, networks are regularly reminded by protests from viewers with young children demanding that "family viewing" be considered by broadcasters.

Farmer's Daughter (1963–1966)

In this series, based on the 1947 film by the same name, down-to-earth farm girl Katy Holstrom (Inger Stevens) went to Washington, D.C., to ask her congressman, Glen Morley (William Windom), for aid for her home-

Inger Stevens and Rory O'Brien in a scene from Farmer's Daughter *(Archive Photos)*

town. She ended up becoming governess to his two sons, Steve (Mickey Sholdar) and Danny (Rory O'Brien).

Predictably, Katy's charm and common sense won over the most pompous politicians and helped advance Morley's career. In November 1965, in an effort to boost failing ratings, Katy married Morley, but the marriage did not save the series, which was canceled at the end of the season.

Stevens won a Golden Globe for Best Actress on Television and was named by *TV Guide* as "Favorite Female Performer." Sadly, after the series ended, Stevens became despondent. In April 1970, at the age of 36, she died of an overdose of sleeping pills.

Fawcett, Farrah (1947–)

The undisputed sex symbol of the mid-1970s, Farrah Fawcett became a media sensation after playing Jill Munroe on *Charlie's Angels* (1976–1981). In 1977, her swimsuit poster sold over two million copies in less than four months, and she joined the ranks of earlier pinup queens Marilyn Monroe, Betty Grable, and Lana Turner.

Born in Corpus Christi, Fawcett worked as a model while attending the University of Texas—first as a microbiology major, then as an art major. She came to Hollywood after a producer saw one of her modeling pictorials. Fawcett began her television career in commercials for Wella Balsam shampoo and the Mercury Cougar. Her first recurring role on television was as Major Roger Healey's girlfriend during the final season of *I Dream of Jeannie* (1965–1970). Before becoming an Angel, she had small roles in a few TV movies such as *The Feminist and the Fuzz* (1971), *The Great American Beauty Contest* (1973), and *Murder on Flight 502* (1975).

From the first episode of Charlie's Angels, the "Farrah Phenomenon" (as it was called in *TV Guide*) gathered energy. She was inundated with merchandising offers and media deals. Like other "instant" successes, Fawcett was buoyed by the tremendous attention and left the series after only one season. She did not have the expected success in feature films.

Her first non-Angel success was in the off-Broadway play *Extremities,* in which she played a rape victim. Fawcett gave an excellent performance in a made-for-television movie, *The Burning Bed* (1984), in which she played a battered wife who finally kills her abusive husband. She then appeared in the feature-film version of *Extremities* (1986).

Fawcett returned to television briefly in a 1991 sitcom, *Good Sports,* costarring her live-in partner, Ryan O'Neal. In 1997, at age 50, she did an

Female Executives

Several high-profile women have executive positions within the television industry, but men make up the majority of decision-makers. A 1996 study indicated that only 16 percent of executive producers were women, and these were mostly on programs they had created, and only 11 percent of directors and 22 percent of writers were women.

In the annual "Women in Entertainment" issue of *The Hollywood Reporter,* the 1997–1998 employment numbers were similarly discouraging. Only 18 percent of series creators were women, with a slightly higher percentage (19 percent) working as executive producer. The number of female producers was higher (29 percent), but the number of directors decreased to only 8 percent. The numbers for women writers decreased to 20 percent and editors numbered 15 percent.

These figures are generally consistent throughout various studies. A statistical study done by Women in Film (WIF) that was released in September 1998 revealed that the number of female producers, directors, and writers was down to 23 percent (from 28 percent) for the 1995–1996 season. Women make up 25 percent of the membership of the Writers Guild of America (WGA),

but hold only 20 percent of the television writing jobs.

Further, a WGA study released in October 1998 concurred with the WIF study. In 1987 female writers worked in 21 percent of the script assignments; ten years later, in 1997, the number had risen to only 23 percent. A similar study conducted by the Directors Guild of America found that women directors filled only 6.8 percent of the directing jobs available in Hollywood (television and feature films).

As long as men make most of the policy and programming decisions, women characters will likely remain second-class citizens in the televisual world. Studies indicate that when women have positions of authority on televsion series or feature films, the dynamics of characterizations change.

With more female input behind the scenes, female characters speak more often, and introduce topics and initiate conversations more frequently. Female writers write scripts that allow female characters to be functional to the story by moving the story line and resolving conflicts or crises rather than being merely supportive or decorative.

appropriately named pay-per-view special, *Farrah Fawcett: All of Me,* for Playboy Entertainment; in a performance art segment she "danced" nude on canvases, using her body as a paintbrush.

Felicity (1998–)

This well-written coming-of-age drama centers around appealingly naive Felicity Porter (Keri Russell), a sheltered 17-year-old. On impulse, Felicity followed a boy, Ben (Scott Speedman), on whom she had developed a crush, to college in New York City. Although she was certain that he was her romantic soulmate, the romance she envisioned between them never materialized, and they both entered into other romantic entanglements—he with her new friend, Julie (Amy Jo Johnson), and she with her dorm floor's resident advisor, Noel (Scott Foley). In the season finale, however, Felicity was forced to choose whether to go with Noel to Germany for the summer or drive across country with the now-interested Ben.

In its first year, Russell won a Golden Globe for Best Actress in a Drama.

FEMALE IMPERSONATORS

Throughout its history, comedy has had a tradition of men dressing as women. Not surprisingly, the history of television has also had its share of female impersonators.

Probably the first to use women's attire for laughs was Uncle Miltie. During the run of his early series (*Texaco Star Theatre*, 1948–1954, and *The Milton Berle Show*, 1954–1956), Berle often dressed as a garish female and played the femme fatale. During the same period, Jack Benny occasionally dressed up as a prim female, complete with pearls and fox stole, when he appeared in skits with other comedians such as George Burns. Many years later, Harvey Korman frequently dressed as a woman in comedy skits on *The Carol Burnett Show* (1967–1977).

On the long-running series *The Beverly Hillbillies* (1962–1971), Max Baer Jr., who played Jethro Bodine, sometimes appeared as Jethro's sister, Jethrene. During the 1968–1969 season, ABC had a series entitled *The Ugliest Girl in Town*, in which Peter Kastner played a talent agent who, after being photographed dressed as a woman in a hippie wig, became a top fashion model in London. Perhaps the best-remembered comedian to appear in drag is Flip Wilson (*The Flip Wilson Show*, 1970–1974). He regularly appeared as sassy Geraldine Jones, who wore skin-tight miniskirts and often spoke of her boyfriend, Killer. This character was so popular that Wilson appeared at the 1974–1975 Emmy awards in Geraldine-drag, and "her" expressions—"the devil made me do it" and "what you see is what you get"—became part of popular slang.

For ten years, Corporal Maxwell Klinger (Jamie Farr) tried to get a section 8 (mentally unfit) discharge from the army by dressing in often outlandish and definitely nonregulation outfits on *M*A*S*H* (1972–1983), perhaps the most popular sitcom of all time. Unfortunately for him, he was more often accepted by the rest of the unusual 4077th personnel, complimented on his outfits, and asked for fashion advice rather than condemned.

Running concurrently with *M*A*S*H* for two years, from 1980–1982, ABC broadcasted *Bosom Buddies*, a series in which Tom Hanks and Peter Scolari dressed as Buffy and Hildegarde (respectively) in order to live in the low-rent Susan B. Anthony Hotel. Remembered chiefly as being one of Tom Hanks's early efforts, the series was relatively popular.

(continued on next page)

(continued from previous page)

Other examples of men who have dressed as women for roles include David Duchovny on *Twin Peaks* (1990–1991) as the transvestite detective Dennis/Denise, Martin Lawrence on *Martin* (1992–1996), and Jaleel White on *Family Matters* (1989–1996). Well-known British female impersonators appearing on American television include Benny Hill and Dame Edna.

In addition to these examples of men in long-running drag roles, several actors have appeared dressed as women in episodic or onetime roles. John Davidson played a murderous schizophrenic female impersonator in an episode of *The Streets of San Francisco* (1972–1977). Both Lee Majors and Doug Barr dressed as WACs in a bounty-hunting scheme on *The Fall Guy* (1981–1986). Many of the male cast members of the long-running comedy series *Saturday Night Live* (1972–) have dressed as women in various comedy skits. Among those who have had onetime or recurring female personas are John Belushi, Dan Aykroyd, Garrett Morris, Joe Piscopo, Martin Short, Dana Carvey, and Billy Crystal.

On the 1997 Halloween episode of *Soul Man,* Dan Aykroyd dressed as Julia Child. Also during the 1997–1998 season, *The Wonderful World of Disney* presented *Mr. Headmistress,* in which Harland Williams played a mob-chased con man who dressed as the headmistress of an exclusive academy to escape retribution. In 1998 a short-lived series, *Ask Harriet,* had recently fired male reporter Jack Cody (Anthony Tyler Quinn) masquerading as Sylvia Coco to get a job as the advice columnist on his old paper. In an episode of *Hercules: The Legendary Journeys* (1994–), Salmonius (Robert Trebor) and Autolycus (Bruce Campbell), friends of Hercules, dressed as women in a Some-Like-It-Hot parody to escape capture by an evil prince.

Finally, it is, of course, well known that everyone's favorite collie, Lassie, was not a lass at all but a laddie. For seven generations, male descendants played the beloved dog in films and television series.

While men such as basketball star Dennis Rodman occasionally dress as women for publicity stunts, others make their names in drag. One of the most recent drag sensations is RuPaul. Elegantly dressed and elaborately made up, "she" is a true media personality. RuPaul made his first TV appearance on a cable access program, *American Music Show,* and appeared in full drag in a wedding performance with the Now Explosion. It took years to perfect his look, and RuPaul spent many years in gender-bending guises before making his national debut on *The Gong Show* in 1988. He went into full-glamour drag in 1989 and was crowned (Drag) Queen of Manhattan in 1990. His résumé includes music albums, music videos, guest shots on episodic television series, and several film appearances, in addition to having written several books. He had his own Christmas special, *Ho Ho Ho: The RuPaul Christmas Special* (1997), on VH1. In addition, he appeared as both himself and his drag alter ego on a 1998 episode of *Sabrina, the Teenage Witch* (1997–) and as an occasional guest star on the *New Hollywood Squares* (1998).

Field, Sally (1946–)

Born in Pasadena, California, Sally Field first came to television viewers' attention as the pixie-faced lead character on *Gidget* (1965–1966). After that series ended, she starred as the eternally optimistic Sister Bertrille on *The Flying Nun* (1967–1970). She had difficulty overcoming her "perky" typecasting, and appeared in a succession of lightweight roles including another sitcom, *The Girl with Something Extra* (1973–1974), in which she portrayed a young wife with ESP.

However, her performance in the 1976 TV movie *Sybil* as the woman with multiple personalities brought her an Emmy and recognition as a dramatic actress—recognition that increased when the film won a Peabody. In 1979 she appeared as union-organizer Norma Rae, a breakout role that earned her an Oscar for Best Actress. She appeared as the overly ambitious reporter in *Absence of Malice* (1981), the troubled widow in *Kiss Me Goodbye* (1982), and the stoic mother in *Places in the Heart* (1984), for which she received her second Oscar for Best Actress.

She established her own production company and appeared in her own projects as well as those of other producers, including *Murphy's Romance* (1985), *Punchline* (1988), *Steel Magnolias* (1989), *Not without My Daughter* (1991), and *Soapdish* (1991). Also in 1991, she produced the Julia Roberts movie *Dying Young*.

Her most recent acting work includes the role of Robin Williams's estranged wife in *Mrs. Doubtfire* (1993) and the voice of Sassy the cat in the *Homeward Bound* movie series. She directed and made a cameo appearance in "The Original Wives Club" segment of Tom Hanks's *From the Earth to the Moon* (1998).

See also *The Flying Nun, Gidget, The Girl with Something Extra, Sybil.*

Fili-Krushel, Patricia (1950–)

Patricia Fili-Krushel is the first woman to head ABC Television Network. As president she is responsible for all programming and every business area of the network.

With an MBA from Fordham University, Fili-Krushel began as a secretary with the network, moving up through the ranks to become program controller of the sports department. She moved to HBO as director of sports administration, and was later named director of sports and specials. She

FIFTIES MOMS

For the baby-boomer generation and, to a lesser degree, the generations who watched syndicated reruns, the moms of the 1950s sitcoms represented the idealized perfect-mother figure. Impeccably dressed, with a requisite string of pearls, and perfectly coifed, these televisual mothers were cheerfully efficient and unerringly supportive.

Several 1950s versions of this icon appeared. Margaret Anderson (Jane Wyatt) was unflappable and ceaselessly understanding on *Father Knows Best* (1954–1963). June Cleaver (Barbara Billingsley) was the loving mother on *Leave It to Beaver* (1957–1963) who left all the important advice-giving to her husband.

Another enduring mother figure was Harriet Nelson of *The Adventures of Ozzie and Harriet* (1952–1966), who never had any adventures but was always there for her family.

Although every family sitcom had its own perfect-mom clone, these three were perhaps the best known and remembered because their shows are still seen in syndication or on cable networks. However, the fact that these moms gave up their own identities to become mothers was never mentioned or alluded to. In one episode of *Leave It to Beaver,* when June talks to her eldest son about her life before getting married, his disbelief prompts her to inform him that she "wasn't born a mother."

Some of the mothers who appeared in later series, such as Donna Stone (Donna Reed) on *The Donna Reed Show* (1958–1966) and Carol Brady (Florence Henderson) on *The Brady Bunch* (1969–1974), were still stay-at-home moms, but many of the later mothers entered the workforce, just as their real-life counterparts did. Abby Bradford (Betty Buckley) on *Eight Is Enough* (1977–1981) was a teacher, Clair Huxtable (Phylicia Rashad) on *The Cosby Show* (1984–1992) was an attorney, and Elyse Keaton (Meredith Baxter) of *Family Ties* (1982–1989) was an architect.

Yet no matter how demanding their careers might be, these mothers always had time for their families and were seldom seen involved in any aspect of their careers. Although the fifties icon changed slightly with the times, Mom's focus continued to be her husband and/or children.

was promoted to director of production for the entire network, and finally to head of original programming business affairs.

In 1988, Fili-Krushel moved to Lifetime Television as senior vice-president of programming and production when it changed its focus to women's programming. She made all decisions on which programs to develop and put on the air.

In 1993, she returned to ABC as president of ABC Daytime. She launched *The View* (1998–), the first successful talk show to appear in the morning period in ten years. She accepted the position of network president in August 1998.

Fisher, Terry Louise (1946–)

Writer/producer Terry Louise Fisher brings her own life experiences to the characters she creates, adding realism and authenticity to their depiction. Fisher was born in Chicago and raised in Los Angeles. She majored in anthropology in college and went to UCLA Law School with the vague goal of eventually practicing law with her husband. Although she divorced before completing her first year, she decided to continue her studies. After graduation, she went to work for the district attorney's office, where she learned firsthand the problems with (in her view) the "dysfunctional justice system."

Realizing that she did not want to continue working within the legal system, Fisher tried to break into screenwriting. She found it difficult to be taken seriously as a screenwriting lawyer, but she wrote two novels that are now out of print, *A Class Act* (1976) and *Good Behavior* (1979). The critics thought her heroines "too strong and independent," and when the third book deal fell through, she turned again to screenwriting, this time with partner Steve Brown.

The two were successful in writing made-for-TV movies such as *Your Place or Mine* (1983) and *This Girl for Hire* (1983). Soon they wrote for *Cagney and Lacey* (1982–1988), but although their professional collaboration flourished, their personal relationship ended.

Next, Fisher teamed with Steven Bochco to create and write *L.A. Law* (1986–1994), in which her past legal experiences were apparent in the stories and characterizations. In this series she was able to overcome some of the problems she had seen with the workings of the justice system and at the same time create well-rounded, strong female characters.

See also *Cagney and Lacey,* Careers for Women on Television.

The 5 Mrs. Buchanans (1994–1995)

A female ensemble comedy in which four women were related by marriage and a shared dislike for their mother-in-law, Emma (Eileen Heckart). Alex (Judith Ivey) was a Jewish New Yorker who ran a thrift shop. Delilah (Beth Broderick) was a sexy southern belle, and Vivian (Harriet Sansom Harris) was a snobbish Midwesterner. Bree (Charlotte Ross), the newest and youngest Mrs. Buchanan, was a blonde Californian who had worked at a Disneylandish park before her marriage.

The women had nothing in common, but they united in their battles against their overbearing mother-in-law, and were generally supportive of one another during the crisis-of-the-week.

Flanigan, Dayna (1950–)

As president of Steven Bochco Productions since 1989, Dayna Flanigan is in charge of all business and production decisions for the estimated $75 million production budget (1997–1998 season), including the development of Bochco's short-lived CBS series *Brooklyn South* and his established hit, *NYPD Blue* (1993–).

Flanigan started in the entertainment industry in 1978 in the business affairs division of Columbia Pictures Television. She moved to the development division of Twentieth Century Fox Television in 1980, becoming executive vice-president of creative affairs. She met Steven Bochco there, and helped him develop *LA Law* in 1985.

Flo (1980–1981)

The character of Flo Castleberry (Polly Holliday), the thrice-divorced, feisty, kiss-my-grits waitress, was such a hit with viewers on the sitcom *Alice* (1976–1985) that the producers gave the character her own show. The series premise had Flo impulsively buying a roadhouse, one of the favorite hangouts from her younger days, and becoming an entrepreneur in her hometown of Cowtown, Texas.

The roadhouse was duly renamed Flo's Texas Rose, and Flo undertook the challenge of running her own business. The problems of being back among her family, operating a business, and dealing with the requisite number of comical regulars and employees were the grist of the episodes' humor.

Although ratings were initially high and critics touted Holliday as a "truly funny woman" and a "talented comedienne," the network moved the series often, scheduling it against one established hit after another until the audience lost track and ratings plummeted. It lasted only a year, but Holliday received her third Emmy nomination as the irrepressible Flo.

The Flying Nun (1967–1970)

This series starred Sally Field as the perpetually cheerful and enthusiastic American novitiate Sister Bertrille, who joined Convent San Tanco in San Juan, Puerto Rico. Unfortunately, Sister Bertrille was quite small, and when the wind caught the winglike cornette worn by the order, she took flight.

The situations she got into as a result of her unusual—and unwanted—ability were the basis of the comedy. Surprisingly, this series, based on the book *The Fifteenth Pelican* by Tere Rios, was commended by some religious orders for humanizing nuns.

Foster, Jodie (1962–)

Although Jodie Foster is better known for her excellent film performances, she first appeared on television at the age of three in a Coppertone commercial. She made her first film when she was eight (*Napoleon and Samantha* in 1972), and received her first Oscar nomination for her portrayal of a teenage prostitute in *Taxi Driver* (1976).

Foster appeared on many popular television series in the 1970s, including *Gunsmoke* (1955–1975), *Mayberry RFD* (1968–1971), *Julia* (1968–1971), *Nanny and the Professor* (1970–1971), *The Partridge Family* (1970–1974), and *Kung Fu* (1972–1975). She had a recurring role in *The Courtship of Eddie's Father* (1969–1972) as Eddie's friend Joey Kelly, and starred in her own short-lived television series, *Paper Moon* (September 1974–January 1975), about a con artist, Moses Pray (Christopher Connelly), and his 11-year-old daughter, Addie (Foster). She appeared in several made-for-TV movies, including *Menace on the Mountain* (1970), *Rookie of the Year* (1973), *Smile Jenny, You're Dead* (1974), and *Svengali* (1983).

Foster won two Oscars: for *The Accused* (1988), in which she portrayed a rape victim, and for *Silence of the Lambs* (1991), in which she portrayed an FBI agent tracking down a serial killer.

After being in show business virtually her entire life, Foster made her directorial debut with an episode of the TV series *Tales of the Darkside* (1984–1988). The first feature film she directed was *Little Man Tate* (1991), the story of a child prodigy, followed by *Home for the Holidays* (1995). She continues to direct as well as star in films, and has formed her own production company, Egg Pictures.

In 1998 she received a Modern Master Award at the 13th Annual Santa Barbara International Film Festival. Foster also became a single mother in 1998.

Francis, Arlene (1908–)

Arlene Francis was one of the many intelligent and charming "personalities" to appear on early television. She and Dorothy Kilgallen (1950–1965) were the first two panelists on *What's My Line?* (1950–1967), later joined by Bennett Cerf (1951–1967) and Steve Allen (1953–1954).

During her 15 years on *What's My Line?* she also appeared on *Blind Date* (1949–1951) and *Fashion Magic* (1950–1951), as well as several dramatic anthologies. From 1953 to 1955 she hosted *The Talent Patrol,* an army recruiting ploy disguised as a military talent show. During this same period she hosted an NBC daytime talk show, *Home* (1954–1957), part of a trilogy that included *Today* and *Tonight.* After *Home* ended, she briefly hosted another daytime series, *The Arlene Francis Show* (1957–1958).

Beginning in 1981, she hosted *The Prime of Your Life* on WNBC in New York. She made guest appearances on series, and appeared on specials such as *NBC's 60th Anniversary Special.*

Frederick, Pauline (1909–1990)

"When a man gets up to speak, people listen, then look. When a woman gets up, people *look;* then if they like what they see, they listen."

The above quote is by one of the first women to break down the all-male barrier of television news reporting. Pauline Frederick was born in a coal-mining town in Pennsylvania and began in newspaper work while still in high school. She eventually received an undergraduate degree in political science and a graduate degree in international law.

Frederick returned to journalism in 1931 with a regular column in the *Washington Star* and later worked for *United States News,* where her beat included the Departments of State, War, and the Navy. She became well known in diplomatic circles, and in 1939 had a radio program of interviews with the wives of diplomats and statesmen.

In 1945 she was one of the first women to go overseas as a war correspondent when she spent two months touring North Africa, Asia, and China.

Later she covered the Nuremburg trials as a freelance reporter (despite her experience and knowledge, network reporting was still closed to women).

She continued to freelance for ABC radio, but was allowed to cover only "women's" news. Few women worked in news, and Frederick was often the only woman present at events. Although she logged many miles and won several noteworthy exclusives, ABC would not hire her full-time.

In 1948, through a fluke, Frederick was sent to cover the convening of the United Nations Council of Foreign Ministers. As she cultivated sources and proved herself trustworthy, she was allowed to report on-air more often. Also in 1948, Frederick was sent to the presidential conventions by ABC's newly formed television news bureau to cover the "women's angle." After her success at the conventions, ABC finally hired her full-time, making her the first woman to work full-time for a television network news division. She even had her own 15-minute program, *Pauline Frederick's Feature Story.*

In 1953 she left ABC to cover the United Nations for NBC, which she did for the next 21 years with such success that her name became linked with the United Nations in viewers' minds. She was a tenacious reporter and earned the respect of her peers for the expertise she developed in international affairs.

In 1967 she wrote *Ten First Ladies of the World,* a compilation of profiles of wives of world leaders. In 1969, at the age of 60, she married for the first time.

Forced to retire from NBC in 1975, Frederick moved to National Public Radio and reported on international affairs, briefly hosting her own radio show, *Pauline Frederick and Colleagues.* In 1976 she became the first woman to moderate a televised presidential debate.

Her excellent reporting garnered her many awards and honors throughout her career. She was the first newswoman to be named to Gallup's list of most admired women, and she was the eleventh recipient of the Alfred I. DuPont Award for "meritorious service to the American people" in 1953. In 1954, Frederick became the first newswoman to receive a Peabody Award for "outstanding work in the field of international understanding." She was named to the Hall of Fame of the professional journalism society (Sigma Delta Chi), and received over 20 honorary doctorate degrees in journalism, law, and the humanities.

In 1980, Frederick received the Paul White Award for distinguished service to broadcast journalism, again the first woman so honored. She was the first woman to serve as president of the UN Correspondents Association. She retired from National Public Radio in 1981, and died in May 1990.

Although not an avowed feminist, by her actions Frederick opened doors for this century's second wave of feminists. She was very conscious of the prejudice that dominated the field of reporting, and blasted the "lookism" of television news, which dictated that people looked first at a woman's appearance before listening to what she had to say. She was the role model for the generations of newswomen who followed her.

See also Careers for Women on Television, News.

Funicello, Annette (1942–)

Annette Funicello was the most popular Mouseketeer of the original *Mickey Mouse Club* (1955–1959). After the debut of her own serial, appropriately named "Annette," a regular feature within the club format, she received over a thousand fan letters each week. Her life as a teenager was a hectic blend of scripts, public appearances, and school.

In many people's minds, she became the epitome of the perfect teen of the 1950s, and many young girls of the 1950s wanted to be "just like her." Her Annette line of Disney-licensed merchandise made the studio a respectable profit, and her recordings, such as *Tall Paul* and *Pineapple Princess,* added to her popularity.

Funicello's serial was based on Janette Sebring Lowry's book *Margaret,* about a small-town girl who is suddenly sent to live in the city and thrust into unfamiliar situations. The character's struggle to find her place and successfully face the challenges of her new life struck a chord with young viewers.

After *The Mickey Mouse Club* ended, Funicello was the only Mouseketeer to remain under contract to Disney Studios. She appeared on early television series such as *Zorro* (1959/1961) and *Wagon Train* (1963), and later on episodes of *Burke's Law* (1963/1965), *Fantasy Island* (1979, 1980, 1981), *Love Boat* (1971, 1978, 1982), and *Growing Pains* (1986). She also had a recurring role in *Make Room for Daddy* (1959). She also appeared in several Disney films, including *Shaggy Dog* (1959), *Babes in Toyland* (1961), *The Misadventures of Merlin Jones* (1964), and *The Monkey's Uncle* (1965).

Annette Funicello and Frankie Avalon in a scene from the movie Beach Party. *(Corbis/Bettmann)*

In the early 1960s, Funicello appeared with teen heartthrob Frankie Avalon in a succession of *Beach Party* movies as the perennial virginal girl-next-door who wore conservative two-piece bathing suits while the other actresses appeared in skimpy bikinis. Her character was reprised in 1987 when she and Avalon made a parody of the early *Beach Party* movies enti-tled *Back to the Beach.* The movie was so popular that it led to a joint con-cert tour the following year.

In 1965, Funicello married, and over the next several years made few appearances as she raised her children. After her eventual divorce, she be-came the spokeswoman for several consumer products, including Mennen baby products and Skippy peanut butter.

In 1992, Funicello disclosed that she had multiple sclerosis, a crip-pling disease of the nervous system. She created the Annette Funicello Re-search Fund for Neurological Diseases to help fund research as well as in-crease public awareness of the disease.

She also created AF Bear Company, which designs and markets lim-ited-edition stuffed bears commemorating people and events in her life. In 1993 she introduced her own line of perfume, Cello, sold at New Orleans Square in Disneyland. She is a role model for disabled people as she con-tinues her involvement in a number of business ventures.

In recent years, Funicello has received several awards. In 1992 she re-ceived the Disney Legacy Award for her contribution to the Disney story, and in 1993 she received her star on Hollywood's Walk of Fame. Also in 1993 she received the Helen Hayes Award from the Saint Clare's Hospital and Health Center in New York City for her career achievements and for her work to raise public awareness of multiple sclerosis. Her most recent award was in 1998 from the Multiple Sclerosis Society for her work in pub-licizing the illness and her fund-raising efforts.

Furness, Betty (1916–1994)

Betty Furness, who became one of television's most recognizable faces dur-ing the early years, began her career as a model and eventually won a screen test in 1932. She subsequently made 35 films in five years for RKO Studios, the most memorable being *Magnificent Obsession* (1935) and *Swing Time* (1936). She spent several years working in the theater before getting her first television show in 1945 on the Dumont network called *Fashions, Com-ing and Becoming,* a weekly 15-minute program on the latest couture col-lections.

The event that probably made her career occurred when she appeared in a play for *Studio One* in 1948. In the early days of television, all commercials were done live, and after seeing how poorly the commercial was being done in rehearsal, Furness offered to step in. The sponsor, Westinghouse, hired her, and soon she regularly appeared on television as the company's only on-air representative, as well as appearing at sales conventions and stores.

In 1951, Furness appeared for a very short time in a dramatic series, *News Gal,* in which she starred as Harriet Hildebrand, a sob-sister reporter. The show was renamed *Byline,* but ran only another two months.

For a brief time, Westinghouse sponsored Furness in a 15-minute talk show entitled *Meet Betty Furness* (1953), featuring celebrity interviews and household hints. After her show ended, she became a semiregular panelist on both *What's My Line?* (1950–1967) and *I've Got a Secret* (1952–1976), and occasionally appeared in dramatic anthologies.

Her tenure with Westinghouse ended in November 1960, and Furness became host of a phone-in talk show, *At Your Beck and Call,* which appeared two hours daily on WNTA-TV in New York. When this series ended after a year, she went on to two radio series that ran concurrently, *A Woman's World* and *Ask Betty Furness.*

Doing commercials for Westinghouse at the presidential conventions in 1952 led to Furness's interest in politics. She entered the Democratic political arena in earnest in 1962, traveling as a Democratic policy representative and promoting such programs as Head Start and VISTA.

In March 1967, the Johnson administration offered her the position of Special Assistant for Consumer Affairs. Although viewed by many as unqualified for the job, Furness soon proved that she was a quick study and dedicated to protecting consumers' interests. During her tenure in office she succeeded in securing laws requiring truth-in-lending, flame-resistant fabrics for children's clothing, improved meat inspection, and credit-rate regulation.

Furness left the White House when Johnson's term ended, and chaired the New York State Consumer Protection Board. She left that position in 1971 and became New York City Consumer Affairs Commissioner from 1973 to 1974.

In 1974 she became consumer reporter for the local NBC affiliate in New York City, the first person to regularly cover consumer issues for a nightly news program. She was not afraid to name dishonest businesses, and often brought cameras when reviewing businesses with questionable practices. She received approximately 400 letters a week from consumers requesting help with problems.

When Barbara Walters left *Today* in 1976, Furness filled in as anchor until her replacement, Jane Pauley, was hired. After Furness's hosting duties ended, she continued as the program's consumer reporter throughout the 1980s. Furness also had her own local weekly consumer show, *Buyline: Betty Furness,* which won a Peabody in 1977.

In March 1992, Furness left broadcasting due to ill health, and died of stomach cancer on 2 April 1994.

G

The Gale Storm Show (1956–1960)

In keeping with the social climate of a period that pointed women to the home as their proper place, this "career woman" comedy featured a frantic, slightly man-hungry single woman. Susanna Pomeroy (Gale Storm) was the social director on the luxury liner SS *Ocean Queen*. She and her friend Elvira "Nugey" Nugent (ZaSu Pitts) constantly got into screwball scrapes and misunderstandings that tried the patience of their captain (Roy Roberts).

Galen, Nely (1964–)

Nely Galen was named president of entertainment for the Spanish-language network Telemundo in 1998. Although the Latino market is virtually ignored by the larger networks, it is the fastest-growing audience in the United States. Galen structures the programming with an eye to Hollywood-style entertainment while keeping Latino cultural values intact.

Born in Cuba, Galen has lived in the United States most of her life. She worked in writing and production before being made station manager of the Spanish-language WNJU-TV in New Jersey in 1986.

Game Shows

For most of the history of television, game-show hosting has been an almost exclusively male arena; very few female hosts can be found in the history of the genre.

Arlene Francis hosted *Blind Date* (1949), in which six male college students (or, during the war, servicemen) vied for the opportunity to date a model in what was arguably the prototype for the later *Dating Game.* Kay Westfall cohosted *Sit or Miss* (1950), which had contestants playing musical chairs; the one who lost his chair had to answer questions or perform a stunt. Arlene Francis took another turn at hosting with *Who's There* (1952), a show that challenged contestants to identify a famous person from possessions or artifacts associated with him or her.

In 1953, Vera Vague hosted *Follow the Leader,* in which she performed a sketch and audience members were asked to reenact it for a prize. In 1954, French actress Denise Darcel hosted a series entitled *Gamble on Love,* in which young couples answered questions for prizes, a possible prototype for the later *Newlywed Game.*

Not until the late 1970s did a woman once again cohost a game show. Sara Purcell appeared with Bill Anderson on the civilized "battle of the sexes" called *The Better Sex.* In 1982, Leslie Uggams cohosted *Fantasy* with Peter Marshall, in which contestants' fantasies were fulfilled. A year later (1983), Betty White hosted *Just Men,* for which she won an Emmy—the first ever given to a woman as the host of a game show.

The most recent shows with female hosts were on MTV. In 1992, Dr. Joyce Brothers hosted *Lip Service,* in which contestants guessed whose lips appeared on video clips. Jenny McCarthy hosted a dating game MTV-style called *Singled Out* (1996–1997).

One of the most popular women to appear as a model-host on a game show is Vanna White from *Wheel of Fortune* (1983–). Although her job consists mainly of highlighting the letters that contestants guess correctly, her popularity and that of the show ensures that whatever she does is news. She often appears in magazines and the less reputable supermarket tabloids.

Garland, Judy (1922–1969)

Born to a vaudevillian family, Judy Garland was already a successful movie star and concert performer when she moved to television. Some consider her the finest singing actress, and her talents shone in such films as *The Wizard of Oz* (1939), *Meet Me in St. Louis* (1944), and *A Star Is Born* (1954). Yet, her career was a series of ups (a special Oscar for her performance as Dorothy in *The Wizard of Oz*) and downs (lost parts and poor performances).

Prior to pursuing a television career, one of Garland's career triumphs was her concert at Carnegie Hall (23 April 1961), the recording of which won five Grammys and appeared on the top-sellers list for 73 weeks.

Her variety show, *The Judy Garland Show* (1963–1964), was to be her comeback vehicle after a bout of career and personal disappointments. Unfortunately, her series was placed in competition with NBC's top-rated series, *Bonanza* (1959–1973), and the lack of a solid format resulted in cancellation after only five months.

Garland continued to perform sporadically, often exhibiting true brilliance, until her death in London of a drug overdose.

See also Variety Programs.

GEN-X TV

While many Xers object to the term *Gen-X*, it is a generalized demographic identifier not unlike *baby boomer, yuppie,* or *senior citizen.* It merely denotes those individuals born during the 1960s and 1970s, who could just as easily have been labeled *boomer babies.*

One thing that many Xers have in common is an astute understanding of television and its conventions, having been raised on the medium as their parents' baby-sitter-of-choice. Another attribute many have in common is an ironic and self-deprecating sense of humor fueled by a basic disbelief in establishment rhetoric.

Most series categorized as Gen-X feature young people who no longer believe that the American dream is achievable for everyone and who know that hard work isn't always rewarded. However, no matter what their situation, the characters do the best they can with the options available to them. Their words often have a harder bite than those of previous characters, but the realities for both characters and viewers are much different from those faced by earlier generations.

When the Fox network premiered, it strongly courted Gen-X viewers. Early Fox programs generally identified with Gen-X include *Married . . . with Children* (1987–1997), which featured a family almost devoid of hope and whose every word reflected cynicism and sexual frustration; *21 Jump Street* (1987–1991), which featured a group of young cops working undercover to rid Los Angeles's schools of predators, a modern version of *Mod Squad* (1968–1973); and *The Tracey Ullman Show* (1987–1990), reflecting the often biting humor identified with this generation.

Spun off from *The Tracey Ullman Show* came the most popular animated series in the history of television, *The Simpsons* (1990–), whose sarcastic and cynical humor instantly appealed to Xers. The series evolved into a parody of popular culture and often lampooned celebrities or media figures even while it used the conventions of popular culture to increase its popularity.

Programs popular with Xers often feature ensemble casts rather than one star. Three of the most popular series of the 1990s—*Roseanne* (1988–1998), *Friends* (1994–), and *Seinfeld* (1990–1998)—were directed to Xers, with their irreverence and media references. *Roseanne*, especially, built episodes around previous series, including an episode in which cast members

(continued on next page)

(continued from previous page)

took the parts of characters from *Gilligan's Island* (1964–1967), and another with the "perfect mothers" from 1950s sitcoms advising Roseanne on mothering skills.

Another popular Xer ensemble series was *Living Single* (1993–1997), created by Xer Yvette Lee Bowser. The program featured a group of friends as they dealt with life experiences and disappointments, and although some cast members were male, the series emphasized the female point of view.

GEN-X SERIES FOCUSED ON FEMALES

My So-Called Life (1994–1995), winner of Best Drama Series from the TV Critics Association in 1995, featured Angela Chase (Claire Danes), a teenage misfit who suffered from an emotional angst that many Xers could understand. The problems faced by Angela and her friends were honest and realistic—not glossed over, as with most previous series.

The successful *Party of Five* (1994–) focuses on the lives of the Salinger siblings as they face life together after their parents are killed in a traffic accident. Several members of the cast have established film careers buoyed by their television popularity.

Caroline in the City (1995–1999) featured cartoonist Caroline Duffy (Lea Thompson) and her group of eccentric friends facing life in New York City in the 1990s. Chronically uncertain and often naively trusting, Caroline was the 1990s embodiment of the popular cartoon character Cathy (created and drawn by Cathy Guisewite).

Naked Truth (1995–1998) featured Tea Leoni as Pulitzer Prize–nominated photographer Nora Wilde, who after divorcing her wealthy but philandering husband and asking only for her freedom, was forced to take a job as a celebrity photographer (aka paparazzi). After the paparazzo became a topic of controversy and the series changed networks, Nora became a less manic advice columnist. Touted as the next Lucille Ball, Leoni has a talent for physical humor that made her expressions as laughter-inducing as the jokes/situations, but the retooling and time changes failed to find an audience.

Another single-woman-making-it-on-her-own series is *Suddenly Susan* (1996–), called by *TV Guide* "the Gen-X *Mary Tyler Moore Show*." The series features Brooke Shields as a young writer who takes a job on the trendy magazine *The Gate*, based in San Francisco, after leaving her fiancé at the altar. Although often insecure and tentative, Susan is an oasis of calm in the midst of an office full of outlandish yet good-hearted coworkers.

See also Bowser, Yvette Lee; *Caroline in the City*; *Roseanne*; Teen Shows.

George, Phyllis (1950–)

The former Miss America for 1971, Phyllis George was the first woman to be a regular on CBS's sports staff (1972–1978). She covered football and other sports before briefly hosting *People* (1978), the televisual version of the magazine, which provided short interviews and profiles of noteworthy people. She later became the First Lady of Kentucky when her husband was elected governor.

Now divorced from her husband, George returned to television in 1999 to host *Woman's Day Television* on PAX-TV. Prior to this series she hosted *American Crafts* on the QVC network and has written a book, *Phyllis George: Living with Quilts* (1999).

Get Christie Love (1974–1975)

This series was the first to feature a black woman as the lead character in a police drama. Christie Love (Teresa Graves) was the only female detective in Los Angeles's Special Investigations Division. Most of her assignments were undercover, so she was free to improvise and rarely did anything according to procedure.

The series was canceled after one season, possibly because the audience felt, as the critics did, that the character was too tough and brash for a woman.

Teresa Graves as the title character of Get Christie Love, *1974. (Photofest)*

Get Smart (1965–1970)

Although this series revolved around and was named for the inept male secret agent Maxwell Smart (Don Adams), his partner, Agent 99 (Barbara Feldon), was an equally important character. Both Smart and 99, as agents for C.O.N.T.R.O.L., battled the evil forces of K.A.O.S. in this tongue-in-cheek spy spoof.

Agent 99 was brilliant, independent, and competent, but inexplicably in love with the bungling Smart. Eventually, they married and had twins before the series ended.

The show was extremely popular, especially with younger viewers, and Smart's expressions "would you believe?" and "missed it by *that* much" entered into the American slang of the late 1960s.

The Ghost and Mrs. Muir (1968–1970)

When the Muir family moved into Gull Cottage overlooking Schooner Bay in New England, the series appeared to be a typical widowed-mother-raising-children-alone-with-housekeeper story, but this show had a twist. Although the mother, Carolyn (Hope Lange), and her children, Candice (Kellie Flanagan) and Jonathan (Harlen Carraher), loved the place, Gull Cottage was still inhabited by the irascible Captain Daniel Gregg (Edward Mulhare), the ghost of the nineteenth-century man who originally owned the house and now resented his privacy being violated.

Until the Muirs moved in, he had frightened off all potential tenants that his cowardly grandnephew, Claymore Gregg (Charles Nelson Reilly), had found to rent the house. Carolyn Muir was made of sterner stuff, and eventually the captain accepted the family's presence and grew fond of them, especially Carolyn. Although there were light romantic moments between the captain and the widow, the series revolved around the Muirs' adjustment to life in the New England town.

Other than Claymore, only Carolyn and the children could see the captain, which led to the requisite gossip by the townspeople of seemingly one-sided conversations and strange goings-on at Gull Cottage.

The series was based on the 1947 movie by the same name that starred Gene Tierney and Rex Harrison.

Gidget (1965-1966)

During a period of growing youth unrest, *Gidget,* based on an earlier series of movies (*Gidget, Gidget Goes Hawaiian, Gidget Goes to Rome*), depicted the perfect, nonrebellious teen. Francine "Gidget" Lawrence (Sally Field) was the perky daughter of widower Russell Lawrence (Don Porter), a professor at a nearby university. Gidget and her father got along well, and the worst disobedience Gidget ever exhibited was breaking curfew, although older sister Anne (Betty Conner) and brother-in-law John (Peter Deuel) always thought the worst.

The series was based on the situations that Gidget and her best friend, Larue (Lynette Winter), regularly got into as they went through the normal passages of life. Each episode ended with Gidget restating the situation and outcome, and bidding the audience "Toodles" until the next week.

Twenty years later, a syndicated sequel was created and called *The New Gidget* (1986–1988). In this series, Gidget (Caryn Richman) and her longtime boyfriend Jeff "Moondoggie" Griffin (Dean Butler) were married, almost-thirty-something professionals. Jeff was an architect for the city and Gidget owned a travel agency, where her still-best friend, Larue (Jill Jacobson), worked.

Most of the series was based on the experiences of Gidget's niece, Danni (Sydney Penny), and Danni's best friend, Gayle (Lili Haydn). Very much a new "Gidget," Danni constantly got into innocent trouble that necessitated her aunt's intervention.

Gidget, the Dog (1994–)

Although portraying a male revolutionary, the spokesdog for Taco Bell is, in fact, a female chihuahua. Gidget has become a hot advertising commodity who is represented by an agent and whose entourage includes a trainer, understudy, and publicist.

Only 18 inches tall and weighing under six pounds, Gidget's image appears on T-shirts, a line of plush toys, cups, and other Taco Bell items. In addition, Gidget has a small role in an Antonio Banderas film and has appeared as a guest on *Good Morning America* (1975–).

See also Commercials, Consumerism.

The Girl from U.N.C.L.E. (1966–1967)

In this spinoff of the popular series *The Man from U.N.C.L.E.* (1964–1968), April Dancer (Stefanie Powers) was another resourceful agent for the United Network Command for Law and Enforcement. This series had the same tongue-in-cheek approach to the spy business, but April and her British partner, Mark Slate (Noel Harrison), never found an audience, and the series lasted only one season.

The Girl with Something Extra (1973–1974)

In this series, Sally Field starred as newlywed Sally Burton, who on her wedding night informed her new husband, John (John Davidson), that she had ESP and could read minds. The comedy revolved around the results of her ability and the difficulty it posed in the couple's attempts to have a normal marriage.

Gish, Lillian (1896–1993)

Lillian Diane Gish made her theatrical debut at the age of five in a play called *In Convict's Stripes* (1901). With her sister Dorothy, she began touring with stock companies in 1902. In 1912, Mary Pickford introduced her to famed filmmaker D. W. Griffith, and Gish subsequently appeared in several of his classic silent films, including *Birth of a Nation* (1915), *Intolerance* (1916), *Broken Blossoms* (1919), *Way Down East* (1920), and *Orphans of the Storm* (1922). She was called "The First Lady of the Silent Screen," and became the symbol of female innocence and vulnerability.

Complimented by Griffith as having "the best mind of any woman," he encouraged her to go beyond acting; as a result, she directed her sister in a film entitled *Remodeling Her Husband* (1920). Between 1923 and 1928, she cowrote and produced several films, including *La Boheme* (1926), *The Scarlet Letter* (1926), and *The Wind* (1928). She did not take screen credit because she did not feel that producing was "any career for a woman."

Temporarily lost in the influx of new talent with the advent of the talkies, Gish moved to Broadway. In 1930 she appeared in Chekhov's *Uncle Vanya*, and later starred in *Camille*. In 1936 she played Ophelia in John Gielgud's landmark production of *Hamlet*. Although Gish returned to movies and moved into television, she continued to appear on Broadway, where at the age of 82 she sang "I Want to Be Loved by You" in the revue *A Musical Jubilee*.

Gish moved to television early in its history by appearing on *Philco Television Playhouse* (1948–1955) in the play "The Late Christopher Bean" (1949), and continued to appear on dramatic anthologies such as *Ford Theatre* (1949–1957), *Pulitzer Prize Playhouse* (1950–1952), *Schlitz Playhouse of Stars* (1951–1959), and *Kraft Television Theatre* (1947–1958). She also appeared regularly on episodic series including *The Defenders* (1961–1965), *Mr. Novak* (1963–1965), and *The Love Boat* (1977–1986).

In 1969, Gish and Helen Hayes appeared as the charming if murderous sisters in a special television production of *Arsenic and Old Lace.* The following year, Gish won a special Oscar for her cumulative work and her "superlative artistry and for distinguished contribution to the progress of motion pictures."

She continued to appear on Broadway, in films, and on television well into her nineties. Her final film, number 104, was *Whales of August* (1987), in which she allowed her demanding costar, Bette Davis, to have (arguably undeserved) top billing with a calm "Let her have it if it's that important to her."

Lillian Gish died at age 99 after a career spanning more than 90 years and including every form of mass entertainment. She wrote of her many experiences in her autobiography *The Movies, Mr. Griffith, and Me* (1969).

The Glass Menagerie (1973)

This adaptation of Tennessee Williams's play emphasized the mother-daughter relationship in the dysfunctional Wingfield family. It starred Katharine Hepburn, in one of her rare television appearances, as Amanda Wingfield, the perpetual southern belle who had "married beneath her," only to be abandoned by her husband and left with two children to raise. Joanna Miles played Amanda's introverted daughter Laura, who had a limp from a childhood illness. Painfully shy, Laura lived in a fantasy world with her collection of glass figurines and was completely uninterested in finding herself a husband—the pursuit that encompassed her mother's life.

See also Hepburn, Katharine.

Gloria (1982–1983)

In this series, Gloria Bunker Stivic (Sally Struthers), the daughter from *All in the Family* (1971–1979), was divorced from Mike "Meathead" Stivic, who had left his family to live in a California commune. She and her son, eight-year-old Joey (Christian Jacobs), lived in Foxridge, New York, where she worked as an assistant trainee for two veterinarians, old Dr. Adams (Burgess Meredith) and liberated Dr. Maggie Lawrence (Jo deWinter).

The comedy predictably revolved around Gloria's adjustments to being single and earning her own way in life for the first time.

The Goldbergs (1949–1954)

The Goldbergs was a popular radio program for over 20 years before moving to television. The television series continued to chronicle the lives of the Goldberg family at 1030 East Tremont Avenue in their six-room apartment (3B) in the Bronx.

The central character was Molly (Gertrude Berg, also the series creator), everyone's favorite Jewish mother, who caused endless trouble as she tried to solve everyone's problems. Her mangled English and malapropisms became known as "mollypropisms," and were part of the humor of the character.

The rest of the family consisted of her husband and two children. As viewers became less centered in metropolitan areas and ethnic humor lost favor, the family moved to the suburbs to bring the show more in line with the viewing public, but the characters had lost their appeal and the series was soon canceled.

See also Berg, Gertrude.

The Golden Girls (1985–1992)

This series was definitely a departure from standard sitcom fare. The series' stars, contrary to general television practice, were all mature women, yet the series consistently placed in the top of the Nielsen ratings.

The Golden Girls revolved around four single women living together in Miami and enjoying their golden years. Blanche Devereaux (Rue McClanahan) owned the house they shared, and was a man-hungry southern belle. Dorothy Zbornak (Bea Arthur) was a strong-willed, outspoken divorcée who occasionally worked as a substitute teacher. Dorothy's mother, Sophia Petrillo (Estelle Getty), was the earthy, wise octogenarian. The final housemate was Rose Nylund (Betty White), a naive, ditsy widow who often misunderstood what was said, and contributed to the conversation things that had nothing to do with the current topic.

In the final episode, Dorothy married Blanche's uncle Lucas (Leslie Nielsen), and the remaining "girls" pooled their money to buy a small art-deco hotel along Miami's trendy South Bay in a series called *Golden Palace* (1992–

GOLDEN AGE OF TELEVISION

This term describes the decade of the 1950s when live dramas were performed on television. Staged in the theater manner, the plays were broadcast from New York and featured both new and established plays such as *Twelve Angry Men, Visit to a Small Planet, No Time for Sergeants, The Miracle Worker, Marty,* and *The Days of Wine and Roses.*

The drama or anthology series dominated all networks' schedules with such offerings as *Kraft Television Theatre* (1947–1958), *Playhouse 90* (1956–1961), *Studio One* (1948–1958), *U.S. Steel Hour* (1953–1963), *DuPont Show of the Month* (1952–1957), and many, many others. The proliferation of these live-drama series acted as a springboard for the careers of many directors and writers as well as actors by enabling them to hone their skills and establish their names. However, by the early 1960s, sitcoms and episodic television were the audience favorites, and live drama faded from the airwaves.

The term was revived in the late 1970s and the 1980s to describe the quality programming produced during that period. To many critics, the term also encompassed comedy as well as drama, as in *The Mary Tyler Moore Show* (1970–1977), *Lou Grant* (1977–1982), *Hill Street Blues* (1981–1987), *Cagney and Lacey* (1982–1988), and *The Golden Girls* (1985–1992).

In the 1990s, the term was revived once more to describe quality dramas of that period, including *Law & Order* (1990–), *Homicide: Life on the Street* (1993–1999), *NYPD Blue* (1993–), *ER* (1994–), and *Chicago Hope* (1994–).

See also *Cagney and Lacey, The Golden Girls, Hill Street Blues, The Mary Tyler Moore Show,* MTM Enterprises.

1993). Unfortunately, instead of becoming landed gentry, they all had to work in the hotel to make the venture profitable. Their managerial difficulties and the strange guests the hotel attracted were the basis of the comedy.

Gould, Cheryl (1952–)

Cheryl Gould, vice-president of NBC News, is the highest-ranking woman in network news in addition to being one of the youngest vice-presidents. She oversees a vast array of business details, including talent contracts, personnel issues, assignments, and overall coverage.

Although she initially set her sights on a career as a newspaper reporter, after graduation from Princeton, Gould first worked at a radio station, then moved to the ABC affiliate in Rochester, New York. She spent a year in Paris as field producer before moving to NBC News.

She started as a producer of the weekend edition of *Nightly News*, then became senior producer of the overnight edition. While working on a D-day documentary, she caught the attention of Tom Brokaw, who requested that she work on a weekday version of *Nightly News*. Gould worked as foreign editor and senior producer, and was the first female executive producer.

Grace under Fire (1993–1997)

After being married for eight years to an abusive alcoholic, Grace Kelly (Brett Butler) got a divorce and built a new life for herself and her three children. She found a house to rent and, thanks to affirmative action, got a job at an oil refinery and became the "quota babe" of her crew.

During the 1996–1997 season, Grace graduated from college and quit her refinery job, only to find another one difficult to come by. She finally accepted employment in a distant city, but soon realized that the strain on her children was too great and quit, thereby becoming unemployed again at the beginning of the 1997–1998 season. She soon had a job in the male-dominated contruction industry as a secretary–cum–office manager for an all-black crew.

Soon after these changes were made, production closed down for a second time amid rumors of Butler's personal problems with substance abuse. Eventually the series was canceled, and Butler returned to the stand-up circuit after receiving help for her addiction.

Grant, Lee (1929–)

Born Lyova Haskell Rosenthal, the only child of a father who worked in education and a Russian mother who had survived Cossack purges as a child, Lee Grant was raised in almost perfect surroundings as her parents exposed her to a variety of artistic and cultural pursuits. After high school, having attended the Julliard School of Music and the High School of Music and Art, she enrolled at Sanford Meisner's Neighborhood Playhouse in New York and found her niche in acting.

As a child she appeared in the opera *L'Oracolo* (1933), and her Broadway debut was *Joy to the World* (1948), before being cast as a shoplifter in *Detective Story* (1949), for which she won a Critics' Circle Award. The 1951 film version garnered acclaim and the Cannes Film Festivals Award for Best Actress.

Lee Grant holds a microphone in her feature-film directing debut on the set of Tell Me a Riddle, *1980. (Filmways Pictures/Archive Photos)*

Just as her star was rising, Grant made a near-career-ending mistake—she spoke out against the blacklist and the House Committee on Un-American Activities. Overnight, her name appeared on the list, although she was told that it would be removed if she would name her then-husband, Arnold Manoff, as a Communist. She refused and did not work again in films for 12 years.

The theater was slightly more resistant to the blacklist, so she was able to get some acting jobs, and she also worked as an acting coach. Occasionally she appeared on the dramatic anthologies that proliferated during the early years of television.

Surprisingly, Grant was removed from the blacklist in the same manner she had been added—overnight. She appeared in a number of episodic television series such as *Ben Casey* (1961–1966), *The Defenders* (1961–1965), *The Nurses* (1962–1965), and *The Fugitive* (1963–1967). Soon she landed a role on the prime-time soap opera *Peyton Place* (1964–1969), and won the Emmy Award for Best Supporting Actress in a Drama in 1965. After *Peyton Place* ended, she appeared on series such as *The Big Valley* (1965–1969), *The Name of the Game* (1968–1971), and *Mod Squad* (1968–1973).

One of the first made-for-TV movies in which Grant appeared, *The Neon Ceiling* (1971), won her a second Emmy. A few years later, in 1975, her role in *Shampoo* (1975) earned her an Oscar for Best Supporting Actress. Also in 1975, she had her own short-lived series, *Fay,* about a divorcée beginning life again.

Although she appeared regularly on television and in films, Grant was drawn to directing and the need to raise consciousness and inform the public about issues that were not generally topics of mainstream films. Her first feature, *Tell Me a Riddle* (1980), dealt with the experience of growing older in a culture that often views aging as a personal failing. Grant followed this with the acclaimed documentary *The Wilmar 8* (1981), which explored the discriminatory employment practices in the banking industry, and *When Women Kill* (1983), which helped change the legal view of spousal abuse.

Her documentary *Down and Out in America* (1986) on HBO portrayed the plight of the homeless and won Grant another Oscar for Best Documentary Feature. This theme was continued in the television features *Homeless* (1989) and *No Place Like Home* (1989), set in Pittsburgh after many of the factories and mills closed during the late 1980s.

Her documentaries and films reflect Grant's search for justice, perhaps partially fueled by her treatment during the blacklist years. *Women on Trial* (1984) exposed the flawed workings of the family court system in Houston, Texas, and the film *Nobody's Child* (1987) dealt with a normal child who was institutionalized because her parents could not control her. It won Grant a Director's Guild of America Award for Best Dramatic Television Special.

She went on to direct *Staying Together* (1989), *Seasons of the Heart* (1994), *Reunion* (1994), and later that same year, *Following the Heart.* Her most recent work included hosting an HBO special that she also directed—*Battered* (1989)—and a documentary on health issues, *Say It, Fight It, Cure It* (1997).

See also Blacklist, McCarthyism.

Grasso, Maria (1962–)

As senior vice-president of comedy development at WB Television, Maria Grasso determines which series ideas to pursue and market to the networks. Through her efforts, WB placed three series on the fall 1998 lineup, with two more debuting midseason.

Grasso worked for MTV in New York for six years before moving to Los Angeles and getting a job in comedy development at Universal Television (later Studio USA). She eventually rose to become senior vice-president of comedy programming before moving to WB late in 1998.

Grindl (1963–1964)

This series was the second sans–Sid Caesar series for Imogene Coca. In this sitcom, Coca played the highly efficient temporary worker Grindl, who was constantly overset by the everyday difficulties of her life. Being a "temp," each week Grindl had a new job, from laundress to ticket taker to baby-sitter to maid to cook.

H

Hallmark Hall of Fame (1951–)

The quality presentations of *Hallmark Hall of Fame* are among the high points of any television season. The first presentation, on Christmas Eve 1951, was funded as a thank-you to all the people who had sent Hallmark Cards; the host was Sarah Churchill, who later hosted the series *Hallmark Television Playhouse* (1952–1955). After Churchill's brief opening remarks, Gian Carlo Menotti's Christmas opera, *Amahl and the Night Visitors*, was presented without further commercial interruption.

Each succeeding year, Hallmark presented quality dramatic programs that ranked among the most popular and critically acclaimed programs of any given season. The first programs were often Shakespearean plays such as *Hamlet* (1953), *MacBeth* (1954), and *Taming of the Shrew* (1956), but the series also offered lighter dramas such as *Alice in Wonderland* (1955), *Born Yesterday* (1956), and *Victoria Regina* (1961). Television viewers were presented with such excellent plays as *Anastasia* (1967), *Winter of Our Discontent* (1983), *Sarah, Plain and Tall* (1991), and its sequel, *Skylark* (1993). In 1993, *To Dance with the White Dog*, starring Jessica Tandy and her husband Hume Cronyn, was the top-rated movie of the 1993–1994 season.

Often cited as a continuation of the company slogan "when you care enough to send the very best," Hallmark Hall of Fame received a Peabody in 1964. Joyce Hall, president of Hallmark Cards, was inducted into the Television Arts and Sciences Hall of Fame in 1985.

Hammer, Bonnie (1957–)

As senior vice-president of Sci-Fi Channel and USA Original Productions, Bonnie Hammer's goal is to make the offerings of the Sci-Fi Channel appealing to both hard-core sci-fi fans and fantasy enthusiasts. Hammer has worked on various prosocial campaigns such as Erase the Hate, and was in charge of enhancing the audience perception of the World Wrestling Federation on the USA network.

Harris, Julie (1925–)

A gifted dramatic actor, Julie Harris has appeared on several television series and has won two Emmys in her television career. In 1958 she won the Emmy for Best Single Performance by an Actress for *Little Moon of Alban* (*Hallmark Hall of Fame*), and in 1961 she won again for her portrayal of Queen Victoria in *Victoria Regina* (*Hallmark Hall of Fame*).

Harris appeared on several of the dramatic anthologies series of the early years of television, including *Actor's Studio* (1948–1950), *The Goodyear TV Playhouse* (1951–1960), *The Philco TV Playhouse* (1948–1955), and *The Starlight Theatre* (1950–1951). Harris also appeared in a short-lived series, *Thicker Than Water* (1973), in which she portrayed the spinster daughter of a pickle baron who must live in the same house with her ne'er-do-well brother and run the family business for five years to be eligible to receive her inheritance.

A few years later, Harris appeared in the dramatic series about life in the South during the Depression, *The Family Holvak* (1975), in which she portrayed a preacher's wife and the mother of two children. Harris next appeared as Nellie Taft in the miniseries *Backstairs at the White House* (1979), which depicted the presidents and their families through the eyes of the domestic staff. In 1981, Harris joined the cast of *Knots Landing* as Lilimae Clements—a role that continued until 1987.

Born in Grosse Point, Michigan, to a wealthy family, as a young woman Harris rebelled against her privileged upbringing by going into acting. She studied acting at Yale before making her stage debut in *It's a Gift* (1945). She later earned an Oscar nomination when she re-created her stage role for the screen in *The Member of the Wedding* (1952). Throughout her career she has been nominated for more than 20 acting awards, receiving five Tony awards and two Emmy awards.

Harris, Susan (1945–)

Susan Harris studied English literature at both Cornell and New York University before writing a script in 1969 that was accepted for the television series *Then Came Bronson* (1969–1970). She worked at Norman Lear's Tandem Productions in the 1970s writing for *Maude* (1972–1978), and was instrumental in having Maude explore issues that had not been dealt with on previous sitcoms, such as vasectomies, abortion, and menopause.

After establishing herself as a writer at Tandem, she began work on *Fay* (1975), about a woman who divorced her husband after 24 years of marriage and started the process of rebuilding her life. Although the series received critical acclaim, it was shown during the family viewing hour, and its topics were much too controversial for that audience. Shortsightedly, the network canceled the series rather than move it to a more acceptable time slot.

Harris's next creation was *Soap* (1977–1981), a parody of prime-time soap operas. The series focused on two sisters and their families—the rich Tates and the blue-collar Campbells. The series ridiculed such topics as homosexuality, incest, impotence, adultery, racism, satanic worship, transsexualism, and transvestitism. Needless to say, civic groups rallied for censorship, but the series placed number 13 in the ratings.

Harris also created *Benson* (1979–1986), based on a character from *Soap*. Benson (Robert Guillaume) was still the glue that held the governor's mansion together, but he was less insolent and more ambitious than the earlier depiction of his character. Eventually, he even ran for governor against his employer.

The next shows that Harris created were less successful. *I'm a Big Girl Now* (1980–1981) starred Diana Canova as a divorcée who moves in with her father (Danny Thomas), who had just been divorced by her mother. *It Takes Two* (1982–1983) starred Patty Duke and Richard Crenna as a husband and wife trying to juggle family and careers (she was an assistant district attorney and he was a chief of surgery). In *Hail to the Chief* (1985), Patty Duke starred as the first female president, Julia Mansfield, who spent more time trying to control the chaos caused by her family than running the country. The premise had promise, but the series was canceled after only seven episodes.

Her next creation turned, figuratively and literally, to gold. *The Golden Girls* (1985–1992) was an almost instant hit. The series focused on four mature women living together in Miami during their retirement years.

Dorothy Zbornak (Bea Arthur) was outspoken and opinionated, while Blanche Devereaux (Rue McClanahan) was a southern belle who never grew out of her "belle" phase. Rose Nylund (Betty White) was naive and conversationally challenged, and Sophia Petrillo (Estelle Getty) was Dorothy's mother, whose "tact cells" were destroyed when she had a stroke. Like previous Harris series, all topics were fair game.

Empty Nest (1988–1995) was set in the same Florida community as *The Golden Girls* and featured eligible widower Dr. Harry Weston (Richard Mulligan) and two of his adult daughters who had come home to live. The stories followed the evolution of the characters' lives, independence, and interdependence.

Harris believed in continuing a winning scenario, so she used the same community to create yet another series, *Nurses* (1991–1994). This sitcom was set in the same hospital in which Dr. Weston worked, and centered on the nurses working there. This series, with a standard character mix, was not as popular as its predecessors.

Harris added her fourth series during this period, the short-lived *Good and Evil* (1991). The series focused on two sisters—good Jenny (Margaret Whitton) and evil Denise (Teri Garr). Reminiscent of *Soap,* the characters were exaggerations and caricatures.

After the end of *The Golden Girls* and Dorothy's marriage to Blanche's uncle, the remaining cast members invested in a small art-deco hotel in a trendy area of Miami. *The Golden Palace* (1992–1993), however, proved to be more of a cash drain than the moneymaker the three had envisioned. Soon Blanche, Rose, and Sophia were working full-time to keep the hotel in business, catering to the needs of an odd assortment of staff and guests.

Harris once again had a sitcom on the schedule with *The Secret Lives of Men* (1998), a short-lived series about three male friends and their efforts to rebuild their lives after divorce.

Hart to Hart (1979–1984)

This series was done in the tradition of the *Thin Man* movies, in which a wealthy couple traveled the world solving crimes and engaging in daring exploits. The 1980s couple consisted of freelance writer-photographer Jennifer Hart (Stefanie Powers) and her millionaire husband, Jonathan (Robert Wagner). Having met in the midst of a murder, the couple married and toured the world as amateur sleuths, solving crimes that baffled the authorities.

Although a beautiful mansion in Beverly Hills was their home base, nearly every week found them traveling to a new location and stumbling across a new mystery to solve. They were assisted by Max (Lionel Stander), their chauffeur and general man-about-the-house.

The series was so popular that ten years after it went off the air, three made-for-TV movies were produced during the 1993–1994 season, in which the Harts were once more globe-trotting sleuths.

Hawn, Goldie (1945–)

Although Goldie Hawn has made a name for herself behind the camera in both television and feature films, she will probably always be remembered as the giggling, bikini-clad go-go girl on *Rowan and Martin's Laugh-In* (1968–1973). One of the first regulars to leave the show, she proved that she was not just another "dumb blonde" by becoming a respected producer and director.

Her first television directorial effort was the TNT film *Hope* (1997), about a 12-year-old dancer coming of age and facing the cruelties of life during the 1962 Cuban missile crisis. Hawn was drawn to the story when she first read it, and persevered during the five years it took to bring the story to the television screen.

She received her grounding as an actor after leaving *Laugh-In* in 1968. One of her first movies was a Disney production, *The One and Only Genuine Original Family Band* (1968), which people seldom remember, but the next year she garnered a Best Supporting Actress Oscar as the wide-eyed ingenue in *Cactus Flower* (1969). For the next 20 years she appeared in several well-remembered and some best-forgotten films, including *There's a Girl in My Soup* (1970), *Butterflies Are Free* (1972), *Sugarland Express* (1974), *Shampoo* (1975), *Foul Play* (1978), *Private Benjamin* (1981), *Swing Shift* (1984), *Wildcats* (1986), *Overboard* (1987), *Bird on a Wire* (1990), *Deceived* (1991), *CrissCross* (1992), *Death Becomes Her* (1992), *The Housesitter* (1992), *First Wives Club* (1997), and *Everyone Says I Love You* (1997).

Hawn was born in Washington, D.C.; her father was a violinist and her mother was a dance instructor. Although she attended American University and studied drama, she left to join the cancan line at the 1965 World's Fair. She moved to Los Angeles and supported herself as a go-go dancer while she tried to break into show business.

She landed a job on the seldom-remembered series *Good Morning World* (1967–1968) as Sandy Kramer, the gossiping neighbor. Although the part was not a large one, she caught the attention of producers, and from there went on to *Rowan and Martin's Laugh-In* as the befuddled, bikini-clad ditz. Partly because of the show's popularity, the public found that confused, naively innocent character the most comfortable and appealing, and her comedies have generally been more popular than the dramatic offerings.

She has received many awards for her work, most recently the Women in Film Crystal Award (1997) and the 12th Annual American Museum of Moving Images Lifetime Achievement Award (1998).

See also *Laugh-In.*

Hayes, Helen (1900–1993)

Helen Hayes, one of the greatest actors of the twentieth century, moved from the theater to television after contracting asthmatic bronchitis, which was aggravated by the dust found everywhere in old theaters. She appeared in several TV movies and won the Emmy for Best Actress in 1952, but is perhaps best remembered for the series in which she starred with Mildred Natwick, *The Snoop Sisters* (1973–1974).

Hayes was born in Washington, D.C., and made her stage debut at age five as Prince Charles in *The Royal Family.* Her New York debut came four years later, at age nine, when she appeared in the play *Old Dutch.* She was an acclaimed actress while still in her teens, and starred in *Dear Brutus* in 1918.

Throughout her stage career, she won numerous awards and portrayed several of the most famous women rulers in history, including Mary, Queen of Scots (in a part especially written for her by Maxwell Anderson); Cleopatra; and Queen Victoria (in the play *Victoria Regina,* which ran on Broadway from 1935 to 1938). She won a Tony the first year it was presented for her role in *Happy Birthday* (1947). She also won a Tony for *Time Remembered* (1958), and in 1980 received the award for career achievement.

Her popularity on Broadway was acknowledged in 1959 when the Fulton Theatre was renamed the Helen Hayes Theatre. Her response to the honor was "an actor's life is so transitory . . . suddenly you're a building." When her namesake theater was torn down in 1982, another building was named for her.

She was never comfortable in Hollywood, but she appeared in several excellent films, including *The Sin of Madelon Claudet* (1931), *A Farewell to Arms* (1932), and *Anastasia* (1956). She won the Oscar for Best Actress for her portrayal of a woman who sacrifices everything for her illegitimate son in *The Sin of Madelon Claudet* and for Best Supporting Actress for her role as the stowaway in *Airport* (1970). She also made regular appearances in Disney films throughout the 1970s.

In addition to her work on *The Snoop Sisters,* Hayes appeared in several drama presentations, including *Dear Brutus* (1956), *Springtime USA* (1956), *One Rose for Christmas* (1958), *Ah Wilderness* (1959), *Woman: The Lonely Years* (1960), and *Four Women in Black* (1961). She also appeared as one of the charmingly murderous aunts in the 1969 television version of *Arsenic and Old Lace.*

In 1988 she was given the Lifetime Achievement Award from the Kennedy Center and received the National Medal of Arts. She wrote three volumes of memoirs: *A Gift of Joy* (1965), *On Reflection* (1969), and *My Life in Three Acts* (1990).

See also *The Snoop Sisters.*

Hazel (1961–1966)

Based on the cartoon character created by Ted Key that appeared in the *Saturday Evening Post, Hazel* starred Shirley Booth as the title character. Hazel was the efficient, all-knowing maid/housekeeper for the Baxters— George (Don DeFore) and Dorothy (Whitney Blake) for the first four years of the series, then Steve (Ray Fulmer) and Barbara (Lynn Borden) for the final year. The home was her domain and no one, not even her bosses, knew better than she what was needed or how to do it. During the five years the series was on the air, Booth won two Emmys for her portrayal.

Booth had previously been a successful Broadway star and appeared on several drama anthologies in the 1950s. She won an Oscar, a Tony, and awards from both the New York Dramatic Critics and the New York Film Critics for her portrayal of Lola Delaney in *Come Back, Little Sheba* (1952). Yet, she is remembered by many people as the ever-meddling Hazel.

Hepburn, Katharine (1907–)

Katharine Hepburn, although generally thought of as a movie star, has appeared in some of the most highly acclaimed TV movies and dramatic presentations in the history of the medium. Thought by many to be one of the most monumental and enduring of all Hollywood stars, Hepburn has always been a role model of independence, courage, determination, and integrity for women.

Although she came to television late in her life, her presence has added style and elegance to all the presentations on which she appears. Her first role was that of Amanda Wingfield in *The Glass Menagerie* (1973), and she won an Emmy for her role in *Love among the Ruins* (1975), which also won a Peabody Award that year. She later appeared in *The Corn Is Green* (1979), *Mrs. Delafield Wants to Marry* (1986), and *Laura Lansing Slept Here* (1988). She also appeared in the special *The Spencer Tracy Legacy: A Tribute by Katharine Hepburn* (1986). She returned in the 1990s to appear in the Christmas movie *The Man Upstairs* (1993), as well as *This Can't Be Love* and *One Christmas* (both 1994).

Hepburn's early life in Hartford, Connecticut, was somewhat unconventional. Her parents were liberal intellectuals who did not rear their chil-

Shirley Booth, as Hazel, catches George Baxter (Don Defore) raiding the refrigerator in the middle of the night in this episode of Hazel. *(Archive Photos)*

HEALTH ISSUES

Other than medical series and soap operas that regularly deal with all manner of human trauma, little attention has been given to health issues within the context of a long-running character. Until recent years, a character seldom had an opportunity to react to and deal with an illness or health condition over an extended period and thus give insight into a human condition.

PREGNANCY

The television industry has come a long way from the days when the word *pregnant* could not be used on *MaryKay and Johnny* (1947–1950), nor later on *I Love Lucy* (1951–1959). However, some believe the pendulum has swung too far the other way. Television has come to the point where motherhood, specifically single motherhood, is nothing more than a plot device.

One of the first central characters to become a single mother within the context of her television series was Molly Dodd (*The Days and Nights of Molly Dodd,* 1987–1991). During the third season, Molly (Blair Brown) became pregnant by her boyfriend, black detective Nathaniel Hawthorne (Richard Lawson). Soon after they decided to get married, he died of a severe allergic reaction, leaving Molly to have the child, Emily, alone during the final season. All this occurred with little notice from the general public.

When Murphy Brown (*Murphy Brown,* 1988–1998) became pregnant by her ex-husband, Jake (Robin Thomas), the entire country seemed to be embroiled in the debate about single motherhood. Vice-president Dan Quayle made Murphy the "poster child" of declining family values

and blamed the problems of society on single-parent, generally mother-headed, families.

Since that time, single motherhood has become an almost-common plot device. One of the most recent single moms is Roz Doyle (Peri Gilpin) on the popular sitcom *Frasier* (1993–). Lifetime premiered an original series, *Oh Baby,* in 1998 that concerns a single businesswoman determined to have a child via artificial insemination.

Critics fault these generally lighthearted portrayals of single motherhood as not truly reflecting the realities faced by single mothers. All the single mothers on television are financially able to care for their child and have extensive support networks, which is often not true for single mothers in the real world.

Although pregnancy is used as a plot mechanism, female actors can be penalized for becoming pregnant in real life. The most famous case involves Hunter Tylo and Aaron Spelling Productions. Tylo had been hired as a vixen character who was to appear for only a few months on the Spelling series *Melrose Place* (1992–1999), but before appearing on the show she learned that she was pregnant. When the production company was informed of her condition, they fired her because, in the words of her termination letter, "your pregnancy is incompatible with this role." Tylo subsequently received a $4.89 million award in a wrongful termination lawsuit.

MENOPAUSE

Menopause is not given much attention on television, partly because older characters are not

(continued on next page)

(continued from previous page)

given central-character attention. Two notable exceptions were characters from Norman Lear productions in the 1970s, the era of reality programming.

When Edith Bunker (Jean Stapleton) in *All in the Family* (1971–1980) started going through "the change," it was the topic of several episodes. Most memorable was the episode in which an exasperated Archie told Edith that she had 15 minutes to "get through the change." Edith's cousin, Maude Findley (Bea Arthur), in *Maude* (1972–1978) also dealt with how menopause affected her life within the context of the series.

Another series that featured older characters dealing with the effects of menopause was *The Golden Girls* (1985–1992). Although the other characters accepted it as a natural part of life, southern belle Blanche Devereaux (Rue Mc-Clanahan) refused to admit that it was part of her life because, in her mind as well as in the minds of some of the viewers, menopause made a woman less than a woman. The events in the episodes were used to show that this belief was unfounded.

CANCER

Cancer, specifically breast cancer, has been given more attention on television in recent years. As the public gains awareness and knowledge of the disease, television characters confront the illness on a personal level.

One of the first series to have a character confront the issue was *Family* (1976–1980), in which Kate Lawrence (Sada Thompson) learned that she had the disease in 1978. The next series was *Cagney and Lacey* (1982–1988), and several episodes dealt with the interpersonal dynamics when Lacey (Tyne Daly) found that she had a lump in her breast.

On *Sisters* (1991–1996), the eldest sister, Alex (Swoosie Kurtz), was diagnosed with breast cancer during the 1993–1994 season. During the year, her experiences with the illness and her family's reaction were documented in addition to other personal problems encountered by the sisters.

In the final season of *Murphy Brown* (1988–1998), Murphy (Candice Bergen) learned that she had breast cancer, and the progression of the illness as well as the characters' reaction to it became the underlying theme for the entire season. After certain episodes, Bergen made public service announcements to raise awareness of the disease, symptoms, and prevention. In happy-sitcom fashion, Murphy learned in the final episode that she was cancerfree, making the outcome happier than it often is for actual sufferers.

dren in traditional sex roles, but rather encouraged them to try new things and expand their abilities. Her father was a physician and her mother an active suffragette, which exposed Hepburn to an expanded view of women's roles from an early age.

Hepburn graduated from Bryn Mawr in 1928, and made her screen debut in 1932 with John Barrymore in *Bill of Divorcement.* She won her first Oscar for her role in *Morning Glory* (1933), but by 1938 had been labeled "box office poison" by theater owners. Not able to get roles in Hollywood, she went to New York, where she appeared on Broadway in *The Philadelphia Story*. Hepburn had the foresight to buy the film rights, which allowed her comeback in the film version (1940) to be on her own terms. In 1951 she starred in *The African Queen* with Humphrey Bogart.

Throughout the 1950s she made a series of light romantic comedies with Spencer Tracy, and won her second Oscar for *Guess Who's Coming to Dinner* (1967), in which she starred with Tracy just before his death. She won her third Oscar for her portrayal of Eleanor of Aquitaine in *A Lion in Winter* (1968), and her fourth for *On Golden Pond* (1981). She continues to hold the record for Oscar wins (4) as well as for Oscar nominations (12).

She wrote her autobiography, *Me,* in 1991.

See also *The Glass Menagerie.*

Here's Lucy (1968–1974)

Although the title changed, the series was actually a reworking of *The Lucy Show* (1962–1968). Now Lucy lived in Los Angeles and worked for Unique Employment Agency as secretary to the president, who also happened to be her brother-in-law, Harrison Carter (Gale Gordon). Lucy was again a widow with two children—this time portrayed by her real-life children, Kim (Lucie Arnaz) and Craig (Desi Arnaz Jr.).

Lucy continued to get into improbable situations and react with outlandish antics.

See also Ball, Lucille; *I Love Lucy; The Lucy Show.*

Hey Jeannie (1956–1957)

This working-class sitcom involved Jeannie MacLennon (Jeannie Carson), a naive Scottish lass who traveled to the United States knowing no one and having no job. On her first day in New York she met cabdriver Al Murray (Allen Jenkins), who offered to sponsor her, so Jeannie moved in with him and his sister Liz (Jane Dulo). Jeannie worked as a waitress while trying to adapt to her new environment and the people of New York.

Hill Street Blues (1981–1987)

Produced in a fast-paced, almost documentary style, *Hill Street Blues* followed the lives of the police officers who worked at the Hill Street Station, a precinct in a ghetto neighborhood of an eastern city. Rather than emphasize crime-fighting as on earlier police dramas, this series detailed the personal lives and relationships of the characters. Although predominantly a male ensemble serial drama, the series had two strong female lead characters.

Attorney Joyce Davenport (Veronica Hamel) was a dedicated public defender who eventually married Precinct Captain Frank Furillo (Daniel J. Travanti), so that their personal and professional lives were played out on the show. The strength and complexity of her character were unusual for television in general during that period, and specifically in the male-dominated arena of police drama.

The other strong female character was Officer (later Sergeant) Lucy Bates (Betty Thomas), a patrol officer who faced the same dangers and problems as her male counterparts. She was so much "one of the boys" that she represented the precinct in the interdepartmental poker finals. Although outwardly tough, her portrayal and various story lines revealed uncertainties and doubts that allowed viewers to identify and sympathize with the character.

The series was a hit with critics before it found a secure audience base, and was awarded a Peabody in its first season. It went on to win 16 Emmys (with eight nominations in the 1982–1983 season alone).

HISPANICS ON TELEVISION

Hispanic females are one of the least represented ethnic groups. In leading roles throughout the history of television, they have been almost nonexistent with little better showing in recurring supporting roles. And, as is often the case with ethnic minorities, frequently Hispanic parts are filled by non-Hispanic actors or Hispanics play non-Hispanic characters.

Perhaps the first Hispanic to have a leading role in a television series was Elena Verdugo in *Meet Millie* (1952–1956). However, the character of Millie Bronson was not Hispanic so the life of a middle-class secretary in Manhattan with a meddling mother was indistinguishable from other early situation comedies. Verdugo later appeared in a supporting role in the popu-

(continued on next page)

(continued from previous page)

lar series *Marcus Welby, M.D.* (1969–1976), as outspoken Nurse Consuelo Lopez. During her seven years on the show, she received two Emmy nominations as Best Supporting Actress in a Drama.

Argentine-born Linda Cristal began her show business career in Spanish-language films at 17 and played a variety of virginal señoritas and Indian maidens in the United States before being cast as Victoria Montoya Cannon on the western drama *High Chaparral* (1967–1971). In a dynastic move, much older Big John Cannon (Leif Erickson) married Victoria, daughter of Don Sebastian Montoya (Frank Silvera) and heiress to his extensive cattle empire. Cristal received two Emmy nominations as Best Actress in a Drama.

Another Hispanic actor, Rita Moreno, spent several years on television in supporting roles. She won an Emmy for her performance as a Polish prostitute in an episode of *Rockford Files* (1974–1980), then went on to play Violet Newstead, a widowed mother with a stereotypical Latin temper in *9 to 5* (1982–1983). She then had a recurring role as Burt Reynolds's estranged wife, Kimberley Baskin, on *B.L. Stryker* (1989–1990), one of the three series that alternated on the ABC Mystery Movie. She also made regular appearances on the educational program *The Electric Company* (1971–).

Rosie Perez, in addition to being an actor, was the Emmy-nominated choreographer for *In Living Color* (1990–1993). Saundra Santiago played undercover Detective Gina Navarro Calbrese on *Miami Vice* (1984–1987), while on *Head of the Class* (1986–1991), Leslie Bega played perfection-driven Maria Borgis (1986–1989), who grounded herself if she got any grade other than an A.

Maria Conchita Alonzo played a spunky Venezuelan waitress turned bookkeeper turned construction worker who married her boss in the extremely short-lived series *One of the Boys* (April—May 1989). In a similar role, Elizabeth Peña played housekeeper Dora Calderon, the feisty illegal alien who married her boss to avoid deportation, on the sitcom *I Married Dora* (1987–1989), which had the dubious distinction of being based on a federal offense (marrying an alien to prevent his or her deportation).

The most visible actor in recent years claiming Hispanic descent was Victoria Principal, who appeared from 1978 to 1987 as the eternally pure and innocent Pamela Barnes Ewing, the wife of good son Bobby on *Dallas* (1978–1991). She became the sexy poster-girl of the late 1970s and early 1980s and had her own line of exercise videos. In addition, she wrote three books on health and beauty (*Body Principal,* 1983; *Beauty Principal,* 1984; and *Diet Principal,* 1987). She went on to appear in several movies-of-the-week including *Mistress* (1987), *Naked Lie* (1989), *Blind Rage* (1990), *Don't Touch My Daughter* (1991), and *Love in Another Town* (1997).

Alex Meneses was added to the cast of *Dr. Quinn, Medicine Woman* (1993–1998), as Mexican schoolteacher Teresa Morales during its final season. And on *FX—the Series* (1996–1998) Jacqueline Torres portrayed Detective Mira Sanchez who worked with the FX crew to stymie the criminals that they encountered.

While Hispanic representation on television is not reflective of their numbers within society, in recent years they have appeared more often and in less menial roles.

Honey West (1965–1966)

This series was truly unusual for the mid-1960s. *Honey West* was cut from the same James Bond–driven spy-sleuth cloth of other campy series of the period, with the exception that its star was female. Honey (Anne Francis) inherited the family detective business from her father and proved to be bright, resourceful, and coolly competent. In addition to being an expert in judo and karate, she had at her disposal an array of interestingly disguised weapons and surveillance devices such as a radio transmitter hidden in her lipstick.

Anne Francis strikes a dramatic pose for her role as Honey West. (Photofest)

She also inherited her father's partner, Sam Bolt (John Ericson), who wanted to marry her if she would ever slow down long enough, but the only male allowed close to her was Bruce, her pet ocelot. Honey's Aunt Meg (Irene Hervey) kept the home fires burning while Honey was out sleuthing.

The character of Honey West was first introduced on an episode of the original *Burke's Law* (1963–1966), where she outsmarted the chief of detectives, Amos Burke (Gene Barry).

See also Action/Adventure Genre, Careers for Women on Television.

Hot L Baltimore (1975)

This series, produced by Norman Lear, was based on an off-Broadway play of the same name written by Lanford Wilson. One of the first sitcoms to bring double entendres into the living room, the characters and subject matter shocked some viewers and critics as much as the dialogue did.

The series was set in the lobby of a run-down hotel in a seedy section of a large city, where the once-grand Hotel Baltimore (the "e" had burnt out and had never been replaced) was now home to an assortment of down-on-their-luck characters. The main characters were April Green (Conchata Ferrell), the requisite hooker-with-a-heart-of-gold, and Clifford Ainsley (Richard Masur), the hotel manager.

Also in residence was Suzy Marta Rocket (Jeannie Linero), a Colombian hooker whose heart was not gold; Bill Lewis (James Cromwell), the desk clerk; Charles Bingham (Al Freeman Jr.), the resident philosopher; Millie (Gloria LeRoy), the unemployed waitress; and George (Lee Bergere) and Gordon (Henry Clavert), the homosexual couple. Rounding out the list of tenants were elderly Mr. Morse (Stan Gottlieb), who was always on the brink of death, and Mrs. Bellotti (Charlotte Rae), whose son Morse was never seen but often talked about by the other tenants.

The episodes concerned the interaction among characters and their unseen experiences as revealed in conversations in the lobby. Often genuinely funny, the subject matter caused too much controversy, and the series was canceled after only six months.

How to Marry a Millionaire (1957–1959)

This syndicated comedy was based on the 1953 movie by the same name, in which three career women live beyond their means in a New York penthouse in an attempt to attract and marry a millionaire. The leader of the group was Mike McCall (Merry Anders in the Lauren Bacall role), with manhunter Greta (Lori Nelson in the Betty Grable role) and nearsighted Loco Jones (Barbara Eden in her first television series playing the Marilyn Monroe role) rounding out the trio.

Lori Nelson left the series after the first season for movie roles that never happened, and she was replaced by Lisa Gaye as Gwen Kirby for the final season.

Howard, Lisa (1930–1965)

Lisa Howard, a former actor, was ABC's first female reporter and anchor of the daily news updates. However, her career came into question when she became publicly involved in the reelection campaign for New York Senator Kenneth Keating in 1964.

She was suspended without pay in September 1964 for "violation of news standards," which required an objective, nonpartisan view of events. In November the suspension became dismissal; Howard filed a $2 million lawsuit against the network, but lost her bid for reinstatement.

During the summer of 1965, Howard committed suicide by overdosing on sleeping pills. Although she had a new job as publicity director for the New York antipoverty program, many considered her dismissal from ABC the major factor in her death.

I Dream of Jeannie (1965–1970)

Jeannie (Barbara Eden) was an incredibly well preserved, 2,000-year-old genie whose bottle home was washed ashore on an uninhabited island. She remained trapped in her bottle until astronaut Tony Nelson (Larry Hagman) took refuge on the island after his space mission was aborted. He unwittingly opened the bottle and became her master, even though he tried to give Jeannie her freedom.

Back home in Cocoa Beach, Florida, Jeannie would not appear to anyone but Tony and, later, Tony's best friend, Roger Healey (Bill Daly). Unfortunately, she was always getting into trouble, and any attempt by Tony to explain Jeannie or any of the many disasters she caused was thought to be a delusion. Tony spent a lot of time talking his way out of the office of the base psychiatrist, Dr. Bellows (Hayden Rorke).

Eventually, Jeannie convinced Tony that he could not live without her and they were married in December 1969, but viewership continued to decline. After the original series ended, an animated series, *Jeannie* (1973–1975), appeared Saturday mornings on CBS.

Several years later, in the late 1980s, Eden reprised her role as Jeannie in a movie that did not include Tony (Hagman was starring on *Dallas*), but did feature their teenage son.

165

Lucy is worn out after a day of trying to sell a vacuum she had bought from a door-to-door salesman in Sales Resistance, *first airing in 1952. (Corbis Bettmann)*

I Love Lucy (1951–1957)

I Love Lucy could arguably be considered the longest-running situation comedy of all time. It has run continuously, in some part of the world, since it was first broadcast, and was the highest-rated TV show of the 1950s.

The list of firsts attributed to this one program is impressive by any standard. It was the first series rated number one in four of its seven first-run seasons (and was never rated lower than number three for its entire run). It was the first sitcom to be performed before a live audience. It was the first series to use three-camera filming (an editing technique developed by Desi Arnaz); filming the series allowed it to endure in syndication. It was the first series to be filmed by an independent production company. It was the first series to be produced in Hollywood. It was the first filmed series, and the second sitcom, to incorporate the star's pregnancy into the story line, although the word itself was never allowed to be spoken.

The series was based on Lucille Ball's radio program *My Favorite Husband,* which ran for three years on CBS. When it became apparent that Ball's marriage to bandleader Desi Arnaz was in trouble, she decided to move the premise to the new medium of television and have Arnaz star as her husband. CBS, however, would not accept Arnaz in the husband role, even though he was her real-life husband, saying that the relationship was "not believable."

To get backing for the proposed series, during the summer of 1950 the Arnazes toured the United States, performing before live audiences to prove that Desi was believable and acceptable as Lucy's husband. Early in 1951 they used their own money to produce the pilot for *I Love Lucy,* and were given the go-ahead to premiere the series the following fall.

The series centered around the zany housewife Lucy MacGillicuddy Ricardo (Ball), who was always getting into trouble by trying to get around some rule or prohibition delivered by her loving and long-suffering husband, Ricky Ricardo (Arnaz). Ricky was a bandleader at the Tropicana Club in Manhattan, and spent a lot of time making sure Lucy didn't sneak onto the club's stage in an effort to break into show business. One of the running jokes of the series was that when Ricky got particularly frustrated with Lucy's machinations, he would abandon his heavily accented English and resort to rapidly spoken Spanish epithets that no one understood.

Lucy was aided and abetted in her schemes by her best friend, Ethel Mertz (Vivian Vance), who with her husband, Fred (William Frawley), owned the apartment building in which the Ricardos lived. Most episodes dealt with the problems that Lucy and Ethel got into and how they were "saved" by their paternalistic husbands.

As the series continued, the Ricardos became more successful, and their lifestyle (and, thereby, the plots) reflected their better circumstances. Ricky received a movie offer that necessitated a cross-country trip with the Mertzes (1954–1955), and the four took a vacation to Europe (1955–1956).

At the beginning of the final season, Ricky got his own club, the Ricky Ricardo Babaloo Club, and later that season, his own TV show.

For years, critics and historians have tried to determine the reasons for *I Love Lucy*'s unparalleled success and longevity. Was it the vision of producer Jess Oppenheimer? Or was it the talent of writers Madelyn Pugh and Bob Carroll Jr.? Was it the chemistry between Ball and Arnaz? Or perhaps the physical comedy of Ball herself? Whatever the reason, no other series has had the success or acclaim that *I Love Lucy* has enjoyed for more than 40 years.

As mentioned earlier, *I Love Lucy* was the number-one show for four years during its initial run (1953, 1954, 1955, 1957). It won the Best Sitcom Emmy in both 1952 and 1953, as well as the Best Comedienne Emmy for Ball in 1952 and the Best Actress Emmy for her in 1955. In 1953, Vivian Vance received the Best Supporting Actress Emmy.

See also Ball, Lucille; *Here's Lucy; The Lucy Show.*

Ilott, Pamela (1935–)

Pamela Ilott was the first female vice-president at CBS News, for many years heading the network's religious programming division, until the virtual demise of noncommercial religious programs in the late 1970s. She worked as executive producer for several weekly series, including *Lamp unto My Feet* (1949–1979) and *Look Up and Live* (1954–1979).

INFOMERCIAL

These programs, which generally air very late at night or on weekend afternoons, ostensibly inform viewers, but are actually very long sales pitches. The topics covered are most often beauty products or business opportunities. The list of personalities who have given "testimonials" for beauty products includes Ali MacGraw, Cher, and Lisa Hartman. Fitness guru Susan Powter established her career on infomercials and Suze Ormond uses the venue to publicize her personal finance books and products.

INFOTAINMENT

Beginning in the 1980s, President Reagan's campaign of deregulation of the television industry created a need for low-cost programming to enhance the more competitive bottom line. Programs such as *Entertainment Tonight* (1981–), *A Current Affair* (1986–), *Unsolved Mysteries* (1988–), *Hard Copy* (1989–), and *Inside Edition* (1989–) were produced similarly to legitimate news broadcasts, with anchors and reporters. Using sophisticated graphics, fast-paced deliveries, and pseudojournalistic styles, topics range from celebrity interviews to gossip to murder to supernatural occurrences.

Appealing to the public's fascination for celebrities and the macabre, these programs are relatively inexpensive to produce, yet popular with viewers. The more the networks use this type of programming in their schedules, the more advertising dollars they bring in with minimal expense.

Isis (1977–1978)

This live-action children's adventure series centered around high school teacher Andrea Thomas (Joanna Cameron), who found a golden amulet on an archaeological dig in Egypt and discovered that she became the personification of the ancient goddess by saying the words "Oh, mighty Isis" while holding the amulet. As Isis she had the power to fly and other powers, enabling her to subdue evildoers while teaching young television viewers moral lessons.

Prior to getting its own series, *Isis* was part of *The Shazam/ Isis Hour* (1975–1977).

Joanna Cameron stars in Isis *on the CBS morning children's show during 1977–1978. (Photofest)*

INTERTEXTUALITY VS. ALLUSION

The theory of intertextuality suggests that one series is viewed and interpreted by the audience in relationship to all previous programs. In the area of popular culture, intertextuality uses culturally accepted images or myths to direct the viewer's understanding of a situation.

However, television generally uses direct textual allusion, that is, it directs the viewer to remember a particular incident from a previous series. For instance, when the character Rhoda Morgenstern (Valerie Harper) tossed her beret in the air during the opening montage of the series *Rhoda* (1974–1978), the scene harkened back to its parent series, *The Mary Tyler Moore Show* (1979–1977), when the character Mary Richards (Mary Tyler Moore) did the same thing. In one episode of *Grace under Fire* (1993–1997), when Grace (Brett Butler) was questioned about what she was going to do about a situation, she whined, "Oh, Rob," as did Laura Petrie (Mary Tyler Moore) on *The Dick Van Dyke Show* (1961–1966).

Similarly, the series *Roseanne* (1988–1998) used several allusions to previous sitcoms. Entire episodes dealt with borrowed concepts, such as when Roseanne was counseled by a group of previous sitcom "good wives/mothers," only to convert them to her "bad" ways, and when Dan's daydream caused the *Roseanne* cast to assume the roles of the castaways of *Gilligan's Island* (1964–1967).

In other episodes, remarks were made relating to previous series, such as the one in which the children were called "Princess, Bud, and Kitten," as were the children on *Father Knows Best* (1954–1963), and when Dan chanted "swimming pools . . . movie stars" from the theme of *The Beverly Hillbillies* (1962–1971). When Lecy Goranson returned to play Becky, she and the actress who had played the part in her absence (Sarah Chalke) did a takeoff from *The Patty Duke Show* (1963–1966), substituting "identical Beckys" for "identical cousins" in the theme song.

Television is a self-referential medium, and certain words and phrases have entered into an almost national understanding. When a character says, "Beam me up, Scotty," few people fail to make the connection to the original *Star Trek* (1966–1969). In fact, the height of self-reference came when some of the cast of *Deep Space Nine* (1993–1999), through the "magic" of computerization, went back in time and appeared in an episode of the original *Star Trek* ("The Trouble with Tribbles").

It's Always Jan (1955–1956)

This series, purportedly loosely inspired by the hit film *How to Marry a Millionaire,* followed the life and times of nightclub singer Janis Stewart (Janis Paige), who was raising her ten-year-old daughter Josie (Jeri Lou James) alone after her husband was killed in the war. Money was tight, so Jan and Josie lived in an apartment with two of Jan's friends, Pat Murphy (Patricia Bright), a secretary for a theatrical producer, and Val Marlowe (Merry Anders), an aspiring actress/model.

Izzicupo, Sunta (1956–)

As senior vice-president of movies and miniseries for CBS, Sunta Izzicupo is in charge of promoting the movie and miniseries franchise. During the 1997–1998 season, 21 of the top 25 movies on television appeared on CBS.

Izzicupo began her career as a producer in Boston and moved to series development at Walt Disney Television in 1986. She spent two years in the movie and miniseries division of Lorimar Television before joining CBS in 1989.

J

Jack and Mike (1986–1987)

This dramedy (comedy-drama hybrid) was a *Moonlighting* clone that hoped to attract the yuppie audience that made the previous series so popular. However, in this series the couple was married instead of single. Jackie "Jack" Shea (Shelley Hack), a columnist for the *Chicago Mirror*, was always on the trail of a hot tip or a heartwarming human-interest story. Her husband, Mike Brennan (Tom Mason), was a restaurateur who owned two trendy cafes and was in the process of opening a third.

Although supposedly very much in love, their respective careers kept them apart, and each became involved in situations that did not include the other. The focus was on their high-pressure careers rather than their marriage, so that their marital status seemed almost superfluous.

Jarvis, Lucy (1917–)

Lucy Jarvis was one of the first female producers in prime-time television, although her route was an indirect one. After being raised in New York City, Jarvis received a degree in home economics from Cornell University (1938) and worked as a dietitian at the University Medical Center.

Before leaving the work environment to raise her two children, Jarvis was a copywriter for Beechnut Foods and associate food editor for *McCall's* magazine, and she wrote *The Pocket Book Cook-Book* (1942). After

173

achieving some success as a fund-raiser for various charities, Jarvis decided to reenter the job market as a producer.

After working a year with the production company Talent Associates, she was hired as women's TV editor for the Pathe news service in 1956. She collaborated with Martha Rountree to develop a program called *Capitol Close-up,* which profiled important political news-makers. Finally, she became producer of a debate program, *The Nation's Future* (1960–1961), on NBC.

In 1962, Jarvis began an ambitious project. Despite numerous political obstacles, she wanted to produce a documentary on the Kremlin in what was still Communist Russia. After many false starts and broken promises, *The Kremlin* aired in May 1963, the first and best program on the historical Russian complex. It won an Emmy and a Golden Mike award.

She next produced a dual tour of the Louvre in Paris and the National Gallery in Washington, D.C. Surmounting the technical difficulties inherent in using a newly deployed communication satellite system, *Museum without Walls* was shown on NBC in November 1963.

After the completion of this project, Jarvis began negotiations to film the first documentary of the history and contents of the Louvre, a feat equal to getting approval to film in Russia. *The Louvre: A Golden Prison* is considered the definitive work on the museum. The film received a staggering amount of awards, among them a Peabody, a Radio-TV Critics award, and six Emmys.

Her later documentaries include several on health issues: *Who Shall Live?* (about kidney dialysis), *Where Does It Hurt?, What Price Health?, Dr. Bernard's Heart Transplant Operations,* and *Cry Help!* (about mental illness among teenagers). She also produced the first film on the rising drug problem in the United States, *Trip to Nowhere* (1970).

Jarvis's next "impossible" project was a film on Scotland Yard and its crime-solving history. Although the Yard had never allowed its internal workings to be filmed prior to her request, *Scotland Yard* was shown in March 1971. After the completion of this film, Jarvis turned her sights on the equally impenetrable Forbidden City in China. As could be expected of her determination, *China and the Forbidden City* was completed in 1973.

Thereafter, Jarvis remained in the United States working on films of social significance (*A Shooting Gallery Called America*) and artistic relevance (*Sophisticated Ladies,* a joint American-Soviet production). Jarvis continues to head two production companies.

The Jean Arthur Show (1966)

This series, lasting only two months, featured the first female attorney in an ongoing role. Patricia Marshall (Arthur) was an extremely successful defense attorney whose newly graduated son, Paul (Ron Harper), returned home to join her practice. Unfortunately, the series was a sitcom, so rather than present her supposed expertise, the plots revolved around her involvement with clients on a personal level and her difficulties with her family.

Jennifer Slept Here (1983–1984)

A takeoff on the successful *Topper* film and television series, this sitcom featured the spirit of sexy movie star Jennifer Ferrell (Ann Jillian) as a well-dressed but bothersome house-haunter.

The Elliot family moved from New York to Beverly Hills and bought Jennifer's former home, unaware that the previous owner had not yet given up residence. Jennifer could only be seen by 14-year-old Joey (John P. Navin Jr.), which resulted in his parents' concern over the fact that their son seemed to be talking to walls and furniture much of the time.

The series had the standard walking-through-walls and floating objects, but most episodes involved Jennifer's relationship with Joey as she helped him adjust to life as a teenager in Southern California.

Johnson, Lucy (1959–)

Lucy Johnson, senior vice-president of daytime/children's programming and special projects at CBS Entertainment, attended Boston University of Fine Arts before becoming an independent producer. She held executive positions at both Lorimar and NBC in daytime and children's programming before moving to CBS in 1989. She was promoted to senior vice-president of daytime programming in 1994 and assumed direction of children's programming in 1996.

Johnson has led CBS's daytime offerings to first place in household ratings and encouraged increased ethnic diversity in daytime programming. She currently oversees the development of child-focused educational programs to be added to the Saturday morning lineup.

Jones, Jenny (1946–)

Jenny Jones was just one of several moderately successful talk show hosts whose shows featured sensationalized topics and confrontational tactics until March 1995, when a show about secret admirers ultimately resulted in the shooting death of Scott Amedure by Jonathan Schmitz, who was found guilty of second-degree murder and sentenced to 25 years in prison. The sentence was overturned on appeal and a new trial ordered. In a later wrongful death trial, the show was found negligent in the death of Amedure and fined $25 million, although most observers expect that the verdict will not be upheld on appeal. The tragedy acted as a wake-up call to talk shows that seemed to be competing for Sleaze of the Year awards, and most toned down their sensationalistic topics and abandoned their ambush tactics (so called because some guests had no advance warning of what would occur, thereby allowing their onstage reactions to be televised).

Jones's first experience in show business occurred when as a teenager she started her own all-girl rock band. Later, she became a backup singer for Wayne Newton. Jones turned to stand-up comedy, and was the first female comic to win the $100,000 first prize in the *Star Search* competition (1986). She became the opening act for Jerry Seinfeld, and eventually was offered her own talk show.

Judge Judy (1996–)

Judge Judy Sheindlin presides over a real courtroom and makes binding decisions on the Small Claims cases for litigants who agree to appear on her program and be bound by her decision. She is known for pithy denouncements of litigants for bad manners or moral instability.

Sheindlin was a prosecutor for ten years, and was appalled by a justice system that often seemed more concerned with the rights of criminals than of their victims. As a judge in Manhattan's family court, she heard more than 20,000 cases in 14 years; she retired in 1996.

The only woman in a class of 126 at American University in Washington, D.C., Sheindlin was first in her class before transferring to New York Law School to complete her degree. In the course of her career she married fellow attorney Jerry Scheindlin, who serves as a justice on the New York Supreme Court. Judge Judy received confirmation that she had entered into the popular culture mainstream when she was parodied on *Saturday Night Live* by Cheri Oteri, making her a bona fide television personality.

Julia (1968–1971)

Diahann Carroll, appearing in the title role as Julia Baker, became the first black female to star in a sitcom in a nondomestic role (the earlier star of *Beulah* was a maid). Contrary to many black Americans' reality at the time, Julia's world was completely integrated, and equality reigned.

Julia Baker was a widow whose husband, an Air Force pilot, had been killed in Vietnam, so she was raising her young son, Corey (Marc Copage), alone. Wanting to start over after her husband's death, Julia moved herself and her son to Los Angeles, where she got a job in the medical office of a large aerospace company.

The focus of the series was Julia's personal relationships at work and within her apartment complex. Dr. Morton Chegley (Lloyd Nolan) was her boss and Hannah Yarby (Lurene Tuttle) was head nurse.

Although seen as innovative because of the integrated cast, the show was blasted by some black leaders as being "too white." Perhaps true in hindsight, the show was nevertheless the first to feature an independent black career woman.

Just Shoot Me (1997–)

After a rocky beginning of ever-changing time slots, *Just Shoot Me* found a "permanent" time slot and the audience followed. A workplace sitcom, the series is set in the offices of *Blush* magazine, a *Cosmopolitan* clone staffed by a quirky group of offbeat personalities.

Although on the surface the characters are out to promote their own personal agendas, fleeting moments of genuine supportive camaraderie occur (vehemently denied). An ensemble effort, the series stars Laura San Giacomo as dedicated journalist Maya Gallo, who, after being fired from her TV news job, swallows her pride to work for her father's fluff magazine. She and her father, Jack (George Segal), have been estranged for years, most recently when he married one of her high school classmates.

Her father is assisted by Nina Van Horn (Wendie Malick), a former supermodel turned fashion editor, and Elliot (Enrico Colantoni), the staff photographer, who is often more interested in dating the models than in photographing them. Rounding out the cast is Jack's calculatingly shallow executive assistant, Dennis Finch (David Spade).

The humor derives from Maya's attempts to infuse some relevance into the magazine's content and the rest of the cast trying to make points off one another.

Cast of the popular television series Just Shoot Me *strikes a pose for this publicity shot. (Fotos International/Archive Photos)*

K

Kate and Allie (1984–1989)

After their respective divorces, Kate McArdle (Susan Saint James) and Allie Lowell (Jane Curtin), friends since high school, decided to share a Greenwich Village apartment to save money and encourage each other in their new single-parent lives. Kate had one daughter, Emma (Ari Meyers), while Allie had a daughter, Jennie (Allison Smith), and a son, Chip (Frederick Koehler). The children were less than enthusiastic about the new communal living arrangement.

The focus of the series was the two friends' adjustment to the changes in their lives and the problems of raising children in a city environment. In addition, Kate and Allie had completely different lifestyles and philosophies; Kate was modern in outlook and worldly, while Allie was old-fashioned and conservative.

After several seasons, Allie received her bachelor's degree, but still found it difficult to find a job, so the two friends started their own catering business. About the same time, their two daughters enrolled in Columbia University, with Emma living in a dorm and later transferring to UCLA (a result of Meyers leaving the show) and Jennie commuting to campus.

In December 1988, Allie married sportscaster Bob Barsky (Sam Freed), and moved with him to a high-rise apartment. When he got a job with a Washington, D.C., television station, Kate once again moved in with Allie and Chip while Bob spent his weekdays in Washington.

The show was praised by many for its realistic depiction of single motherhood.

Kate Loves a Mystery (1979)

In the 1970s, one of the most popular series was *Columbo,* about a rumpled, supposedly absentminded detective (Peter Falk) who always solved the crime-of-the-week. When the first incarnation of the series went off the air in 1977, the producers tried to capitalize on its popularity by introducing a series about his often-mentioned but never seen wife.

In this perpetually revamped series, Kate Columbo (Kate Mulgrew), whose last name was changed to Callahan when producers decided to cut ties to the previous series, worked as a reporter for a weekly community newspaper, *The Valley Advocate,* while raising her daughter, Jenny (Lili Haydn). Being a reporter, she was constantly involved in mysteries, which she solved in much the same low-key manner as the character from *Columbo.*

In an effort to save the series, which received mixed reviews and limited audience attention, the series went through three title changes. It was first entitled *Kate Columbo,* then renamed *Kate the Detective,* and finally, *Kate Loves a Mystery.* Unfortunately, none of the reworkings brought a larger audience, and the series was canceled after a combined run of only seven months.

Kate McShane (1975)

This short-lived series, lasting only three months, is noteworthy as being the first network drama to feature a female lawyer as the lead character. Kate McShane (Anne Meara in her first dramatic role) was an independent and dedicated lawyer who was also empathetic and caring, which meant she became too involved with her clients. She was aided in the resulting dilemmas by her father, Pat (Sean McClory), a former cop, and her brother, Ed (Charles Haid), a Jesuit priest and law professor.

Kauffman, Marta (1950–)

As a partner in the production company Bright/Kauffman/Crane, Marta Kauffman is responsible for some of the most popular series on television. The first series that she and partner David Crane created for television was *Dream On* (1990–1995). With Kevin Bright they created *Friends* (1994–), *Veronica's Closet* (1997–), and *Jesse* (1998–).

After receiving a degree in theater from Brandeis University, Kauffman began her career as a writer on Broadway, where she worked on the musical version of *Arthur.* She and Crane moved to Hollywood to try writing for television on the advice of their agent.

Kilgallen, Dorothy (1913–1965)

Dorothy Kilgallen was an early television personality who appeared as a guest on various talk and variety shows.

Kilgallen was a journalist and gossip columnist by profession, but she became a regular panelist on the popular game show *What's My Line?* from its first airing in 1950 until her death from an accidental medication overdose after appearing on the 7 November 1965 telecast.

Kilgallen was the subject of a 1997 episode of *Dark Skies* (1996–1997), the NBC series concerning a government conspiracy and cover-up after the Roswell incident, and the resulting alien invasion. In the episode, Kilgallen had information documenting the government's activities and was murdered to keep her from writing about her findings.

Koplovitz, Kay (1945–)

As founder, president, and CEO of USA Network, Kay Koplovitz became the first woman to head a network. She graduated Phi Beta Kappa from the University of Wisconsin before receiving her master's in communications from Michigan State University. In 1973 she opened her own communications management and public relations firm, later becoming a producer-director for WTMJ-TV in Milwaukee. She also worked at ComSat in Washington, D.C., prior to becoming vice-president and executive director of United Artists–Columbia Satellite Services.

In 1977 she created Madison Square Garden Network, an all-sports channel and precursor to the USA Network. The channel was renamed in 1980, and became the highest-rated cable network in prime time under her policy of aggressively financing new series and TV movies. Koplovitz also created USA's sister network, the Sci-Fi Channel, and orchestrated the expansion of both into the European, Latin American, and African markets, with plans to expand into the Asian market.

Koplovitz left USA in 1998 to return to independent media ventures, forming Kay Koplovitz & Company.

Kukla, Fran & Ollie (1948–1976)

This well-loved children's program ran at various, if not consecutive, periods for almost 30 years. The show was done live and the dialogue was unscripted, flowing naturally among the characters. It had the distinction of being the first series to broadcast in color.

Fran Allison was the hostess who ad-libbed conversations with the Kuklapolitan Players, the puppets of Burr Tillstrom. Chief among these were the solemn Kukla, who made worry an art form, and Oliver "Ollie" J. Dragon, a happily extroverted dragon who embraced life with as much enthusiasm as Kukla worried about it. Other characters included Fletcher Rabbit; Mme. Ophelia Oglepuss; Beulah Witch; Colonel Crackie; Ollie's cousin, Delores Dragon; and Ollie's grandmother, Olivia Dragon.

Most interactions focused on prosocial attitudes and behavior, but occasionally the troupe presented full-dress productions, ranging from satires of established series to movies to light operettas, and even original musical plays such as *St. George and the Dragon* (1953), with music supplied by Arthur Fiedler and the Boston Pops.

This series was so enormously popular that by 1950 it had more than six million viewers. When the network canceled it in 1954, audience outrage forced them to reconsider. Through its long run, the series won an Emmy and was awarded a Peabody for excellence in children's entertainment.

See also Allison, Fran; Educational Programming.

L

La Femme Nikita (1996–)

Based on the 1991 French movie by the same name and the American film version, *Point of No Return* (1993), the televisual version of *La Femme Nikita* offers a slightly different main character and a dark, noirish style. The series follows a young street-dweller (Peta Wilson) who is sent to prison for a murder she did not commit (in both film versions she *was* a murderer). Her death is staged by a group of covert operatives from an organization known only as Section One, or simply Section, who recruit her to fight their "shades of gray" war against criminal elements with tactics and operations not very different from the criminals or terrorists they fight.

Thinking Nikita a cold-blooded murderer, the group gave her an ultimatum—work for them or be canceled (their euphemism for be killed). To survive, Nikita learned their methods and became as lethal as any of the others, but she could never completely bury her humanity. Eventually, as she voiced her dissatisfaction and reluctance, she was ordered canceled in the final episode of the first season. However, Michael (Roy Dupuis), one of the team leaders and Nikita's sometimes-romantic interest, staged events to make it seem as though she were killed, while she escaped the agency's control.

Of course, in the second-season opener she returned to Section after escaping from a terrorist group who had tracked her down and kidnapped her. She saved Michael from an ambush staged by the same group, and had one night of passion with Michael. Their relationship, which was really what brought her back to the group, did not go well, and by midseason they were back to a romance of insinuation and glance amid an almost adversarial stance.

Throughout the 1998 season, Nikita gained experience and was even put in charge of a mission, but her concern for the innocent victims of Section's operations made her loyalty questionable. The second season ended with Nikita once more ordered canceled for her part in an attempt to shut down Section, orchestrated by a woman who had been one of the organizers of the group. Finally, they decided that killing her would only give her actions and belief more credence with the other operatives, so she was given more missions with the hope that the inevitable would happen.

A huge hit for the cable network, USA, the cast's low-key acting enables the sometimes horrific situations to seem logical and normal.

Lady Blue (1985–1986)

In this short-lived series, Detective Katy Mahoney (Jamie Rose), called "Dirty Harriet" by some critics, was tough and efficient, but hardly feminine. She worked the more corrupt side of Chicago and was not afraid to use her .357 Magnum. The brutality of her life left little room for expressions of a more sensitive side, which is de rigueur with critics and viewers for all female characters in nontraditional professions.

Lansbury, Angela (1925–)

Although Angela Lansbury has been in the entertainment business, in both classic films and Broadway musicals, for many years, she will probably be most remembered as Jessica Fletcher, the mystery-writing sleuth in *Murder, She Wrote* (1984–1997).

Born in England, Lansbury moved to the United States during World War II. She won a Best Supporting Actress Oscar for her first film role in *Gaslight* (1944). She appeared in supporting roles in several films, and was nominated for a second Oscar for her role as the overbearing mother in *The Manchurian Candidate* (1962).

Next, she tried Broadway, and won Tony awards for her roles in such acclaimed musicals as *Mame* (1966), *Dear World* (1969), *Gypsy* (1975), and *Sweeney Todd* (1979). She moved to television in 1983 and appeared in *Lace*, and in 1984 accepted the role of Jessica Fletcher, a part she may have prepared for when she appeared as Agatha Christie's Miss Marple in *The Mirror Crack'd* (1980).

She also had roles in miniseries and made-for-TV movies such as *Shell Seekers* (1990), *The Love She Sought* (1990), and *Mrs. 'Arris Goes to Paris* (1992). In addition, she lent her voice to animated characters in the Disney movies *Beauty and the Beast* (1991) and *Anastasia* (1997).

Although production of *Murder, She Wrote* ended in 1997, several movies were planned for the future, the first being *South by Southwest* (November 1997). In 1995, Lansbury was inducted into the Television Hall of Fame, and in February 1997 she was awarded the Lifetime Achievement Award from the Screen Actors Guild. Later in 1997 she received the National Medal of the Arts from President Clinton.

Her production company, Corymore Productions, signed a development agreement with Universal Television to develop other projects in addition to the *Murder, She Wrote* movies for CBS.

See also *Murder, She Wrote;* Older Women on Television.

Laugh-In (1968–1973)

Hosted by Dan Rowan and Dick Martin, this innovative and creative program broke traditional rules to become a television classic. Fast-paced and satirical, the series appealed to younger viewers and launched the careers of many female actors, including Goldie Hawn, Lily Tomlin, Ruth Buzzi, Judy Carne, JoAnne Worley, Teresa Graves, and Chelsea Brown.

People who have never seen the program may find it difficult to understand the impact this program had during its original run. The frantically paced one-liners, the sight gags, and the topical graffiti (sometimes painted on dancing bodies) that made up each week's program were unlike anything on television up to that time. Each episode was made up of over 300 jokes rapid-fired at the viewers. It was the perfect blend of comedy, with psychedelic overtones that crystallized the period in which it appeared.

As is often the case with popular programs, it was responsible for introducing several phrases into the American slang lexicon of the period, including "Sock it to me," "You bet your bippy," "Ver-r-r-y interesting," "Here come de judge," and "Look *that* up in your Funk and Wagnall."

Although often copied and even resurrected in a short-lived updated version in 1979, nothing has ever come close to the original.

Laverne and Shirley (1976–1983)

A spinoff of the hugely successful sitcom *Happy Days* (1974–1984), *Laverne and Shirley* was part of the nostalgia craze of the 1970s for the supposed innocence and harmony of the 1950s. Highly influenced by the slapstick comedy of an earlier era, the series depicted the everyday occurrences in the lives of Laverne DeFazio (Penny Marshall) and Shirley Feeney (Cindy Williams), who worked on the assembly line at Shotz Brewery but had dreams of making it big in life.

Laverne was sarcastic and defensive but had a vulnerability that always shone through her armor, while Shirley was naive and believed in the good in everyone. In the first two seasons, the cast lived in Milwaukee, but in the third season the cast moved to California, where Laverne and Shirley worked at odd jobs while they pursued careers in the movies.

In 1982, Cindy Williams, who was pregnant at the time, left the show after years of reported rivalry between the stars; the series ended in 1983.

Laybourne, Geraldine (1947–)

Geraldine Laybourne, president of Disney/ABC Cable Network from 1996 to 1998, received her undergraduate degree in art history from Vassar and her master's in elementary education from the University of Pennsylvania before beginning her career as a teacher. Interested in establishing a bridge between education and the media, she cofounded Media Center for Children, a nonprofit resource library for schools and media producers.

In 1980 she worked for the fledgling noncommercial cable network Nickelodeon as program manager, and assumed the responsibilities of president in 1989. After the network was bought by Viacom, it went to a commercial-inclusive format, and Laybourne was instrumental in broadening its base and audience by creating, among other features, the Nick-at-Nite vintage-TV series programming. Known as Boss Lady to the readers of *Nickelodeon* magazine, Laybourne viewed her responsibility to the network's young viewers as the most important aspect of her job.

She moved to Disney/ABC Cable Network in 1996 to assume the duties of president of the newly merged organization, the second largest media conglomerate. Laybourne oversaw the operations of the Disney Channel as well as ABC's involvement in Lifetime, A&E Networks, the History Channel, and E! Entertainment Television. One of the aspects that most drew her to the new position was the power to shape the views of future generations through the programming she endorsed and the services the organization offered. She was instrumental in the development of the series *Bear in the Big Blue House,* named the best new children's show of 1997 by *TV Guide.*

Laybourne left Disney/ABC Cable Networks in 1998 and created Oxygen Media, which now owns the top three on-line sites for women: Thrive, a healthy-living site; Electra, a full-service site; and Moms Online, a parenting site. She has also been involved in planning a new interactive women's cable channel, due to be launched in 2000, also called Oxygen.

Leave It to the Girls (1949–1954)

Created by Martha Rountree, who also created *Meet the Press* (1950–), this program was first aired on radio from 1945 to 1949 as a serious discussion of male-female problems by a rotating panel of career women. When it moved to television in 1949, it was little more than male-bashing, with a representative male panel member defending and representing the male view. In keeping with the era in which it was produced, occasional programs dealt with hints on how to catch a man.

Moderated by Maggi McNellis, the show had no permanent panel members, although Eloise McElhone, Vanessa Brown, and Florence Pritchett frequently appeared. All panelists were, as *TV Guide* noted, "glamorous, well-dressed showbiz types."

Leave It to the Girls was first seen as a local New York program in 1947, then moved in 1949 to NBC, where it appeared until December 1951. It moved to ABC from October 1953 to March 1954 and was produced briefly as a syndicated daytime program during the 1962–1963 season. In 1971 a half-hour version was aired under the title *Mantrap,* and continued the female-panelists-grilling-male-guest format, but with a male host (Alan Hamel).

In 1981 another version appeared, this time with the more politically correct title of *Leave It to the Women.* Hosted by Stephanie Edwards, the series explored more controversial topics than previous incarnations had been able to do, but the panel-against-guest format remained.

Lennon Sisters

Publicity shot of Kathy, Dianne, Peggy, and Janet Lennon (L–R) for the 1969–1970 musical television series Jimmy Durante Presents The Lennon Sisters Hour. *(Archive Photos)*

Before the Jackson Five, before the King Family, were the Lennon Sisters. From Christmas Eve 1955 to 1968, the Lennon Sisters—Dianne (b. 1939), Peggy (b. 1940), Kathy (b. 1942), and Janet (b. 1946)—appeared on the *Lawrence Welk Show* (1955–1971).

They were "discovered" when Lawrence Welk's son Larry was dating Dianne. Larry couldn't get his father to take the time to audition the act, so when his father was home ill, he brought the sisters to the house to sing. They were signed for the next show.

The quartet continued until 1960, when the eldest, Dianne, left to be married. The act continued as a trio until Dianne returned in 1964. The Lennon Sisters represented the perfect young people for many of the older viewers. The sisters even had their own paper doll series and coloring books that featured supposed events in their daily lives.

They were so popular that a series was planned that would feature all of them. However, because of scheduling constraints, the series became *My Three Sons* (1960–1972).

LESBIANS ON TELEVISION

Although hints have been dropped about certain characters' sexuality in the past and even some male characters were "out," until recently sexual orientation was never an issue. Growing pressure from gay and lesbian organizations resulted in more characters being written to reflect these orientations.

One of the first characters to reveal her nontraditional orientation was C. J. Lamb (Amanda Donohoe) on *L.A. Law* (1986–1994). An admitted bisexual, that aspect of her personality was never developed because her major relationship during the series was with a man. On *Roseanne* (1988–1998), the character Nancy (Sandra Bernhard) appeared for several seasons, and during one of them, her love interest was played by Morgan Fairchild, who shared a much-hyped kiss with Roseanne. In one of the many strange plot twists of the final season, Bev (Estelle Parsons), Roseanne's mother, decided that she was a lesbian. Of course, the *Ellen* (1994–1998) debate lasted an entire season, culminating in a humorous and well-done "out" episode.

A review of 1998–1999 series revealed several established and new lesbian or bisexual characters. On *Friends* (1994–), Ross's ex-wife, Carol (Jane Sibbett), and her partner, Susan (Jessica Hecht), have been recurring characters for several seasons. On the same network (NBC), another established couple was on *Mad about You* (1992–1999), in which Paul's sister Debbie (Robin Bartlett) and her partner, Joan (Suzie Plakson), appeared for years.

More recently, on *NYPD Blue* (1993–), Officer Abby Sullivan (Paige Turco) joined the precinct, and on *ER* (1994–), intern Maggie Doyle (Jorja Fox) and nurse Yosh Takata (Gedde Watanabe) joined the staff at County General.

Lewis, Shari (1934–1998)

Shari Lewis, thought by some to be a better ventriloquist than the famed Edgar Bergen, made her television debut with her wooden dummy, Samson, on *Arthur Godfrey's Talent Scouts* in 1952 as a teenager. She went on to star in a local children's show, *Facts 'n Fun* (1953), on WRCA, and in *Kartoon Fun* (1954), followed by *Shari and Her Friends* (1954).

Appearing as a guest on *Captain Kangaroo* in 1956, Lewis was asked to bring something softer than her regular wooden dummy. Lewis created Lamb Chop, her sock-puppet sidekick, soon followed by Hush Puppy and Charlie Horse.

She and her puppet friends starred in a succession of children's programs, beginning with *Shariland* (1956), *The Shari Lewis Show* (1960–1963), *Shari at Six* (1968–1976), and *The Shari Show* (1976–1977). Her most recent series was *The Charlie Horse Music Pizza,* which premiered on PBS in

1998. The new series, geared to ages three to eight, endeavored to teach the elements of music and encourage individual experimentation with instruments in an effort to fill the gap left when many schools eliminated music from their curriculum.

In addition to her many series, Lewis wrote several books, beginning with *The Shari Lewis Puppet Book* (1958) and including *Fun with Kids* (1960), *Folding Paper Toys* (1963), and *Dear Shari* (1963). She also coauthored the Head Start series: *Looking and Listening, Thinking and Imagining,* and *Knowing and Naming* (all 1966). In addition, she made several children's recordings.

A multitalented individual whose titles included not only puppeteer, ventriloquist, and writer but also producer, conductor, musician, actress, and screenwriter, Lewis won 12 Emmys throughout her career. Her first Emmys were for Best Local Program and Outstanding Female Personality in 1957, followed by many in the area of children's programming and as an outstanding personality. She also won a Peabody in 1960 and a Kennedy Center award in 1983. She even broke into sports television in a minor way when she appeared with Lamb Chop in the half-time show at the Aloha Bowl in 1998. Lewis died in August 1998.

See also Educational Programming.

Life with Elizabeth (1953–1955)

This series was the first starring role for Betty White, whom *TV Guide* called "America's sweetheart" because of her "fresh good looks." Produced by White's own production company, the series originated as a local Los Angeles program, but was picked up by NBC and broadcast nationally.

Each program consisted of three unrelated miniplays dealing with the married life of Elizabeth (White) and her husband, Alvin (Del Moore). The action emphasized light comedy and conversational interaction over the more physical humor popular during the period. The narrator, Jack Narz, often had conversations with Elizabeth, leaving Del in the dark as to what was happening.

See also White, Betty.

Lifetime

Lifetime, the self-proclaimed cable network for women, was launched in February 1984. Although the network denies being feminist, it agrees that it represents the feminine side of television by predominantly featuring programs with female characters who are "strong-willed, smart, funny, and compassionate as well as passionate." Lifetime sees its mission as presenting programs that are "positive and empowering" for women.

To this end, Lifetime specializes in original programming as well as reruns of syndicated series deemed popular with women, such as *The Golden Girls* (1985–1992), *L.A. Law* (1986–1994), *Designing Women* (1986–1993), *Chicago Hope* (1994–), and *Ellen* (1994–1998); the network debuted the series *Any Day Now, Maggie,* and *Oh Baby* in 1998. The network has succeeded in creating a niche for itself by providing "innovative entertainment and informational programming" that offers insights into topics of interest to women, ranging from romance and relationships to careers and personal growth.

Lifetime consistently offers talented women a means to express their creativity and visions as actors, directors, and producers. Lifetime's original movies include such award-winners as *Wildflowers* (1991), directed by Diane Keaton and starring Patricia Arquette; the Emmy-winning *Stolen Babies* (1993), starring Mary Tyler Moore; and *Almost Golden: The Jessica Savitch Story* (1995), which starred Sela Ward and was the most watched movie on basic cable to that time.

Their documentary series cover a wide range of topics, including *Dying for Love: A Lifetime Special on the Impact of AIDS on the American Woman* (1987); *Child Abuse: Innocence on Trial* (1988); *Gangs: Not My Kid* (1988); *Against Her Will* (1989), which looked at campus rape; *Jennifer's in Jail* (1992), examining the day-to-day life of female juvenile delinquents; and *Broken Hearts, Broken Homes* (1992), on the problems of the foster-care system.

Lifetime also offers programs geared to education and self-improvement. *The Main Ingredient* features easy recipes as well as timesaving tips and nutritional information, *Handmade by Design* shows craft projects that can easily be done at home, and *Everyday Workout* offers both low-impact and high-intensity workouts, using a split screen to demonstrate both methods.

The network presents concerts and specials focusing on female talent in addition to programs about parenting and children (*What Every Baby Knows* and *Kids These Days*). Their public-awareness campaigns bring a variety of topics to the viewer's attention, ranging from politics to breast cancer prevention. Lifetime also offers such past and present series as *Perspectives on Lifetime,* a forum for discussion and dramatization of issues of importance to women, and *Picture What Women Do,* a program that encouraged more community involvement by women. *Talk It Over,* hosted by Blair Brown and Toukie Smith, was an advocacy and talk show focused on issues relevant to women and their lives.

In 1994, Lifetime began sponsoring sports teams and televising women's sporting events, which were often ignored by other networks. It sponsors the Colorado Silver Bullets, the only women's professional baseball team, and Lyn St. James, a professional auto racer and the only woman driver to be named Rookie of the Year at the Indianapolis 500. Lifetime also broadcasts the games of the Women's National Basketball Association and is an official sponsor of USA Basketball's Women's National Team.

Lifetime has earned over 200 award nominations and has won Cable ACE awards in categories such as public-service campaigns, as well as individual categories such as best actress and best original movie.

See also *Any Day Now, Maggie, Oh Baby.*

Littlefield, Nancy (1925–)

In 1952, after passing a grueling battery of tests, Nancy Littlefield was the first woman to become a member of the Director's Guild of America (DGA). For the next 14 years, she was the only female assistant director who was a member.

Littlefield worked on several television series, including episodes of *Naked City* (1958–1963) and *The Defenders* (1961–1965). In 1979 she produced a documentary on teenage pregnancy, *And Baby Makes Two,* for which she won an Emmy.

Loesch, Margaret (1946–)

Margaret Loesch was chair and CEO of Fox Kids Network before leaving in 1997 to assume the position of president and CEO of Odyssey Channel. Odyssey—owned jointly by National Interfaith Cable Coalition, Liberty Media, Hallmark Entertainment, and the Jim Henson Company—describes itself as a network for "today's family with an added commitment to exploring faith and the human condition." Loesch moved to Fox Kids Network in 1990, overseeing all aspects of the network including their print (*Totally Kids* magazine) and production divisions. She was responsible for increasing viewership and visibility of Fox Kids Network by moving the franchise into the United Kingdom, Australia, and Latin America.

After being reluctantly promoted to the position of vice-chair of Fox Kids Worldwide in 1997 and having many of her responsibilities taken over by a recently hired male executive, Loesch resigned from the network that she had in essence created.

After graduating from the University of Southern Mississippi with a degree in political science, Loesch started as a film clerk for ABC, eventually becoming head of on-air creative services (1971–1974). She worked for NBC as director of children's programming (1974–1979) and Hanna-Barbera Productions as executive vice-president for programming (1979–1984). From Hanna-Barbera she moved to Marvel Productions, assuming the responsibility of president and CEO in 1984.

The Lucy Show (1962–1968)

This series, Lucille Ball's first after her divorce, was loosely based on the book *Life without George* by Irene Kampen. Ball played a widow, Lucy Carmichael, with two children, Chris (Candy Moore) and Jerry (Jimmy Garrett). She and her best friend, divorcée Vivian Bagley (Vivian Vance), were always trying to get rich or find the perfect man.

This time, Lucy's exasperated male was her boss, Theodore Mooney (Gale Gordon), president of Danfield First National Bank. The situations were still far-fetched, and much of the comedy was physical (facial mugging and exaggerated pratfalls and movements), but the audience still loved Lucy.

The beginning of the 1965–1966 season showed some cast changes and a different locale. Vivian Vance retired to appear as an occasional guest, and the setting moved to San Francisco, where Lucy and Mr. Mooney now worked at Westland Bank. Lucy found another coconspirator, her new friend Mary Jane Lewis (Mary Jane Croft).

Ball won two Emmys over the course of this series for Outstanding Continued Performance by an Actress in a Leading Role in a Comedy Series (1967 and 1968).

See also Ball, Lucille; *Here's Lucy; I Love Lucy.*

Lunden, Joan (1950–)

Joan Lunden appeared on *Good Morning America* (1975–) for more than 20 years—first as a reporter, then as cohost for 17 years (1980–1997). Reportedly, she left the show to spend more time with her three daughters.

As part of her lightened workload, she began working on investigative specials under the title *Behind Closed Doors* (1997–). Lunden has written two books, *Healthy Living* (1997) and *A Bend in the Road Is Not the End of the Road* (1998), and is the commercial spokesperson for Claritin allergy medicine.

Lupino, Ida (1918–1995)

Ida Lupino could well be called a renaissance woman. She was an actor, writer, director, producer, composer, and artist. Born in London during a Zeppelin raid, hers was a show-business family that could trace its artistic heritage back 500 years to Grimaldi, the Italian Renaissance clown.

Ida Lupino looks through the camera during the shooting of her film Mother of a Champion. *(Corbis/Bettmann)*

Her future unquestionably lay in show business, so she lied about her age and entered the Royal Academy of Dramatic Arts in 1931. Her first film was in 1933, *Her First Affair,* in which she played a blonde ingenue gone bad—a role she would play many times. She was soon called "the English Jean Harlow."

After coming to the United States in 1933, Lupino was not offered the kinds of film roles she wanted, so she acted on radio, wrote short stories, and composed *Aladdin Suite,* which was performed by the Los Angeles Philharmonic. Her real break in American movies came after she stopped dying her hair blonde. She appeared in the 1939 film *The Light That Failed,* and in several other films varying in quality. She won a New York Critics' Award for her role in *The Hard Way* (1943).

Lupino became an American citizen the same year she formed Emerald Productions, 1948. Unable to find the types of scripts she wanted, she began writing her own on subjects not generally talked about, much less filmed during that period. The production company's first film was *Not Wanted* (1949), a commercially successful film about a young girl who gives up her baby for adoption (Lupino directed after the original director died). However, the company was dissolved, and Lupino formed another company that same year, the Filmakers.

Lupino was now producer-actor-writer-director, and her company continued to document subjects unusual for the time. The next year, 1950, they released *Never Fear,* about a young dancer stricken with polio, and *Outrage,* which addressed the taboo subject of rape. *Hard, Fast and Beautiful,* the story of a young tennis prodigy and her pushy mother, came out in 1951. Many view the 1953 film *The Hitch-Hiker* as Lupino's best directorial effort, and it was the company's most financially successful venture. It concerned two middle-class men who pick up a hitchhiker and are tormented by the person, who turns out to be a murderer.

Lupino was both director and actor in the company's next movie, *The Bigamist* (1953), about a man with two wives. In Lupino's final film for Filmakers, *Private Hell 36* (1954), she wore three hats: writer, producer, and actor. Later in 1954, Filmakers went bankrupt due to the high cost of distributing the finished films.

Lupino moved into television and was one of four rotating hosts of the dramatic anthology series *Four Star Playhouse* (1952–1956). From 1957 to 1958, Lupino starred with her then-husband, Howard Duff, in *Mr. Adams and Eve,* an Emmy-nominated situation comedy about two Hollywood stars trying to have a normal home life.

In 1959, Lupino got her first chance to direct television with an episode of NBC's *On Trial* (1956–1959), a series in which actual legal cases were dramatized. After this successful venture, Lupino directed several episodes for Richard Boone's popular Western series *Have Gun, Will Travel* (1957–1963). She excelled at handling action scripts, making her a natural for the crime and Western drama series prevalent at the time.

The next series Lupino directed was *Thriller* (1960–1962), a suspense anthology hosted by Boris Karloff. After it ended, she worked on the gangster series *The Untouchables* (1959–1963). In 1964 she became the only woman to direct an episode of *The Twilight Zone* (1959–1965).

Lupino was one of the busiest directors in television. The list of series on which she worked includes some of the most popular programs of their times—*Dr. Kildare* (1961–1966), *The Virginian* (1962–1971), *The Fugitive* (1963–1968), *Mr. Novak* (1963–1965), *Bewitched* (1964–1972), *The Rogues* (1964–1965), *Gilligan's Island* (1964–1967), *The Big Valley* (1965–1969), and her final effort in 1969, *The Bill Cosby Show* (1969–1971).

Although she no longer directed, Lupino continued to make appearances in movies and on television. Her final guest appearance on television was on an episode of *Charlie's Angels* in 1977. Lupino's final years were spent in relative seclusion, although she did grant on occasional interview. As her health declined, she became victim to the darker aspect of her bipolar personality, which she had attempted to control with tranquilizers and alcohol. Lupino died in August 1995 of colon cancer.

M

Mabrey, Vicki (1964–)

Vicki Mabrey is one of the chief correspondents for the new *60 Minutes II*, which premiered early in 1999. Prior to that, Mabrey covered such important events as the storming of David Koresh's compound in Waco, the Midwest floods, the Oklahoma City bombing, and the death of Princess Diana.

After graduating from Howard University, Mabrey joined a training program at the CBS affiliate in Washington, D.C., WUSA, and became a reporter for WBAL in Baltimore, where she stayed for nine years. After this apprentice period, she moved to larger assignments with the network news division.

See also News.

McCarthyism

In the years following World War II, roughly from 1945 to the early 1960s, Americans became aware of a supposed threat to national security and the American way of life: Communists in our midst. Egged on by President Truman and Congress, the media rolled out story after story of "red devil" Communists whose aim was to take over "God-fearing" America. During this volatile period, anyone who did not conform to a national ideal or who disagreed with the majority was suspect and could face ruin, imprisonment, or, in the saddest cases, death.

In an effort to control the populace, loyalty oaths became required— first of government workers, then educators, and finally the general public.

Anything even slightly controversial or nonconformist became subversive. Suspect books were banned or burned, and elements of popular culture were analyzed for hidden meanings. Informers were everywhere, and no one was exempt from scrutiny. The climate was such that war-era relocation camps were readied as possible places to send supposed leftist radicals in a clean-sweep plan suggested by ultraconservatives.

The so-called Hollywood Ten, a group of writers and other film workers, was called before Congress in 1947. Originally numbering 19, only 10 faced the House Committee on Un-American Activities, the "permanent" tribunal that investigated subversive activities from 1945 to 1957.

When asked the dreaded and oft-intoned question, "Are you now or have you ever been a member of the Communist Party?" the Ten pleaded either the Fifth Amendment, which protects against self-incrimination, or the First Amendment, which guarantees free speech and free association. Their lack of cooperation resulted in each person serving jail sentences for contempt of Congress and being blacklisted, which in essence denied them future employment.

However, the real thrust of what would later be called the American Inquisition or "a surrealistic morality play" began in 1950 with the announcement by a previously obscure senator from Wisconsin, Joseph McCarthy, that he had a list of Communists working for the State Department. In the following five years, McCarthy was a power to be feared and reckoned with as he orchestrated a campaign of smear and innuendo using hyperbolic rhetoric and unsubstantiated allegations.

Although he never had proof for his charges, the suspicion was enough to destroy lives and careers as those seeking to protect themselves denounced or distanced themselves from the accused, thereby giving the blacklist its power. As further indication of the atmosphere of the period, by 1954 over 300 federal, state, and local laws had been enacted to regulate subversive activities, and passports were denied anyone critical of American policy.

Once the Army-McCarthy hearings were televised in 1954 and the nation saw firsthand McCarthy's questionable methods and abusively belligerent attitude, his power waned. After being criticized by respected newsman Edward R. Murrow on his *See It Now* (1952–1955) series and challenged by special counsel to the Army Joseph Welch with "Have you no sense of decency, sir?" McCarthy was finished. Historically, his name is associated with an era known for indiscriminant charges and unsubstantiated allegations.

McCarthy is often vilified, but he was not alone in this crusade. He was aided and abetted by the most powerful men in the country, and heavily backed by millionaire and future presidential father Joseph Kennedy—until he became more liability than asset. To this day, politicians raise questions about opponents' allegiances to bring doubt to others' minds, even though communism is not considered the bugaboo it once was.

MacCurdy, Jean (1949–)

Jean MacCurdy, as president of WB's TV animation division and Hanna-Barbera Studios since 1992, was instrumental in the creation of Kids' WB!, where she is now president in charge of programming. She manages over 60 series (6,500 half-hour episodes), including the Emmy-winning *Animaniacs,* as well as 1,500 shorts of classic Looney Tunes cartoons for network distribution domestically, in syndication, and in 175 overseas markets.

Under her direction, the WB and Hanna-Barbera shows swept the 1996 animation Emmys in both daytime and nighttime categories, bringing the total number of Emmys earned under her leadership to 20, as well as a Peabody award, an Environmental Media award, and several Annie awards. In addition, she is credited with propelling Fox Kids' Network to first place in children's programming. In 1997, MacCurdy received the prestigious Women in Film Lucy Award for her industry accomplishments.

MacCurdy began her career in the children's programming department at NBC in 1974, and moved to Warner Brothers Cartoons in 1979 as director of animation programming. She worked for both Hanna-Barbera Productions and Marvel Productions before returning to Warner Brothers in 1988.

McEnroe, Kate (1947–)

As president of AMC Networks, Kate McEnroe is responsible for *American Movie Classics, Romance Classics,* and *American Pop* franchises. She believes that the female viewer will be a very important influence in the future of television because, as a demographic, women make up more than 50 percent of the population.

McEnroe was honored in 1998 by the Women in Cable and Telecommunications for "her tireless campaign to ensure that the cable industry better serve its female customers."

McGrady, Phyllis (1953–)

Phyllis McGrady, vice-president and executive producer of ABC News, has worked on most of ABC's newsmagazines, including *20/20* (1978–), *Primetime Live* (1989–), *Turning Point* (1994), and the *Barbara Walters Specials.* She has won two DuPonts—the equivalent of an Oscar for the TV-news industry.

She was in charge of the network's Century Project, which documented the events of the twentieth century over several hours, and appeared on both the History Channel and ABC prime time. Prior to her current position, McGrady was executive producer of *Primetime Live.*

After graduation from Northwestern University, McGrath worked for the Metromedia news program *Panorama,* which was totally run by women. In 1977 she joined *Good Morning America* (1975–) and eventually moved to *Primetime Live.*

McGrath, Judy (1952–)

Judy McGrath became president of MTV in 1994. She began working at MTV in 1981 as an on-air promotions writer, and moved up through the ranks from editorial manager to executive vice-president to creative director before assuming her current title.

Under her direction, the network has expanded from music videos to game shows and episodic series, as well as publishing and home videos. In addition, she was responsible for the development of the popular "Unplugged" concept, and was involved in the introduction of the new network M2.

Her current projects include bringing MTV more actively into the feature film market and revamping the network to more accurately reflect its target audience of young adults (18- to 34-year-olds), who view music as an important part of their lifestyle.

McHale, Judith (1955–)

As president and CEO of Discovery Communications, Inc., since 1995, Judith McHale has responsibility for all Discovery networks, including the Learning Channel, Animal Planet, and Travel Channel. She was instrumental in forging Discovery's alliance with the BBC, a venture that was touted as a major strategic move for both companies.

McHale received a law degree from Fordham Law School before becoming general counsel for MTV Networks. She moved to Discovery Communications as general counsel in 1987.

Maggie (1998–)

At the beginning of the series , Maggie Day (Ann Cusack) is a 40-year-old wife and mother whose family doesn't need her, so she returns to school to become a veterinarian and gets a part-time job at a nearby animal hospital. However, at her job she meets a man, Richard (John Slattery), and her feelings for him cause her to question her marriage. Through the first season, her questioning and her resulting therapy led to her divorce after 20 years of marriage, and she began to start her life over.

Mama (1949–1956)

An ethnic comedy transplanted from radio, *Mama* (also known as *I Remember Mama*) was a warmhearted, humorous look at the daily life of a Norwegian-American family during the early 1900s in Victorian-era San Francisco. Each week the series opened with daughter Katrin (Rosemary Rice) turning the pages of the family album as she recalled the family members and ending with the phrase "but most of all, I remember Mama."

The five members of the Hansen family were Papa Lars (Judson Laire), Mama Marta (Peggy Wood), son Nels (Dick Van Patten), and daughters Katrin and Dagmar (Iris Mann, 1949; Robin Morgan, 1950–1956, who went on to become a well-known feminist writer). Although the shows involved all the family members, the focal point was the strict but loving Mama as she solved her family's problems over the ever-present pot of Maxwell House coffee, the show's sponsor. The gentle and nurturing Mama became the prototype for mother characters that dominated the 1950s family sitcoms.

The series was based on the book *Mama's Bank Account,* written by Kathryn Forbes, which was made into a successful play (1944) and movie (1948). The series, produced by Carol Irwin, was one of the first to be produced by a woman. Because it was broadcast live for most of its run, few reruns are available, and the episodes must generally be relived in narrative accounts.

Mandabach, Caryn (1949–)

As president of Carsey-Warner Company, Caryn Mandabach is responsible for generating and developing new projects, including feature films after the company established a film division in 1995. She also oversees the continued production of established series such as *Cosby* (1996–), *3rd Rock from the Sun* (1996–), and the new hit, *That 70's Show* (1998–).

Mandabach began her career as a producer for Norman Lear's Tandem Productions in 1970, and eventually created her own production company, working in television and on humorous commercials. When Marcy Carsey created her own company, she hired Mandabach to produce some of the first series offerings, including the first three seasons of *The Cosby Show* (1984–1992), which earned an Emmy for Outstanding Comedy Series in 1985.

Mandabach was named president and partner of Carsey-Warner Company in 1987.

See also Female Executives.

Mandated Educational Programming

Since 1996 the Federal Communications Commission (FCC) has required stations to broadcast at least three hours of programming per week that "serve(s) the educational, cognitive, social and emotional needs of children 16 and younger." The ruling was an attempt to offset the product-hyping and violence-ridden cartoons that dominated children's programming in the past.

Although some cable channels devote substantial programming to attract the younger viewer, only the networks that broadcast on public airwaves are required to abide by the ruling.

However, networks are given extreme leeway on the programs they offer to comply with the ruling. In the past, networks offered series ranging from sports (*Sports Illustrated for Kids*) to celebrity interviews in supposed compliance with the FCC requirement. Cartoons are hyped as teaching tolerance and offering insight into the tough issues faced by young people today. One station even claimed that tabloid talk shows are educational because they explore current cultural issues.

Although some stations "push the envelope," most programs adequately fulfill the "social and emotional" component, even though the "educational" component is lacking. Critics cite the lack of educational material, but in 1998 the FCC indicated that it believes that programming for children is getting better and moving toward adhering to the ruling.

Manheim, Camryn (1961–)

Camryn Manheim, in her acceptance speech upon winning the 1998 Emmy for Best Supporting Actress for her role on *The Practice* (1997–), accepted the award for "all the fat girls" in the viewing audience and became the self-professed "poster child for fat acceptance." A few months later, she won a Golden Globe for her role. Manheim's character, Ellenor Frutt, is a pants-suited lawyer with faults, needs, and idiosyncrasies like everyone else in the world, who just happens to be overweight.

In 1999 Manheim published her autobiography, titled *Wake Up, I'm Fat.*

Marge and Jeff (1953–1954)

A 15-minute sitcom seen five nights a week on the Dumont Network, the series followed the daily lives of newlyweds Marge (Marge Green) and Jeff (Jess Cain, who changed his name to Jeff during the series). Written and produced by Marge Green, the series was seen primarily in New York.

Margie (1961–1962)

The series dealt with the coming-of-age trials of Margie Clayton (Cynthia Pepper) and the similarities between her life and that of her friend, Maybelle Jackson (Penney Parker), a former flapper who had grown up during the Roaring Twenties. Subtitles, similar to those seen in silent films, were interspersed during the episodes to alert viewers to upcoming situations, which might involve such teen staples as conflicts with parents, school troubles, or the meaning of friendship.

Marin, Carol (1949–)

Carol Marin, one of the most popular news anchors at NBC's Chicago affiliate, WMAQ-TV, resigned in 1997 after 12 years to protest the station's hiring of Jerry Springer, best known for his "shock" talk show, as a periodic commentator. Marin, who had won 15 local Emmys during her career, supposedly resigned rather than share the anchor dais with someone having so little credibility. However, later reports released by the station claimed she had tendered her resignation *before* Springer was hired.

Marshall, Penny (1943–)

Penny Marshall went from starring in the most popular series of the 1977–1978 season to directing several successful films. She first appeared on television when she was a young girl on such programs as *Ted Mack's Amateur Hour* (1948–1960) and *The Jackie Gleason Show* (1952–1959) with her mother's dance troupe.

Marshall appeared on a succession of television series before getting her own series. Her first role was as Myrna Turner, Oscar Madison's secretary, on *The Odd Couple* (1971–1975). During the same period (1972–1973), she also appeared as Miss Larson, one of Dr. Hartley's neurotic patients, on *The Bob Newhart Show* (1972–1978). The next year she appeared as Paul Sand's sarcastic sister-in-law, Janice Dreyfuss, in *Friends and Lovers* (1974–1975).

Finally, Marshall got her own series, *Laverne and Shirley* (1976–1983), spun off from the hugely successful series *Happy Days* (1974–1984), set in 1950s Milwaukee. She played Laverne DeFazio, a working-class young woman with little education but big dreams for her future who lived with roommate Shirley Feeney (Cindy Williams). Both worked at Shotz Brewery while waiting for their dreams to come true. During this series, Marshall had her first directing experience.

After the series ended, Marshall turned her sights to a directing career. Her first movie was *Jumpin' Jack Flash* (1986), which starred Whoopi Goldberg as a reluctant but effective secret agent of sorts. Her next movie, *BIG* (1988), starring Tom Hanks, was very successful and proved her talent as a director to the powers-that-be who had fired her from her first directing assignment, *Peggy Sue Got Married* (1986), supposedly for inexperience.

Her next project was *Awakenings* (1991), starring Robin Williams as a doctor whose miracle drug awakens a man from a catatonic stupor after more than ten years. Then came *A League of Their Own* (1992), which moved to television for an abbreviated run before Marshall began working on *Renaissance Man* (1994) with Danny DeVito.

Marshall continues to appear on television in Kmart commercials, alone and with Rosie O'Donnell.

Mary Martin "flies" through the air in a 1955 television production of Peter Pan. *(Corbis/Bettmann)*

Martin, Mary (1913–1990)

Although she appeared in many well-known Broadway plays such as *One Touch of Venus* (1943–1945), *South Pacific* (1949–1951), *The Sound of Music* (1959–1961), *Hello Dolly* (1965–1966), and *I Do! I Do!* (1966–1969), to many people who grew up in the 1950s and 1960s she is best remembered for her role in the television version of *Peter Pan.*

She first appeared as Peter Pan in the live 1955 broadcast, followed the next year by another live broadcast that was taped, which allowed for regular rebroadcasts until the mid-1960s. The broadcast in 1956 won an Emmy for Best Single Program of the Year.

Martin appeared in other television specials, including the television version of *Annie Get Your Gun* and her own musical specials (*Magic with Mary Martin* and *Mary Martin at Easter Time*). Martin won three Tony Awards for her work on Broadway: *Annie Get Your Gun* (1948), *Peter Pan* (1955), and *The Sound of Music* (1960).

Mary Hartman, Mary Hartman (1975–1978)

Created by "envelope-pusher" Norman Lear, this late-night syndicated soap opera satirized the entire soap opera genre and led the way for the later, equally satirical *Soap* on ABC. Mary Hartman (Louise Lasser) was a less-than-bright housewife living in Fernwood, Ohio, where she planned her life around television commercials, which she believed were completely true and reflective of reality. Pigtailed, plain, and excessively insecure, she floated from one plot line to another in a string of far-fetched incidents that bordered on the absurd. Obsessed with "waxy yellow buildup" on her floor and depressed because her life was not as attractive or interesting as those she saw on TV, Mary moved through life in a haze.

MaryKay and Johnny (1947–1950)

This series, broadcast live, concerned the lives of a newly married couple, MaryKay and Johnny Sterns, who lived in a New York apartment. MaryKay was the traditional screwball wife of that period, constantly in need of help from her banker-husband, Johnny. During the course of the series, MaryKay (who was actually married to Johnny) became pregnant, and the baby (Christopher) was written into the script; he appeared on the show when he was only a month old.

In an incident that pointed up the importance of the new medium, the show's longtime sponsor, Anacin, wanted to know how many people actually viewed the show, so they offered a free mirror to the first 200 people to send in their comments. The company ordered 400 mirrors to be sure they would have enough, and were amazed when over 8,900 letters poured in.

The Mary Tyler Moore Show (1970–1977)

One of the first sitcoms to go beyond light or farcical entertainment, *The Mary Tyler Moore Show* presented reality-based episodes in an effort to expose the audience to the day-to-day issues in the life of a thirtysomething single career woman in the 1970s. Mary Richards (Mary Tyler Moore) was a symbol of female liberation for many viewers during the seven years the series was originally produced, and she was hailed as one of the first credible representations of the new female reality.

Cloris Leachman (Phyllis Lindstrom) and Mary Tyler Moore (Mary Richards) from a 1971 episode of The Mary Tyler Moore Show. *(Corbis/Bettmann)*

The series' opening montage expressed much about the premise of the show and the characterization of Mary Richards. The first theme song questioned, "How will you make it on your own" in a world that is "awfully big," and the second version, introduced during the third season, affirmed: "You're going to make it after all." Although the words affirmed Mary's independence, the majority of the visuals presented the character in stereotypically feminine pursuits or surrounded by symbols traditionally associated with femininity. In addition, the coworkers-as-family scenario was established by shots of Mary enthusiastically hugging boss Lou (Ed Asner), writer Murray (Gavin MacLeod), and news anchor Ted (Ted Knight).

The series explicitly depicted Mary Richards as a single woman with a responsible, possibly glamorous job and no driving need to find a man to marry for validation. Her seriousness and dedication to her job were traits that endeared her to some feminists of the period because it showed that women could have productive and well-lived lives beyond marriage and home. Yet, while unstated, it was understood by most viewers that eventually Mary would meet Mr. Right and marry. The fact that Mary never had a steady boyfriend subtly reinforced the traditional view that a woman could have a career or a family—but never at the same time.

Ostensibly on her own, Mary was surrounded by surrogate family members. At home she had sister/friend, Rhoda (Valerie Harper), as well as her landlady, Phyllis (Cloris Leachman). At work she had Lou (father), Murray (older brother), and Ted (younger brother). Even though she was miles away from her family of origin, Mary was never without caring, supportive family members.

From the beginning of the series, Mary was established as the interpersonal rock for those around her. If a relationship problem arose among her friends, Mary was always available to counsel and advise. She was unfailingly supportive and caring as she helped deal with the troubles faced by her friends, and her door was literally always open to them.

The traditional female role was subtly reinforced in the work environment even while independence was explicitly celebrated. Over the seven years of the series, Mary rose from associate producer to producer, but the work she was shown doing was that of a glorified gofer-secretary: handling mail, taking messages, filing, or acting as office receptionist. Although projects she supposedly worked on were occasionally mentioned, she was seldom shown actively involved in them. The viewer saw Mary only in the socially acceptable roles of secretary and caretaker of her coworkers.

Further examination indicates that Mary's relationship with her newsroom boss, Lou Grant, reinforced the traditional role of women most strongly. Although she might temporarily assert herself and her rights, she eventually deferred to Lou, and was unfailingly submissive to his judgment and experience. In all the years they worked together, she was virtually incapable of calling him anything but Mr. Grant, while all the other characters called him Lou.

Mary's wardrobe was another area in which the traditional female role was subtly reinforced. Although explicitly filling a managerial position, Mary did not dress for success in the manner of first-time women executives of the period. Rather than the skirted suits that were the female managerial uniform, she wore clothes ascribed to clerical workers: dresses, jumpers, skirts, and occasionally pantsuits. While the men in the office wore somber, refined colors, Mary wore brightly colored outfits accented with large pieces of jewelry. Again, while the explicit message was "executive," the implicit message was "clerical worker."

Although the premise of the show—a young, single woman working as an executive in a male-dominated field—was outwardly a challenge to traditional roles, adequate feminine symbols remained to reassure viewers that the status quo was not being threatened. The show was very popular, and received numerous awards during its original production.

Genuinely a high point in television, the series was extremely well written, the acting exceptional, and the characters well developed. Yet, when all the layers are peeled away, Mary Richards was a 1950s nurturing mother transplanted to the work environment of the 1970s, an improvement in the limited roles allowed women, but not a radical change.

M*A*S*H (1972–1983)

This series, which premiered while American soldiers were still fighting in Vietnam, had a strong antiwar tone. Based on the novel and hit movie by the same name, the series followed the members of the 4077th Mobile Army Surgical Hospital (MASH) as they worked through the insanity and futility of war. It became the most successful sitcom in the history of television up to that time.

The episodes, which alternated between funny and serious, offered no neat solutions to the problem-of-the-week as do most sitcoms, but seemed to indicate that with humor all things were possible, or at least endurable.

Women were well represented among the cast, but the male doctors were in charge, and women were viewed as sexual entities to be propositioned or to have problems that male cast members could help solve. The televisual version of Margaret "Hot Lips" Houlihan (Loretta Swit) was the most positive female character; she was depicted as evolving from a sex-starved Army brat to a multifaceted woman who grew through love, marriage, and divorce.

Matriarchs

See Older Women on Television

Maude (1972–1978)

The series was a spinoff of the hugely popular *All in the Family* (1971–1983), and featured Edith's cousin, Maude Findlay (Beatrice Arthur), a character modeled after Frances Lear, the late editor of *Lear's* magazine and former wife of creator/producer Norman Lear. The series followed the life and experiences of many-times-divorced Maude, an outspoken archliberal, who was accurately described in the series theme as "enterprising, socializing, everything but compromising." Along with her fourth husband, Walter (Bill Macy); Carol Traynor (Adrienne Barbeau), her adult daughter who lived with them; and grandson, Philip (Brian Morrison, 1972–1977; Kraig Metzinger, 1977–1978), Maude faced the challenges of life in the 1970s. Her favorite admonition when disappointed—"God'll getcha for that!"—entered into the slang of the period.

The series took on topics considered taboo by most programs, such as birth control, unwanted pregnancy, abortion, depression, alcoholism,

Adrienne Barbeau (Carol) joins Beatrice Arthur (Maude), Rue McClanahan (Vivian), and Hermione Baddeley (Mrs. Naugatuck) in a rousing song on this 1975 episode of Maude. *(CBS/Archive Photos)*

and menopause. In keeping with Lear's reputation for challenging the status quo, Maude became the first television character to have an abortion—a year before abortion was protected by *Roe v. Wade*—which brought heavy viewer protest but did not change the series' attitude toward controversial topics.

Meadows, Audrey (1925–1996)

Audrey Meadows is best remembered as Alice Kramden, the wife of blustery Ralph Kramden (Jackie Gleason), in *The Honeymooners* (1952–1956). Although *The Honeymooners* was a stand-alone series for only one season (1955–1956), it had been a skit on several of Gleason's series since 1951.

When Gleason was casting for a new Alice, he turned down Meadows as being too attractive, so she had photos taken of herself with uncombed hair, no makeup, and old clothes as she fumbled around the kitchen. Upon seeing the photos, Gleason gave her the job, saying that a woman willing "to be seen like that for a job deserves it."

In fact, she was perfect for the role of the practical Alice as opposed to Gleason's pie-in-the-sky Ralph. Her timing was excellent, and she was quick-witted enough to react to the unpredictable Gleason, who hated to rehearse and often ad-libbed during a skit.

After the end of *The Honeymooners,* Meadows appeared on television specials and episodic series. She even costarred in the short-lived series *Uncle Buck* (1990–1991), but will always be remembered as Alice.

She exhibited her business savvy by being the only cast member to ask for lifetime royalties from the show—a move that left her financially comfortable for decades.

Meet Corliss Archer (1951–1952/1954–1955)

Another radio transplant, *Meet Corliss Archer* had been a successful radio series since 1943. The series revolved around the coming of age of an all-American girl (Lugene Sanders, 1951–1952; Ann Baker, 1954–1955) and her apple-pie perfect family. As with other series from that period, the plots were simplistic (the Christmas episode involved the family members' attempts to keep their gifts hidden from one another) and reinforced the ideal of suburban family life.

CBS canceled the series in 1952, and it was reprised in first-run syndication during the 1954–1955 season.

Meet Millie (1952–1956)

This series originated on radio in 1951 and moved to television the following year. Millie Bronson (Elena Verdugo) was a young, attractive secretary working in Manhattan and trying to live her own life while living with her matchmaking mother (Florence Halops) in a brownstone apartment. Although Millie had a boyfriend, Johnny (Ross Ford), her mother suggested Millie as a potential spouse to every eligible man she met.

Michaels, Helene (1962–)

Helene Michaels, executive vice-president of Columbia TriStar Television, began her career as a journalist for the CBS news division. She moved to Columbia Tri-Star Television and rose through the ranks to become vice-president of development, then vice-president of current programming, before attaining her current position. Michaels oversees comedy and drama development as well as overall programming and talent for the company.

Under her leadership, Columbia Tri-Star Television placed all 15 of its pilots on network schedules in the 1997 fall season. Michaels was also instrumental in developing established hits: *The Nanny* (1993–1999), *Mad about You* (1992–1999), and the critically acclaimed *Party of Five* (1994–).

Mitchell, Pat (1947–)

Pat Mitchell, president of CNN Productions, Turner Original Productions, and Time, Inc. Television, came to television after she lost her writing job when *Look* magazine went out of business in the early 1980s. She has been with Turner Broadcasting since 1992.

Over the years, Mitchell worked for all three major broadcast networks and several cable channels producing reality-based specials and news segments. She substituted briefly for Jane Pauley on *Today* (1952– , NBC) and appeared occasionally on *Sunday Morning* (1979– , CBS) as the arts correspondent. Before coming to Turner Broadcasting, she hosted the talk show *Woman to Woman,* which won an Emmy in 1984 for Outstanding Talk or Service Series.

Mod Squad (1968–1973)

Although not a female-centered series, this successful program presented three icons of the 1960s hippie generation, one of which was female. The Mod Squad ("one white, one black, and one blonde") was comprised of Pete (Michael Cole), a rich kid gone wrong; Linc (Clarence Williams III), a ghetto kid from a family of 13 arrested during the Watts riots; and Julie (Peggy Lipton), the vagrant daughter of a prostitute. The three were recruited by Police Captain Adam Greer (Tige Andrews) to work undercover in the youth culture and search out adult offenders preying on the young and leading them astray.

The Mommies (1993–1995)

Originally based loosely on the stand-up routine of stars Marilyn Kuntz and Caryl Kristensen, this series was about female bonding and family life in the suburbs. As the series continued, the stand-up comedy was abandoned for a more standard sitcom format of kids and pesky neighbors.

Marilyn was married to Jack Larson (David Dukes) and had two children, Adam (Shiloh Strong) and Kasey (Ashley Peldon). Caryl, pregnant at the start of the show, was married to Paul Kellogg (Robin Thomas, 1993–1994; Lane Davis, 1995) and was mother to Blake (Ryan Merriman) and Danny (Sam Gifaldi). In the final few months of the series, Marilyn and Jack divorced, allowing the stars to add dating jokes to their repertoire.

After the series was canceled, Kuntz and Kristensen had their own talk show, *Caryl & Marilyn: Real Friends* (1996–1997). When it was canceled, the two returned to the comedy circuit, playing college and university campuses, and became commercial spokeswomen.

Mona McCluskey (1965–1966)

Mona Carroll (Juliet Prowse) was a movie star making $5,000 a week who fell in love and married an Air Force sergeant, Mike McCluskey (Denny Miller), who made $500 a month. To save her husband's pride, Mona lived with him in a two-bedroom apartment and could not use any of her money to help with expenses. The series dealt with her efforts to improve his financial situation without him realizing it, and her adjustment to life as a military wife.

MONSTER FAMILIES

In the mid-1960s, two series premiered that featured families comprised of "monsters." Both started within the same week, and both were removed from the schedule in the same week. In both series the female lead (the wife) was depicted as the more logical and resourceful family member.

Arguably the more popular of the two was *The Addams Family* (1964–1966), based on Charles Addams's cartoons, which appeared in the *New Yorker.* It featured the ghoulish Addamses and their unconventional, often bizarre lifestyle. Morticia (Carolyn Jones) generally wore a full-length black gown and was "deathly pale" from her "moon tan." Her husband, Gomez (John Astin), was fabulously wealthy and childishly enthusiastic about his hobbies.

Their children—Pugsley (Ken Weatherwax) and Wednesday (Lisa Loring)—tried to at least marginally fit in with the world outside their hilltop mansion. Grandmama (Blossom Rock) was a witch whose spells sometimes went wrong, and Uncle Fester (Jackie Coogan) could literally light up a room. The family was taken care of by Lurch (Ted Cassidy), the seven-foot-tall butler of few words.

The Addams Family was more popular among young people, and after it left the airwaves, two cartoon programs (1973–1975, 1992–1995) continued the family's adventures. In addition, two movies, *The Addams Family* (1991) and *Addams Family Values* (1993), featured the characters (although not the original cast) in further family chronicles, achieving moderate success.

The second family, *The Munsters* (1964–1966), was comprised of level-headed, vampire-looking Lily (Yvonne DeCarlo) and her husband, Herman (Fred Gwynne), who resembled the Frankenstein monster and worked as a gravedigger. Their son, Eddie (Butch Patrick), was a wolf-boy, and Grandpa (Al Lewis) was a 350-year-old vampire who changed into a bat in tense situations. The final member of the family was the normal-looking Marilyn (Beverly Owen, 1964; Pat Priest, 1964–1966), who caused the family some concern over her "strangeness."

Although definitely the less popular of the two series, more than 20 years after the demise of the first series, *The Munsters Today* (1988–1991) began syndicated production. The family supposedly woke up after a 20-year sleep to find themselves in the 1980s. The family still comprised Lily (Lee Merriweather), Herman (John Schuck), Eddie (Jason Marsden), Grandpa (Howard Morton), and Marilyn (Hilary Van Dyke), but the show had a more modern look.

MONTAGE

A montage is the opening sequence of a series where program credits are shown and the series' soundtrack or theme song is played. Music for dramas is generally instrumental, but situation comedies often have songs with lyrics that reflect the show's theme or outlook, such as *All in the Family*'s version of "Those Were the Days" and *The Mary Tyler Moore Show*'s "Love Is All Around."

The visual sequence of the montage falls into three general categories. The action montage shows the characters participating in activity typical of the series and hints at the focus and/or location of the program. The star montage identifies the series' stars against a backdrop of typical series action or location. Finally, the combination montage begins by identifying the stars and ends with action sequences.

The montage is used to enhance the regular viewer's identification with a series and its characters. In addition, by displaying the stars and/or typical action sequences, it acts as a preview for new viewers unfamiliar with the program, and hopefully will be of sufficient interest to motivate them to watch the episode.

Moonlighting (1985–1989)

A postmodern romantic comedy–cum–battle of the sexes in the context of absurdity and parody played out against the backdrop of a detective agency, *Moonlighting* was one of the most popular programs on television for its first years. Unfortunately, the series ended when it became a victim of egos and ill-conceived story lines.

After her financial manager disappeared with her accumulated fortune, former international fashion model Maddie Hayes (Cybill Shepherd) became the reluctant active employer/partner of brash David Addison (Bruce Willis) in the Blue Moon Detective Agency, one of the few assets Maddie's manager had left her. The sexual attraction of the two lead characters was expressed by arguing and stylistic door-slamming, and the romantic tension drew many to watch in "will they or won't they" anticipation. Other regular characters included Agnes Dipesto (Allyce Beasley), their rhyming receptionist, and Herbert Viola (Curtis Armstrong), their clerk/wannabe-detective.

A true comedy-drama hybrid, the show had many innovative moments. One excellent example was the *Taming of the Shrew* takeoff in 1986 entitled "Atomic Shakespeare," in which contemporary sayings were interlaced amid Elizabethan dialogue in iambic pentameter. At other times the characters directly addressed the camera and audience to discuss story developments or, in one case, fan letters calling for an intimate encounter between Maddie and David.

Unfortunately, once the producers gave in to audience pressure and let the Maddie-David attraction lead to bed, the series became unbearably mediocre and the plot convoluted. As the "supposed" producer explained to Maddie and David in the final episode that captured the show's essence and decline, "a case of poison ivy is more fun than watching you two lately . . . people don't want laughs, they want romance . . . and romance is a very fragile thing . . . once it's over, it's over and I'm afraid for you two, it's over . . . people fell in love with you two falling in love, but you couldn't keep falling forever . . . sooner or later you had to land someplace."

Moore, Mary Tyler (1936–)

Mary Tyler Moore brought to life two of television's favorite, if not beloved, female sitcom characters: Laura Petrie (*The Dick Van Dyke Show,* 1961–1966) and Mary Richards (*The Mary Tyler Moore Show,* 1970–1977). However, she first attracted the public's attention when a photograph of her, at age one, won first prize in a Kodak–*New York Times* contest.

Born in New York City to a remote father and a fun-loving but later alcoholic mother, Moore was raised by an extended family that included her grandmother and maternal aunt Bertie, who was more her mother than her biological mother. Moore began singing and dancing at family gatherings as early as age six. She was molested by a family friend during this time, but her accusation was ignored by her mother, who stated, "It didn't happen."

A few years later the family moved to Los Angeles in search of work in the entertainment industry, and Moore took dancing lessons. Her devotion to dance brought stability and accomplishment, which offset to some degree her unstable family life.

Moore appeared in Hotpoint commercials for the television series *The Adventures of Ozzie and Harriet* (1952–1966) soon after graduating from high school. Her career as Happy, the Hotpoint elf, quickly ended when she became pregnant soon after her marriage to Dick Meeker.

Once her son, Richie, was a toddler, Moore returned to dancing and appeared on such successful television variety series as *The Eddie Fisher Show* (1957–1959), *The Jimmy Durante Show* (1954–1957), and *The George Gobel Show* (1954–1960). After realizing that she wanted to be an actor, not just a chorus dancer, she turned once more to commercials while audition-ing for acting roles.

Her first role of note was that of Sam, the answering service operator on the *Richard Diamond* (1957–1960) detective series. Although her face was never seen, her sultry voice and long legs made her a hit with male viewers. Unfortunately, she soon learned that anonymity was not condu-cive to advancement; she was replaced after 13 episodes when she asked for more money.

Although she lost the role of Danny Thomas's daughter on *The Danny Thomas Show* (1953–1965), Moore made such a favorable impression that when it came time to cast the wife on the new series *The Dick Van Dyke Show* (1961–1966), she was called in to audition. In the role of Laura Petrie, Moore was the perfect wife and mother, and was responsible for creating a "capri fad" by appearing in slacks around the house rather than in the dress-and-high-heels uniform of previous sitcom wives.

As Moore proved her comedic talent, her part, which had originally been conceived as merely a straight man for Dick Van Dyke, was enlarged. She was given pivotal scenes, and the stories moved increasingly from the work setting to the home setting.

During the show's first season, Moore divorced her first husband and soon married Grant Tinker, former advertising executive turned program-mer at NBC. Professionally, she continued to hone her craft, and in 1964 won the Emmy for Best Actress in a Comedy Series.

Moore moved into movies with the role of shy Miss Dorothy in *Thor-oughly Modern Millie* (1965) and to Broadway as Holly Golightly in the musical version of *Breakfast at Tiffany's*. She returned to Hollywood to costar with Elvis Presley in *Change of Habit* (1969) as one of three nuns who work in street clothes with underprivileged youths in the inner city. Moore was not particularly successful with other mediums, so she returned to television.

During this time, Moore was diagnosed with Type I (insulin-depen-dent) diabetes. Moore continued her career without letting the public know of her illness. Years later she went public and served as international chair of the Juvenile Diabetes Foundation, making public service announcements and lobbying Congress for research funding.

In 1969, Moore developed the character with which she would be most identified, that of Mary Richards, single career woman of the 1970s. To ensure creative control of the series, Moore established her own pro-duction company, MTM Enterprises, to produce the show. MTM Enterprises became synonymous with quality television and produced some of the most critically acclaimed series on television. Moore sold it in 1988, netting an estimated $85 million, although a large portion of the money was in stock options for the purchasing corporation, which went bankrupt before the options realized any value.

Moore took a few months off after the end of *The Mary Tyler Moore Show* in 1977, then attempted a comeback in a musical variety show entitled *Mary* in 1978. *Mary* was canceled after only three episodes and another attempt, *The Mary Tyler Moore Hour,* was canceled after eight episodes. It was a difficult period for Moore: her series had both fizzled, she learned that her son had a drug problem, and her second marriage failed.

Not one to give in to adversity, Moore made her dramatic debut as the grieving mother in *Ordinary People* (1980), for which she won an Oscar nomination, followed by a five-month run on Broadway in *Whose Life Is It Anyway?* as a quadriplegic suing for the right to die. During her Broadway appearance, her life was threatened by an overzealous fan who "loved" her so much that he wanted to grant her wish (from the play) to die. Luckily, the man was apprehended before he could harm anyone.

Soon after the end of the play, Moore's son, Richie, accidentally shot himself and died of the wounds. This final tragedy increased Moore's growing dependence on alcohol. Nevertheless, Moore began in earnest to build an independent life for herself during what was only the second time since she was born that she had not been living with either her father or one of her husbands (the first time was the six-month period between marriages).

While Moore's parents were visiting her in New York, her mother became ill, and Moore found herself attracted to the doctor, S. Robert Levine, who treated her mother. Although initially put off by their age difference (she was 18 years older), they eventually married.

Moore appeared in the movie *Heartsounds* (1984) as the wife of the dying Hal Lear (James Garner) before beginning her third series, *Mary* (1985), set in a Chicago newspaper office. The writing never met her standards, and she requested that the series be canceled. Moore returned to films and appeared in *Finnegan Begin Again* (1985) and in *Just between Friends* (1986) as the wife who learns that her best friend had been having an affair with her deceased husband and was now pregnant with his child.

Moore appeared in Gore Vidal's miniseries *Lincoln* (1988) as Mary Todd Lincoln before starting her fourth series, *Annie McGuire* (1988), about a divorced mother who remarries and the humorous adjustments needed to blend two households. This series was canceled after two months and marked the fourth consecutive series failure for Moore.

Finally in 1989, Moore was ready to confront her alcoholism and, with her husband's support, began the long steps to recovery by checking into the Betty Ford Clinic. Although the program was difficult, Moore persevered and remains sober to this day. Buoyed by her success with alcohol, Moore also gave up smoking, as did her husband.

Moore has virtually retired from acting, although she occasionally appears in television productions. She won the Emmy for Outstanding Supporting Actress in a Miniseries for her role in *Stolen Babies* (1993). She returned to series television in *New York News* (1995), an hour-long dramatic series in which she portrayed the driven publisher of a daily tabloid, but the series was soon canceled.

Throughout the years, rumors have been persistent that she and Valerie Harper will reunite in a series featuring Mary Richards and Rhoda Morgenstern, but the projected 1998 debut was postponed.

See also *The Mary Tyler Moore Show;* MTM Enterprises.

The Mothers-in-Law (1967–1969)

The conservative Hubbards and the freewheeling Buells had been best friends and neighbors for 15 years. Now their children, Jerry (Jerry Fogel) and Susie (Deborah Walley), were married and attending college. Unfortunately for the young couple, both Eve Hubbard (Eve Arden) and Kaye Buell (Kaye Ballard) had definite ideas on how the young couple should live their lives and were not hesitant in sharing their opinions.

The series was a vehicle to showcase the comedic talents of both Arden and Ballard, who had been popular comediennes in the 1950s.

Mr. Adams and Eve (1957–1958)

Starring Ida Lupino as Eve Drake and her (then) real-life husband, Howard Duff, as Howard Adams, this series focused on the events in the professional and private lives of husband-and-wife film stars. Although exaggerated to fit sitcom requirements, some of the events in the episodes were reportedly based on real events in the Duffs' lives.

See also Lupino, Ida.

MORNING SHOWS

Morning shows are among the top money-makers for any television network, so it is understandable that the networks fight for morning supremacy. For the last five years, NBC's *Today* (1952–) has been the highest-rated show; according to a *New York Times* report, it earned more than $100 million in 1998.

In January 1999, ABC moved news-veteran Diane Sawyer to *Good Morning America* (1975–) in an effort to challenge *Today*. ABC hoped to regain the top slot it ceded to NBC several years earlier when *Good Morning America* lost its identity by introducing too many changes at once. The CBS early entry, *This Morning*, is clearly an also-ran in the morning sweepstakes.

With the return of former coanchor Charlie Gibson and the introduction of Sawyer, *Good Morning America* was poised to take the program, as Gibson said on the 18 January broadcast, "back to the future and reinforce the sense of familiarity" from its past glory days. ABC even reintroduced a cozy living room–like set to invite viewers to stop and visit awhile.

The organization of the 7 to 9 A.M. program is fairly standard regardless of the network on which it runs. The programs begin with 30 minutes of hard news and recent developments, then lighten coverage to general topics such as health and exercise, cooking, or interviews. Each show even allots a certain amount of time for snappy repartee and/or self-disclosure among the hosts so that viewers feel a bond with them.

After the early-morning shows end, early talk shows begin. These shows are lighter than the programs seen later, in keeping with the friendly morning objective. Such programs as *Regis and Kathie Lee* (1989–) and *The View* (1997–) on ABC, *Leeza* (1994–) and the *Roseanne Show* (1998–) on NBC, and *Martha Stewart Living* (1992–) on CBS fill in the morning hours prior to the daily soap opera fest.

Mr. and Mrs. North (1952–1953/1954)

Pamela North (Barbara Britton) was the somewhat naive wife of mystery publisher Jerry North (Richard Denning), who also dabbled in helping the police solve baffling crimes. Supposedly an average Greenwich Village couple, murders happened around them regularly. Much to everyone's chagrin, Mrs. North generally solved the mystery before her husband or the police.

The series was seen on CBS for the first year, then moved to NBC for its final months.

Mrs. G Goes to College (1961–1962)

This series, which changed its name to *The Gertrude Berg Show* after a few months, concerned Sarah Green (Berg), a matronly woman who returned to college after her husband's death to fulfill her desire for a formal education. Her adjustment to academic life and her effect on the younger students around her formed the basis of the comedic situations.

Unfortunately, viewers still "saw" Berg as Mollie Goldberg, so the series never found an audience; it was canceled after seven months.

MTM Enterprises

Founded in 1970 by Mary Tyler Moore (hence the name), her then-husband, Grant Tinker, and Arthur Price, MTM Enterprises (MTM) was considered by many to be the driving force for the so-called second golden age of television. The company's philosophy was to allow its creative staff to be creative without interference from corporate "suits." This concept was central to the MTM blueprint for a quality program and continues to be imitated by other production companies.

The graduates of the MTM "school" of writing, producing, and directing include some of the most influential people in television since the 1970s: James Brooks, Allan Burns, James Burrows, Glen and Les Charles, Jay Sandrich, Jay Tarses, Steven Bochco, and Linda Woodward. Although the company put out some of the best series on television, as this partial list demonstrates, it was not a haven that encouraged female creativity—even though the head of the company was a woman.

MTM produced such hit sitcoms as *The Mary Tyler Moore Show* (1970–1977), *The Bob Newhart Show* (1972–1978), and *Rhoda* (1974–1978), but by 1977 the company turned its attention to social dramas such as *Lou Grant* (1977–1982) and *The White Shadow* (1978–1981). With the success of its social dramas, MTM moved into reality-based dramas such as *Hill Street Blues* (1981–1987) and *St. Elsewhere* (1982–1988).

While the company was at its peak, it received four Peabody awards for its programs: *The Mary Tyler Moore Show* (1977), *Lou Grant* (1978), *Hill Street Blues* (1981), and *St. Elsewhere* (1984). Sadly, the company was sold in 1988, and an era ended. The creative personnel dispersed to other companies or started their own production companies, and MTM ceased to exemplify a product of exceptional quality.

MTV

When MTV began as a standard cable network in 1981, it was merely a showcase for videos advertising and promoting recording artists' songs. As videos became more popular, their content was regularly challenged by feminists and other cultural critics for the misogynistic bent that featured abuse of women as entertainment.

In 1984, just three years after its inception, the National Coalition of Television Violence released a report critical of the amount of violence depicted in the network's videos. The study found an average of 17.9 acts of violence per hour; 22 percent of the videos showed violence between men and women (with women generally being the victims) and 13 percent depicted sadistic violence. The media coverage surrounding this report prompted MTV to cut back on videos featuring heavy-metal bands because they featured the greatest amount of violence.

In 1986, MTV introduced veejays—the first being J. J. Jackson and Nina Blackwood. In 1987, MTV went international, first into Europe, then Asia in 1991 and China in 1995.

In an effort to move beyond its musical base, its first original series, *Real World,* was introduced in 1992. Seven individuals were recruited to live in a large apartment, at MTV's expense, and allow film crews to follow them for three months. This series and the versions that followed documented the roommates' lives through job hunting, college stress, dating and relationships, and simply adjusting to life in a coed commune atmosphere.

Also in 1992, MTV introduced an animated series entitled *Beavis and Butthead,* about two less-than-intelligent male teenagers and their view of the world. Criticized by most adults, it was a hit with the younger viewers, until the duo was "killed" in 1997. MTV's next animated series, *Daria,* was a spinoff of the previous series, and featured an alienated 16-year-old girl who feels superior to and separated from the rest of the world and her family.

MTV continued to broaden its operations base in the 1990s. MTV Productions was created in 1993 to produce its own series and specials, and it moved into other ethnic markets with MTV Latino that same year. The network went on-line in 1994, and soon followed with MTV Interactive. Other programs included *Mouth to Mouth* (a talk show), *Club MTV* (an updated show similar to *American Bandstand*), *The Week in Rock* (a rock music newsmagazine), and *Remote Control* (a game show).

Although seldom popular with older viewers, MTV revolutionized the music industry and the means of promoting music. The network has matured during its years of existence, but it continues to target younger viewers with its more diversified program offerings.

See also Representation of Women.

Murder, She Wrote (1984–1996)

Jessica Fletcher (Angela Lansbury) was a middle-aged widow from Cabot's Cove, Maine, who began writing mystery novels after her husband's death and her retirement from teaching. Her first novel, *The Corpse Danced at Midnight,* became a best-seller, and she embarked on a new career. Often mentioned during series episodes, her supposed literary output was remarkable—29 books over the course of the series.

No matter how mundane the initial event of an episode might seem, in the classic formula of Agatha Christie's Miss Marple mysteries, Jessica always came upon a body or other mysterious circumstance that needed her attention. The pacing was similar to an earlier series, *Ellery Queen* (1975–1976), with clues revealed to lead the viewer to "whodunit."

In 1991, changes were made to the original premise. Although she did not give up her home in Cabot's Cove, Jessica lived in Manhattan during the week, which enabled her to teach criminology during the day at Manhattan University and creative writing at night school. This change in venue allowed Jessica to encounter a wider variety of people.

Jessica Fletcher was a role model of sorts for the aging population. She was intelligent and charming, but most of all she was active. Exciting things happened to her as she met life head-on and tried new things. In a world of contradictions and shades of gray, her mysteries were neatly solved, with evil being punished and morality upheld.

The Jessica character was so popular that even after the series ended, the franchise continued with *Murder, She Wrote* TV movies. The first, entitled *South by Southwest,* premiered in November 1997 and featured Jessica matching wits with smug government types to find a woman who had witnessed the murder of a government whistle-blower.

Murphy Brown (1988–1998)

Murphy Brown debuted in 1988 during a period of backlash when women were nearly eliminated from television by all-male buddy shows; it was one of the few series to focus on a female character that year. Created, produced (in the first five years), and, for many episodes, written by Diane English, it was the first truly well-rounded portrayal of a career woman in a situation comedy.

Murphy Brown was the story of a driven journalist and her "family" of coworkers on a weekly news program, *FYI*. Murphy was portrayed by Candice Bergen, an actress who had actually worked as a photojournalist (her work appeared in *Time* and *Life*). Murphy was an alumna of the Betty Ford Clinic, where she overcame drinking and smoking addictions honed from years as a hard-driving journalist. Murphy was most comfortable with men, perhaps because of her highly competitive nature, and her closest friends were coworker and investigative reporter Frank Fontana (Joe Regalbuto) and house painter-turned-permanent-fixture Eldin Bernecky (Robert Pastorelli), who eventually served as Murphy's son's nanny even after he sold one of his paintings for $1 million.

Coanchor Jim Dial (Charles Kimbrough) was a newsman from the Edward Murrow cloth, who for 25 years had been respected by peers such as Cronkite and Rather. Corky Sherwood (Faith Ford) was the naive former Miss America (by default) who was brought onto *FYI* to add youth and energy to the "aging" triumvirate by covering human-interest stories of dubious value. *FYI*'s producer for the first eight years was Miles Silverberg (Grant Shaud), a neurotic wonder-kid who had been in elementary school when Jim, Murphy, and Frank started their journalistic careers. He eventually married Corky, but left the show at the end of the 1996 season to take a network job in New York (he continued to be spoken of but never seen). His replacement was Kay (Lily Tomlin), the no-nonsense newsroom veteran, who could be as abrasive as Murphy.

Unlike the typical sitcom that avoids topical or controversial issues, this series dealt with homelessness, political correctness and oversensitivity, the downside of celebrity, ecology, First Amendment protections, and single motherhood and family values. Not only did the series readily address issues of substance, it often made a statement.

Murphy Brown differed from the standard sitcom formula in other ways. Unlike most television series, no opening montage appeared to establish program premise or central characters. Each week the episode be-

Murphy Brown, played by Candice Bergen, holds her newborn son, Avery, in a Murphy Brown *story line that generated controversy over family values and single motherhood. (Corbis/Bettmann)*

gan with a few bars of music and the words "Murphy Brown," followed by program credits as the action began to unfold. By using this stylistically simple introduction, *Murphy Brown* avoided the initial boundaries of characters and program established by montage sequences.

Some sitcom characters, from both the past and the present, are often still looking for their niche or ideal lifestyle, but Murphy had reached the pinnacle of success in the field of journalism, having been the coanchor of *FYI* for more than 20 years. She was an insightful and hard-hitting investigative reporter known (and feared) for her relentless pursuit of the truth.

The series' willingness to take a stand on issues and deal with controversial topics allowed the character Murphy Brown to become a symbol of either the reality of our times or the problem with family life and declining values. During the 1991–1992 season, the still-unmarried Murphy became pregnant, although the baby was given quasi-legitimacy by making the father Murphy's ex-husband.

Murphy was a fictional character, but she became the topic of heated debate within the media, and the target of conservative politicians and religious groups. The character transcended the boundaries between make-believe and reality by the unexpected attention given to Murphy's pregnancy by (then) Vice-President Dan Quayle in speeches on family values during the 1992 presidential campaign.

Murphy Brown, as an unwed mother, was held up as a symbol of the declining family values in the United States in speeches given throughout the country. After this unexpected reaction to a plot device, Murphy "appeared" in a variety of national magazines, from *U.S. News and World Report* to *Christian Century.* In a hyperreal episode from the 1992 fall season, Murphy replied to Quayle's comments in a segment of *FYI* that featured real-life nontraditional families.

The unforeseen celebrity acquired by the Murphy Brown character illustrates the authenticity that a fictional character can assume from extensive exposure. Television is such a popular and pervasive part of American life that the boundaries between actual and imaginary are sometimes easily blurred.

Although in many ways Murphy was a feminist role model, her character was not without the typical conflicting signals and symbols found in female characters. Although she was shown to be extremely successful, her predominant personality traits—independence, bluntness, excessive self-confidence, and ambition—are those most often ascribed to males in American society. In addition, she was professionally successful, but her private life was depicted as nearly nonexistent. The implicit message was that to be successful, a woman must be masculinized, thereby losing many aspects of her femaleness, resulting in an empty personal life.

Because of her powerful characterization, Murphy's pregnancy might be viewed as an effort to soften her personality by aligning her with the socially accepted role of motherhood—albeit single motherhood. However, her son, Avery, and her role as mother seldom appeared in the story line beyond the pregnancy and birth episodes, so the reason for this plot shift is unclear beyond the fact that 1989 heralded the beginning of a televisionwide baby boom.

During the show's final season, Murphy was faced with another challenge. She learned early in the season that she had breast cancer, and in addition to the typical work-related stories, many of the episodes chronicled her battle and how she dealt with this new crisis in her life. At the end of several episodes, Candice Bergen made public service announcements concerning the subject.

In the final episode, Murphy learned that she was cancer-free. After much soul-searching and questioning of her priorities, she decided that doing her job was when she was most content and fulfilled, and she pledged to continue *FYI*. Perhaps the most satisfying scene to longtime viewers was the one in which she returned to her townhouse to find Eldin, who had left seasons earlier to paint in Spain, once more painting her den. The series had come full circle, and Murphy's family was intact.

Murphy Brown offered a nontraditional role model of female success even though conflicting messages of masculinity and femininity were present. Murphy was depicted as a survivor of her dysfunctional childhood and her professional journey of hard knocks. This resiliency and persistence might well have been the most positive and beneficial aspect of her character for the viewing audience.

My Friend Irma (1952–1954)

Marie Wilson was one of the entertainment industry's favorite dumb blondes of the period, and perhaps her most famous role was that of Irma Peterson, a role she created for radio in 1947 and which moved to television five years later.

Irma Peterson (Wilson) was an illogical, screwball legal secretary who, instead of having the standard understanding husband, had an understanding and levelheaded roommate, Jane (Cathy Lewis). Irma and Jane shared an apartment at the boardinghouse owned by Mrs. O'Reilly (Gloria Gordon).

The final season brought cast changes as Jane moved to Panama and Irma got a new roommate, Kay (Mary Sharp), who was a reporter. In addition, Irma's seven-year-old nephew, Bobby (Richard Eyer), came to live with her.

My Little Margie (1952–1955)

Willful Margie Albright (Gale Storm) shared a Fifth Avenue apartment with her attractive and eligible father, Vernon (Charles Farrell). Most of her time was spent trying to protect her widower father from the clutches of various scheming women while trying to make him more settled and circumventing his parental control over her life.

In a reverse of the usual progression, the series went from television to radio in December 1952, airing different, but concurrent, episodes for the remaining three years.

My Living Doll (1964–1965)

Perhaps one of the most sexist series concepts of all time, this series had Julie Newmar as the scantily clad (for the period) robot Rhoda, who sometimes took words literally and instantly obeyed any order she was given—in other words, a male fantasy come to television.

The AF709 (Newmar) was designed by Dr. Carl Miller, who left his creation in the care of a psychiatrist, Dr. Robert McDonald (Robert Cummings), when he was sent to Pakistan on assignment. Bob moved the newly named Rhoda into his home with the explanation that she was Dr. Miller's niece, and began the process of turning her into his version of the perfect woman. Unfortunately, Bob's neighbor, Peter (Jack Mullaney), fell in love with the obedient and seldom-speaking Rhoda, and Bob had to go to great lengths to keep the secret from him.

My Sister Eileen (1960–1961)

The series concerned the two Sherwood sisters, who moved from Ohio to Manhattan to pursue their dream careers. Ruth (Elaine Stritch) hoped to become a writer, while younger sister Eileen (Shirley Boone) wanted to be an actress, so they found an agent and began adjusting to life in the city.

The serious and sensible Ruth contrasted with Eileen, who was beautiful but naive and too trusting. To make ends meet while waiting for their big break, Ruth worked for a publisher, Mr. Beaumont (Raymond Bailey), and spent most of her time keeping her sister out of trouble.

The series was based on a book by Ruth McKinley that had earlier been made into two movies (1942, 1955).

My Sister Sam (1986–1987)

Samantha "Sam" Russell (Pam Dawber) was a 29-year-old commercial photographer living in San Francisco whose 16-year-old sister, Patti (Rebecca Schaeffer), came to live with her. The episodes involved their adjustment to living together and Sam's uncertainty over which role she should fill in her sister's life—sister, friend, or surrogate-mother.

Schaeffer was murdered by a fan-turned-stalker in 1989.

N

Name Game: Females with Male Names

An interesting phenomenon exists on television in relation to some female characters who work in nontraditional, male-dominated careers: A large percentage of these characters are given nicknames that are either male names or sexually ambiguous.

The central character in *Murphy Brown* (1988–1998), a successful reporter on a prime-time newsmagazine with an already ambiguous name, was called Murph or Slugger by her friends and coworkers. During the first two seasons of *Profiler* (1997–), Dr. Samantha Waters was an accomplished forensic psychologist who was called Sam. Detective Rose Phillips (*Under Suspicion,* 1994–1995) was called Phil by everyone except her father. *Foley Square* (1985–1986) featured a female assistant district attorney named Alexandra who was called Alex.

Even the two women detectives on the successful series *Cagney and Lacey* (1982–1988) were known by their last names, a common practice among adolescent boys. Murphy Brown was further degendered when one of her romantic partners called her Brown.

One of the few nontraditional professions to escape this degenderization is that of physician, possibly because as doctors the female characters are involved in nurturing and caring for others, a traditionally female activity.

Besides the earlier mentioned Alex on *Foley Square,* the characters portrayed as attorneys seem to be divided between male-sounding names and traditional names. *The Client* (1996–1997) featured Reggie, and the central character in *Ally McBeal* (1997–) also has an ambiguous name. Interestingly, most of the characters who have recognizably female names are not central characters, but one of many in ensemble casts.

Nancy Drew Mysteries (1977–1978)

Based on the series of novels featuring a teenage sleuth who regularly outwitted all adult investigators, this program starred Pamela Sue Martin as Nancy Drew, the 18-year-old daughter of renowned criminal lawyer Carson Drew (William Schallert). With her best friend, George (Jean Rasey, 1977; Susan Buckner, 1977–1978), and Ned (George O'Hanlon, Jr.), her father's law student aide turned investigator for the district attorney's office, she traveled the world solving exciting but always nonviolent mysteries.

Pamela Sue Martin as Nancy Drew on the television series The Nancy Drew Mysteries. *(Photofest)*

The series alternated with *The Hardy Boys Mysteries* on Sunday nights, and occasionally the casts of both series appeared in one episode. However, in January 1978, Martin left the show prior to both shows being combined permanently into one program. By the fall of 1978, the Nancy Drew character (now played by Janet Louise Johnson) was dropped, and the series reverted to *The Hardy Boys Mysteries.*

The Nanny (1993–1999)

Fran Fine (Fran Drescher) was the epitome of the New York Jewish woman; her mother, Sylvia (Renee Taylor), constantly harped on her daughter's unmarried status while eating junk food nonstop, and her grandmother, Yetta (Ann Morgan Guilbert), was in another reality entirely.

Appearing at the Manhattan mansion of successful theatrical producer Maxwell Sheffield (Charles Shaughnessy) to sell cosmetics, Fran was mistaken for a nanny applicant to care for Sheffield's three motherless children—Maggie (Nicolle Tom), Brighton (Benjamin Salisbury), and Grace (Madeline Zima). Talking her way into the job, Fran moved into the mansion and proceeded to turn the well-ordered British household upside down. Fran's ally was the family butler, Niles (Daniel Davis), and her nemesis was Maxwell's lovelorn assistant, C. C. (Lauren Lane).

Uneducated and uncultured by most standards, Fran had the common sense and traditional values to meet the challenges of the Sheffield household. As the series progressed, Maxwell fell in love with the eager Fran, and the 1997–1998 season featured the slow progression to marriage, culminating in the much-anticipated wedding. The final season chronicled their marriage and Fran's anticipated motherhood.

Nanny and the Professor (1970–1971)

Phoebe Figalilly (Juliet Mills) was the British nanny with uncanny psychic abilities and a knack for keeping the chaotic Everett household in order. She was hired by Professor Everett (Richard Long), who was desperate after losing his fifth housekeeper in less than a year. The rest of the household was made up of eldest son Hal (David Doremus), who was always conducting unusual scientific experiments; precocious Butch (Trent Lehman); and Prudence (Kim Richards), a musical prodigy who practiced one melody constantly.

The episodes were consistently bright and cheerful, and centered around the everyday occurrences in the lives of the family members.

National Velvet (1960–1962)

Based on the classic adolescent novel, the television version of *National Velvet* was set not in England, but in the American Midwest, where 12-year-old Velvet (Lori Martin) dreamed of competing in the Grand National Steeplechase with her chestnut thoroughbred, King. Her family and an ex-jockey, Mi Taylor (James McCallion), shared her dream.

Most episodes involved the adventures encountered by Velvet and King as they trained for the national competition.

Nevins, Sheila (1949–)

Sheila Nevins, senior vice-president of documentaries and family programming at HBO, has seen her projects receive 13 Emmy Awards and six Oscars. Nevins, an early convert to the cable network career path, believes that qualified women had more opportunity to prove themselves because men were reluctant to leave the established networks for cable, considered an upstart in the early years.

NEWS

With few exceptions until the end of the 1960s, television reporters and broadcast anchors were male. Some intrepid women worked in television journalism, such as Marlene Sanders, Barbara Walters, Liz Trotta, Sylvia Chase, and Nancy Dickerson, but for the most part the viewing audience received their news from men. The 1970s ushered in the era of affirmative action, and networks actively searched for female reporters for their news bureaus.

It became normal to see female reporters reading news or delivering on-site reports. In 1976, the male domain of news anchor was opened for women by Barbara Walters. At the local level it became standard practice to have both a male and a female anchor news broadcasts.

In this more inclusive, if grudgingly accepting, environment, many women entered the news industry in the 1970s and 1980s. Some made their names in hard news, while others became known as celebrity interviewers or "talking heads."

See also Chase, Sylvia; Chung, Connie; Craft, Christine; Dickerson, Nancy; Howard, Lisa; Pauley, Jane; Roberts, Cokie; Sanders, Marlene; Savitch, Jessica; Sawyer, Diane; Stahl, Lesley; Trotta, Liz; Walters, Barbara.

NEWSMAGAZINES

One of the most predominant genres on television today is newsmagazines. Networks flood the airwaves with this type of programming because newsmagazines are relatively inexpensive to produce, approximately $600,000 per hour as opposed to $1 million and up for other types of series. Low costs mean higher profit.

The first newsmagazine to appear was *60 Minutes* (1968–). With the popularity of this series, other series were created following the same format and concept. Of those programs still on the air, *20/20* premiered in 1978, *Dateline NBC* in 1992, *48 Hours* in 1988, and *Primetime Live* the following year.

In fact, the genre is so popular that in 1999, CBS launched *60 Minutes II* to increase their offering time. As of early 1999, three hours of newsmagazines were offered on NBC, three hours on ABC, and four hours on CBS, that does not even include tabloid offerings.

The Project for Excellence in Journalism conducted a study during the fall of 1997 to determine the types of stories covered by the five top series. Most often covered for all series were human-interest and personality profiles, not the hard news touted in promotional advertising by the networks.

In fact, *48 Hours* spent almost half its broadcast time on human-interest stories and no time on government or foreign affairs. *60 Minutes* spent the largest segment of its time on personality profiles, while *Primetime Live* was heaviest on human-interest stories. Two areas that were almost uniformly ignored were government and the economy.

What kind and quality of information are being dispensed by these newsmagazines? Recent investigations indicate that mistakes are standard, and inaccurate or misleading information is common. The lives of some individuals have been ruined by an erroneous story that was edited for broadcast so that their words were out of context.

Nichols, Nichelle (1936–)

Nichelle Nichols was the most prominent black female on television during the late 1960s. As Communications Officer Uhura (*Star Trek*, 1966–1969), she portrayed the first nondomestic black female in a leading role on a dramatic series.

Granted, the world Uhura inhabited was a future one where Russians, Americans of all races, and even aliens existed in equality and peace—far distant from the turbulent reality of the 1960s. The future depicted on *Star Trek* was a hopeful one, and the Uhura character allowed women and minorities to feel a part of it. Uhura was beautiful, but most importantly, she

1967 photograph of Nichelle Nichols as Lieutenant Uhura on Star Trek. *(Corbis/ Bettmann)*

was intelligent, dignified, and capable, as exemplified by the fact that she was an officer and the head of communications for a starship.

Nichols began her show business career as a singer and dancer, studying classical ballet as well as more contemporary forms of dance. As a teenager, she played clubs in the Chicago area, and following high school, did some road touring in the United States and Canada. After an attempted sexual assault, she stopped touring.

She moved to Los Angeles, where she appeared in clubs to augment her work in feature films. Her first film break was a small part in the film version of *Porgy and Bess,* which brought her to the attention of the black stars of the era, including Sammy Davis Jr., Pearl Bailey, Dorothy Dandridge, and Sidney Poitier. After that film she worked in local theater as well as on Broadway and the New York club circuit, appearing in some of the best clubs in the era, including the famous Blue Angel.

Nichols first worked with Gene Roddenberry, the father of the *Star Trek* empire, in 1963 while appearing in an episode of his earlier television series, *The Lieutenant* (1963–1964). While he was devising and refining his *Star Trek* concept, she continued to work in films and made appearances in Europe. During her tour in Paris, she was called back to Hollywood to appear in the pilot of *Star Trek.*

She was accepted and respected by the other actors and crew members of the series, but she soon became disheartened by racism and prejudice from the management of Desilu Studios, where *Star Trek* was produced. After much thought, Nichols decided to quit the series. Dr. Martin Luther King, an Uhura fan, encouraged her to remain on the series as a role model for black children and as a representative of black Americans for the rest of the world.

In an episode from the final season of *Star Trek* entitled "Plato's Stepchildren," Nichols participated in the first interracial kiss ever to appear on network television. The script called for Uhura and Captain Kirk (William Shatner) and Spock (Leonard Nimoy) and Nurse Chapel (Majel Barrett) to be forced to "perform" romantically for the powerful but jaded Platonians. Even though the kiss was clearly an act of coercion by the Platonians, the network was greatly concerned that the public would object to it. However, no negative reaction came from the viewers, and a television first occurred without most people being aware of it.

Star Trek was canceled in 1969, and the "Star Trek phenomenon" began to form. The series went into syndication almost immediately, appearing on television screens in more than 66 countries. The fans, from loyal to rabid, began organizing and attending conventions, keeping the *Star Trek* universe alive. A convention held in Chicago in 1975 was attended by more than 30,000 fans.

After the end of the series, Nichols became involved in Kwanza, a charitable organization that raises funds to support worthwhile projects such as providing food, toys, clothing, and other necessities to disadvantaged families. In addition to her charitable work, in 1976 she began writing and producing educational films and programs using music, her first love, as a teaching tool.

In 1977, after many years as a promoter of space exploration, she was appointed to the board of directors of the National Space Institute (NSI), an organization founded by Wernher Von Braun. Through her work with the NSI, she encouraged NASA to open the space program to women and minorities. Soon she was helping NASA with its recruitment of astronauts for the space shuttle project.

In 1978 filming began on the first *Star Trek* movie. *Star Trek: The Motion Picture* premiered in Washington, D.C., in December 1979. The first movie was followed by *Star Trek II: The Wrath of Khan* (1982), *Star Trek III: The Search for Spock* (1984), *Star Trek IV: The Voyage Home* (1986), *Star Trek V: The Final Frontier* (1989), and *Star Trek VI: The Undiscovered Country* (1991).

When she was not working on one of the *Star Trek* movies, Nichols continued to sing; she created a two-act musical that showcased black singing legends. In 1992 she hosted a 13-part series on the SciFi Channel entitled *Inside Space*.

Not one to rest on her laurels, Nichols added "novelist" to her impressive list of accomplishments, which include singer, dancer, actor, producer, and educator, with the publication of her science fiction novel *Saturn's Child* (1995), and is working on an as-yet-untitled sequel. She has also designed a line of accessories that includes jewelry and scarves.

Nightingales (1989)

Although only produced for four months, this series is famous for alienating the nursing profession and for being a failed attempt by Aaron Spelling to resurrect the 1970s "T&A" viewer mentality on which his success was based. The series ostensibly focused on student nurses studying at Wilshire Memorial Hospital in Southern California.

The characters were a collection of sad stories and stereotypes. Bridget (Susan Walters) was in the witness protection program, Sam (Chelsea Field) was a recovering alcoholic who moonlighted as a dancer, Allyson (Kim

Ulrich) was an oversexed blonde, Yo (Roxann Biggs) was the obligatory ethnic minority (Latino), and Becky (Kristy Swanson) was the innocent from the South.

The students were clearly more interested in their romantic lives than in dealing with patients or learning anything. In fact, they were depicted as little more than scantily clad sex-kittens watched over by Christine Broderick (Suzanne Pleshette), Director of Student Nurses, and Head Nurse Lenore Ritt (Fran Bennett).

The blatant exploitation of the student nurses brought protests from nursing professionals and organizations that eventually spelled the end for the series.

9 to 5 (1982–1983/1986–1988)

Loosely based on the hit movie from 1980, this series had many incarnations and casts. The series premise was the same as the movie without the direct action against the boorish boss: three overworked secretaries tried to change the sexist environment in which they worked.

Originally, Violet (Rita Moreno), Doralee (Rachel Dennison), and Judy (Valerie Curtin) were the secretaries, but in 1983, Judy was replaced by Linda (Leah Ayres), who worked and lived with Violet and Doralee. When the series began syndicated production, the Doralee and Judy characters were reprised by the original actors, and Marsha (Sally Struthers) joined the group.

Nixon, Agnes (1927–)

Agnes Nixon sold her first radio play while attending Northwestern University, and was hired by Irna Phillips as a dialogue writer for *Woman in White* (1938–1942). Nixon moved to New York City to write for the dramatic anthologies that personified the early years of television, including *Studio One* (1948–1958), *Hallmark Hall of Fame* (1952–), *Cameo Theatre* (1950–1955), and *Philco TV Playhouse* (1948–1955).

As episodic series gained popularity, Nixon elected to remain in the East because her husband had an established career in Philadelphia. As writing jobs became more scarce, Irna Phillips once again offered Nixon work, writing for *The Guiding Light* (1952–), Phillips's soap opera based in New York City. Nixon eventually became the program's head writer, although she seldom ventured to New York, preferring to send her plot outlines to dialoguers to write.

By the late 1960s, Nixon was second only to Phillips in the soap opera genre. By 1968, when Nixon took over Phillips's *Another World* (1964–), she had acquired a reputation for saving troubled serials. Through introducing new characters and stories, Nixon propelled the failing program to become the second most popular daytime serial. In that same year, *One Life to Live* (1968–), the first soap opera to be created, written, and produced by Nixon, was introduced.

Although Nixon did not alter the basic soap opera format introduced by Phillips on radio, which focused on a few families and the people around them, she brought the soap opera into a new period in which the story lines were more reflective of current cultural conditions, rather than those of an idealized world. Under her influence, the soap opera world became populated by a more culturally and racially diverse society.

In fact, *One Life to Live* was the first soap opera to offer a black character in a central role. Carla Gray (Ellen Holly) was a light-skinned black woman who pretended to be Italian to gain acceptance into Llanview society. To add viewer interest, Nixon included stories that called for location shots, thus moving the characters out of the limited sets previously used.

Her next serial was *All My Children* (1970–), in which she introduced such issues as abortion, infertility, cancer in women, depression, child abuse, and the effects of the Vietnam War on the returning soldiers. Plots with more relevance increased viewership by appealing to more people, adding men as well as younger viewers to the women who traditionally watched. As daytime serials came to be considered "legitimate," some actors became stars.

To appeal to the younger viewers, Nixon introduced *Loving* (1983–1997), set on the fictional Alden University campus. The writing reflected more-explicit sexual tones, ushering in an era of steamy, provocative stories and near-X-rated scenes.

Nixon continues her work in soap operas, and her serials remain among the most popular with viewers.

Northern Exposure (1990–1995)

Although very much an ensemble program, this offbeat hit, set in the fictional Alaskan town of Cicely, had several strong, albeit eccentric, female characters. Maggie O'Connell (Janine Turner) was an independent air-taxi pilot who had extremely bad luck with boyfriends (they all died under bizarre circumstances); many believed she was under a "love curse." Shelly Tambo (Cynthia Geary) was the 18-year-old beauty queen (at the start of the series) madly in love with Holling Vincouer (John Cullum), the sixtyish owner of the town's tavern.

Ruth-Anne Miller (Peg Phillips) was a wise crone archetypal character who ran the general store while she dispensed advice and accepted the other characters' quirks. Marilyn Whirlwind (Elaine Miles) was the enigmatic Eskimo receptionist-assistant at the local medical office who seemed to possess psychic abilities and dispensed native homilies with the medications.

The story lines ranged from bizarre to mundane to surreal, but the characters remained likable for all their idiosyncrasies. Popular with critics and the viewing audience, *Northern Exposure* won an Emmy for Outstanding Drama Series in 1992, several Golden Globes, two Peabody awards, and was named Program of the Year by the Television Critics Association in 1992.

Nurses (1991–1994)

Miami's fictional Community Medical Center was the site of this quasi-spinoff of *Empty Nest* (1988–1995). Most of the series' action took place at the third-floor nurses' station or their breakroom; the characters were seldom shown actually working with patients, although they were always portrayed as harried and overworked.

Annie (Arnetia Walker), a working mom, tried to keep the rest of the shift's nurses in line and focused on the job. Sandy (Stephanie Hodge) was cynical and world-weary, Julie (Mary Jo Keenan) was neurotic and germphobic, Gina (Ada Maris) was the wise Latina immigrant, and Greg (Jeff Altman) was the flaky male nurse. The nurses' commonsense wisdom generally showed up the incompetent doctors, except for Dr. Riskin (Florence Stanley), an older female doctor, who was wise and compassionate.

In the series' last season, with much fanfare Loni Anderson joined the cast as Casey MacAfree, the new hospital administrator, after the hospital was bought by an HMO. Also in the final season, Gina became pregnant by the longtime object of her affections, Dr. Hank (Kip Gilman), and after many months of refusing his proposals, married him prior to the baby's birth.

The Nurses (1962–1964/1965–1967)

Filmed in New York City, this series focused on the professional and personal lives of head nurse Liz Thorpe (Shirl Conway) and student nurse Gail Lucas (Zina Bethune) as they worked at Alden General Hospital. In the fall of 1964, the title changed to *The Doctors and the Nurses* when two male doctors joined the cast to advise the nurses on medical and ethical problems.

The series became a daytime serial (1965–1967) with a complete cast change, although the setting stayed the same.

O

Occasional Wife (1966–1967)

In this series, aspiring painter Greta Patterson (Patricia Harty) agreed to pretend to be the wife of Peter Christopher (Michael Callan), an executive at the very conservative and family-oriented Brahms Baby Food Company, to help his career, which had stalled because he was single. Peter rented an apartment two floors above his for her, and paid for her art lessons in return for Greta's appearance as his wife whenever his boss, Max Brahms (Jack Collins), was around—which necessitated a lot of traffic on the fire escape connecting the two floors.

Naturally, most episodes dealt with the problems and confusing logistics caused by this arrangement.

O'Donnell, Rosie (1962–)

Rosie O'Donnell's talk show premiered to the highest ratings of any daytime talk show and ranked as the number-one program in 14 major markets in its first week. It remains in the top 20, and O'Donnell has been given the title "Queen of Nice" because of her genuine, friendly style. The show uses the celebrity-driven format of decades past, and O'Donnell's rule of not telling a joke about anyone that "she would not tell to their face" is a welcome relief from the usual confrontational talk show atmosphere.

O'Donnell was raised on Long Island, one of five children; her mother died when she was only ten, and as the eldest daughter she became

243

Rosie O'Donnell poses with actor Tom Cruise on the set of her talk show, The Rosie O'Donnell Show *in 1998. (Reuters/Ho/Archive Photos)*

the surrogate mother to her younger siblings. In reaction to her mother's death and her father's alcoholic withdrawal, she turned to television for her idealized family.

Even with this less-than-perfect home life, she managed to be voted prom queen, homecoming queen, and class president at her high school. She enrolled at Dickinson College as a prelaw student before transferring to Brown University as a drama major. Eventually, she quit college to pursue a career in comedy.

She wrote her own stand-up routines, and won the *Star Search* competition five times in 1987. Her first television role was as the Kaniskys' New York neighbor, Maggie O'Brien, in *Gimme a Break* (1981–1987) during its last season. She became a VJ on VH-1, and hosted VH-1's *Stand-Up Spotlight.* In 1992 she briefly starred on *Stand by Your Man,* a black comedy about two sisters-in-law living together while their husbands were in prison.

Her first film was the hit *A League of Their Own* (1992), after which she appeared in *Sleepless in Seattle* (1993) and *The Flintstones* (1994). In 1994 she appeared on Broadway as Rizzo in the revival of *Grease* and in the less-than-memorable *Exit to Eden,* followed by *Now and Then* (1995), *Beautiful Girls* (1996), and *Harriet, the Spy* (1997).

During the mid-1990s, O'Donnell adopted the first of her two children (Parker and Chelsea). She needed a more settled schedule than moviemaking allowed, so she circulated a proposal for a talk show.

Her talk show has made her a household word, as has her work for disadvantaged children. She has received many accolades during recent years, but none more special to her than the Kids' Choice Award she won in 1997. During that year she also won the American Comedy Award as funniest female performer on a television series, was named Number 1 Entertainer of the Year by *Entertainment Weekly,* and won the first of two Emmys as Outstanding Talk Show Host.

Oh Baby (1998–)

In this Lifetime network series, Tracy (Cynthia Stevenson) is 35 years old and has a successful career with a software company. However, her biological clock is sounding a major alarm and her current relationship is going nowhere, so she decides to be artificially inseminated. The season's episodes follow Tracy's experiences with her developing pregnancy and the situations that result from her condition.

Supported by her best friend, Charlotte (Joanna Gleason), and questioned by her mother, Celia (Jessica Walters), Tracy prepares for single motherhood. In the final episode of the first season, Tracy gives birth to her child (a son) and her commitment-phobic boyfriend proposes. This ending ties the series up in a neat family-friendly wrapping and ends any single-mother controversy.

Oh Madeline (1983–1984)

In this series Madeline Wayne (Madeline Kahn), a settled housewife, was bored by her mundanely routine life in the suburbs, so she decided to give the trendy lifestyle a try. Each episode focused on a different fad that Madeline embraced.

Faintly reminiscent of *I Love Lucy,* the show featured slapstick comedy and harmless marital misunderstandings as Madeline tried to add some excitement to her life, which always resulted in the need for her rescue by her understanding husband, Charlie (James Sloyan), who wrote romance novels under the pseudonym Crystal Love.

The series was based on the popular British series *Pigs in the Middle.*

One Day at a Time (1975–1984)

With the success of *The Mary Tyler Moore Show* (1970–1977), many networks hurried to develop their own woman-on-her-own series. One resulting effort, *One Day at a Time,* was the first successful prime-time sitcom to feature a divorced woman as the central character. Divorced after 17 years of marriage, Ann Romano (Bonnie Franklin) began rebuilding her life with her two teenage daughters, Julie (Mackenzie Phillips) and Barbara (Valerie Bertinelli).

The episodes centered around the coming of age for all the characters. Ann struggled not only with being a single working mother, but becoming her own person, since she herself had been married since she was 17. Sheltered and controlled her entire married life, Ann had to learn quickly how to maintain and succeed in a world that was unfamiliar to her in many ways. She was, as creator Norman Lear called her, an "emerging woman" like many of those in the viewing audience, trying new things and learning from her mistakes. In the midst of her own difficulties, Ann had to help her daughters adapt to their own changes and navigate through their growth dilemmas.

OLDER WOMEN ON TELEVISION

As the baby boomers get older, the 45-and-up age segment of the population gets substantially larger. Because women generally outlive men, the female segment of the older population is also growing. Older women often live alone because of divorce or spousal death. Their incomes are generally low; even if they worked during their lifetimes, their salaries were normally less than those of males, making both Social Security and pension payments smaller.

Even as a growing population segment, the representation of older women on television has been virtually nonexistent until relatively recently. In the past, when older women were represented, the characterization was seldom accurate or flattering. Their true economic and social situations were ignored, and they were often depicted as members of extended families or intact nuclear families—a phenomenon that occurred less frequently in real life.

One of the first series to feature an older woman as the lead character was *December Bride* (1954–1961). In this series, Spring Byington portrayed the vivacious widow Lily Ruskin, who had an active social life and many friends. Although the depiction of an older woman was very positive, the series and its character were not seen as typical.

Early television had occasional supporting characters who were older females, such as nurturing Aunt Bea (Frances Bavier) on *The Andy Griffith Show* (1960–1968) and the sagacious Granny (Irene Ryan) on *The Beverly Hillbillies* (1962–1971), as well as the lovable but befuddled Aunt Clara (Marion Lorne) on *Bewitched* (1964–1972).

On dramatic series, older women, though rarely present, fared better. Victoria Barkley (Barbara Stanwyck) was the respected matriarch of the Barkley clan on *The Big Valley* (1965–1969), and Grandmother Walton (Ellen Corby) was a valued member of *The Waltons* (1972–1981). An early precursor to the popular series *Murder, She Wrote* (1984–1997) was *The Snoop Sisters* (1973–1974), part of the rotating *NBC Mystery Movie* quartet, in which sibling mystery writers Ernesta (Helen Hayes) and Gwen (Mildred Natwick) constantly became embroiled in crimes and mysteries despite their advanced years, and to the chagrin of the authorities were generally able to solve the mysteries before the younger investigators.

Although their portrayal on dramatic series was more favorable, older women were only a very small fraction of the older people depicted on television, and no racial minorities were portrayed. In one research study, characters over age 65 constituted only 2 percent of all the characters on television—and of that 2 percent, only 9 percent were female. Worse yet, many of those characters were powerless, feeble, befuddled, and often victimized.

In the 1980s, the depiction of older women improved, although not realistically, and the characters were given fuller lives. No longer confined to family units, they often had jobs and active social lives. Unfortunately, while early television depictions were limited and distorted on the negative side, older female characters in the 1980s were often shown in an excessively positive light.

On the prime-time soap operas that proliferated during that decade, older women were

(continued on next page)

(continued from previous page)

well represented by Miss Ellie (Barbara Bel Geddes, Donna Reed) on *Dallas* (1978–1991), Angela Channing (Jane Wyman) on *Falcon Crest* (1981–1990), and Victoria Cabot (Anne Baxter) on *Hotel* (1983–1988). Unfortunately, most of these characters were wealthy, powerful, abundantly self-confident, and sometimes villainous, so although older women were no longer devalued or victimized, the picture was still distorted.

Perhaps the most realistic portrayal of an older woman was that of Jessica Fletcher (Angela Lansbury) on *Murder, She Wrote*. Although Jessica was a successful writer, she was not excessively rich or powerful. True, she constantly found dead bodies and uncovered mysterious circumstances, but the character was unabashedly an older, nonglamorous woman who was active, resourceful, intelligent, and dignified.

On the comedy front, the debut and success of *Golden Girls* (1985–1992) brought older women to the attention of television viewers. Dorothy Zbornak (Bea Arthur), Rose Nyland (Betty White), Blanche Devereaux (Rue McClanahan), and Sophia Petrillo (Estelle Getty) showed that older women could be active, empowered, and busy socially. In contrast, older women's sexuality was played for laughs in the oversexed characters of Blanche and Mona Robinson (Katherine Helmond) from *Who's the Boss* (1984–1992).

In the 1980s, then, older female characters were seen more often and more positively, but the depictions were still not reflective of reality. Unlike her real-life counterparts, the older character had an adequate income, faced no age discrimination, and had no health problems. As television moved into the last decade of the twentieth century, older female characters once again became scarce.

Few older women appeared on any series in the 1990s, and those who did often did not last very long. Eileen Heckart appeared as the mother-in-law from hell in *The 5 Mrs. Buchanans* (1994–1995), and Rose Marie returned to television as the owner of a baseball team in the short-lived *Hardball* in 1994. One of the few nonwhite older female characters was portrayed by Amy Hill as the scene-stealing Grandma on *All-American Girl* (1994–1995). Betty White costarred as Marie Osmond's meddling mother in *Maybe This Time* (1995–1996), Maxine Stuart played the aging grandmother on the short-lived *Pursuit of Happiness* (1995), and Doris Roberts plays the meddling mother on *Everybody Loves Raymond* (1996–).

On the dramatic front, older women fared little better. Della Reese plays the head angel on the extremely popular *Touched by an Angel* (1994–). However, Cicely Tyson appeared only briefly as the idealistic small-town lawyer in *Sweet Justice* (1994–1995).

As the decade closed, older women on television were once again a virtually invisible segment of the population. Even as the population ages and its numbers grow, the realities and issues of older women are ignored by the industry that validates reality for many viewers.

For the first four seasons, Ann's quest for self-actualized fulfillment and independence meant that she had no long-term male partner. During the 1979–1980 season, the now-married Julie was written out of the show on the pretext that her husband, Max (Michael Lembeck), had accepted a job in Houston (it was really done to allow Phillips to go to the first of many drug rehabilitation centers).

After several years as an advertising account executive, Ann became partners, both professionally and romantically, with Nick Handris (Ron Rifkin) in a freelance advertising agency. However, Nick soon died in an automobile accident, leaving Ann with temporary custody of his son, Alex (Glenn Scarpelli).

Eventually, Barbara married Mark (Boyd Gaines). When Phillips returned to the show, Julie and Max returned from Houston and soon had a daughter, Annie (Lauren/Paige Maloney). Not long after her granddaughter's birth, Ann married Barbara's divorced father-in-law, Sam Royer (Howard Hesseman). In 1983, Phillips was once again written out of the show for "health" reasons, and her character, Julie, abandoned her family.

However, as the focus of the series shifted from Ann's personal growth to her work life and the adult lives of her daughters, the feminist undertones of the series were lost, as was the loyalty of the viewing audience. The show ended in 1984 with Ann and Sam moving to London so that Ann could accept a fantastic job offer.

Open House (1989–1990)

This series took the female leads of the romantic sitcom *Duet* (1987–1989) and placed them on their own, reversing their starring positions. Linda (Alison LaPlaca), whose husband, Richard (Chris Lemmon), bowed out after only a few episodes, worked for a high-priced real estate office in Los Angeles, while former *Duet* star Laura (Mary Page Keller), who was separated from her husband, attempted to support herself as an apprentice agent.

Most episodes focused on Linda's effort to make top sales agent in her cutthroat sales office.

Oprah Winfrey Show (1985–)

Like all talk shows in the 1980s, the *Oprah Winfrey Show* presented sensationalistic topics. However, from the beginning of the series, Winfrey approached her viewers and audience as "friends." The show, as it developed, became the prototype for the confessional-personal programs that proliferated during the late 1980s and early 1990s.

If an issue or event is important to her, she shares it with her audience of friends. With this approach, her viewers have shared her trials and triumphs with her weight and her endeavors to improve her life as well as the lives of her viewers. Her self-proclaimed ministry is to improve the lives of women.

In 1996, Winfrey began Oprah's Book Club, in which she recommends a book to her audience and invites the author on her show to discuss the book and answer questions from the audience. By her endorsement, two dozen books, some of which might have remained obscure, have become best-sellers.

In 1997, Winfrey initiated the Angel Network to encourage her viewers to volunteer within their communities and help the less fortunate. In 1998 she began a segment entitled "Remembering Your Spirit" to highlight spiritual issues and encourage viewers to nurture that area of their lives.

At the start of her thirteenth season, when it was revealed that Jerry Springer had taken the talk show crown from her, Winfrey told her audience that she did not want to add to the craziness that already existed on the airwaves. She hoped that the new season would be a positive influence on the viewers' lives and uplift rather than drag people down.

See also Winfrey, Oprah.

Our Miss Brooks (1952–1956)

This series originally premiered on radio in 1948 and proved so popular that the concept was moved to television four years later; episodes continued to air on both through the mid-1950s. The series focused on high school English teacher Connie Brooks (Eve Arden), whose lethal one-liners set her targets back on their heels. In addition to trying to teach English to a group of mostly disinterested students, she spent much of her time trying to attract the shy, bumbling biology teacher, Philip Boynton (Robert Rockwell), while conducting a battle of wills with the school principal, Osgood Conklin (Gale Gordon).

This series was extremely popular with educational organizations as well as the general public. Arden became a popular speaker at educational groups and PTAs, and even received actual job offers from schools around the country.

The setting of the series changed from Madison High School to Mrs. Nestor's Private Elementary School at the start of the final season. This time, Miss Brooks was the one being pursued—by the school's physical education teacher, Gene Talbot (Gene Barry). When the new romantic interest did not appeal to the audience, Mr. Boynton was brought back, but the series ended soon after his return.

After its demise, a movie was made in 1956 that tied all the loose ends together. Mr. Boynton finally proposed.

P

The Patty Duke Show (1963–1966)

This series offered lighthearted family fare about two identical cousins growing up in Brooklyn Heights, with both characters played by Patty Duke. Patty Lane was an average, fun-loving, if slightly irresponsible, teenager, while her "cousin" Cathy was a prim and proper Scottish intellectual who tried vainly to keep Patty out of trouble. Although Cathy was the voice of reason between the two, she was talked into many escapades by the persuasive Patty, who often proposed switching identities.

The show was very popular with young viewers, and the occasional guest appearance by popular singers of the period (Bobby Vinton, Chad & Jeremy, and Frankie Avalon) increased its appeal to youth.

Pauley, Jane (1950–)

Jane Pauley was one of a number of women who entered the hallowed halls of television journalism on a crest of affirmative action in 1972. She began as a reporter for WISH-TV in Indianapolis, then moved to WMAQ-TV in Chicago as an anchor and reporter in 1975.

The next year she joined the cast of *Today* (1952–) and was coanchor for almost 15 years (1976–1990). During this time she was also a writer/reporter, as well as the substitute anchor, for *NBC Nightly News* (1980–1982).

After leaving *Today*, Pauley appeared on *Real Life with Jane Pauley* (1990–1991), a newsmagazine-interview program. After that series ended, she joined the cast of *Dateline NBC* (1992–) as coanchor. In 1996 she began an occasionally seen series, *Time & Again*, which looked at current news events in a historical context.

See also News.

Pearl (1996–1997)

For this series, Rhea Perlman tried to recapture the magic that had made her character, Carla, so successful on *Cheers* (1982–1993), but on a gentler level. Perlman played Pearl, a middle-aged widow who attended college at night to achieve her long-held dream of earning a college diploma while managing a loading dock during the day.

Her nemesis was one of her instructors, Professor Pynchon (Malcolm McDowell), and the comedy derived from their interactions and misunderstandings as well as Pearl's dealings with fellow students and coworkers. Unfortunately, Pearl was a nicer, more reasonable character than Carla, and the viewing audience did not accept the change from wisecracking sarcasm to assertive vulnerability.

Peter Loves Mary (1960–1961)

This series had real-life married couple Peter Lind Hayes and Mary Healy playing a show business couple, Peter and Mary Lindsey, living in the suburbs and trying to bridge the gap between the fast-paced life of New York City and the quiet life of suburbia. Peter missed living in the city, but Mary was eager to become a "normal" suburbanite.

Most episodes revolved around the difficulties encountered by working in the city while living in the country, and differences in the two environments. Also featured in the series were Wilma (Bea Benaderet), the Lindseys' housekeeper, and their two TV children—Leslie (Merry Martin) and Steve (Gil Smith).

A decade earlier, the couple had a short-lived series entitled *The Peter Lind Hayes Show* (1950–1951). Guests came to a replica of the couple's home for dinner, and their "acts" were worked into the scripts.

Peter Pan

Although the classic story by James M. Barrie is the story of a boy who refuses to grow up, the part of the ever-young Peter Pan, for many years and many succeeding generations of youngsters, belonged to Mary Martin. The live play was restaged on NBC in 1955, 1956, and in 1960, when it was finally videotaped in color and subsequently rebroadcast many times from 1961 to 1973, and again in 1989. In a statement issued in 1992 by the New York Museum of Television and Radio, the play was praised as "high on the list of the most memorable broadcasts in television history."

A restaged version of the play in 1976 with a different cast and a different score was received less warmly and was never rebroadcast.

Phillips, Irna (1901–1973)

Irna Phillips was known to many as the "Queen of the Soaps"; she is perhaps the person most responsible for the proliferation of daytime soaps on television. She loved acting, but studied education at the University of Illinois after being told she was not attractive enough for an acting career. After receiving a graduate degree from the University of Wisconsin, she taught speech and drama in Dayton, Ohio, while moonlighting as a writer for a radio talk show, *Thought for the Day.*

While working on the talk show, she was asked to create a family drama for radio. Soon her first ten-minute "soap," *Painted Dreams,* the story of a widow struggling to raise her large family, premiered on WGN radio in Chicago.

From 1933 to 1938, Phillips wrote, and briefly starred in, radio's most popular daytime serial, *Today's Children,* virtually a carbon copy of her earlier serial, *Painted Dreams,* which she had left over a control dispute with WGN. Phillips canceled the serial when her mother, who had inspired the main character, died suddenly. Five years later, however, she brought back the series for an additional seven-year run (1943–1950).

In 1937 she created *Guiding Light,* the longest-running soap in broadcast history, which moved to television in 1952 and is still seen daily. The original focus of the serial was a preacher and his efforts to minister to his congregation and deal with the problems within his own family. A popular part of the early serial was the reverend's sermons, which were collected into a book that sold more than a quarter of a million copies. Eventually the pastor was killed, and the series evolved into its current form.

In the latter years of radio's monopoly on home entertainment, Phillips created several serials, including *Woman in White, The Road of Life,* and *The Brighter Day,* the latter two adapted for television. In 1956 she created *As the World Turns* (1956–), followed by *Another World* (1964–), *Days of Our Lives* (1965–), and *Love Is a Many Splendored Thing* (1967–1973).

Phillips was the innovator of such soap staples as tease endings, which developed into the season-finale cliff-hangers used on television programs other than soaps, and the use of dramatic background music to enhance mood. In addition to being an innovative force, she wanted to use her shows to promote issues of social significance and uphold the ideals of marriage, home, and family.

During her career, she helped many writers just starting out in television. Perhaps the most prominent of them is Agnes Nixon, who created and wrote many of her own soaps.

See also Soap Operas, Daytime.

Phyllis (1975–1977)

In this spinoff of the popular series *The Mary Tyler Moore Show* (1970–1977), former landlady Phyllis Lindstrom (Cloris Leachman) moved back to her hometown of San Francisco following the death of her never-seen husband, Lars. Because of reduced circumstances, Phyllis and her daughter, Bess (Lisa Gerritsen), were forced to move in with her scatterbrained mother-in-law, Audrey (Jane Rose), and her second husband, Judge Jonathan Dexter (Henry Jones).

Phyllis continued to be a self-interested busybody and, in a truly upwardly mobile ideal, went from working as an assistant at a photography studio (1975) to being an administrative assistant to Dan Valenti (Carmine Caridi), a member of the San Francisco Board of Supervisors (1976–1977). As ratings began to fall, Bess married Valenti's nephew, Mark (Craig Wasson), but even the addition of newlywed adjustment stories did not help; the show was canceled at the end of the season.

Pistols 'n' Petticoats (1966–1967)

The Hanks family of Wretched, Colorado, could outgun any outlaw or gunslinger for miles, and regularly did. Except for city-bred Lucy (Carole Wells), all the Hanks—Lucy's mother, Henrietta (Ann Sheridan), Grandpa (Doug-

Studio shot of radio star and writer Irna Phillips, *1935. (Photofest)*

las Fowley), and Grandma (Ruth McDevitt)—were experts with firearms. The town sheriff, Harold Sikes (Gary Vinson), was no match for anyone carrying a gun, so the Hanks were called in to restore order each week.

Police Woman (1974–1978)

One of the first series to focus on a female officer, albeit within stereotypical lines, was *Police Woman*. Sergeant Suzanne "Pepper" Anderson (Angie

Dickinson) was an undercover officer for the Los Angeles Police Department's Criminal Conspiracy Division.

Her job usually consisted of posing as a decoy, such as a prostitute or girlfriend, in sting operations. Although she carried a gun, she was more often threatened than threatening. She was often in need of saving by one of her male partners, making her role even less threatening.

Dickinson later appeared in a similarly premised, though short-lived, series entitled *Cassie & Company* (1982), in which she played a former police officer turned private detective.

See also Careers for Women on Television; Detective/Police Drama Series.

Prime Suspect (1992–1996)

This series was created by writer Lynda La Plante after she called New Scotland Yard to determine how many of their more than 100 chief inspectors were women, and the response was "Oh, quite a few. Four." This British program, broadcast on PBS, featured intelligent and driven Detective Chief Inspector (later Detective Superintendent) Jane Tennison (Helen Mirren) as she battled the "ol' boys" system of New Scotland Yard to rise through the detective ranks. Equal time was spent on solving murders and showcasing the office politics that often interfered with the work of catching criminals. Tennison's personal demons and challenges were used to add depth to the character.

Not subservient, glamorous, or eccentric, Jane Tennison is believed by many to be the first realistic female police detective on television. Although often bad-tempered, the tough-minded Tennison was shown working on realistic cases that seldom had happy endings.

Consistently popular, the ongoing program was originally broadcast on *Mystery!* in miniseries format before it moved to *Masterpiece Theatre* in 1995 and was changed to movie format. The series won two Emmys for Outstanding Miniseries (1992–1993, 1994–1995).

See also Detective/Police Drama Series.

Private Benjamin (1981–1983)

Based on the movie of the same name, this series featured spoiled socialite Judy Benjamin (Lorna Patterson), trying to survive basic training and adjust to military life after somewhat impulsively joining the army. Judy shared the recruit life with a variety of other women—Maria Gianelli (Lisa Raggio) had been given the choice of joining the army or going to jail, Rayleen White (Joyce Little) came from a Detroit ghetto, Barbara Ann Glass (Joan Roberts) was a shy country girl, and Carol Winter (Ann Ryerson) was an unrepentant brownnoser.

Eventually, after several cast changes, the recruits made it through basic training and assumed jobs on post. For the final months of the series, Judy worked as an administrative assistant for Captain Lewis (Eileen Brennan) in the public affairs office.

Private Secretary (1953–1957)

In this series, efficient secretary Susie McNamara (Ann Sothern) was always trying to run her boss's life—both in the office and outside. Her boss, Peter Sands (Don Porter), was a successful talent agent in New York who suffered more than he was helped by her "assistance."

Besides getting her boss into countless embarrassing situations, Susie and her best friend, Vi Praskins (Ann Tyrrell), were always on the lookout for any marriage-eligible men. Competing with Susie for men was friend and rival Sylvia (Joan Banks).

Profiler (1996–)

This series, part of the "Thrillogy" lineup on NBC, featured in the first three seasons forensic psychologist Samantha "Sam" Waters (Ally Walker) as the profiler for the elite FBI Violent Crimes Task Force (VCTF) headed by Bailey Malone (Robert Davi). During that time, the series featured three strong female characters with diverse personalities.

Each week the VCTF is called in to investigate a new serial criminal— be it a killer, rapist, or arsonist. In addition to the psycho-of-the-week, Sam was stalked by a serial killer known as Jack, who killed not only her husband prior to the start of the series, but also Sam's romantic interest during the 1997–1998 season, fellow officer Coop (A. Martinez). Sam is haunted by the realization that she is the catalyst for many of Jack's murders. In one case, Jack murdered the doctor who had delivered Sam more than 30 years earlier.

For all her academic credentials, Sam is first and foremost the concerned mother of young Chloe (Caitlin Wachs, 1996–1998; Evan Rachel Wood, 1998–), who is the only person to have seen Jack and lived. One of the most well-rounded female characters in a nontraditional role on television, Sam is intelligent, courageous, and "the best" at her job, but she is also caring, nurturing, and loyal—an equal blending of traits without making the character deficient in some manner because of her successful career. While far from perfect, Sam is allowed to be capable as well as nurturing, and her sensitivity is crucial to her career success.

Sam's best friend since childhood and housemate for the first two seasons was Angel (Erica Gimpel), an artist who opened her home to Sam after the murder of Sam's husband. Because of her closeness to Sam, Jack threatened Angel in his obsession to be the only one in Sam's life. When Jack broke into their lakeside home, the three went into hiding in a firehouse turned apartment under 24-hour guard and constant video surveillance.

Although Angel was dedicated to her art, she provided a stable, centering environment for both Sam and Chloe, and her whimsical side was a perfect counterpoint to Sam's intense seriousness. Sadly, when Jack was finally apprehended, Sam and Chloe moved into a house of their own and the Angel character was written out of the series.

The final powerful female character is Grace Alvarez (Roma Maffia), a forensic pathologist assigned to the VCTF, who became a first-time mother during the second season. Dedicated to her work, Grace is relentless in her quest to get all possible information from evidence found, and this thoroughness often results in her finding the crucial information needed to break the case.

In the final episodes of the 1997–1998 season, Jack was finally caught, and he turned out to be someone with whom Sam had gone to Sunday School when she was a child. Although Jack was held in high-security isolation, he continued to play mind games with Sam and, via the Internet, enlisted a presumed "disciple" to continue his killing spree. At the end of the third season, however, it was revealed that this disciple was the real Jack and he had cornered Sam in an isolated cabin.

Although sometimes grimly realistic, the series is a positive improvement over previous series because it features strong female characters interacting or working with male coworkers on a truly equal basis. It is one of the few programs in which each member of the ensemble cast is pivotal to the success of both the stories and the series.

See also Careers for Women on Television; Detective/Police Drama Series.

Pruitts of Southampton (1966–1967)

This series revolved around the unlikely scenario of the IRS allowing a family of Long Island highbrows to live in their 60-room mansion even though the family owed over $10 million in back taxes. Explained by claiming that the IRS feared a stock market crash if the world knew that the "wealthy" Pruitts were broke, the episodes dealt with the efforts of the matriarch, Mrs. Poindexter Pruitt (Phyllis Diller), to keep the family secret while maintaining the illusion of wealth.

The title was changed to *The Phyllis Diller Show* after only three months, and the mansion was turned into an upscale boardinghouse to raise money to repay the IRS. Unfortunately, these changes did not stop the series' cancellation a few months later.

The series was based on the novel *House Party* by Patrick Dennis.

Q

QUIZ SHOWS

Quiz shows, in which contestants win money or prizes for correctly answering questions, were extremely popular in the early years of television. Popular with networks and sponsors because they were inexpensive to produce and exciting to watch, they proliferated throughout the airwaves.

Big-money programs such as *$64,000 Question* (1955–1958), *Twenty-One* (1956–1958), and *$64,000 Challenge* (1958) became national obsessions. Successful contestants who won big money even became popular culture celebrities and were featured in magazines and on interview programs.

However, when "Wizard of Quiz" Charles Van Doren admitted that he had been coached on the answers to the questions when he appeared on *Twenty-One,* the reign of sponsor-produced quiz shows ended and the nation lost its innocence. Because the tainted programs were sponsor-controlled, networks no longer allowed single sponsors to fund a program; instead, they sold advertising "spots," thereby allowing the networks to remain in control of the programs.

For several years, quiz shows were replaced by game shows, which the viewers believed were less fixable. However, the quiz show made a comeback in 1964 when the perennial favorite *Jeopardy!* premiered; it remains one of the most popular shows on television.

See also Game Shows.

R

RATING SYSTEM FOR PROGRAMS

The content of television programs and the need to regulate the content of programs potentially viewed by children have been a contested issue for many years. In 1996 the government encouraged the industry to label programs as to their suitability for children and to schedule at least three hours of children's educational programs each week.

Although the ratings system was not universally used, by 1997 some voluntary compliance was evident in the use of TV-Y (all children), TV-Y7 (appropriate for children 7 years or older), TV-G (general audience), TV-14 (14 or older), TV-MA (mature audiences), and TV-PG (parental guidance suggested). Further notations used to indicate content included D (suggestive dialogue), L (coarse language), S (sex), and V (violence). In addition, some networks ran verbal disclaimers before programs, stating that the program "may not be suitable" for younger viewers.

The increased attention to program content did not cause a noticeable decrease in violent or sexually suggestive programs as some groups hoped. However, proponents of the ratings system believe that the introduction of the proposed V-chip component into new television sets by the year 2000 will eventually cause ratings to drop on objectionable programs as parents block these programs from viewing by their children.

RELEVANT PROGRAMMING

A trend developed from the late 1960s into the 1970s to depict situations and characters that were more realistic and reflective of the real world. More socially conscious series were typified by such programs as *Storefront Lawyers* (1970–1971), *The Bold Ones* trilogy (*The New Doctors,* 1969–1973; *The Lawyers,* 1969–1973; and *The Senator,* 1970–1971), and *The Young Lawyers* (1970–1971).

The characters in these programs were generally young and always very earnest idealists who worked to change the establishment while aiding the poor and downtrodden in mostly urban settings. Unfortunately, relevance was not entertaining; by 1971 these series were history, and television once more offered lighter viewing.

Remington Steele (1982–1986)

Laura Holt (Stephanie Zimbalist) was a brilliant and resourceful private detective who found it difficult to attract clients because she was female. To soothe her potential clientele, she invented an elusive, never-seen male boss whom she named Remington Steele; hidden behind this fictitious man, her agency became very successful.

However, the agency's success meant that more people demanded to meet Mr. Steele. Finally, Laura was forced to produce her "boss" to accept an award, so she hired a suave and charming Bogart fan with a mysterious past (Pierce Brosnan, in pre-007 days) to stand in for one night. Once introduced as "Mr. Steele," he decided to stay on, assuming the identity over Laura's objections.

Initially inept and more hindrance than help, he quickly learned the trade and became an uninvited partner on all the cases. However, as the episodes played up the romantic attraction between Laura and Steele (his real name was never revealed), Laura ceased to be the independent career woman and became the beautifully clothed and coifed helpmate rather than the driving force of the agency.

After the show was canceled, NBC aired two two-hour movies in which Steele's past was partially revealed and their romantic relationship played out as they solved cases that called for them to travel the world.

This general premise was used in Pamela Anderson's series, *VIP,* which premiered in 1998. She plays Vallery Irons, who, in an effort to save the reputation of a cowardly action star, pretended to be a bodyguard-to-the-stars. She was recruited to be the figurehead-boss of a protection agency that bore her name. Not surprisingly, she became more involved in the cases and more than a figurehead.

REPRESENTATION OF WOMEN

Since the 1970s, many feminists and television critics have done content analyses to determine the representation of women on television. One of the earliest was by Nancy Tedesco (1974), and revealed that men outnumbered women two to one, and that 75 percent of women on television were relegated to comedic roles.

Perhaps of more concern than the ratio is the characterization of women on television. Since the second wave of feminism occurred in the 1960s, women characters were routinely given jobs outside the home, but the jobs were generally low-paying, low-status jobs, with only a slight increase in female professional characters. Of those female characters depicted with a job/career, more than 54 percent were shown in a purely interpersonal context and were portrayed as more interested in a romantic or personal involvement than in their careers.

Female characters are shown as acting out of a desire for romance or marriage, while male characters are motivated by beliefs or ideological principles. Male characters rely on authority or violence, often against women, to get what they want, while female characters, who generally have lower status and less authority, use dependence behaviors or sex. Female characters continue to be defined by marital status or their relationship to a male character.

Some people might believe that things have improved over the years since Tedesco's study, but in 1996, Dr. Martha Lauzen (San Diego State University) examined 65 prime-time series (39 sitcoms and 26 dramas) from the 1995–1996 season and determined that males made up more than 63 percent of the characters on television; only 43 percent of the major characters on television at that time were female.

A look at some of the current popular shows reveals that not much has changed in the intervening years from 1974. The main character on *Suddenly Susan* (1996–) is a reporter, but she is most concerned with her romantic situation. *Caroline in the City* (1995–1999) featured a female cartoonist who is more involved with her and her friends' romantic lives than with her career. On *Ally McBeal* (1998–) the female lawyers focus on interpersonal relationships.

So, while female characters are being brought into the work world (albeit in generally low-status jobs), their chief concern continues to be depicted as interpersonal relationships. Even those few characters who are given status positions, such as lawyer or doctor, remain more focused on relationships and maintaining the work/social environment than in career advancement, and are generally secondary to the male characters on the show.

Overall, the professions are still very much a male enclave. More than 93 percent of the doctors portrayed on television have been male, and 87 percent of the lawyers. Judges have been overwhelmingly male (97 percent), and 86 percent of the characters classified as business executives have been male.

Rhoda (1974–1978)

In this spinoff of the popular *Mary Tyler Moore Show* (1970–1977), a trim and self-confident Rhoda Morgenstern (Valerie Harper) returned to New York to visit her family. She met and fell in love with Joe Gerard (David Groh), the owner of the New York Wrecking Company, and decided to return to New York permanently.

She moved in with her younger sister, Brenda (Julie Kavner), and began working as a window dresser for a nearby store. In a special hour-long episode on 28 October 1974, Rhoda married Joe. The newlyweds moved into the building in which Rhoda had shared an apartment with Brenda prior to her marriage, and Rhoda became a stay-at-home wife; Brenda became the resident manhunter.

Rhoda chafed at the inactivity, and soon decided to open her own window-dressing business with her high school friend Myrna (Barbara Sharma). It soon became apparent to the producers that a happy marriage was not very funny, so Rhoda and Joe started having difficulties and decided to separate. This allowed Rhoda to go through the adjustment to single life again and have a series of impermanent boyfriends.

By 1977, Rhoda and Joe had divorced, the first prime-time couple to go through the ordeal within a series, and Rhoda had a new job at Doyle Costume Company and a new boyfriend named Benny Goodwin (Ray Buktenica). Rhoda's single status did not help the ratings as the producers had anticipated.

At the start of the final season, even Rhoda's mother, Ida (Nancy Walker), was single after longtime husband Martin (Harold J. Gould) deserted her. Even this collection of eccentric singles (Rhoda, Brenda, and Ida) could not save the series, and the final episodes aired in December.

Interestingly, one of the show's most popular characters was never seen on camera. The perpetually inebriated doorman in the building in which Brenda, Rhoda, and Joe lived was a hit with viewers. He always announced himself over the intercom, "This is Carlton, your doorman." Carlton's voice was done by Lorenzo Music, one of the show's producers.

Rivers, Joan (1937–)

Joan Rivers began her career as a stand-up comic in the 1960s, and at one time was considered the heir apparent to Johnny Carson's late-night talk show. In fact, she won an Emmy in 1983 for guest-hosting *The Tonight*

Show. However, she and Carson had a falling-out, and in 1989, Rivers premiered her own show, *The Joan Rivers Show* (1989–1994), for which she won another Emmy in 1990.

She also hosted several shows on cable networks, including *Gossip, Gossip, Gossip* (1992–1993) on USA Network, and she frequently hosts entertainment specials on E! Entertainment. In addition, she brought out her own line of jewelry, which is sold on the home-shopping channel, QVC.

Rivers began her comedic career as a member of the Second City comedy troupe and was voted Las Vegas Comedienne of the Year in 1976 and 1977. In 1989, she was given her star on Hollywood's Walk of Fame.

Rivers has written several books, including *Having a Baby Is a Scream* (1975), *Enter Talking* (1986), and *Still Talking* (1991). Her most recent book, *Bouncing Back: I've Survived Everything . . . and I Mean Everything . . .and You Can Too!* (1997), deals with how Rivers has overcome the many travails of her life.

Roberts, Cokie (1944–)

Cokie Roberts, ABC News' chief congressional analyst since 1988, grew up amid politics and the Washington scene. Known and respected for her thoughtful and balanced analyses, Roberts was named "favorite talking head" by the readers of *George* magazine in 1997.

Roberts has appeared on several ABC newscasts, including *This Week with David Brinkley* and *World News Tonight with Peter Jennings.* Most recently, she coanchors *This Week with Sam Donaldson and Cokie Roberts* and frequently substitutes on the anchor desk of *Nightline.* In addition, Roberts serves as a news analyst for National Public Radio and writes a syndicated newspaper column with her husband.

Before joining ABC, Roberts was a contributor to PBS's *MacNeil-Lehrer Hour* and a correspondent for CBS based in Athens, Greece. She also worked for several years as a producer and host of a public affairs program on WRC-TV in Washington, D.C.

Rolle, Esther (1920–1998)

Best remembered for her portrayal of Florida Evans—first on *Maude* (1972–1978), then on *Good Times* (1974–1979)—to many viewers Esther Rolle represented the quintessential black matriarch. One of her primary concerns about the characters she played was that they accurately depict black life.

The cast of Good Times *poses for a publicity shot in 1976. Pictured clockwise from left are Jimmie Walker, Ja'Net Dubois, Ralph Carter, BernNadette Stanis, and Esther Rolle.*

That concern, plus the impact of each characterization on the viewing audience, led Rolle to leave her successful sitcom *Good Times* in 1977 to protest the buffoonish depiction of her television son, JJ (Jimmie Walker), who is best remembered for his catch-phrase, "dy-no-mite," and his improbable schemes. She reportedly told producers, "I did not agree to do a clown show for you to degrade young black men." After the character was altered, Rolle returned to the series for its final season.

One of 18 children, Rolle was one of the original members of the Negro Ensemble Company, and found success on Broadway before landing a regular role on ABC's daytime drama *One Life to Live* in 1971. In 1972 she began playing the acerbic maid, Florida, and her character became so popular that she was spun off on her own show, which focused on Florida's family life.

Rollin, Betty (1936–)

Betty Rollin is a journalist, news correspondent, and writer who has appeared on several NBC programs (*Nightly News, Women Like Us,* and many news documentaries).

Born in New York City, Rollin has lived all her life in its suburbs. In eighth grade, Rollin began attending Fieldston Ethical Cultural School, a private school that encouraged intellectual investigation and competitiveness among its students. She attended Sarah Lawrence College, where the climate was one of freethinking and experimentation.

Acting was one of the careers with which she experimented, appearing off-Broadway in *The Country Wife* during the summer of her graduation. She even made a pilot for a television series in 1961.

While her acting supported her, Rollin compiled a collection of original wedding vows in a book entitled *I Thee Wed,* which sold very well. Her second book was *Mothers Are Funnier Than Children,* which was also a moderate success. Deciding that writing was her talent, Rollin talked her way into a job as associate feature editor with *Vogue* magazine, moving to *Look* magazine a year later.

When *Look* stopped publishing in 1971, Rollin moved to television journalism and was hired immediately by NBC. Her first jobs were associate producer of *First Tuesday* (1969–1973), a two-hour monthly newsmagazine, and drama critic for the local NBC affiliate (WNBC-TV).

She began training as a news correspondent, and was assigned to the northeastern bureau in 1973. She found that she preferred in-depth stories to spot news coverage, and began specializing in "soft news."

After covering Betty Ford's battle with breast cancer in 1974, Rollin learned that she too had the disease, and she underwent a mastectomy. She took a leave of absence from NBC and wrote a book about her experiences with cancer, *First You Cry.* The book was later made into a television movie starring Mary Tyler Moore as Rollin.

Roseanne, John Goodman, and their television children pose on the living-room set of the television show Roseanne in 1988. (Corbis/Lynn Goldsmith)

Roseanne (1988–1997)

Roseanne, one of the biggest hits of the late 1980s and the 1990s, was a program that viewers either loved or hated. Some felt it was a realistic depiction of a post-Reaganomics, blue-collar family with its seemingly constant fight to maintain a decent style of living. Others felt *Roseanne* was the poster program for dysfunctional family life and an endorsement for childless adulthood. Perhaps it was both.

Instead of making viewers envious of their lifestyle as previous "ideal family" sitcoms had done, the Conner family allowed the viewer to feel superior. The Conners' existence was definitely hand-to-mouth, and they made a virtual game out of juggling their final-notice bills. Constantly short of money and precariously employed, the episodes often had a little-people-against-the-Establishment flavor.

Contrary to previous father-centered sitcoms, the center of the Conner family was the grudging mother, Roseanne (played by the former stand-up comic and self-described "domestic goddess" of the same name), whose scathing one-liners could be directed at any of her family members or an unlucky cultural institution. As the producers and others involved with the series always stressed, the insults and put-downs were delivered with a smile or a laugh within a "loving" family.

Roseanne's husband of many years was Dan (John Goodman), and they had three children: Becky (Lecy Goranson; Sarah Chalke), Darlene (Sara Gilbert), and D. J. (Michael Fishman). Also regularly seen were Roseanne's sister, Jackie (Laurie Metcalf), and their mother, Bev (Estelle Parsons).

The episodes followed the Conners' everyday struggle to stay semi-solvent and the coming-of-age problems of their children, as well as the problems faced by family members Jackie and Bev, all of whom seemed to be searching for their place in the larger world. As the series progressed, Becky eloped with boyfriend Mark (Glenn Quinn), and Darlene went away to school only to return, get pregnant, and eventually marry the father, on-again/off-again boyfriend David (Johnny Galecki). Both Jackie and Roseanne had babies within the scope of the show, but the series ended before D. J. could fully exhibit any teenage angst. During the final season, Jackie and Roseanne's mother, Bev, decided that she was gay after 60-odd years. Through all the multifaceted problems, the family remained supportive of one another in a sarcastic, seemingly demeaning and almost exploitative way.

In the final season, the Conners supposedly won the lottery and began to live the good life, rubbing elbows with the rich and famous. This concept and the entire season alienated most fans, and those who weren't put off by the concept switch in the ninth season were offended by the hour-long finale, in which Roseanne's voice-over revealed that the entire ninth season was a figment of her imagination, a way to get over Dan's death (from a heart attack at the end of the eighth season), except that Darlene did have a baby and Bev did decide that she was gay. The sitcom that came in with a roar went out with a whimper.

Over the years, the series and the stars received much popular and critical acclaim, including Emmys, Golden Globes, American Comedy awards, and Peabody awards. In addition, Roseanne won the Eleanor Roosevelt Award for being an outstanding American woman.

Throughout its nine years, the series was marked by bitter battles between Roseanne and producers and network executives over control of the series and scripts. Stranger even than the offbeat final season was the behavior of Roseanne off-screen.

She screeched the national anthem at a Padres game in 1990, ending her "performance" by scratching her crotch and spitting, actions that caused a public outcry. She claimed to be an incest survivor (an allegation denied by all her family members). As an explanation for her bizarre behavior, she claimed to have multiple personalities. She sent obscene faxes to critics of her show. She verbally attacked anyone who took exception to her behavior or lifestyle. Even so, she claimed that she was not as outrageous as she should have been.

After the end of her series, Roseanne went to Madison Square Garden in New York to play the Wicked Witch of the West in a remake of *The Wizard of Oz*. After the end of that show, she considered a career as the first large-sized supermodel, but settled on creating an afternoon talk show, *Roseanne*, which premiered in 1998.

Rountree, Martha (1912–1999)

Martha Rountree was one of the first women to work in network news. As a freelance writer she helped develop *Meet the Press*, first as a radio program, then moving to television in 1947; *Meet the Press* remains the longest-running series on television.

In addition to serving as one of the writers and producers, Rountree was one of its first moderators (1950–1952), until she sold her interest in the series in 1953. She later hosted *Press Conference* (1956–1957), whose format was similar to that of her previous creation.

Rural Women

During the 1960s, rural female characters were prevalent on television. As the country suffered social unrest and cultural changes, many viewers were drawn to the innocence and simplicity that the idealized "country" represented, as depicted by these characters.

The first series to feature a rural family was *The Real McCoys* (1957–1963), which starred character actor Walter Brennan as cantankerous Amos McCoy, who lived with his grandson and extended family. Although panned by critics, the NBC series was extremely popular with viewers, ranking as the number-five television show of the 1960–1961 season.

With its success, CBS rushed to create other rural-inspired clones. Each had the requisite female character, but three series featured prominent female characters. In *Petticoat Junction* (1963–1970), matriarch Kate Bradley (Bea Benaderet) and her three nubile daughters operated the Shady Rest Hotel outside Hooterville. Two years later, CBS spun off another series set outside Hooterville, *Green Acres* (1965–1971). In this series, Oliver (Eddie Albert) and his non-domestic wife, Lisa (Eva Gabor), moved from their Manhattan penthouse to a run-down farm and tried to adapt to their new environment.

The show that introduced one of the most enduring of rural television families—the Clampitts—was *The Beverly Hillbillies* (1962–1971). The matriarch of this clan was Daisy "Granny" Moses (Irene Ryan), a feisty woman whose simple wisdom put most of the show's city slickers to shame. Along with the rest of her family—Jed (Buddy Ebsen), Jethro (Max Baer Jr.), and Elly Mae (Donna Douglas), Granny tried to make sense of city ways. The series was the most popular of the rural comedies, ranking number one in its first two seasons.

In 1971, CBS hired a new program executive who decided that viewers wanted more sophisticated programs, and canceled all rural-inspired series. Demographically, rural series appealed more to audiences in nonmetropolitan areas (thereby not the favored target audience), but the programs that followed lacked the sensitivity and humanness of the rural comedies.

S

Saarinen, Aline B. (1914–1972)

Aline Saarinen became the first woman to head a network overseas news bureau when she was named chief of NBC's Paris office in 1971. She began her career with NBC as art and architecture editor in the early 1960s, and in 1964 she became a correspondent on "women's matters," moderating a panel show called *For Women Only*.

Born in New York City, Saarinen graduated Phi Beta Kappa from Vassar College in 1935 and went on to receive a graduate degree in the history of architecture from the Institute of Fine Arts at New York University in 1941. From 1944 to 1948 she was an art editor for *Art News* and associate art editor and critic for the *New York Times* (1947).

Saarinen won several awards for art criticism, including the American Federation of the Arts Award for best newspaper criticism in 1953, and wrote several books, including *500 Years of Art* (1946) and *The Proud Possessors* (1958). In 1964 she was offered the post of ambassador to Finland, which she declined.

Salhany, Lucie (1946–)

Lucie Salhany became the first woman to head a network when she was named chair of Fox Broadcasting in 1993. After attending Penn State University, she began her career as a secretary at WKBF-TV in Cleveland in 1967. She moved to WLVI in Boston as program manager, and then spent six years (1979–1985) as vice-president of television programming at Taft Broadcasting. Her next position was as president with Paramount Domestic Television, where she was responsible for the development of *Star Trek: The Next Generation* (1987–1994). She also negotiated the syndication of *Cheers* (1982–1993) and *Family Ties* (1982–1989).

Salhany moved to Fox in 1991 and assumed the chair responsibilities two years later. She oversaw all operations of the network, including syndication and cable production and distribution. In 1994 she moved to the fledgling network UPN as president and CEO, becoming instrumental in expanding its market saturation to 93 percent of the country.

Despite her achievements, in 1997 she was edged out of her leadership role after a reorganization at Viacom and Chris-Craft.

See also Female Executives.

Sally (1957–1958)

Sally (Joan Caulfield) was the stabilizing force in the life of her slightly madcap boss, Mrs. Myrtle Banford (Marion Lorne, who later played Aunt Clara on *Bewitched*). As traveling companion to the wealthy widow, Sally tried to keep her employer out of trouble as they traveled the world.

A few weeks before the series ended, the two returned home to help run the Banford-Bleacher Department Store, and Sally became Mrs. Banford's administrative assistant.

Sanders, Marlene (1932–)

In 1964, Marlene Sanders became the first woman to anchor an evening newscast on network television—albeit only as a substitute for the regular male anchor. During that same period, Sanders had her own daily newscast, *Marlene Sanders with the Woman's Touch,* and anchored the five-minute *ABC Midday Report* (1964–1968).

Sanders began her television career in 1955 as a production assistant on a local news program in New York City. By 1956 she was associate producer of a celebrity interview series, *Night Beat Featuring Mike Wallace.* In 1962, while she was the assistant director of news and public affairs at WNEW radio station (NYC), she wrote a documentary entitled *The Battle of the Warsaw Ghetto,* for which she won a Writers Guild of America award.

She joined ABC-TV in 1964, and at one time was the only female foreign correspondent covering Vietnam. During the early 1970s she produced the first network television documentary on the women's liberation movement (*Women's Liberation,* 1970), and other documentaries including *The Hand That Rocks the Ballot Box* (1972); *Woman's Place* (1973), about sex-role stereotyping and cultural expectations of women; and *The Right to Die* (1974). Their success led to her promotion, in 1976, to vice-president of news and director of television documentaries.

She moved to CBS in 1978 and worked as a correspondent and reporter with that news division, becoming an outspoken critic of women's second-class status and treatment in the industry. In 1987 she was fired for not fitting the network's arbitrary standard of "charisma, looks, or age" and for refusing to be shuffled off to the radio division. Actually, CBS called it "mutual termination" in an effort to "streamline the news division."

After leaving CBS, she joined WNET, the PBS station in New York City, and produced several documentary series, one of her most successful being *Profiles in Progress* (1991) for Discovery Channel.

See also News.

Sara (1976)

This short-lived, female-centered Western focused on a strong-willed schoolmarm, Sara Yarnell (Brenda Vaccaro), who moved from her stuffy home in the East to Independence, Colorado, in the 1870s to battle injustice and ignorance. A possible thematic precursor to the later *Dr. Quinn, Medicine Woman* (1993–1998), Sara's sometimes militant actions met with various degrees of approval and disapproval by the townspeople, although she received glowing admiration from students in her one-room school.

Sara (1985)

This short-lived comedy focused on the professional and personal life of Sara McKenna (Geena Davis), a San Francisco lawyer who shared her storefront office with three other lawyers—her best friend, Rozalyn (Alfre Woodard), and two men.

Saralegui, Cristina (1948–)

Spanish talk show host Cristina Saralegui poses at The American Foundation for AIDS Research's benefit in honor of her efforts in AIDS education within Latino communities, 1997. (Reuters/Fred Prouser/Archive Photos)

Cristina Saralegui is the most popular talk show host on Spanish-language television. Her daily talk show is broadcast on Univision, the nation's fifth largest television network, and reaches approximately 1.3 million viewers a day in the United States.

El Show de Cristina premiered in 1989, and is shown in most Spanish-speaking countries, with a worldwide viewership estimated at 100 million. As perhaps the most influential media personality in the Latino community, Saralegui makes more than $6 million annually and controls an empire that includes her TV show (she's executive producer), a monthly magazine, and daily radio commentaries heard in over 90 countries.

Born in Cuba, Saralegui comes from a family that was once one of the most powerful in that country; they fled after the Communist takeover and have not returned. One of Saralegui's first jobs was as a copywriter for *Vanidades* magazine. When *Cosmopolitan* launched a Spanish-language edition in 1973, she became the first staff writer; six years later, she was named editor.

In addition to her daily show, she has a prime-time series shown on Monday nights, *Cristina: Edición Especial,* which reaches about 2.6 million viewers. Her autobiography, *Cristina: My Life as a Blonde* (1998), made the Spanish-language best-seller list soon after it was released.

Outspoken and intelligent, two traits in women that are not viewed with approval in traditional Latino communities, Saralegui has brought many topics into Latino homes that are viewed as controversial and inappropriate. She has led discussions on infidelity, homosexuality, incest and child abuse, AIDS, and women's equality—all considered taboo by Latino cultural norms. Her goal is to open minds and educate the Latino community by presenting real issues in plain language, and with their consequences clearly shown.

Saralegui is also a tireless fund-raiser for various Latino charities, especially AIDS research and treatment. She even created her own foundation, Up with Life/Arriba La Vida, dedicated to AIDS awareness and education.

Although she has a contract with Univision to produce her show through 2001, she has indicated an interest in starting a media company that would give Latino artists and writers an outlet for their work.

Savitch, Jessica (1947–1983)

Jessica Savitch was a woman who seemed to have everything, and was even voted "one of the most riveting news faces in television history" by her viewing audience, but slowly—before the eyes of the news-viewing public—she lost it all. An overachiever from a very early age, Savitch was raised in a dysfunctional environment. She was taught that success and perfection, whether real or illusionary, were all that mattered.

While still in high school, Savitch cohosted a youth-oriented radio show, *Teen Corner,* in New Jersey. She soon was disc jockey of her own show from noon to eight on Sundays in addition to emceeing at dances and other events. Her first news spot was delivered on 22 November 1963 on the teen reaction to President Kennedy's assassination.

Highly self-critical and driven to succeed, Savitch attended Ithaca College and focused on becoming a broadcast journalist. In essence, she created herself in the image that she thought would be an on-air success. Her first job after graduating was as an administrative assistant (in her case a glorified gofer) with CBS in 1968.

She went to KHOU in Houston in 1971 as a reporter, and a year later moved to the fourth largest television viewing market as a reporter with

KYW, the NBC affiliate in Philadelphia. She got her first anchor job—and began her dependency on drugs to smooth out the rough edges of her life and give her the energy to withstand the grueling pace that both she and the network set. Unfortunately, the drugs caused her already unstable psychological condition to worsen.

After becoming a media star at KYW, she moved to the Washington, D.C., bureau of NBC in 1977, then the New York bureau in 1979. In New York she anchored the Saturday edition of *Nightly News* as well as daily *Updates,* and occasionally filled in as host on the *Today* show. She hosted the *Prime Time Sunday* newsmagazine from 1979 to 1980, and in the years that followed she anchored other news broadcasts on a fill-in basis. In January 1983 she began hosting *Frontline,* a series of hour-long documentaries.

The constant pressure from the network to outshine other networks' female reporter-anchors effectively dehumanized her, and her depressive personality began to take its toll, physically as well as mentally. On the personal side, two failed marriages—one ending in the suicide of her husband—further caused her life to spin out of control.

On 3 October 1983, the viewing audience saw the facade fall away to reveal the lost soul that Savitch had become as she stumbled over words and miscued her reports. Amid rumors of drug dependency and speculation of imminent dismissal, Savitch died after the car in which she was riding overturned into a canal in a freak accident on 23 October 1983.

See also News.

Sawyer, Diane (1945–)

Diane Sawyer is one of the most visible female journalists on television as coanchor of *Good Morning America* since the beginning of 1999, and reporter for various prime-time newsmagazines. Prior to her assignment to *Good Morning America,* Sawyer was coanchor on *Prime Time Live* (ABC, 1989–) and *Turning Point* (1994), excelling at investigative reports and no-nonsense interviews.

In 1997 she was inducted into the television Hall of Fame for "two decades of outstanding journalistic work as a network news correspondent for CBS's *60 Minutes* and ABC's *Prime Time Live.*" She is, in the words of an ABC official, a top talent, although some might say that being called "talent" demeans her journalistic expertise.

Sawyer's first job in television was as a general reporter and weather-person in Louisville, Kentucky, in 1967. She held several administrative press positions within the Nixon administration and assisted Nixon in writing his memoirs.

See also News.

Scarecrow & Mrs. King (1983–1987)

Mrs. Amanda King (Kate Jackson) was a suburban divorcée whose quick wits and vivid imagination supposedly made her very good at espionage and subterfuge. Scarecrow, the code name for agent Lee Stetson (Bruce Boxleitner), took her as his partner, and together they outfoxed the bad guys between her PTA meetings and family grocery shopping.

When her live-in mother, Dottie (Beverly Garland), began to notice her absences, she got a job at International Federal Film Company (the cover name for Scarecrow's employer, the Agency). She eventually completed agents' school, and became Scarecrow's official partner.

As is often the case in TV series, the episodes were full of innuendos and hints of romantic interest between Scarecrow and Mrs. King. Finally, in February 1987, they married, but no one could be told in order to protect Amanda's family from Scarecrow's many enemies.

See also Action/Adventure Genre.

Schaeffer, Rebecca (1967–1989)

Although she was considered a promising actress, Rebecca Schaeffer is remembered as one of the first victims of the type of obsessed fan known as a celebrity stalker. Although most celebrities are only inconvenienced or frightened by their stalkers, Schaeffer was murdered.

Born in Eugene, Oregon, Schaeffer went from model to actress, and first appeared on *One Life to Live* (1984) before finding work in feature films and prime-time television. She appeared as younger sister Patti Russell with Pam Dawber in *My Sister Sam* (1986–1988).

The man who had stalked her appeared on her doorstep to declare his devotion. When she tried to close her door, he shot her and fled. He was caught, tried, and convicted of her murder.

Schultheis, Mindy (1962–)

As executive vice-president of comedy at Twentieth Century Fox Television, Mindy Schultheis works on the development and production of all the organization's comedy projects. One of her more recent efforts is the ABC hit *Dharma and Greg* (1997–).

Schultheis has always worked in the comedy field, starting with Viacom before going to Columbia Television in 1992. In 1996 she moved to Twentieth Century Fox Television as senior vice-president of comedy.

SCIENCE FICTION

For the most part, science fiction is very much a male genre. Early television series such as *Captain Video* (1949–1953), *Tom Corbett—Space Cadet* (1950–1952), and *Space Patrol* (1951–1952) did not include any female characters. Even later series such as *Voyage to the Bottom of the Sea* (1964–1968) and *The Invaders* (1967–1968) were male enclaves of adventure.

Science fiction anthologies such as the original *Twilight Zone* (1959–1965) and the original *Outer Limits* (1963–1965) featured female characters in their stories, but not until *Lost in Space* (1965–1968) did female characters become regular cast members. Of course, since *Lost in Space* featured the Robinson family in a modern rendition of the Swiss Family Robinson, the fact that female characters appeared—mother, Maureen (June Lockhart); eldest daughter, Judy (Marta Kristen); and youngest daughter, Penny (Angela Cartwright)—was easily accepted.

The next year, the original *Star Trek* (1966–1969) appeared, and communications officer Lieutenant Uhura (Nichelle Nichols) became a vanguard for women's and minority equality. Other series from that period, such as *Time Tunnel* (1966–1967) and *Land of the Giants*

(1968–1970), continued to include female characters only as damsels-in-distress or for occasional romantic interest.

The late 1970s included two science fiction series that were greatly promoted, if not widely viewed. *Battlestar Galactica* (1978–1979) was a male-dominated series, but during its first season had two token female characters in Athena (Maren Jensen), the daughter of leader Adama (Lorne Greene), and Cassiopea (Laurette Sprang), a stereotypical reformed-hooker-with-a-heart-of-gold. *Buck Rogers in the 25th Century* (1979–1981), like its original version (1950–1951), featured Wilma Deering (Erin Gray), now a colonel and commander of Earth's defenses against the evil Draconian princess, Ardala (Pamela Hensley). In the first season, Ardala was set on taking over Earth with the help of her henchmen. The second season, Wilma and Buck went off into the galaxy to search for survivors of the great holocaust of the late twentieth century.

An almost instant cult hit of the mid-1980s, *V* (1984–1985) began as a miniseries and evolved into a weekly series. It featured Dr. Julie Parrish (Faye Grant) as one of the leaders of the resis-

(continued on next page)

(continued from previous page)

tance against alien visitors bent on conquering Earth and eating the population. The aliens were led by incredibly evil Diana (Jane Badler), who was challenged for leadership by alien military leader Lydia (June Chadwick).

The *Star Trek* franchise returned to television with *Star Trek: The Next Generation* (1987–1994), supposedly set 78 years after the original voyages of the USS *Enterprise*. As in the original, several female characters appeared in important recurring roles: Lieutenant Tasha Yar (Denise Crosby) was the head of security for the first season until her murder by a strange alien life-form, Dr. Beverly Crusher (Gates McFadden) was the ship's chief medical officer, and Counselor Deanna Troi (Marina Sirtis) was a half-Betazoid who could sense others' feelings.

In the final years of the series (1988–1993), Guinan (Whoopi Goldberg) was the intuitive bartender of Ten Forward Bar aboard the (new) *Enterprise,* which had a crew and dependent complement of over 2,000 people.

The next *Star Trek* series was *Deep Space Nine* (1993–1999), which concerned the inhabitants of a space station orbiting Bajor and guarding a wormhole that allows instant transport to other quadrants of the galaxy. Among the crew were Major (later Colonel) Kira Nerys (Nana Visitor), who had been a Bajorian freedom fighter before being named first officer on the space station, and Chief Science Officer Jadzia Dax (Terry Ferrell), a Trill who had been joined with a symbiont life-form that needed a host to survive. When Jadzia was murdered at the end of the fifth season, the life-form was joined to Ezri Dax (Nicole de Boer), a young Trill who had not gone through the conditioning generally required before joining, and as a result, was

a mass of conflicting feelings and memories (the symbiont had lived several hundred years in both male and female hosts).

In 1995 another *Star Trek* series premiered: *Voyager.* This series featured the first female captain, Kathryn Janeway (Kate Mulgrew), who commanded a small (crew complement approximately 150) federation ship. *Voyager* was hurled 75,000 light-years from federation space in a plasma storm created by a superior alien life-form while chasing a Maquis terrorist ship, which was also caught in the storm. To maximize the possibility of reaching home, the two factions join forces and merge crews before beginning the long trek home.

Besides Captain Janeway, the *Voyager* has several female crew members: Chief Engineer, and former Maquis, B'Elanna Torres (Roxann Biggs-Dawson) is half-human, half-Klingon, and must constantly fight to control her Klingon side; Kes (Jennifer Lien) was a short-lived Ocampan who, through her experiences on *Voyager,* was able to reach a higher plane and become solid energy at the end of the second season; and Seven-of-Nine (Jeri Ryan), a former Borg-assimilated-human whose nanaprobes had been removed to allow her humanness to reestablish itself, joined the crew.

Other than the *Star Trek* series, most science fiction series continue to be male-centered, with no female characters central to the story lines. One such series was *Alien Nation* (1989–1991), based on the 1988 movie by the same name. The two main characters were male detectives Matt Sikes (Gary Graham) and George Francisco (Eric Pierpoint), who happened to be a Newcomer from the planet Tencton. The two female

(continued on next page)

(continued from previous page)

characters on the show included George's wife, Susan (Michele Scarabelli), who worked in advertising, and Cathy Frankel (Terri Treas), a Newcomer biochemist living in the same building as Matt, who found her attractive.

Another popular series, which eventually went to the SciFi cable channel, was *Sliders* (1995–). Again the main character was male— Quinn Mallory (Jerry O'Connell) discovered a way to travel to parallel universes, but once he started traveling ("sliding"), he was unable to get home. (In one episode the travelers did get home, but didn't realize it was *their* dimension.) During the first three seasons, Wade Wells (Sabrina Lloyd), a fellow student and computer whiz, was one of the hapless travelers. The final original episode had Quinn getting shot and dying in Wade's arms. A later version of the show replaced all the characters except Rembrandt "Crying Man" Brown (Cleavant Derricks), a singer inadvertently caught in the time-travel vortex.

In a rarity for a science fiction series, the short-lived *VR5* (1995) featured a female protagonist. Sydney Bloom (Lori Singer) accessed the fantasy level of virtual reality that affected life in the real world, and had to protect herself from virtual villains as well as real-world crooks.

Another series conceived by *Star Trek* creator Gene Roddenberry premiered in 1997: *Earth— The Final Conflict*. Although predominantly male-centered, the series has a strong female presence in the character of Captain Lili Mar-quette (Lisa Howard), a former marine fighter pilot who was not only on the personal staff of Da'an, the American Taelon ambassador, but was also working for the resistance. Interestingly, while Taelons appear androgynous, both major Taelon characters are played by women— Da'an (Leni Parker) and Zo'or (Anita LaSalva). In the 1999 season finale, it appeared that all the main characters had been killed—either in a Taelon sweep against the resistance or when Lili, thinking the resistance had been crushed, set a bomb to destroy the Taelon Mothership.

Another syndicated series is *Stargate: SG-1* (1997–), based on the movie by the same name. Among the four-person main team (SG-1) is Captain Samantha Carter (Amanda Tapping), a theoretical astrophysicist assigned to the project from the Pentagon.

In 1999 the SciFi Channel announced the development of two original series. *First Wave* centers on Cade Foster (Sebastian Spence), who escaped from an alien-laboratory experiment and tries to convince others of the alien threat. *Farscape* focuses on an intergalactic battle for supremacy. Two of the resistance fighters are female: Pa'u (Priestess) Zotoh Zhaan (Virginia Hey) is a blue-toned Delvian spiritualist and Aeryn Sun (Claudia Black) is a former Peacekeeper (the bad guys) working to overthrow her former comrades.

See also *Star Trek; Star Trek: Deep Space Nine; Star Trek: The Next Generation; Star Trek: Voyager.*

SCREWBALL WIVES

A stereotypical characterization mostly popular in the early years of television, screwball wives (and a few screwball singles) were based on the heroines of the popular screwball comedies of the 1930s. These characters, unpredictable and scatterbrained, dealt with the world in a different, seemingly illogical manner, yet were sincere and likable.

The screwball wife was always getting into difficult and embarrassing situations because of her unique way of viewing life and the world. This often led to an erroneous interpretation of a person or circumstance, and the need to be saved by her long-suffering husband.

One of the first screwball wives was MaryKay Sterns (playing herself) of *MaryKay and Johnny* (1947–1950), the unpredictable wife of staid banker Johnny Sterns. During that same period, on the same short-lived Dumont network, another screwball wife, known only as Mrs. Payne (Judy Parrish, 1948–1949; Elaine Stritch, 1949), on *The Growing Paynes* (1948–1949) caused havoc in the life of her insurance sales-

man husband. The character Lucy Ricardo (Lucille Ball) of *I Love Lucy* (1951–1957) could technically be classified as a screwball wife, although the portrayal went beyond the general category into a realm all its own.

Other screwball wives over the years include Joan Stevens (Joan Davis) of *I Married Joan* (1952–1955), Liz Cooper (Joan Caulfield, 1953–1955; Vanessa Brown, 1955) of *My Favorite Husband* (1953–1955), Gladys Porter (Cara Williams) of *Pete and Gladys* (1960–1962), Glynis Granville (Glynis Johns) of *Glynis* (1963), Paula Hollister (Paula Prentiss) of *He & She* (1967–1968), and Debbie Thompson (Debbie Reynolds) of *The Debbie Reynolds Show* (1969–1970).

The screwball wife characterization is seldom seen today on television because it is now politically incorrect to portray a woman in such a condescending manner, yet elements of the screwball personality can still be noted in certain characters, such as Carol Foster (Suzanne Somers) of *Step by Step* (1991–1996).

Sheena, Queen of the Jungle (1955–1956)

This series, a weak parody of the Tarzan concept, had jungle excitement, wild animals, and hilariously trite dialogue (even by 1950s standards). The series is best remembered as being the second program to feature a woman as the lead in an action series.

Supposedly set in Kenya but filmed in Mexico, this series featured Sheena (former model Irish McCalla) as White Goddess, protector of beasts and natives. Instead of the Tarzan yell, she had a hunting horn to announce her imminent arrival. In a reversal of normal roles, Sheena was always saving her trader friend, Bob (Christian Drake), with the aid of her chimpanzee companion, Chim.

SEXISM

Sexism is defined in Webster's Collegiate Dictionary as (1) prejudice or discrimination based on sex, and (2) behavior, conditions, or attitudes that foster stereotypes of social roles based on sex. An examination of female television characters reveals that these characters have not "come a long way, baby!"

Although female characters are no longer relegated to being merely wives and mothers or wanna-be wives, neither have they been released from these roles. Female characters are still classified by their relationship to the male characters on the program—haves (wives or girl-friends) and have-nots (single and looking).

Female characters are no longer depicted as helpless without a man, but they are still shown as being happiest when a man is in their lives. The old adage "success means nothing without someone to share it with" is very evident in the portrayal of female characters.

A female character can have a job or a family—but never both successfully. One aspect always suffers from the attention given the other. Well-remembered characters Claire Huxtable (*The Cosby Show,* 1984–1992) and Elyse Keaton (*Family Ties,* 1982–1989), both professional women (lawyer and architect, respectively), were always shown within the home, with little attention given to the careers they had worked so hard to achieve.

Even if the female character is shown in a professional light, such as Dr. Samantha Waters (*Profiler,* 1996–), the story line makes it clear that her private life suffers from her dedication to her career. Ally McBeal (*Ally McBeal,* 1997–) is depicted as an endearing neurotic who obsesses about her social/love life.

Balanced is not a word used to describe female characters on television.

The series was based on the popular comic strip created by S. M. Iger and Will Eisner in the 1930s. McCalla eventually left show business and became a successful artist and designer.

Sheilah Graham in Hollywood (1951)

In the early 1950s, many programs on both radio and TV were only 15 minutes in length. This series, hosted by syndicated gossip columnist Sheila Graham, was a combination of movie news, star gossip, fashion news, and star interviews. The show was broadcast live in Los Angeles, and later rebroadcast nationally on NBC using a kinescope made during the local broadcast.

Actress Irish McCalla in leopard skins as Sheena in the 1955–1956 series Sheena, Queen of the Jungle. *(Archive Photos)*

Shephard, Greer (1967–)

Born in New York, Greer Shephard studied English and French at Amherst College, where she graduated Phi Beta Kappa, but went into entertainment because of her interest in literature and storytelling. As vice-president of drama series development at ABC until 1998, her awareness of television's influence on social beliefs regarding such topics as gender, class, and race greatly influenced the development of new series.

Shirley Temple's Storybook (1958–1961)

Shirley Temple, the most popular child star of the 1930s, was host, narrator, and occasional star of this dramatic anthology of fairy tales and popular children's stories. The show was a semiregular program through 1956, then monthly through 1959. In 1960 it became a weekly program and was renamed *The Shirley Temple Show.*

Shirley's World (1971–1972)

This short-lived series starred movie actor Shirley MacLaine in her only weekly sitcom effort. She played a modern reporter-photographer based in London, who traveled the world on various assignments for the fictitious *World Illustrated* magazine.

Her impulsive nature led her to become overly involved in the lives of her subjects, ranging from spies to movie stars, with predictably comic results. One of the main attractions of the series was that it was filmed in various exciting locations in England, Scotland, Tokyo, and Hong Kong, among other glamour spots around the world.

Shore, Dinah (1917–1994)

Dinah Shore spent most of her career on television. Her southern charm and easy friendliness made her a natural for the imaginary intimacy of television. Her pure-pitched singing voice made her popular on the early musical-variety shows before she received her own series.

Her first series, *The Dinah Shore Show* (1951–1957), was a 15-minute musical show aired twice weekly after the nightly NBC news broadcast. Concurrently with this series during the last year, Shore appeared on an hour-long series, *The Dinah Shore Chevy Show* (1956–1963). This longer format enabled her to feature guests and include skits and production numbers.

After this series ended, she did not have another show of her own until *Dinah's Place* (1970–1974). This series was a combination talk show and down-home country advice forum. Her guests not only talked, but shared a favorite pastime with viewers. On one show, Joanne Woodward shared needlepoint, and on another, Ethel Kennedy played the piano. The show won an Emmy in 1973 for Outstanding Program Achievement in Daytime.

After being inexplicably canceled by NBC in 1974, the show went into syndicated production and changed the name to simply *Dinah!* (1974–1980). The show was available in either 60- or 90-minute formats and featured almost every popular performer of that period.

In 1991, Shore was inducted into the Television Hall of Fame.

Short, Short Dramas (1952–1953)

This 15-minutes series hosted by model and cover girl Ruth Woods aired twice weekly. Woods introduced the storyteller/cast member, who in turn established the background and setting of the playette, then joined the rest of the cast and started the play. The offerings alternated between serious and light, and the cast was made up of relative unknowns, some of whom later became stars, such as E. G. Marshall, Cliff Robertson, Tony Randall, and Leslie Nielsen.

The Singing Lady (1948–1950)

Irene Wicker had been a radio favorite for more than 20 years before she brought her program of children's stories and songs to television. The topics emphasized good behavior and moral lessons as acted out by the Suzari Marionettes.

In June 1950, Wicker's name appeared in *Red Channels,* a right-wing publication purporting to list Communist sympathizers. Although her series was still popular with viewers, in August 1950 her program was canceled. All citations were proved erroneous, but her career was destroyed because, even after being proved innocent, she was still controversial at a time when conformity was the only way to prosper.

See also Blacklist; McCarthyism.

Sisters (1991–1996)

Set in Winnetka, Illinois, this series involved the Reed sisters' lives and families. Alex (Swoosie Kurtz) was the eldest sister, married to a plastic surgeon who was also a cross-dresser. Georgie (Patricia Kalember) was a real estate agent whose husband was unemployed. Teddy (Sela Ward) was the family free spirit and an artist. Frankie (Julianne Phillips), the youngest, was a marketing analyst in love with Teddy's ex-husband.

Each episode began with the sisters in a steam room discussing their lives and included stylized flashbacks in which their younger and adult selves interacted. The stories unfolded in soap opera fashion from one improbable situation to another.

In April 1993, the sisters discovered that their father had an illegitimate daughter, Charlie (Jo Anderson), who had become a doctor and had enough problems to make her eligible to join the family. And then there were five.

SITUATION COMEDIES

Despite the social and cultural shifts of recent decades, the situation comedy (sitcom) remains popular and consistently represented on program schedules. Essentially two ten-minute acts and an epilogue separated by commercials, one of the main appeals of the sitcom is the guaranteed resolution of all problems, because conflicts and disagreements are never serious. Another attraction of the sitcom is the familiarity derived from character predictability and the use of limited sets. These elements encourage the viewers' identification with the series' characters and their world.

Sitcoms have historically been a genre in which women are easily included because the story line generally involves a family or pseudo family setting. This offers women an obvious, if limiting, showcase for their talents. In fact, in the early years of television, 80 percent of the women appearing on television were in sitcoms.

The sitcoms of the 1950s and early 1960s were vehicles of postwar socialization as well as entertainment. To get socially approved messages across to the public, two stock characters or archetypes were developed: the scatterbrained wife and her exasperated but loving and understanding husband. The programs of the era emphasized that a woman's place was in the home, and that women needed men to protect and guide them.

As a result, women in sitcoms of that period were generally portrayed as little more than children, who could do nothing without the guidance and direction of their paternalistic husbands-cum-fathers. This was made acceptable and even ideal by portraying the husbands' loving tolerance.

The first sitcom developed for television that was not transplanted from radio was *MaryKay and Johnny* (1947–1950), concerning the lives of real-life married couple MaryKay and Johnny Sterns. In the soon-to-be-traditional role for sitcom wives, MaryKay was scatterbrained and in need of husbandly direction. The plots involved real-life issues faced by a young married couple in the postwar years while promoting traditional values.

As mentioned above, many programs moved to the new medium from radio. Early hits included *Mama* (1949–1956), about a Norwegian immigrant family in San Francisco, and *The Goldbergs* (1949–1954), about a Jewish family living in New York (and later, as a reflection of the urban exodus of the 1950s, in the suburbs). Other popular shows included *The George Burns and Gracie Allen Show* (1950–1958), concerning the duo's "everyday" lives, and the megahit *I Love Lucy* (1951–1957), about the Ricardos and Mertzes' lives, and the trouble Lucy and Ethel inevitably got into trying to circumvent Ricky's rules.

Another archetypal character from the early period created to promote the postwar women-back-to-the-homes ideology was the single, working-woman wannabe-wife, such as Connie Brooks (*Our Miss Brooks*, 1952–1956) and Sally Rogers (*The Dick Van Dyke Show*, 1961–1966). No matter how fulfilling or rewarding her job might seem, the working woman was never satisfied or content because she was unmarried. Although the real-life single working woman threatened the ideal of the stay-at-home housewife, the threat was lessened by the televised depiction of her as really wanting to be married and relentless in her pursuit of a husband.

In the late 1950s and early 1960s, the urban-based husband-wife sitcoms were replaced by the

(continued on next page)

(continued from previous page)

middle-class suburban family sitcom. These re-volved around the "normal" problems of white, middle-class daily life, and emphasized child-rearing and socialization while touting postwar consumerism. These programs showcased the suburban ideal of contentment and made the family-centered, middle-class lifestyle seem to be the only acceptable version of the good life.

While every perfect family needed a mother, these roles were strictly window dressing: sup-portive of husband as head of household and decision-maker. The nurturing mother was a staple character of the period and was exempli-fied by such well-remembered characters (thanks to syndication) as June Cleaver (*Leave It to Beaver,* 1957–1966), Margaret Anderson (*Father Knows Best,* 1954–1963), Harriet Nelson (*The Adventures of Ozzie and Harriet,* 1952–1966), and Donna Stone (*The Donna Reed Show,* 1958–1966). These televisual wives, while no longer scatterbrained, relied to one degree or another on their husband's advice and guidance. The child-rearing philosophy of "wait until your father gets home" was implicit.

The sitcom world of that period could only be described as picture-perfect. Located wholly within the suburban landscape, the work world was almost entirely ignored. Yet, these programs all presented an idealized world where Ameri-can values and the Puritan work ethic were re-warded with middle-class affluence.

The characterization changed little through-out the 1960s, although the idealized nuclear family was enlarged to include domestic help as surrogate mothers. Therefore, Hazel (*Hazel,* 1961–1966), the managing maid, mothered the Baxter family, and Katy Holstrom (*Farmer's Daughter,* 1963–1966) was governess to Con-gressman Morley's two young sons. Life on sit-coms was tranquil and serene, even while the country experienced violent protests and angry movements against the war in Vietnam, pov-erty, racism, and sexism. Except for the reality shows of Norman Lear, the sitcom world remained unaffected by the social unrest of the period.

In what seemed to be a response to the women's movement, the networks eliminated women from programs by creating male-only environments. The few shows that did feature women in prominent roles portrayed them as supernatural beauties who lived to serve their men (*I Dream of Jeannie,* 1965–1970, and *Be-witched,* 1964–1972) or who were innocent and not particularly bright (*The Beverly Hillbillies,* 1962–1971, and *Petticoat Junction,* 1963–1970). Even the supposedly ground-breaking series *That Girl* (1966–1971), praised for being about a single career woman, was actually the story of Daddy's little girl becoming (her) fiancé's little girl.

The 1970s brought the advent of the work-place sitcoms with the premiere of *The Mary Tyler Moore Show* (1970–1977), but even into the 1980s, television presented females as primarily home-centered no matter what their career sit-uation, or as office wives who took care of their coworkers. As long as women remained relegat-ed predominantly to sitcoms, their issues and problems could be trivialized by comedic treat-ment, which sometimes allowed derogatory rep-resentations under the guise of laughter.

The 1980s reflected a nationwide backlash against women and the women's movement. Female-centered programs declined dramati-cally, while all-male programming increased.

(continued on next page)

(continued from previous page)

However, with the debut of *Murphy Brown* (1988–1998), a forceful, independent woman was presented in prime time. After the popularity and success of *Murphy Brown,* other work-family sitcoms have been introduced revolving around female characters. Still, women in sitcoms are usually family- or relationship-focused even though they are involved in various careers, subtly reinforcing the myth that "a woman's place is in the home."

See also *Bewitched; Farmer's Daughter; Fifties Moms; The Goldbergs; Hazel; I Dream of Jeannie; I Love Lucy; Mama; The Mary Tyler Moore Show; MaryKay and Johnny; Murphy Brown; Our Miss Brooks;* Rural Women; and *That Girl.*

Smith, Maureen (1956–)

Maureen Smith, now general manager of Fox Kids Network and executive vice-president of Fox Family Worldwide, was one of the original employees at the fledgling Fox Network in 1986. She began in research and marketing, and was eventually named vice-president of children's research.

She moved to Fox Kids Network in 1996 as vice-president of planning, responsible for scheduling and station relations, before being named to her current position in May 1998.

The Snoop Sisters (1973–1974)

Elderly sisters Ernesta (Helen Hayes) and Gwen (Mildred Natwick) Snoop were successful mystery writers with a penchant for finding "real" mysteries. A possible inspiration for *Murder, She Wrote* (1984–1996), the sisters provided the brainpower, while their bodyguard-chauffeur, Barney (Lou Antonio), or policeman-nephew Steve (Bert Convy) did the physical work.

An early senior-citizen offering that alternated with three other series on NBC's *Mystery Movie,* the series not only featured two gifted actors in Hayes and Natwick but portrayed older women who were as intelligent as they were gracious and charming.

See also Action/Adventure Genre; Older Women on Television.

So This Is Hollywood (1955)

This series featured two women trying to make it in show business and the difficulties they encountered. Queenie Dugan (Mitzi Green) was a veteran stuntwoman who knew her way around, and realizing that she would never be a star, was eager to promote her roommate's career. Her roommate was Kim Tracy (Virginia Gibson), a talented newcomer who worked as an extra while waiting for her big break.

The humor derived from the problems encountered by the roommates and the manipulations in which they engaged to bring Kim to the attention of various producers and directors.

Soap Operas, Daytime

Humorist James Thurber defined the soap opera as "a kind of sandwich; between thick slices of advertising, spread 12 minutes of dialogue, add predicament, villainy, and female suffering in equal measure, throw in a dash of nobility, sprinkle with tears . . . and serve five times a week."

Estimated to bring in anywhere from 55 to 75 percent of all network revenue, the soap opera didn't receive professional recognition until 1974 when the daytime Emmys were established. The genre was further legitimized in an article in *Time* (January 1976) entitled "Sex and Suffering in the Afternoons."

Known for their excessive, often extreme plot structures, soap operas focus on issues of importance to women and emphasize personal relationships and emotions. The plots are, at their core, merely good versus evil played out in a town populated by doctors, lawyers, millionaires, and business magnates.

Although long the cornerstone of daytime schedules, in recent years soap operas have steadily declined in viewership. In the first week of January 1997, the three networks' total soap opera viewership was approximately 14.1 million, but during the same period in 1998 the viewership was down to 12.4 million.

This trend and the concern that the established audience is aging have motivated the introduction of younger characters involved in "relevant" story lines in an effort to attract younger viewers. Of further concern is the popularity of program websites and periodicals where viewers can keep up with the action without watching.

History

More than any other genre, the soap opera can be credited to, or blamed on, one individual—Irna Phillips. Through her own creations and those of the people she trained, the soap opera has become a staple of daytime television. Serial stories date back to the early 1800s, when newspapers and magazines printed monthly installments of longer works. Then came comic strips with continuing stories, radio, and finally television.

After losing control of her first effort, *Painted Dreams,* in 1937, Phillips created *The Guiding Light,* the longest-running soap opera in broadcast history. In a story line originally based on small-town minister Rev. John Ruthledge and his parishioners, Phillips established the major elements of the genre: a continuous series of first

(continued on next page)

(continued from previous page)

and second acts, and a constant juggling of dominant and secondary stories. She also employed the quintessential element of the soap opera, the cliff-hanger, to keep the audience tuned in for new developments.

By 1939 the genre was regularly referred to as "soap opera," probably because the main sponsors were manufacturers of household products and cleansers whose target audience consisted of housewives. From the appearance of the first soap opera, psychological professionals voiced concern over the audience's fascination with the characters' misfortunes and unhappiness. A New York psychiatrist, D. Louis Berg, likened the soap opera to Hitler's propaganda machine, and charged that both destroyed the human nervous system.

After World War II, the soap opera moved to the new medium of television. The first soap operas were shown on the Dumont Network and were radio transplants: *Big Sister* and *Aunt Jenny's True Life Stories.* In 1946, Dumont created *Faraway Hill,* but the new series lasted only three months. Even Phillips's reworking of *Painted Dreams* failed.

The first successful soap opera was *Search for Tomorrow,* which premiered in 1951 and ran until 1986. By emphasizing close-ups and limited sets, the audience became emotionally attached to and comfortable with the characters.

Soon Phillips brought *The Guiding Light* to television ("*The*" was dropped in 1977). It no longer focused on a religious community; the core family was now the Bauers, a German-American family looking for a better life.

Soap operas were still 15 minutes in length until 1956, when Phillips created *As the World Turns* and initiated the half-hour program. This longer format allowed Phillips to emphasize two tenets of the genre: The most important part of the story is the exchange of feelings and memories among characters, and any incident should affect the entire community in some manner. In addition, the longer format allowed more characters from differing backgrounds to be introduced and explored.

In 1963, ABC premiered *General Hospital.* Produced in Hollywood, it introduced the more polished production techniques of filmmaking to the genre. In 1965 another Hollywood product was introduced: *Days of Our Lives,* the first soap opera to be broadcast in color.

By the 1960s, Phillips was sharing the soap opera limelight with one of her protégés, Agnes Nixon. After reviving the tired story line of the established serial *Another World,* Nixon created *One Life to Live,* in which she introduced racial diversity into the soap opera world. Nixon created the character of Carla Gray (Ellen Holly), a young black woman passing for white, and in the process made soap opera history with the first black actor to appear as a main character.

Another Phillips protégé, Bill Bell, created two successful soap operas, *The Young and the Restless* (1973–) and *The Bold and the Beautiful* (1987–). By the 1980s, soap operas were being created using real locations, so that *The Bold and the Beautiful* was set in Los Angeles in the fashion industry.

Together, this soap opera triumvirate created one of the most familiar and defining soap opera characters: the bitch goddess. A woman who will stop at nothing to achieve her own happiness and uses her sexuality as a weapon to achieve her goals, this harridan has lit up the

(continued on next page)

(continued from previous page)

soap opera world since the early 1960s. Two such "bitches" are Rachel Davis (Robin Strasser, 1967–1972; Victoria Wyndham, 1972–) of *Another World* and Erica Kane (Susan Lucci) of *All My Children*. (In 1999, Lucci finally won the daytime Emmy for Best Actress after being nominated for 17 years without winning.)

One analysis of story lines revealed that the three most popular themes for soap opera stories are (1) mystery and intrigue, (2) crime and punishment, and (3) romance, love, and sex. Of course, these themes are often combined or paired with other themes to create variety and fit the environment of the series.

Soap operas have been able to explore issues and topics denied to prime-time television until more recently, partly because they are seen during the day. Racism was explored in the 1960s, and spousal abuse was included in the story line of *One Life to Live* in the 1970s. Other controversial topics include homosexuality, abortion, white supremacy, rape, the right to die, interracial romance, Native American beliefs, and Alzheimer's disease.

Many soap operas have been aired over the history of television, and currently 11 daytime soap operas appear in one-hour productions and one in a half-hour series: *All My Children* (ABC, 1970–), *As the World Turns* (CBS, 1956), *The Bold and the Beautiful* (CBS, 1987–), *Days of Our Lives* (NBC, 1965–), *General Hospital* (ABC, 1963–), *Guiding Light* (CBS, 1952–), *One Life to Live* (ABC, 1968–), *Port Charles* (half-hour, ABC, 1997–), *Sunset Beach* (NBC, 1997–), *The Young and the Restless* (CBS, 1973–), and the newly created *Passions* (NBC, 1999–). Of these, eight were created by Irna Phillips, Agnes Nixon, or Bill Bell—together or individually.

PAST SOAP OPERAS

Another Life, 1981–1984
Another World, 1964–1999
Ben Jarrod, 1963
The Bennetts, 1953–1954
The Best of Everything, 1970
Bright Promise, 1969–1972
The Brighter Day, 1954–1962
Capitol, 1982–1987
The Catlins, 1983–1985
The Clear Horizon, 1960–1962
Concerning Miss Marlowe, 1954–1955
Dark Shadows, 1966–1971
The Doctors, 1963–1982
The Edge of Night, 1956–1984
The Egg and I, 1951–1952
Fairmeadows, USA, 1951–1952
The First Hundred Years, 1950–1952
First Love, 1954–1955
Follow Your Heart, 1953–1954
From These Roots, 1958–1961
Full Circle, 1960–1961
Generations, 1989–1991
Golden Windows, 1954–1955
The Greatest Gift, 1954–1955
Hawkins Falls, 1951–1955
Hidden Faces, 1968–1969
How to Survive a Marriage, 1974–1975
Kitty Foyle, 1958
Love Is a Many Splendored Thing, 1967–1973
Love of Life, 1951–1980
Lovers and Friends, 1977–1978
Loving, 1983–1997
Miss Susan, 1951
Moment of Truth, 1965

Morning Star, 1965–1966
Never Too Young, 1965–1966
The Nurses, 1965–1967
One Man's Family, 1954–1955
Our Five Daughters, 1962
Paradise Bay, 1965–1966
Portia Faces Life, 1954–1955
Return to Peyton Place, 1972–1974
The Road of Life, 1954–1955
The Road to Reality, 1960–1961
Ryan's Hope, 1975–1989
Santa Barbara, 1984–1993
Search for Tomorrow, 1951–1986
The Secret Storm, 1954–1974
The Seeking Heart, 1954
Somerset, 1970–1976
Texas, 1980–1982
These Are My Children, 1949
Three Steps to Heaven, 1953–1954
A Time for Us, 1964–1966
A Time to Love, 1954
Today Is Ours, 1958
Tribes, 1980
Valiant Lady, 1953–1957
Where the Heart Is, 1969–1973
A Woman to Remember, 1949
Woman with a Past, 1954
A World Apart, 1970–1971
The World of Mr. Sweeney, 1954–1955
Young Dr. Marlowe, 1958–1963
The Young Marrieds, 1964–1966

See also Dark Shadows; Nixon, Agnes;
Phillips, Irna; Soap Operas, Prime-Time.

SOAP OPERAS, PRIME-TIME

Like all soap operas, the prime-time versions focus on the characters' personal lives and the story lines are incredibly complex. The first prime-time soap opera was *One Man's Family* (1949–1952), centering on the well-to-do Barbour family in San Francisco.

The next to appear on prime time was *Peyton Place* (1964–1969), which was loosely based on the 1956 novel by Grace Metalious. Peyton Place was a small New England town in which Allison MacKenzie (Mia Farrow) lived—a hotbed of extramarital affairs, conspiracies, and betrayals. At the height of its popularity, the series aired original episodes up to three nights a week and had a cast of over 100 in recurring, if not starring, roles.

Nighttime soap operas did not appear again until the late 1970s. Although shown very late at night, generally after the 11 o'clock news, the first soap opera parody—*Mary Hartman, Mary Hartman* (1975–1978)—was very popular. On this series, Mary Hartman (Louise Lasser) was the impressionable housewife who based her life on the "truths" found on television, and armed with this "wisdom" was able to calmly, or obliviously, meet the challenges of living in Fernwood, Ohio.

The next year, soap operas once again hit prime time when ABC created the serial drama *Family* (1976–1980), which followed the lives of the Lawrence family in a middle-class neighborhood in Pasadena, California. The next prime-time soap opera was another parody of the genre, entitled *Soap* (1977–1981). The series followed the preposterous events in the lives of the wealthy Tates and the middle-class Campbells, joined together by sisters Jessica Tate (Katherine

Mia Farrow on the phone in TV's Peyton Place, *1964–1969. Based on Grace Metalious's popular novel, which had been made into a movie in 1957. (Archive Photos)*

Helmond) and Mary Campbell (Cathryn Damon).

When a soap opera again appeared on prime time, a middle-class environment in a small town was not good enough. Now the characters were larger than life and richer than Croesus. The first "oil" opera, originally conceived as a five-part miniseries, was *Dallas* (1978–1991). The series centered on the megarich Ewing family and the people they encountered in their quest for more money (greed) and more love

(continued on next page)

(continued from previous page)

(lust and sex). The character who turned the miniseries into a prime-time fixture was the evil and unscrupulous heir to the Ewing fortune, J. R. (Larry Hagman), although the program had been intended as a vehicle for Victoria Principal, who played Pam Ewing, "good wife" to "good brother" Bobby Ewing (Patrick Duffy).

With the popularity of *Dallas,* other soap operas about the rich, greedy, and dysfunctional followed. The first was *Knots Landing* (1979–1993), a spinoff centered around the weak-willed, middle Ewing brother, Gary, and his family. They lived a middle-class life on an event-laden cul-de-sac called Seaview Circle. Although less well remembered than *Dallas,* at the time it ended, *Knots Landing* was the third-longest-running series in television history (after *Gunsmoke* and *Dallas*).

The next oil-clone was *Dynasty* (1981–1989). This series featured the overt personification of good and evil. The "good" was Krystal (Linda Evans), the glamorous young wife of oil magnate Blake Carrington (John Forsythe), while the "evil" was Alexis (Joan Collins), Blake's ex-wife and villainess incarnate.

Although the confrontations between Krystal and Alexis kept the viewers happy for several years, especially the seasonal catfights, in 1984 a new character was added: Dominique Devereau (Diahann Carroll), the first (self-described) "black bitch" on television. She was less overt about her evilness than Alexis, but she had more reason to plot Blake's end—she was his illegitimate half-sister.

Close on the successful heels of *Dallas* and *Dynasty* came other, less successful prime-time soap operas: *The Colbys* (1985–1987), a weak *Dynasty* spinoff; *Flamingo Road* (1981–1982), a middle-class version of sex and corruption; and *Falcon Crest* (1981–1990), featuring lust and greed among a wealthy wine-making family.

After the oil operas lost favor, soap operas again passed from the prime-time schedule for a few years. Then, a teenage soap opera called *Beverly Hills 90210* (1990–) appeared and caught the favor of viewers. The teen-angst drama originally dealt with realistic issues facing teenagers and, as the characters grew older, the problems faced by college students . . . then young professionals . . .

Following on this success, *Melrose Place* (1992–1999) was created. This serial followed the romantic antics and backstabbing among the upwardly mobile inhabitants of an apartment complex in Los Angeles. After a drop-off in ratings, the producers introduced a villainess in Alexis's mold: Amanda (Heather Locklear), who kept everyone in turmoil and betrayed everyone with abandon.

SPORTS

The coverage of sporting events still focuses primarily on male teams, although women's sports are slowly receiving network attention and fan support. Women's golf, tennis, track, and basketball are receiving increased exposure, while women's gymnastics and figure skating have long been popular with both the viewing audience and sponsors. Names like Debbie Thomas, Nancy Kerrigan, Michelle Kwan, Tara Lipinski, and Kerri Shrug are as familiar as, if slightly less famous than, John Elway. Female athletes such as the WNBA's Cynthia Cooper have begun to appear in product endorsements.

One of the first sporting events to be broadcast was the roller derby, which featured both a male and female squad on each team, and was a hit through the early 1960s. Various cities had teams (such as the Los Angeles Thunderbirds and the San Francisco Bombers) that competed in one of the first examples of "sports entertainment." Sports entertainment was later used to depict choreographed competitions with the competitor as actor.

Such women as Joanie Weston, Ann Carvello, Gerry Murray, and Midge "Toughie" Brasuhn were the stars of the sport, and as popular with viewers as any of the male stars. In 1999, *RollerJam* premiered on TNN, bringing back competitions among such teams as the California Quakes, the Florida Sundogs, the Nevada Dice, and the New York Enforcers (the designated "bad" team). Filmed at Universal Studios in Florida, the competitions are still "sports entertainment," featuring athletes from speed skating, ice hockey, and other contact sports skating on rollerblades.

As the century neared its end, women entered into previously male sporting events. Female wrestlers became more prevalent as competitors, rather than as fashionable accessories to a male entourage. Boxing, long thought to be a male domain, incorporated a women's division.

Not only did broadcast time allocated to women's sporting events increase, but so did women's presence and involvement in male sports. Women have joined the ranks of sportscasters, covering football as well as female sporting events. Leslie Visser was the first female football anchor.

Julie Moran (1962–), a former track and basketball athlete, was the first female to host *The Wide World of Sports* (ABC, 1994–1995) after cohosting *Inside Stuff* (1990–1991) with Ahmed Rashid, before eventually joining *Entertainment Tonight* as a correspondent. Robin Roberts (1960–) hosts *In the Spotlight* (ESPN, 1994–), as well as *The Wide World of Sports* (ABC, 1998–) and the Sunday edition of *Good Morning America* (ABC, 1998–). Pam Oliver (Fox), Michele Tafoya (CBS), and Bonnie Bernstein (CBS) deliver sideline reports and features during NFL games.

Since 1992, Hannah Storm has filled several broadcast roles for NBC Sports, including interviewer, sideline reporter, and host for baseball and basketball, as well as special Olympic coverage.

Stahl, Lesley (1941–)

Lesley Stahl was one of many women who entered television news as a result of pressure brought to bear on the industry by the women's movement. These women are sometimes referred to as "the class of '72."

She began as a reporter for CBS based in Washington, D.C. She covered the White House for eight years (1978–1986), gaining fame and public attention during Watergate, and was CBS's national affairs analyst (1986–1989). Concurrently with these positions, Stahl was anchor and interviewer on *Face the Nation* (1983–1990).

Stahl appears on *60 Minutes* as a correspondent, and has served as coeditor since 1991. In 1998, Stahl published her memoirs, *Reporting Live*.

See also News.

Star Trek (1966–1969)

Arguably the most successful television series of all time when measured by its lasting impact on popular culture, *Star Trek* resulted in several successful spinoffs and a feature film franchise of more than seven movies.

Star Trek was the first program to feature an integrated cast—racially and planetarily. Although plagued by production difficulties and personality conflicts during its first run, it developed a cult following and has been perpetually seen in syndicated reruns since the series ended in 1969.

Most of the major cast members were male, but the series boasted one female of command rank. Lieutenant Uhura (Nichelle Nichols), the communications officer, was notable as being both a female and a black role model. Although she generally needed to be saved by male crew members, she was portrayed as efficient and extremely competent at her job.

After the cancellation of the series, the crew continued to "go where no man has gone before" in an animated version of the series that was broadcast for two years (1973–1975) and featured the voices of the original cast members, except Lieutenant Pavel Chekkov (Walter Koenig). Although the stories were thought to be too complex for young viewers, the show was popular with older viewers and the faithful cult following of the original *Star Trek*.

See also Nichols, Nichelle; Science Fiction.

Star Trek: Deep Space Nine (1993–1999)

This series centered around the events on a space station orbiting Bajor after a Cardassian occupation of that planet. The space station was commanded by Benjamin Sisko (Avery Brooks), but the first officer was Major (later Colonel) Kira Nerys (Nana Visitor), a former Bajorian freedom fighter. On the station for the first five seasons was Chief Science Officer Jadzia Dax (Terry Ferrell), a Trill who was killed not long after she married Worf (Michael Dorn), a Klingon Star Fleet officer first seen on *The Next Generation*. After her death, her symbiont was joined to Lieutenant Ezri Dax (Nicole deBoer), a young Trill who had never undergone training to be joined, and was deeply conflicted by her new condition.

The series ended with the Federation winning the war against the Dominion and Sisko joining The Prophets (an advanced race to which his mother belonged), leaving Colonel Kira in charge of the station until his return. Ezri had solved many of her inner conflicts and was free to pursue a relationship with the station's chief medical officer, Julian Bashir (Siddig El Fadil).

See also Science Fiction.

Star Trek: The Next Generation (1987–1994)

This series began where the original *Star Trek* left off. Supposedly 78 years had passed since the first *Enterprise* missions, and the new USS *Enterprise* held a crew and dependent complement of over 2,000 people.

As in all Gene Roddenberry series, several female characters were seen in recurring roles. Lieutenant Tasha Yar (Denise Crosby) was head of security until her death by a mysterious alien life-form. Dr. Beverly Crusher (Gates McFadden) was the ship's chief medical officer and spent one year as head of Star Fleet Medical, during which time she was replaced aboard the *Enterprise* by Dr. Kate Pulaski (Diana Muldaur, 1988–1989).

Counselor Deanna Troi (Marina Sirtis) was half-Betazoid and could sense others' feelings and motivations. For the final years of the series, Guinan (Whoopi Goldberg) joined the crew and ran the Ten Forward Bar.

See also Science Fiction.

Publicity shot of the cast from the first season of Voyager. *Pictured clockwise from top left are Garrett Wang, Robert Duncan McNeill, Tim Russ, Roxann Dawson, Robert Picardo, Robert Beltran, Ethan Philips, Kate Mulgrew, and Jennifer Lien. (Photofest)*

Star Trek: Voyager (1995–)

The fourth series to evolve from the original *Star Trek* (1966–1969) concept, this series features the first female captain of a Federation starship who appears on a weekly basis. Although *Voyager* is a small ship by *Enterprise* standards, the crew numbers more than 150.

While chasing a Maquis terrorist ship, both *Voyager* and the Maquis ship were caught in a plasma storm that hurled them 75,000 light-years away to the Delta quadrant of deep space. When the Maquis ship was destroyed, the crews joined forces to find a way home.

The captain of *Voyager* is Kathryn Janeway (Kate Mulgrew), a graduate of Star Fleet Academy, who made Chakotay (Robert Beltran), the captain of the Maquis ship, her first officer and integrated the rest of the crew according to their specialties. Another Maquis who was given command status was B'Elanna Torres (Roxann Biggs-Dawson), a half-Klingon/half-human in charge of engineering.

For the first two years, Kes (Jennifer Lien) was also a member of the crew. She was an Ocampan whose life expectancy was nine years, but in her final episode, she became a formless life-energy that went into space after propelling the *Voyager* several light-years toward Earth. To fill her place on the crew, Seven-of-Nine (Jeri Ryan) was introduced during the 1997–1998 season. A human who had been assimilated into the Borg, she was rescued by Captain Janeway, and her Borg technology removed to allow her to become more human.

See also Science Fiction; *Star Trek*.

Stewart, Martha (1942–)

After a successful career as a stockbroker on Wall Street, Martha Stewart started a home-based catering business that eventually led to her becoming the ubiquitous priestess of refined living. Her empire has grown to include magazines, books, television, the Internet, radio, merchandise endorsements with Kmart, and a line of latex paint.

Martha Stewart Living (1992–) appears daily on more than 200 stations nationally and features experts in areas of home decoration and home improvement. Her magazine, which predates the television show by two years and is also titled *Martha Stewart Living,* is published monthly. Stewart has published 21 books, the most recent being *Martha Stewart's Healthy*

STEREOTYPES

Characters depicted on television are generally stereotyped representations of individuals. The nurturing mother, the brilliant child, the bumbling father, the street-smart black—these are all easily identified by viewers because they abound in cultural entertainment.

When characters are not allowed to reflect current changes in the cultural climate because networks fear they might alienate some viewers, the use of stereotypes belittles the forces of change as well as the particular group being limited by the stereotype. On television, women have always been depicted as family-centered and other-focused. Even in the 1990s, when perhaps more female characters appeared in series than at any other time in television's history, most of these characters were more interested in their romantic situation than in career advancement or personal growth. Women continue to be defined, overtly or covertly, by their marital status, while men are defined by their occupation.

Studies indicate that repeated images in popular culture, modeled over time, can become internalized by the audience, and this pervasive, institutionalized depiction of women may well contribute to the inability of some to discern women as capable and competent individuals rather than a "homogenized-same."

Depicting female characters, even career women, as preoccupied with their romantic rather than professional lives limits the perceived options available to women. The television world seems to say that working is fine for women, but only as a prelude to real feminine fulfillment through a husband and family.

Quick Cook (1997) and *The Best of Martha Stewart Living: Handmade Christmas* (1998).

A 1997 biography, *Martha Stewart: Just Desserts,* presented a picture of a perfectionist with sometimes disturbing and abusive behavior. Purporting that Stewart reinvents her past, the book exposed several inconsistencies between her life and the spins she gives it.

Superheroines

See *The Bionic Woman; Wonder Woman; Xena, Warrior Princess*

Supernatural Women

See *Bewitched; I Dream of Jeannie*

Sweeney, Anne (1957–)

Anne Sweeney became president of Disney/ABC Cable Networks in August 1998 when Geraldine Laybourne left the network. Previously, Sweeney had been executive vice-president of the Disney Channel, where in her first year (1996), she increased viewership of the premium channel by 33 percent.

She received her undergraduate degree from the College of New Rochelle and her graduate degree in education from Harvard University. She worked as a page in the New York office of ABC before moving to Nickelodeon/Nick-at-Nite, where she became senior vice-president of program enterprises in 1981, responsible for the introduction of Nickelodeon to the United Kingdom. She became vice-president of acquisitions for MTV Networks in 1990, and in 1993 moved to Fox's fX Networks as chair and CEO. She was instrumental in the launch of both fX and its sister network, fXM: Movies.

Sweet Justice (1994–1995)

This series was an idealistic legal drama about former Wall Street lawyer Kate Delacroy (Melissa Gilbert), who moved back to her southern hometown to join the law firm of Battle-Ross & Associates, headed by an early civil rights advocate, Carrie Grace Battle (Cicely Tyson). The stories revolved around the two women's fight to achieve justice for their disadvantaged clients while wrestling with their own personal and family problems.

Michael Warren and Cicely Tyson as Carrie Grace Battle in Sweet Justice *(Fotos International/Archive Photos)*

Sybil (1976)

Sally Field left her Gidget and Sister Bertrille personas far behind when she appeared as a woman with 16 distinct personalities in this fact-based movie produced by Jacqueline Babbin and broadcast on NBC in 1976. Joanne Woodward, who had appeared in a similarly premised movie in 1957 (*The Three Faces of Eve*), appeared as Sybil's psychiatrist. Field won an Emmy, critical acclaim, and the respect of the industry for her portrayal of the tormented Sybil.

The movie itself won a Peabody award for Outstanding Dramatic Program.

T

TABLOID TELEVISION

This genre of television became popular during the deregulation years of Reagan's presidency with the introduction of Fox Network's *A Current Affair,* which was nationally syndicated in 1986 as an inexpensive filler for local stations during nonnetwork hours. Called by some the "classic tabloid" that defined the genre, the series typically used lurid and/or controversial stories to attract viewers. These programs became staples in early-evening programming, although critics target them for appealing to viewers' voyeuristic tendencies.

A Current Affair was quickly followed by *Hard Copy* (1989–1999), which became known for its glitz and brashness, and *Inside Edition* (1989–), which approached its stories in a less exploitative manner. *America's Most Wanted* (1988–) dramatized selected crimes each week and profiled fugitives in an effort to encourage viewers to supply information that would lead to their capture. Hosted by John Walsh, whose own son had been murdered, the series has proven to be effective in apprehending fugitives, with more than 350 arrested since the show began.

A similarly premised program, *Unsolved Mysteries* (1988–), hosted by Robert Stack, dramatizes crimes and profiles missing-person stories and mysterious circumstances, then invites viewers to call an 800 number if they have any information on the incident or person. *Cops* (1989–) follows law enforcement personnel in various cities and presents reenacted "day in the life" videos. *Rescue 911* (1989–), hosted by William Shatner, reenacts actual rescue operations by emergency agencies.

All these programs came after the success of *Entertainment Tonight* (1981–), a celebrity-based series shown during early nonnetwork hours during the week and on weekends. Pre-

(continued on next page)

(continued from previous page)

sented in newscast format, the stories range from new-movie hype to celebrity love lives. Much publicity was garnered for the show with the report that cohost Mary Hart's legs had been insured for $1 million, and that special lights were aimed at her legs during broadcasts to make them more photogenic.

Taco Bell Chihuahua

See Gidget, the Dog

TALK SHOWS

Originally, the talk show was a means for film and other celebrities to promote their current projects. These shows were cordial and relaxed, offering the illusion of getting to know celebrities better. Later, some shows focused on audience members, elevating the audience to actor.

One of the first of this type of daytime talk show was *Art Linkletter's House Party* (1952–1970), which featured interviews with audience members and children as well as celebrities and experts. Also in 1952, *For Women Only*, a 15-minute informational series hosted by Amy Sedell, premiered, but did not receive high enough ratings to remain on the air.

Talk shows remained mostly a male domain until Virginia Graham hosted a daily program, *Girl Talk* (1962–1970), which some critics charged was nothing more than "a bitch session" in which Graham and her two female guests expressed their feelings about life, current events, and one another. Graham was replaced during the final year of the series by Betsy Palmer.

The next successful talk show to be hosted by a woman, *Dinah's Place* (1970–1980), was hosted by singer Dinah Shore and won an Emmy for Outstanding Program Achievement in Daytime in 1973 for its blend of celebrity interviews and guest involvement in studio activities. During this time, other women hosted talk and informational series, such as *Take My Advice*, with Kelly Lange (1976), but generally the programs did not fare well against the soap operas that ruled the airwaves during the late morning and early-afternoon hours.

In the 1980s, talk shows moved toward sensationalism and exploitation of guests who seemingly had no shame or restraint. Guests vied to see who could present the most dysfunctional story, and confession turned to confrontation. Proponents claimed the programs were cathartic and rooted in the consciousness-raising of the 1960s women's movement. Far from calling them "trash TV," proponents claimed that by sharing personal problems, the guests allowed larger cultural and social problems to be examined.

(continued on next page)

(continued from previous page)

Critics, however, charged that the programs not only exploited guests, but featured only abnormal people, who made the trivial seem important and the significant seem trivial. They further charged that the programs promoted feelings over reason and suggested quick fixes for complex issues. A final charge was later proved accurate when guests admitted that some events had been staged for maximum effect. Topics during the sleaze period of talk show included support-group junkies (*Oprah Winfrey Show*), aging strippers, gay men in search of rich lovers, marriage with a 14-year-old, and sisters who strip (*Sally Jesse Raphael*).

The *Oprah Winfrey Show,* later shortened to *Oprah*, premiered in 1985 in Chicago and went into national syndication the next year. The first nationally broadcast topic was "How to Marry the Man of Your Choice," and Winfrey became known for her seemingly prosocial, intimate conversational style. Her show won many Emmys and became the show to emulate.

Although Sally Jesse Raphael started her talk show a year before Winfrey, her program never attained the popularity that *Oprah* did. An early proponent of shock topics, Raphael's show was often more exploitative than informational.

With the success of *Oprah*, the airwaves were inundated with imitators. After a relatively unsuccessful attempt at a talk show in 1969, Joan Rivers returned to daytime television to host a talk show based in New York City, *The Joan Rivers Show* (1989–1994). Ricki Lake became a successful host of a show that premiered in 1993 and was geared to a younger audience. Rosie O'Donnell became a talk show sensation after her show premiered in 1996, and she soon earned the title "Queen of Nice" because of her nonconfrontational, earnest style.

O'Donnell's show premiered after the talk show genre was brought into close scrutiny by an incident on *Jenny Jones* in March 1995. Although the Jenny Jones show initially covered innocuous topics like fashion and self-image, ratings dictated a more aggressive approach, and the producers turned to more provocative topics such as "same-sex crushes."

During the taping of an unaired episode in what was called an "emotional ambush," Scott Amedure revealed that he had a crush on Jon Schmitz. Although Schmitz seemed to take the revelation well, three days later he shot and killed Amedure, citing his humiliation as a cause. Schmitz was sentenced to prison, but the verdict was overturned on appeal and a new trial ordered, in the course of which Schmitz was convicted a second time. However, as a result of the murder and its aftermath, many talk shows reexamined their approach and questioned their methods.

At one time, it seemed that any person with minimal celebrity had a talk show. Some programs were better than others, but none lasted very long. Singer Vicki Lawrence had a moderately successful series with her celebrity-driven program *Vicki* (1992–1994). Caryl (Kristensen) and Marilyn (Kentz) followed their failed sitcom *The Mommies* with a brief stint as talk show hosts with *Real Friends* (1996–1997). Leeza Gibbons, formerly of *Entertainment Tonight,* hosted an issues-oriented talk show, *Leeza* (1994–1997), while actors Marsha Warfield, Tempestt Bledsoe, and Gabrielle Carteris had short-lived series.

(continued on next page)

(continued from previous page)

One reason for the profusion of talk shows is that they are relatively inexpensive to produce, yet bring in large amounts of advertising revenues. Because their audience is largely female, most recent hosts have been women.

One of the newest and most popular talk shows is *The View* (1998–), created and hosted by Barbara Walters. She is joined by Meredith Vieira, Joy Behar, Star Jones, and, for the first year, Debbie Matenopoulos for a multigenerational discussion of gossip, social issues, and celebrity and pop news.

Although talk show producers claim social benefit by purporting to disseminate useful information to the viewing audience, the true potential for learning and information has been overlooked in favor of ratings. Further, the marginally investigative nature of some of the topics allows for the claim of journalistic credibility when, at best, topics are presented as infotainment, with audience participation lending an air of personal involvement.

See also Jones, Jenny; O'Donnell, Rosie; *Oprah Winfrey Show;* Rivers, Joan; Winfrey, Oprah.

Tammy (1965–1966)

In this series, based on the 1957 movie *Tammy and the Bachelor* starring Debbie Reynolds and the sequels starring Sandra Dee, the backwoods sage (played by Debbie Watson) worked for wealthy John Brent (Donald Woods) and lived with her grandfather (Denver Pyle) and Uncle Lucius (Frank McGrath) in their houseboat on the bayou.

Predictably, Tammy beguiled her way into everyone's hearts, except for John Brent's neighbors, the Tates—Lavinia (Dorothy Green), her daughter Gloria (Linda Marshall), and son Peter (David Macklin). Stories emphasized that good intentions and a pure heart were powerful against the jealousy and greed of the Tates, who regularly received their comeuppance.

After the series was canceled, the principals reprised their TV roles in a 1967 TV movie, *Tammy and the Millionaire*.

Tarnofsky, Dawn (1960–)

After graduating with a degree in journalism from Florida International University in Miami, Dawn Tarnofsky worked as vice-president of development at Kushner-Locke and then president of Michael Jacobs Productions before moving to Twentieth Century Fox Television as senior vice-president in 1984. She was responsible for the development of many successful series, including *King of the Hill* (1997–) and *Buffy: The Vampire Slayer* (1996–); she was also involved in developing Chris Carter's *Millennium* (1996–1999).

In 1996, Tarnofsky moved to Lifetime Television as senior vice-president in charge of programming and production. Known for her "relentless pursuit of excellence," she is developing several comedy and drama series concepts in an effort to increase original programming to 80 percent by 2001, and expand the number of *Intimate Portraits* the network produces annually. One of the new series launched by Lifetime in 1998, *Any Day Now*, has won critical praise and a loyal following.

Although known as the network geared to women, Lifetime has a 35 percent male viewership, which Tarnofsky believes must be increased to establish Lifetime as a well-rounded network.

See also *Any Day Now;* Lifetime.

Jamie Tarses, president of ABC's entertainment division, seen with Ted Harbert, chairman of ABC's entertainment division, shortly after Harbert's resignation announcement, 1997. (Reuters/Fred Prouser/Archive Photos)

Tarses, Jamie (1964–)

Jamie Tarses, daughter of producer Jay Tarses and a Williams College graduate, became the first woman president of an entertainment division of one of the Big Three networks when she became head of ABC's entertainment division in 1996. She began in the television industry in 1985 as a production assistant on *Saturday Night Live,* then worked in the casting department of Lorimar before moving to NBC, where she eventually became a senior vice-president overseeing prime-time series development. She is known for her work with youth-oriented urban sitcoms such as *Mad about You* (1992–1999), *Friends* (1994–), *Caroline in the City* (1995–1999), and *NewsRadio* (1995–1999).

Less than a year after making headlines as a media darling and the savior of the faltering ABC network, Tarses made more headlines as a media target in a succession of articles declaring that she was "paying the price for her youth and gender," and was unfit for the position of president of a major network. Considering the number of other women in executive positions in the television industry, the venom aimed at Tarses from the beginning of her tenure is difficult to understand. Traits praised in men when exhibited by a woman have traditionally been viewed as detriments and deserving of being labeled, in the trump card of censure, "unfeminine." In her case, Tarses goes from unfeminine to "too feminine," depending on the article.

After achieving programming successes at NBC, chiefly the development of *Friends,* Tarses was frantically wooed by ABC to bolster its sagging ratings and stem the mass audience defection it had been suffering for years. Although she invigorated the 1997–1998 season with programs like the drama *Nothing Sacred* and the offbeat comedy *Dharma & Greg,* her expertise in urban, thirty-something comedies did not mesh well with the Disney philosophy of family-oriented entertainment. In addition, in July 1997 she was "trashed" in an article in the *New York Times* that caused executives at Disney, ABC's parent company, to again take frantic, if knee-jerk, action.

She is no longer viewed by the powers-that-be as a youthful—and better yet, female—miracle worker, but as a "young, naive *girl*" not seasoned enough for the responsibilities of her position. The old-boy network closed ranks and placed a man in a created position, effectively demoting Tarses to a number-two position within the division.

Tarses's accession as president has been mired in difficulties from the outset. Many at ABC viewed her as being dumped on them by Disney president Michael Ovitz, who hired her, shortly after Disney bought ABC and not long before he left Disney under a controversial cloud. Others believe that Disney set Tarses up for a fall by dropping her into what amounted to a hostile environment with no support mechanisms. Added to that, she was allowed to leave NBC only after rumors of a threatened lawsuit surfaced. With the inflated expectations placed on her, she was playing against a stacked deck.

She received criticism for her *male* predecessor's prime-time lineup, and in the process of adjusting to her new position, she had to contend with Disney chairman Michael Eisner and ABC president Bob Iger, who both had their own agendas and expectations.

In 1998, Tarses stated that the "difficult" period of adjustment was over and that she was relieved to be able to focus on her job: making ABC's prime-time offerings competitive and representative of current audience tastes. However, after further reorganizing at ABC, Tarses resigned in August 1999, declining to disclose future plans.

Tassler, Nina (1959–)

Nina Tassler, senior vice-president of drama at CBS Entertainment since early 1998, is responsible for the development and production of all drama series at CBS Productions. She was instrumental in getting three new drama series on the 1998 prime-time lineup: *To Have and to Hold*, *L.A. Doctors*, and *Martial Law*.

Tassler worked with Triad Artists from 1985 to 1990, first as a talent agent and then as director of motion pictures–TV administration. She moved to Lorimar Television as vice-president of drama before going to CBS in 1997.

TEEN SHOWS

Since the inception of television, series have been made to appeal to the teenage audience. One of the first youth-oriented series to focus on the everyday life of a young girl was *Meet Corliss Archer* (1951–1952; 1954–1955). The series chronicled the events in the lives of Corliss (Lugene Sanders, 1951–1952; Ann Baker, 1954–1955), her boyfriend, and her family.

While children and teenagers were often included in comedies about family life, the next series to focus exclusively on a young girl was *Karen* (1964–1965), part of an anthology that was broadcast as *90 Bristol Court*, named for the fictitious apartment complex in which the characters lived. Karen (Debbie Watson) was an energetic 16-year-old who was always getting into improbable situations.

In the following year, *Gidget* (1965–1966) was introduced, based loosely on the popular film character. In the televisual version, Francine "Gidget" Lawrence (Sally Field) was the same exuberant teenager, who now found herself embroiled in others' lives and troubles as well as her own. The concept was reintroduced in a se-

ries entitled *The New Gidget* (1986–1988), which centered on Gidget's niece, Danni (Sydney Penny), who was very much like her aunt and encountered similarly improbable situations as she grew up.

In 1975 another *Karen* came to television. Lasting only one season, this time Karen (Karen Valentine) was an idealistic young woman working for a citizens' action group, Open America, in Washington, D.C. Four years passed before the premiere of another girl-centered sitcom, *Facts of Life* (1979–1988). The series focused on the girls (originally ages 11–15) attending preppy Eastland School. Through the course of the series, the girls—Blair (Lisa Whelchel), "Tootie" (Kim Fields), Jo (Nancy McKeon), and Natalie (Mindy Cohn)—grew up and moved on to adult lives.

One of the first series to focus on the escapades of twins was *Double Trouble* (1984–1985). Although 16-year-old Kate (Jean Segal) and Allison (Liz Segal) were identical, their personalities were polar opposites. Allison was serious and

(continued on next page)

(continued from previous page)

responsible, while Kate was a spirited trouble-maker who enjoyed getting both of them into improbable situations.

Two girl-centered series appeared in 1991. *Clarissa Explains It All* (1991–1994) premiered on the cable network Nickelodeon and centered around Clarissa Darling (Melissa Joan Hart), an energetic high school student who each week explored one of the mysteries of teenage life such as love, friendship, boys, and parents, and reported the results to the viewers. Meanwhile, on NBC, *Blossom* (1991–1995) focused on the coming-of-age events in the life of the older-than-her-years, 13-year-old Blossom Russo (Mayim Bialik). She met life with grit and occasional fantasies in which she received advice from "experts" like Sonny Bono, ALF (Alien Life Form), Little Richard, and Phil Donahue. After each episode, the resulting new knowledge was recorded in her video diary during the epilogue.

Another twin series premiered in 1994—first on ABC, then NBC. *Sister, Sister* (1994–1999) was set in Detroit and focused on a set of twins, Tia and Tamara (Tia and Tamara Mowry), who were separated at birth and adopted into different families. After 14 years they find each other at a mall sale and refuse to be separated again. To satisfy the girls, their now-single parents decide to try blending their families to allow the girls to live together.

In an effort to appeal to its young viewers, Nickelodeon created a girl-centered series, *The Secret World of Alex Mack* (1995–), in which Alexandra Mack develops superhuman powers after being accidentally sprayed with a chemical called GC-161. It enables her to zap electricity from her fingers, morph into a silvery blob, move objects with her mind, and glow unexpectedly.

On the same network, *The Mystery Files of Shelby Woo* (1996–) focuses on Shelby (Irene Ng), who constantly becomes involved in mysteries and solves them with the help of her friends Cindy (Preslaysa Edwards) and Noah (Adam Busch). In 1999, Shelby and her grandfather, Mike Woo (Pat Morita), moved from Cocoa Beach to Wilton, Massachusetts, so Shelby has new mysteries to solve in a new town.

In keeping with WB's attempt to appeal to urban young people, it premiered *Moesha* (1996–), which chronicles the events in the life of Moesha (Brandy) as she meets the challenges of life as a teenager trying to find her place in the 1990s. On a fantasy plane, *Sabrina the Teenage Witch* (1996–) follows Sabrina (Melissa Joan Hart), who on her sixteenth birthday is told that she is a witch and, guided by her eccentric aunts (Caroline Rhea and Beth Broderick), must learn to control her powers while learning the other lessons of teenage life. Based on the hit movie, *Clueless* (1996–1998) continued the saga of Cher (Rachel Blanchard) as she shops and matchmakes her way through high school, and becomes involved in outlandish situations with her friends.

For younger viewers the ever-popular Olsen twins (Mary Kate and Ashley) premiered in a new series, *Two of a Kind* (1998–1999). Mary Kate played an athletic tomboy, while Ashley was the deb-in-training; both lived with their widowed father.

Teen-ensemble series have also increased, such as *Buffy: The Vampire Slayer* (1996–) and *Dawson's Creek* (1998–). *Dawson's Creek* is often cited as too sexual for younger viewers, but it made history as one of the first teen series to

(continued on next page)

(continued from previous page)

introduce a gay character, Jack McPhee (Kerr Smith), into its midst. Amid its supernatural mayhem, *Buffy* depicts the problems of teen life and the characters' endeavors to find their place in the larger world.

Another fantasy series featuring an ensemble cast of young people premiered on Fox in the afternoons: *Mystic Knights of Tir Na Nog* (1999). Princess-warrior Deirdre (Lisa Dwan) and a group of young warriors fought to rid their home of the evil invaders of Queen Maeve.

Many popular teen series have had book series follow their heroines' further exploits, such as those for *Buffy: The Vampire Slayer; Clueless; Moesha; The Mystery Files of Shelby Woo; Sabrina; The Secret World of Alex Mack; Sister, Sister;* and *Two of a Kind.*

TELEVISUAL WORLD

Found in more than 99 percent of all homes, television is the most pervasive entertainment form in American life. Popular shows are often discussed to such a degree that even those who do not watch a particular show find it becomes part of their life experience because they are familiar with it from others' discussions. Television is truly the common thread that runs through the country's population regardless of racial, economic, or social class.

Studies indicate that television can affect a viewer's worldview, and that the more one watches, the more one is affected because the images often work at a subconscious level. Television is the babysitter of choice for many busy families, and young children learn about the world in which they live by what they see on television. With women and children watching slightly more television than men, what is it they see?

SELF-IMAGE

Males continue to dominate the airwaves, with the majority of characters, especially in functional roles, being men. Of the female characters depicted, many are directly or indirectly motivated by males, since too often the female characters' goals include finding or pleasing Mr. Right. These repeated images send messages that it is indeed still a man's world, and that happiness or success must include a man. The popular *Ally McBeal* (Fox, 1997–) portrays a young woman with an interesting and rewarding career but whose love life, or lack thereof, can nullify all the good aspects of her life.

Equally damaging to the female viewer is the proliferation of beautiful characters with perfect bodies. Since the majority of the female population (approximately 60 percent) is a size 12 or larger, the repeated televisual endorsement of bodily perfection can lead to dissatisfaction with one's own body and, as a result, life in general. With more than one million adolescent girls watching television each night, this emphasis on bodily perfection prepares another generation to value appearance over all else.

(continued on next page)

(continued from previous page)

SOCIAL CLASS

Although all social classes have been portrayed on television, the majority of characters inhabit a vast middle-class stratum. However, at various times, groups of people other than the homogeneous middle class have been in vogue.

In the early years of television, most viewers lived in urban centers, and ethnic comedies were popular. Both *Mama* (CBS, 1949–1956) and *The Goldbergs* (CBS/NBC/Dumont, 1949–1956) followed the lives of working-class families who somehow never seemed to go without or be deprived, even though the families were large and the only breadwinner had a menial job.

The dramatic anthologies that were popular during the early years covered all classes and economic situations, but later two popular sitcoms included a blue-collar family and a middle-class family. *The Honeymooners* (CBS, 1955–1956) followed the lives of an irresponsible bus driver, Ralph Kramden (Jackie Gleason), and his logical and sensible wife, Alice (Audrey Meadows). At a slightly higher economic level, *I Love Lucy* (CBS, 1951–1957) portrayed the lives of nightclub entertainer Ricky Ricardo (Desi Arnaz) and his starstruck wife, Lucy (Lucille Ball). Both series featured a "battle of the sexes," in which the economically deprived Alice was shown to be more powerful within the marriage because of her levelheadedness than the materially better-off but "screwball" Lucy, who only got her way through tears.

In later series, working-class families were completely displaced by suburban middle-class families. Such series as *Father Knows Best* (CBS/NBC/ABC, 1954–1963), *Leave It to Beaver* (CBS/ABC, 1957–1963), *The Adventures of Ozzie and Harriet* (ABC, 1952–1966), and *The Dick Van Dyke Show* (CBS, 1961–1966) depicted families living the comfortable good life.

As the setting for sitcoms moved into the realm of the workplace long shown by dramatic series, the workers were depicted as belonging to the middle class, with comfortable, well-furnished homes. Even the irregularly employed Ann Marie of *That Girl* (ABC, 1966–1971) lived in a spacious apartment in New York and dressed in the height of fashion. Similarly, the title character on *Alice* (CBS, 1976–1985) worked as a waitress in a small diner, yet she and her son had a comfortable, well-furnished apartment. More recently, on the blue-collar sitcom *Roseanne* (ABC, 1988–1998), discussions of deprivation and utility disconnections were more often than not discussions only—the Conner family not only had the bare necessities of life, but enjoyed some consumer toys as well.

According to the televisual world, American society is divided into two social and economic classes: the extremely wealthy, as in *Dallas* (CBS, 1978–1991) and *Dynasty* (ABC, 1981–1989), and a vast middle class that includes professionals, teachers, secretaries, and waitresses, who live comfortable lives regardless of how low-paying their jobs are.

Tellem, Nancy (1953–)

Nancy Tellem, entertainment president of CBS since 1998, is the first woman to be named to that position. She received her promotion after serving as executive vice-president, at which time she was the highest-ranking female in the entertainment division.

Tellem received her undergraduate degree from Berkeley and her doctorate in law from Hastings College before practicing business law for four years. She joined the legal department of Columbia Television in 1983, then moved to the business affairs division of Lorimar Television in 1987, eventually being named head of Lorimar/Warner Brothers Television's business department, where she was responsible for negotiating all contracts for movies and weekly series. She left Lorimar to accept a position with the CBS entertainment division.

That Girl (1966–1971)

This entertaining and inoffensive series, produced during a period of social unrest in the United States, presented a female character who was young, naively innocent, and pursuing her dream of being a Broadway actress. Starring Marlo Thomas as Ann Marie, the virginal all-American daddy's girl, the series introduced having a career as an option to the traditional daughter-wife-mother progression shown on previous shows. As a result of this innovation, the series has been touted as the prototype for all independent-woman programs that followed.

Although *That Girl* overtly showed a young woman working and living alone in New York City, the series' themes and underlying characterizations implied less independence and self-determination than contemporary media coverage indicates. Although Ann Marie did not live with her parents, several supportive neighbors lived in her apartment building, and her father, Lou Marie (Lew Parker), was only minutes away by train and an ever-present figure via frequent telephone calls. Further nullifying her purported aloneness, from the first episode she was paired with boyfriend Donald Hollinger (Ted Bessell), who was also only a phone call away.

Supposedly pursuing a career as an actress, Ann was seldom shown working at her craft. When she was shown working, it was generally at a stereotypically feminine temporary job while she waited for her big break. Interestingly, although she seemed to work only minimum-wage-type jobs, she lived in an attractive one-bedroom apartment that boasted a huge living room with fireplace, a large dining alcove, and a well-appointed kitchen, and she always dressed in the most fashionable clothes. How she managed to afford such an apartment and dress in such a manner in New York City on minimum wage was never addressed and definitely gave the viewers an inaccurate view of "being on your own."

The Ann Marie character, on closer examination, differed little from previous female sitcom characters. She was protected and guided by either her father or Donald. She never lost her little-girl quality, as exemplified by her referring to her father as "Daddy" and her naively trusting approach to life—even in New York City, the epitome of an impersonal metropolis.

Although Ann's approach to life could be endearing, if impractical, it is disheartening to realize that television's first independent career woman was a "dippy would-be actress" as expressed in a contemporary article by Betty Rollin. In essence, the character of Ann Marie followed the well-established televisual pattern of the scatterbrained wife; the series simply brought that character into a more contemporary focus. Interestingly, while other people were protesting unpopular government and social policies, indulging in a variety of psychedelic drugs, and otherwise "doing it" if it "felt good," Ann was the kind of daughter that many parents dreamed of having—she was, according to the song from her opening montage, what every girl should strive to be.

The weekly humor resulted from Ann's misunderstanding or misinterpreting an event, person, or thing, much like previous scatterbrained wives. Each week she was saved, consoled, and petted by either her father or Donald—or both.

The innovative aspect of the series, Ann's singleness and career focus as opposed to marriage focus, was virtually nullified by her reliance on her father or her boyfriend, and the fact that much of the action took place in her apartment or other nonwork environment. The series seemed to say that women could pursue their own dreams and push social and cultural boundaries, as long as they stayed childlike and ultimately incapable of sustained autonomy. This seemingly contradictory depiction became a model for future female characters in nontraditional roles.

thirtysomething (1987–1991)

A series aimed at the "Yuppie" audience—in their 30s and establishing successful careers—that advertisers thought were high consumers. The soap operaish stories followed the lives of a group of friends—an ensemble cast of two couples and three singles—in Philadelphia. In essence, a series that spotlighted 30s angst, *thirtysomething* focused on career and relationship travails and the characters' constant questioning of the "true meaning" of their lives when not obsessing about their lost youth.

Only moderately popular with viewers though successful in attracting a "cult" following, the series was loved by many critics. It won several Emmys its first year out—Outstanding Drama Series, Outstanding Writing in a Drama Series, Outstanding Supporting Actress in a Drama Series (Patricia Wettig), and Outstanding Guest Performance in a Drama Series (Shirley Knight). In 1988 the series won the award for Outstanding Writing in a Drama Series and Outstanding Supporting Actress (Patricia Wettig) and Outstanding Supporting Actor in a Drama (Timothy Busfield).

Thomas, Betty (1947–)

An Emmy-winning actress, Betty Thomas has gone on to direct feature films as well as television series. Best remembered as Officer (later Sergeant) Lucy Bates on *Hill Street Blues* (1981–1987), Thomas honed her directorial craft while on the set of the series, although she was never allowed to direct an episode.

Her directorial debut was *Only You* (1992), and she worked on the Emmy-winning series *Dream On* (1990–1995). She later directed *The Brady Bunch Movie* (1995) and *Private Parts* (1997). She won a Director's Guild of America Award for Outstanding Directorial Achievement in a Dramatic Special for her work on *Late Shift* (1996) for HBO, after being nominated in 1993 (*Silent Night, Holy Cow*) and in 1994 (*My Breast*).

Her most recent project was a remake of *Dr. Dolittle* (1998), starring Eddie Murphy.

Three's Company (1977–1984)

This series was a stereotypical, slapstickish comedy about two women and a man platonically sharing an apartment. Filled with sexual innuendos and double entendres, the show was a sophomoric hit.

Originally, the threesome was made up of serious Janet (Joyce De-Witt), who worked at a flower shop; airheaded Chrissy (Suzanne Somers), a typist; and Jack (John Ritter), a student-chef who over the run of the series eventually opened his own place, Jack's Bistro. Costar Somers became a media celebrity, only to fade from network television when the producers refused her salary demands in 1980. Chrissy was replaced by Chrissy's cousin Cindy (Jenilee Harrison), in turn replaced in 1981 by Terri (Priscilla Barnes), who worked as a nurse.

The series ended in 1984 when Janet got married and Terri moved to Hawaii, while Jack moved to a different series, *Three's a Crowd* (1984–1985), based on the popular British series *Man about the House*. In fact, the first episode was almost an exact duplicate of the British series' first episode except for using American idioms and slang.

After being released from the series, Suzanne Somers went on to a career in infomercials, creating her own exercise equipment line, and later, her own cosmetics line. Eventually she returned to network television as the mother in *Step by Step* (1991–1996), about two single parents who marry and combine their families.

To the Queen's Taste (1948–1949)

One of the first cooking shows to appear on network television, this series featured cooking expert Dione Lucas, who owned the Cordon Bleu Restaurant in Manhattan at the time. Lucas showed viewers how to prepare exotic dishes from a variety of countries and cultures.

The series, also known as *The Dione Lucas Show*, started locally in New York in October 1947 and went to network distribution in May 1948, then continued locally after its network cancellation in 1949.

Tomlin, Lily (1939–)

"The trouble with the rat race is that even if you win, you're still a rat" (Lily Tomlin, actress and comedian). Lily Tomlin got her television start on *The Garry Moore Show* in 1967 after dropping out of a premed program to pursue a cabaret career. Her big break came when she became a regular on *Rowan and Martin's Laugh-In* (1968–1973) with her characterizations of Edith Ann, a mischievous five-year-old, and Ernestine, the snorting switchboard operator.

Tomlin left the show in 1972, but continued to appear in comedy specials, winning several Emmys. She debuted in movies with *Nashville* (1975), for which she won a New York Film Critics Circle Award, and received a Best Supporting Actress Academy Award nomination. She appeared on *The Late Show* (1977), *9 to 5* (1980), *All of Me* (1984), *Big Business* (1988), and *The Search for Signs of Intelligent Life in the Universe* (1991).

She also appeared in one-woman shows in clubs and on university campuses. She made a successful transition to Broadway, winning Tony awards for both of her one-woman offerings, *Appearing Nightly* (1977) and *The Search for Signs of Intelligent Life in the Universe* (1986), on which the film was based.

Her 1996 animated special, *Edith Ann's Christmas,* won a Peabody for "confronting today's family problems." She returned to television in 1997 by joining the cast of *Murphy Brown* (1988–1998) as the producer of *FYI.*

A Touch of Grace (1973)

Shirley Booth, who had won awards for her performances on Broadway, television, and feature films, returned to television in this sitcom as Grace Simpson, a fun-loving, sixtyish widow living with her staid daughter, Myra (Marian Mercer), and son-in-law, Walter (Warren Berlinger). The concept was more than faintly reminiscent of an earlier series, *December Bride* (1954–1959).

The humor derived from the contrast between the youngish Grace and the old-before-their-time Myra and Walter, whose views on how a widow should behave were at odds with Grace's joyful attitude. The series was based on a British hit, *For the Love of Ada.*

Touched by an Angel (1994–)

At the beginning of the series, Monica (Roma Downey) was a newly promoted angel caseworker. Her mission was to inspire and guide people to change their lives for the better, thereby solving their problems. Along with her supervisor, Tess (Della Reese), she traveled the country in a vintage Cadillac convertible helping mortals face the stresses and challenges of life.

The heartwarming stories and hopeful messages of the episodes made the series an almost instant hit. Its success focused attention on the guardian angel belief, and an angel craze swept the country. Soon, books on angels and mortals' experiences with them, angel jewelry, angel dolls, and other angel merchandise flooded the market.

The Trials of Rosie O'Neill (1990–1992)

Successful attorney Rosie O'Neill (Sharon Gless) left her Beverly Hills law practice after divorcing her husband-partner and became a public defender. Of course, she didn't really fit in with the other public defenders, who thought she was slumming. Her family couldn't understand why she would take a low-paying and frustrating job when it wasn't necessary.

As a result, she suffered constant angst, and most episodes opened with Rosie in her analyst's office talking about her problems and her attempts to achieve justice for her clients.

Trotta, Liz (1938–)

Liz Trotta was one of the first female news reporters to appear on television, before the affirmative action impetus of the 1970s. She began her career as a writer for Associated Press and the *Chicago Tribune* before going into broadcast news in 1965 with NBC's New York affiliate. Trotta was that network's first female foreign correspondent during the Vietnam War from 1968 to 1971.

After her tours in Vietnam, Trotta was bureau chief in Singapore from 1971 to 1973, and then moved to the London bureau as a general correspondent until 1975, when she moved to CBS.

Known in the business as aggressive and often abrasive, Trotta was unpopular with some in the industry, not because she was completely dedicated to her job but because she demanded to be respected for her ability and experience regardless of her sex.

See also News.

Tucker's Witch (1982–1983)

Rick (Tim Matheson) and Amanda (Catherine Hicks) Tucker were partners in a private detective agency. Rick relied on conventional methods to solve cases, while Amanda used witchcraft. Since her spells seldom worked as she expected, she often caused more problems than she solved.

Tyson, Cicely (1933–)

Cicely Tyson first appeared on television in *East Side, West Side* (1963–1964) as Jane Foster, who worked as a secretary in a welfare agency in New York City. She then went on to a career in films that included *The Comedians* (1967), *The Heart Is a Lonely Hunter* (1968), *Sounder* (1972)—for which she received an Oscar nomination as Best Supporting Actress—and *Fried Green Tomatoes* (1992).

On television, she starred in *The Autobiography of Miss Jane Pittman* (1974), which won an Emmy as Outstanding Special; Tyson won an Emmy as Outstanding Actress in a Special. Later, she appeared as Coretta Scott King in *King* (1978), as well as in *The Marva Collins Story* (1981) and *The Oldest Confederate Widow Tells All* (1994).

She returned to series television in *Sweet Justice* (1994–1995) as Carrie Grace Battle, a civil rights lawyer in the South fighting for the rights of the less fortunate. The series also starred Melissa Gilbert as Kate Delacroy, a former Wall Street lawyer who returned to her hometown and joined Battle-Ross & Associates.

Tyson was born in New York City to Caribbean immigrants and grew up in Harlem. She started a successful modeling career in her late teens before turning to acting. She won the Vernon Rice Award in 1961 for her role in *The Blacks.*

U

Ullman, Tracey (1959–)

First coming to television in her own series on the fledgling Fox Network, Tracey Ullman is a multitalented performer—singer, actress, mimic and master of dialects, and comedienne. Ironically, Ullman won an Emmy for Outstanding Performance in a Variety or Musical Program two weeks after her series, *The Tracey Ullman Show* (1987–1990), was canceled.

Ullman worked for many years in Europe before coming to the United States. She was a member of a German ballet company before going into musical comedy and receiving the London Theatre Critics' Award for Most Promising New Actress in 1981. In 1983, she received a British Academy Award for her work on BBC Television, including her comedy-variety series *Three of a Kind,* from which Ullman had two hit songs: "You Broke My Heart in Seventeen Places" and "They Don't Know."

Tracey Ullman balances her 1998 American Comedy Award on her head while talking to reporters after her presentation. (Deidre Davidson/Saga/Archive Photos)

327

Upon moving to the United States, she appeared in several movies, including *Jumpin' Jack Flash* (1986), *I Love You to Death* (1990), *Death Becomes Her* (1992), and *I'll Do Anything* (1994). Ullman returned to television with her HBO series *Tracey Takes On . . .* , for which she won another Emmy in 1997.

Her most recent appearance on television has been as the offbeat, extremely unconventional psychiatrist on *Ally McBeal,* beginning in 1997.

Under Suspicion (1994–1995)

This TV-noir series was about Rose "Phil" Phillips (Karen Sillas), the first female homicide detective in an all-male precinct in Portland, Oregon. An intelligent and competent detective, the series showed her vulnerable side and her uncertainties as a woman in a male-dominated profession.

Her male coworkers were mostly old-boy sexists who resented her promotion and blamed her for the death of her partner, Frank (Peter Onorati), who died in the pilot. Although a "good cop," she often worried about getting too tough. Several episodes analyzed her motivations and personality while she solved the crime at the center of the episode.

Throughout the series she had an on-again/off-again romance with Internal Affairs Detective James Vitelli (Philip Casnoff), although there were hints that she had loved her slain partner, with whose family she remained in close contact. In the season finale, when it was uncertain whether or not the show would return, she was shot. As she lost consciousness, she talked to Frank about the field of flowers that she "saw."

The series did not return the next season, not because it was not well written and well acted, but because the network thought it "skewed too old," meaning it didn't appeal to the young audience that advertisers sought. In addition, Sillas had indicated that she was interested in leaving to pursue a film career.

See also Detective/Police Drama Series.

V

VCR

The VCR was a boon to home entertainment and the entertainment industry in general. Although the first VCRs were rather bulky and expensive units, they enabled people to record a television program for later viewing, an ability that greatly increased the impact and audience of the daytime soap opera. Feared by some to portend a decline in television viewership by allowing households the option of renting or purchasing a wide variety of filmed entertainment (documentaries, recent feature films, and a plethora of self-help videos), the VCR has in some cases actually increased viewership by allowing viewers to tape one program while watching another, thereby eliminating the need to choose between two competing programs.

Veronica's Closet (1997–)

Starring Kirstie Alley, the series is about the life of recently divorced Veronica "Ronnie" Chase (aka the Queen of Romance) who owns a mail-order lingerie company and writes books on how to have a great love life while never finding a satisfying relationship herself.

The office staff is the usual assortment of eccentrics, with her assistant, Violet (Kathy Najimy), being the only sane person on her staff. Ronnie's father insists on working as her chauffeur, a spot of "common man" in her otherwise luxurious facade.

VARIETY PROGRAMS

Variety series went out of viewer favor in the 1970s, with occasional entries until 1982, when *Barbara Mandrell and the Mandrell Sisters* was canceled, opening the way for prime-time soap operas and newsmagazines. Until viewers lost interest, variety shows were among the most popular programs on television.

The first variety series appeared during television's infancy: *Hour Glass* (1946–1947), hosted by Helen Parrish on NBC. The program was an experimental collection of songs, skits, interviews, monologues, and commercials—one lasted more than four minutes!

In 1950, Hazel Scott, a well-known jazz pianist at that time, had a 15-minute series on the Dumont Network, becoming the first black woman to host a network show. Several years later, another woman got her own show when *The Dottie Mack Show* (1953–1956) premiered, with Mack and her assistants pantomiming songs from the Hit Parade.

Other female-hosted series followed, including *The Dinah Shore Show* (1951–1957), a 15-minute program that featured songs and gossip. Known for her friendly style, Shore moved to a longer format with *The Dinah Shore Chevy Show* (1956–1963), which became a weekly series after first appearing as monthly specials.

Although not long-running, *The Patti Page Show* (1956) was the summer replacement for *The Perry Como Show* (1948–1963). Surprisingly, when Judy Garland came to television with a variety show in 1963, it lasted only a few months.

Perhaps the most successful variety series hosted by a woman was *The Carol Burnett Show* (1967–1978). With a combination of comedy sketches, dancing, and singing, Burnett was able to exploit her versatility and act as the focal point for her cast of regulars and guests.

Leslie Uggams hosted a short-lived variety program, *The Leslie Uggams Show* (1969). Lasting only two months, the series featured singing, dancing, and a continuing comedy skit, Sugarhill. Except for Dennis Allen, the entire cast was made up of black performers.

In the years that followed, variety series featured female and male duos or groups such as the original *The Sonny and Cher Comedy Hour* (1971–1974), *Tony Orlando and Dawn* (1974–1976), *The Captain and Tennille* (1976–1977), and the first *Donny & Marie* (1976–1979). The next woman to host her own series was Barbara Mandrell (1980–1982). A country-western star with a string of hit records, Mandrell was joined by her sisters Louise and Irlene in a combination of songs and comedy sketches.

See also Burnett, Carol; Cher; Shore, Dinah.

Previously, Alley portrayed Rebecca on *Cheers* (1987–1993), for which she won a Golden Globe, a People's Choice Award, and an Emmy for Outstanding Actress in a Comedy Series (1991). In 1997, Alley also starred as the conflicted tooth fairy in the Disney production *Toothless*.

Vieira, Meredith (1954–)

Meredith Vieira is a CBS news correspondent who appears on the live daytime panel-talk show *The View* (1997–) with ex-prosecutor and *Court TV* analyst Star Jones and Barbara Walters. Vieira also appeared on the primetime series *Verdict* (1991), which reported on actual courtroom trials and showed excerpts from the proceedings.

From 1989 to 1991, Vieira also worked as a coeditor on *60 Minutes,* but when she tried to cut back on her hours after becoming pregnant in 1991, executive producer Donald Hewitt released her. This prompted charges of sexual discrimination and countercharges of deficient work performance, although the "deficiency" had never been mentioned before.

Vieira began her broadcasting career as a radio announcer for WORC Radio in Worcester, Massachusetts, in 1975. She was a news reporter and anchor for WJAR-TV in Providence, Rhode Island, before moving to WCBS-TV in New York as a reporter. In 1983 she moved to Chicago as a reporter for the local CBS bureau and was promoted to correspondent in 1984. From 1985 to 1989 she was a principal correspondent for the CBS program *West 57th.*

VIOLENCE

On average, a regular network television viewer sees more than 10,000 violent acts per year. A recent study (1997) indicated that by the time a child completes elementary school, he or she will have "witnessed" 8,000 murders and seen over a million acts of violence. An analysis of television series further indicated that as much as 60 percent of prime-time shows include at least one act of violence.

The two most often committed crimes on television are murder and assault, as opposed to burglary and larceny (the two crimes actually most often committed). Further studies indicate that the per capita assault rate has increased more than seven times from the level in 1958—when television was not the most pervasive part of American life and the baby-sitter of choice for generations.

Of deep concern to women's groups is the fact that often the victims of these criminal acts are women. Violence in the world of television makes violence in the real world seem to be the normal and acceptable method to resolve differences. This fact, added to other cultural and social messages, may lead viewers to accept and expect women to be treated violently.

Unfortunately, not all violent acts are committed by criminal elements within the story. Often the violence is perpetrated by characters

(continued on next page)

(continued from previous page)

representing law enforcement, with little attention given to due process or individual rights. A recent National Television Violence Study reported that violent acts on television, which are often gratuitous, are often committed by role-model characters, and that these actions are often glamorized and the results downplayed.

This concern with the effect of watching violence on television is not new. In 1954 the Kefauver Congressional Hearings studied whether violence on television contributed to the growing crime rate. Throughout the 1960s, several congressional investigations were held into the "rampant and opportunistic use of violence" on television, resulting in a five-volume report on the effect of television violence on children in 1969.

In 1972 the Pastore Hearing clarified that television violence seemed to have a causal effect on violent behavior in children. This report led to the institution of "family viewing hours," which was supposed to limit violence to non–prime-time programs.

Of course, the family hours were soon abandoned, and violence once more became the stock-in-trade of television series. In 1990 the Television Program Improvement Act was passed, allowing for "developing and disseminating voluntary guidelines designed to alleviate the negative impact of violence in telecast material."

Although violence is still present on television, most networks put ratings in the upper corner to warn viewers of the content. The V-chip, a device that will allow certain stations and programs to be blocked from viewing, is in final development.

W

Walden, Dana (1964–)

As executive vice-president of drama at Twentieth Century Fox Television since 1996, Dana Walden is in charge of all drama programs produced by Fox, including such established hits as *The X-Files* (1993–) and *Chicago Hope* (1994–), as well as the development of new drama series such as *Buffy: The Vampire Slayer* (1996–), *Millennium* (1997–1999), *Ally McBeal* (1997–), and *Nothing Sacred* (1997–1998). Under her direction, 1996–1997 was Fox's most successful drama season to date.

Walden began her career in the entertainment industry as a publicist at Bender, Goldman & Helper, then moved to Arsenio Hall Communications at Paramount as marketing vice-president. She moved to the media relations division at Fox in 1992, and rose to vice-president of current programming in 1994.

Although she has script approval, Walden views her role more as a facilitator whose job is to do whatever is necessary to allow producers to create a top product.

Walters, Barbara (1931–)

Barbara Walters, arguably the most well known of television newswomen, was the first woman to coanchor an evening network news broadcast (1976). She continues to appear on celebrity interview specials as well as the daytime talk show she created, *The View* (1998–).

In 1961, Walters started as a writer and researcher for *Today* (1952–), but by 1964 she was not only writing the words but also delivering them on camera as the "Today Girl," and eventually cohosted the program until 1976. While appearing on *Today,* Walters also hosted a discussion series called *Not for Women Only* (1972–1976). She moved to ABC and signed a five-year contract for $1 million a year—the highest amount paid to any broadcaster to that time—and coanchored the *ABC Evening News* with Harry Reasoner (1976–1978), but hard news was not her niche.

She served as a correspondent for *20/20* (1979–1984) before joining the series as cohost with Hugh Downs, and continues to anchor that program. With its combination of newsworthy topics and entertainment, the series fits Walters's style better than a more somber news program. In addition, Walters has four interview specials each year, in which she interviews the "hot" people of the period, be they celebrities or politicians.

Walters has won many awards throughout her career, including Broadcaster of the Year (1975) and several Emmys. In 1989 she was inducted into the Television Hall of Fame, and in 1992 was honored for her "outstanding contribution to the television medium" by the American Museum of the Moving Image.

For all her success in television, Walters originally planned to become a teacher. However, following her graduation from Sarah Lawrence, she worked at an advertising agency, and decided that writing suited her better. Her first job in the television industry was as assistant director of publicity at WNBC and WNBT in New York. After a year, she was named a producer of the newly formed special-events division at NBC and began producing a local series, *Ask the Camera,* in 1953.

Waters, Ethel (1896–1977)

Born into poverty in Chester, Pennsylvania, Ethel Waters was married before she was 13, and by age 17 was a featured singer at the Lincoln Theatre in Baltimore. She appeared on stage and in clubs as one of the great blues singers of her time, billed as Sweet Mama Stringbean, popularizing such blues standards as "Dinah," "Stormy Weather," and "Heat Wave."

Waters was nominated for an Academy Award for Best Supporting Actress for her role in *Pinky* (1949). She received a New York Drama Critics' Circle Award for her role in *A Member of the Wedding* in 1950. She went on to appear in the film version of *A Member of the Wedding* (1952) as well as *The Sound and the Fury* (1959).

WANNABE-WIVES

The wannabe-wife was a stock character during the early years of television situation comedies. These female characters thought that life would not be complete for them until they found a husband, and they would do just about anything to find one.

Most of the single female characters on television during the 1950s and early 1960s held matrimony as their own personal Holy Grail. Connie Brooks (Eve Arden) of *Our Miss Brooks* (1952–1956) lived and breathed to snare the shy biology teacher, Mr. Boynton (Robert Rockwell). Susie McNamara (Ann Sothern) of *Private Secretary* (1953–1957) searched for Mr. Right when not making the life of her boss (Don Porter) more difficult. Sothern played a similarly romance-conscious character on *The Ann Sothern Show* (1958–1961) as the efficient assistant hotel manager, Katy O'Connor.

The next well-known wannabe-wife was Sally Rogers (Rose Marie) on *The Dick Van Dyke Show* (1961–1966). Although Sally was a well-paid and successful comedy writer, she was always looking for a "fella" to make her life more meaningful. Of course, Jeannie (Barbara Eden) on *I Dream of Jeannie* (1965–1970) lived to please her master (Larry Hagman) in the hopes that he would marry her.

As the women's movement of the 1960s gained attention and converts, female characters became less obsessed with getting married—at least overtly. However, while Ann Marie (Marlo Thomas) of *That Girl* (1966–1971) was supposedly pursuing her acting career, she was safely paired with boyfriend Donald (Ted Bessell) from the first episode. Female characters were given jobs and/or careers but, with few exceptions such as Murphy Brown, their focus remained long-term relationships, if not marriage.

Even with Mary Richards (Mary Tyler Moore) on *The Mary Tyler Moore Show* (1970–1977), the televisual epitome of the 1970s career woman, viewers had an understanding that she would one day find Mr. Right and marry. This trend continued in the 1990s. Caroline (Lea Thompson) of *Caroline in the City* (1995–1999) is much more interested in her romantic life than her professional one, and Susan (Brooke Shields) of *Suddenly Susan* (1996–) is likewise primarily concerned with her personal relationships.

The list is not limited to sitcoms. Many female characters in dramas, from medical to legal, are relationship-focused to a much greater degree than male characters.

She moved to television, appearing on *Beulah* (1950–1953), the first television series to feature a black woman in a title role. For two years she played the conscientious and long-suffering maid to the basically incompetent Henderson family. After she was replaced as Beulah, Waters made guest appearances on television until her death in 1977.

She wrote two volumes of her autobiography—*His Eye Is on the Sparrow* (1951), followed by *To Me It's Wonderful* (1972).

Radio entertainer Ethel Waters stands next to a microphone in this 1920s photograph. (Corbis/Bettmann)

Weitz, Julie Anne (1957–)

Julie Anne Weitz joined TNT as vice-president in charge of original pro-gramming in 1995, eventually being named executive vice-president of that division in 1996. She is in charge of the development and production of all original movies, miniseries, and specials for TNT, emphasizing strong, of-ten controversial topics from American history. In 1996 she supervised the production of the miniseries *Samson and Delilah,* as well as the critically acclaimed movies *Buffalo Soldiers, George Wallace Story,* and *Honor and Glory.*

Weitz earned her undergraduate degree in political science from UCLA and her graduate degree in communications management from USC be-fore becoming an A&R manager at CBS Records. She moved to the televi-sion industry and became director of development at Hearst Entertainment, and later president of von Zerneck/Sertner Films. In 1992 she moved to ICM, where she was head of long-form (that is, movie and miniseries) packaging.

Wendy and Me (1964–1965)

Wendy Conway (Connie Stevens) was the screwball bride of airline pilot Jeff (Ron Harper). They lived in an apartment building purchased by George Burns (who played himself), so that he would have a place to rehearse his act—just in case someone asked him to perform again.

Similar to the earlier Burns and Allen series from the 1950s, Burns (with his trademark cigar) served as on-screen narrator as he commented on Wendy's activities and dilemmas or entered the action himself. Unfortunately, Wendy was no Gracie, and the series ended after one season.

The Wendy Barrie Show (1949–1950)

Celebrity interviews and gossip were the main components of this program. Hosted by Wendy Barrie, a former movie starlet and one of television's first "personalities," the series took place on a set that supposedly duplicated her Manhattan apartment. The tone was definitely low-key as she welcomed her guests for what seemed to be a friendly chat. She signed off each show with the phrase "Be a good bunny."

The series went through several name changes during the months it was telecast. Originally produced in cooperation with the magazine, it was first called *Inside Photoplay* while on the Dumont Network, then became *Photoplay Time* when it moved to ABC late in 1949. Two months later, it was changed to *The Wendy Barrie Show,* and when it moved to NBC in August 1950, it was again changed, this time to *Through Wendy's Window.*

West, Betsy (1952–)

As vice-president of prime time for CBS News, Betsy West is in charge of all news programs shown during the evening hours, including *48 Hours* (1988–), *60 Minutes* (1968–), and the new *60 Minutes II* (1999–). Prior to joining CBS in 1998, West was a 23-year veteran with ABC News.

Her first job after receiving her master's from Syracuse's Newhouse School of Communications in 1975 was as a news writer for ABC News radio. She moved into field-producing for *World News Tonight* (1970–), and from 1983 to 1989 worked as senior producer for overseas coverage on *Nightline* (1980–). West has won 18 Emmys over her producing career.

White, Betty (1922–)

Betty White was born in Oak Park, Illinois, but moved to Southern California before she was two. She originally wanted to become a writer, but her interests soon turned to acting. After graduating from Beverly Hills High School and unsuccessfully trying to break into films, she turned to radio, reading commercials and playing bit parts for as little as $5 a show.

As television got its start, White began getting jobs on the small screen, first as a singer and then on a local Los Angeles game show, *Grab Your Phone.* In November 1949 she was hired as girl Friday for a local talk show, where she did everything from booking guests to reading commercials to singing. When the original host and his replacement left the show, White took over as sole host.

Concurrently with working on the talk show, White formed Bandy Productions with KLAC (later KCOP) station manager Don Fedderson and writer/director George Tibbles in 1952. Her first sitcom, *Life with Elizabeth* (1952–1955), was a combination of songs and witty dialogue around three vignettes that explored "life with Elizabeth." For KCOP's fiftieth anniversary telecast, White once more appeared in a short vignette as an updated Elizabeth.

Soon, NBC hired her away from the local KLAC, and in February 1954, *The Betty White Show* (1954–1955) premiered and ran concurrently with *Life with Elizabeth.* The new series was a 30-minute combination of songs and celebrity interviews.

After both her series ended, White became a regular guest on several game shows, including *To Tell the Truth* and *What's My Line?* For the next 20 years, beginning in 1955, White hosted the Tournament of Roses Parade from Pasadena, California, on New Year's Day. For ten years, White hosted the Macy's Thanksgiving Day Parade.

In 1957, Bandy Productions produced White's second sitcom, *A Date with the Angels.* The stories revolved around the life of newlywed couple Vicki (White) and Gus (Bill Williams) Angel and the well-intentioned schemes that Vicki dreamed up. The series was canceled after only six months, and a revamped *Betty White Show* took over the time slot. However, this series was also canceled after six months.

John Hillerman (John Elliot), Betty White (Joyce Whitman), and Georgia Engel (Mitzi Maloney) star in the short-lived 1977 revamped The Betty White Show. *(Photofest)*

White returned to being a guest panelist on various game shows and a regular on *The Jack Paar Show* for the next three years. For a brief time she hosted a radio program, *Ask Betty White,* which replaced *Ask Betty Furness* after Furness left to become involved in politics.

Unable to sell a network on a series concept, White continued as the perennial game show guest and toured in summer stock. In 1971, she briefly hosted an interview program, *The Pet Set,* which featured celebrities and their pets.

Finally, in 1973, White returned to prime time as the "Happy Homemaker," man-crazy Sue Ann Nivens on *The Mary Tyler Moore Show* (1970–1977). Although not appearing regularly (fewer than half of each season's episodes), White became identified with the calculating and catty Sue Ann.

She won back-to-back Emmys as Best Supporting Actress in a Comedy (1975, 1976).

After *The Mary Tyler Moore Show* went off the air in 1977, White briefly had her own series, *The Betty White Show,* about an out-of-work actress and her extended family. Unfortunately, placed against *Monday Night Football,* the series lasted only five months.

After this series ended, White returned to the game show arena, hosting a *Match Game*–type show called *Just Men!* where prime-time "hunks" helped contestants win a car. That year she became the only woman to win an Emmy as Best TV Game Show Host, even though the show lasted only six months.

In 1985, at age 63, White became associated with the biggest hit of her varied career. On 14 September 1985, she entered television history as the less-than-bright Rose Nyland on *The Golden Girls* (1985–1992). In 1985, White again won an Emmy, this time as Best Actress in a Comedy Series.

After *Golden Girls* ended, White appeared on *Golden Palace* (1992–1993), in which three of the characters from *The Golden Girls* (Blanche, Sophia, and Rose) bought a Miami hotel. Lacking the bite and wit of the previous series, it lasted only one season.

White is active in humane organizations, and in 1983 her first book was published: *Betty White's Pet Love.* Her next book was a collection of autobiographical remembrances entitled *Betty White—In Person* (1988). Her third book, *The Leading Lady: Dinah's Story,* about blind performer Tom Sullivan's seeing-eye dog, was published in 1991.

In 1994, White became the tenth woman to be inducted into the Television Hall of Fame. In that same year, she published her autobiography, *Here We Go Again: My Life in Television.* In September 1995, *Maybe This Time* premiered, in which White played Marie Osmond's matchmaking mother, but the series lasted only a season.

White, Vanna (1957–)

Vanna White has become a popular culture icon virtually without saying a word. White was a model and sometimes-actress who in 1982 landed the job of a lifetime. In 1982 she became the letter-turner on *Wheel of Fortune,* the highest-rated syndicated series in the history of television.

Other than talking briefly with host Pat Sajak at the beginning and end of the program, White achieved celebrity with little effort on her part.

She was so popular with viewers that she was named cohost in the early 1990s.

Her popularity made her tabloid-fodder as the supermarket newspapers avidly followed her romantic travails and, after she married, her efforts to have children. In 1998 she widened her horizons by authoring a book, *Vanna's Afghans A to Z,* which presents some of her favorite crochet patterns.

The Whoopi Goldberg Show (1992–1993)

In this late-night talk show, which had Goldberg welcoming a new guest to her informal set every night, no controversial or challenging questions were allowed. This laid-back interview show featured current news-makers as well as celebrities. Goldberg's encouraging demeanor and nonconfrontational style might well have won her the title "Queen of Nice" if the accolade had existed when this series aired.

In 1998, Goldberg returned to television to appear as the center square on *The New Hollywood Squares,* which is produced by her production company, One Ho Productions. Several high-profile celebrities appear on the program, with donations going to their chosen charities in lieu of regular salaries.

Who's the Boss (1984–1992)

In a role-reversal series, former baseball player Tony Micelli (Tony Danza) tended the house, and advertising executive Angela Bower (Judith Light, a two-time Emmy winner for her role on *One Life to Live*) was the stressed professional.

In the first episode, divorcée Angela hired widower Tony to manage her house and "active" son, Jonathan (Danny Pintauro), thus giving Tony and his daughter, Samantha (Alyssa Milano), a home. Along with Mona (Katherine Helmond), Angela's oversexed mother, they formed a televisual reconstructed family unit.

The episodes dealt with the everyday problems encountered by the family members, as well as the growing attraction between Angela and Tony. It took them seven years to decide that they had indeed fallen in love, and then they almost broke up when Tony took a coaching job in Iowa. After trying several alternatives, Angela realized that she couldn't give up the challenge of her lifestyle and settle down in the backwoods of Iowa.

Giving up on the relationship, Angela once again advertised for a housekeeper, only to have the ad answered by Tony. In a final role-reversal, he had decided that his job was not as important as their love and the life they could spend together.

In a further reversal of normal events, where British series are imported to American television, this series was adapted for British tastes and was a huge success called *The Upper Hand*.

Willy (1954–1955)

Arguably the first drama to feature a female lawyer, the plots of this series did not involve serious legal issues. When her small hometown in New Hampshire did not supply enough cases to keep newly graduated attorney Willa Dodge (June Havoc) busy, she accepted an offer to represent a show business organization. This necessitated a move to New York City, with the typical small-town-girl-in-the-big-city fare. However, the series never found an audience, and it was canceled after one season.

WINDOW DRESSING

A term used, generally, by feminist television critics for female characters who are included in action series only to attract male viewers. These characters are seldom functional or important to the plot or action, but rather, often become damsels-in-distress for the main male characters to save.

This type of character has become less prevalent in recent years, but was often found on early adventure series such as *The Alaskans* (1959–1960) and *Hawaiian Eye* (1959–1963). Singer Rocky Shaw (Dorothy Provine) was the feminine interest on *The Alaskans*, and singer-photographer Cricket Blake (Connie Stevens) offset the swinging detectives on *Hawaiian Eye*. Interestingly, most of these characters were often named after spices (Cinnamon, Pepper), small creatures (Cricket), or given male-sounding nicknames (Rocky).

Winfrey, Oprah (1954–)

One of the richest women in the entertainment industry, Oprah Winfrey was born to a single mother and lived the first six years of her life with her grandmother on a pig farm in rural Mississippi. Because her grandmother tutored her, she was able to do arithmetic, read, and write before she entered school. Fond of the spotlight, she participated in church plays and dramatizations.

In 1960, Winfrey went to live with her mother, Vernita, in a Milwaukee rooming house, sharing a room with her mother and her younger half-sister, Patricia. In 1962, after Vernita's current boyfriend refused to marry her, Winfrey was sent to live with her father, Vernon Winfrey, and his wife in Nashville.

1997 photograph of television personality Oprah Winfrey. (Corbis/Mitchell Gerber)

Her father and stepmother brought stability into her life, and they were adamant about her getting an education. While living in Nashville she made her first "professional" appearance, a dramatic speech before a church group for which she received $500. She was seven years old.

Winfrey visited her mother during the summer, and Vernita decided that she did not want her daughter to return to Nashville. Uprooted once again, Winfrey moved in with her mother, Patricia, and a new baby brother, Jeffrey, in a two-room apartment that they shared with Vernita's new boyfriend.

When Winfrey was nine (or 12, depending on the source), she was raped by a 14-year-old cousin who lived with her family in the cramped apartment. Submitting to sexual attention from male relatives and their friends brought her the attention she craved but could never get from her mother.

Winfrey continued to excel at school, and in 1968 she was given an Upward Bound scholarship to an all-white high school in Fox Lake, a suburb of Milwaukee, more than 20 miles away. She had access to better educational facilities, but she also began to run wild, and her mother could no longer pretend that she controlled her 14-year-old daughter.

She was sent back to Nashville and her father's family. Soon after she arrived, her stepmother discovered that she was pregnant. Winfrey miscarried the male fetus, an event that haunted her for years.

At her father's, her life revolved around school, the church, and family. She was assigned outside reading by her stepmother and had to report to her on the books. In addition, she had to learn 20 new words a week.

Winfrey not only excelled in academics, she was also popular with her peers and was elected student council president. She continued to give dramatic recitations at churches and civic groups several times a month. While still in high school, Winfrey was hired by a local radio station (WVOL) to read news reports for $100 a week. At this radio station, she got her first technical experience with show business.

Winfrey entered Tennessee State University on a four-year scholarship after she won the title Miss Black Tennessee in 1972. However, in 1973 Winfrey accepted a job with WTVF-TV, the CBS affiliate in Nashville, which necessitated dropping out of school. This job made Winfrey the first female and the first black newscaster in Nashville.

Three years later she moved to WJZ-TV, an ABC affiliate, in Baltimore. The qualities that made her popular in Nashville—her concern for others and her conversational style—made her a pariah in Baltimore. The station tried to "make her over," but only succeeded in undermining her confidence.

In 1977, Winfrey began cohosting a new show on WJZ-TV, *People Are Talking.* To everyone's surprise, the show beat the established juggernaut, *Donahue,* in local ratings. The show's success reaffirmed to Winfrey that her style had an audience.

Winfrey moved to Chicago in 1984 to host the half-hour *A.M. Chicago* at WLS-TV. Within six months of her first appearance, she "owned" her time slot, and the program was expanded to an hour. By 1985, she controlled all aspects of the show, from topics to guests to behind-the-scenes activities.

Winfrey appeared in her first film that same year. She was cast as the strong-willed Sophia in *The Color Purple,* based on the book by Alice Walker. The role earned Winfrey an Oscar nomination for Best Supporting Actress.

Although WLS-TV had released her to appear in the film, the experience made Winfrey realize that she needed control of the show to control her own future. As she completed filming, negotiations began to syndicate *A.M. Chicago* as the *Oprah Winfrey Show.*

In 1986, Winfrey formed her first production company to produce the show, giving her further control of her "product." During that same year she appeared in another film, *Native Son,* as a mother whose son strikes back at racism by killing a white girl. By the end of the year, the first that her show was shown nationally, Winfrey had grossed $30 million, and she won the Emmy for Best Talk Show (1987).

In the late 1980s, like other talk shows, *Oprah!* presented sensationalized programs ranging from satanic worship to sex surrogates to auto-erotic asphyxia. Jenny Jones is "credited" with one murder, but Winfrey is credited with two suicides.

In 1989, Winfrey produced her first miniseries, *The Women of Brewster Place,* in the new facilities for her renamed production company, Harpo Studios. The miniseries became a series on ABC, but lasted only one month. By building her own facilities, Winfrey became the first African American and the third woman (after Mary Pickford and Lucille Ball) to own a production facility.

Also in 1989, Winfrey opened an extremely popular restaurant, The Eccentric, in the Chicago area, further diversifying her interests. In 1991, Winfrey won a grand slam of Emmys—one for Outstanding Host, one for Outstanding Talk Show, and one for Outstanding Director.

Also in 1991, Winfrey began working for the passage of the National Child Protection Bill, which would allow employers to check for a history of child abuse in a job applicant's past. When the bill failed in Congress, Winfrey was instrumental in getting a 1992 special produced, entitled *Scared Silent: Exposing and Ending Child Abuse.*

In 1993, Winfrey became the first black woman to be inducted into the Television Hall of Fame. A few years later her production company signed a six-movie deal to produce films under the "Oprah Winfrey Presents" umbrella. The first, *Before Women Had Wings* (1997), dealt with child abuse. Next came *Tuesdays with Morrie* (1998), followed that same year by remakes of *David and Lisa* and *The Wedding.*

Also in 1998, Winfrey produced and starred in *Beloved,* based on Toni Morrison's novel, Winfrey's first effort that was not extremely successful. About the same time, Winfrey lost her talk show crown to Jerry Springer and his aggression-based talk show, only to have both talk shows lose the crown to the syndicated court series *Judge Judy.*

Still, Winfrey has enough clout to create best-selling books simply by recommending them to the audience in her Book Club segment and can influence her audience's buying preferences by endorsing certain products.

In November 1998, Winfrey became a partner in the Oxygen Channel, a new network for women slated to launch in 2000.

Wizard of Oz (1939)

Until recently, when the movie went into limited video release, the broadcast of this 1939 movie starring Judy Garland, Ray Bolger, Jack Haley, Bert Lahr, Margaret Hamilton, and Frank Morgan was an almost annual prime-time tradition. In fact, it was the movie's repeated television exposure that elevated a coolly received movie when first released into the classic it is considered today.

The film appears seven times on Nielsen Media Research's 1991 listing of the "top rated Network Prime-Time Feature Films," garnering no less than a 49 percent share of the viewing audience in all its outings.

Wonder Woman (1976–1979)

Based on the comic-book character created by Charles Moulon in the 1940s, the series appeared intermittently on ABC before moving to CBS in 1977 as a weekly series. On ABC, Wonder Woman (Lynda Carter), like her comic-book alter ego, fought Nazi agents and other World War II–era criminals to protect mortals and especially Major Steve Trevor (Lyle Waggoner), for whom Wonder Woman worked as secretary in her mortal guise as Yeoman Diana Prince.

When the show moved to CBS, the time period was contemporary, and Diana, who didn't age like mortals, now worked for the Inter-Agency Defense Command (IADC) with Steve Trevor Junior, who looked exactly like his father. Trevor was eventually promoted to the position of Diana's boss, which meant that she went on missions alone to fight terrorists and other threats to the American way of life.

The series never lost its comic-book approach to plots or took itself too seriously, which allowed it to spoof the genre it depicted.

Working Girl (1990)

This very short-lived series is notable only as the television debut of San-dra Bullock, who later hit it big in such movies as *Speed* (1994), *While You Were Sleeping* (1996), and *Hope Floats* (1998).

The concept, based on the hit 1988 movie of the same name, was that Tess McGill (Bullock) was an independent, gutsy secretary who charmed her way into a junior executive position, then had to survive hostile corpo-rate politics and the antagonism of her boss, Ms. Newhouse (Nana Visitor).

X

Xena, Warrior Princess (1995–)

Xena, Warrior Princess, the most popular syndicated series in syndication history, is a spinoff of *Hercules: The Legendary Journeys* that premiered in September 1995. The series is the first to feature a female in a superhero odyssey-action format. In just a few years, it has spawned a Xena cult, with avid fans who flock to conventions and are eager consumers of merchandise from the Xena-verse.

Xena (Lucy Lawless) is a former evil mercenary leader who has renounced her previous lifestyle and is on a quest to make amends for the pain and destruction she once caused. She has turned her back on her former patron god, Ares (Kevin Smith), and defends the people on whom she had previously preyed.

Xena is the first series to feature a female action hero in the true sense of the word. She is an expert in martial arts and uses all forms of weaponry. Xena is not confined to strictly defending the downtrodden; she goes on the offensive when necessary, and can be as lethal and ruthless as those she defends against.

Yet, for all her strength and cunning, Xena has a sensitive and compassionate side. She is haunted by her murderous past, and believes that no matter how much good she does, she can never make up for the death and destruction she caused in her former life.

In the first episode, Xena met Gabrielle (Renee O'Connor), an innocent young woman who joined Xena to see the world and seek adventure.

Along the way, Gabrielle learned about herself and helped Xena learn about her own inner qualities, long hidden by her hard facade. During their travels, a deep familial bond formed, and they became sisters in the true meaning of the term.

Xena is not the first female fantasy character (Sheena, Queen of the Jungle, Wonder Woman, and Bionic Woman are others), but the Xena character, in addition to being more independent and lethal, is not perfect. The issues from her past enable the character to explore her flaws and through soul-searching become stronger.

She perhaps is more heroic because she is not innately good—she must work at overcoming her inner demons to achieve goodness. Her inner quest—her mistakes and her attempts at redemption—makes Xena appealing to a wide variety of viewers. The series does not take itself too seriously, but maintains a balance between being camp and meaningful.

Although the stories involve Xena battling evildoers or mythical beasts, the time period is completely fluid in a time warp known as the Xena-verse. Any person or event even faintly mythical or classical is fair game for inclusion in the Xena-verse. Xena has been involved with or fought against Julius Caesar, David and Goliath, Ulysses, the Lost Mariner, the Ark of the Covenant, Mary and Joseph, Hippocrates, Prometheus, Helen of Troy, and Homer.

Lucy Lawless stars in the fantasy series Xena, Warrior Princess. *(MCA TV Int'l/Archive Photos)*

The X-Files (1993–)

Although not a female-centered series, the female character of this science fiction/fantasy drama, FBI Agent Dana Scully (Gillian Anderson), is one of the most self-reliant and emotionally strong women ever to appear on television.

Scully, a medical doctor with a grounding in physical sciences, and her partner, Fox Mulder (David Duchovny), investigate cases involving situations and phenomena that defy conventional explanation, such as UFOs, aliens, mutants, and clones.

Scully faces all manner of life-threatening circumstances with a calm belief that a scientific explanation exists for everything. Her skepticism perfectly offsets Mulder's easy belief and acceptance of all things bizarre and incredible.

A tremendous cult hit, the series has spawned fan conventions, books, and, in 1998, a movie. It was the first science-fiction program to win a Golden Globe for Best Dramatic Series (1994–1995) and has been nominated for numerous Emmy awards.

Gillian Anderson and David Duchovny as Agents Dana Scully and Fox Mulder in the popular The X-Files. *(Michael Grecco/FOX/ Photofest)*

Y

Young, Loretta (1913–)

Loretta Young was one of the most successful anthology hostesses of the early years of television. Her series, *The Loretta Young Show* (1953–1961), was a favorite with the public and earned Young three Emmys.

Each episode opened with Young sweeping on-screen in a full-length dress to introduce the evening's presentation. Each play ended with Young reading a poem, a passage from the Bible, or a saying by Confucius that restated the episode's theme.

Whether serious or amusing, all the plays concentrated on celebrating the human spirit and taught "wholesome," socially accepted values. Young once said that she went into television to present a role model for young girls, and because she had complete control of her series, she could do just that.

The year after her first series ended, she starred in *The New Loretta Young Show* (1962–1963), in which she portrayed Christine Massey, a widowed writer with seven children trying to raise her family alone while continuing her career. Most episodes centered around Christine, but other family members were sometimes the focus of episodes.

Young first made a name for herself in films before moving to television. Although she had a small part in *Sweet Kitty Bellairs* (1916), she didn't pursue an acting career until she was 15. A small role in *Naughty but Nice* (1927) earned her a screen contract, and her first major film role was in *Laugh, Clown, Laugh* (1928).

She appeared in many popular films of the Depression and war years, winning the Best Actress Oscar for her role in *Farmer's Daughter* (1947). She was nominated for the award again in 1949 for her role in *Come to the Stable.* She retired from feature films to work on her television show, and when the series ended, she devoted her time to Catholic charities.

Z

Zarghami, Cyma (1960–)

Cyma Zarghami, executive vice-president and general manager of Nickelodeon, has been with the network for 14 years, working in the programming, scheduling, and acquisitions divisions. She was named general manager in 1996 and spearheaded the launch of Nick Jr., SNICK (Saturday Night Nickelodeon), TV Land, and Nicktoons.

Zirinsky, Susan (1950–)

As executive producer of *48 Hours*, Susan Zirinsky is credited with revitalizing the ailing newsmagazine to make it competitive with the ratings giant *ER*, which it faces in its time slot. She also worked as a senior producer for *The Evening News* and supervised special-events coverage, including the network's political reporting.

After graduating from American University, Zirinsky went to work for Ed Koch, then a congressman from Manhattan. At the height of the Watergate period, Zirinsky began working part-time at CBS News' Washington bureau. She soon worked for CBS full-time, and has moved steadily up the ranks. She is not interested in an executive management position because, at the end of the day, she likes to view the broadcast and "see the house [that] I helped build."

Directors

Adams, Catlin

    Beverly Hills 90210 (1991)

Addison, Anita

    Sisters (1990)

    Knots Landing (1990)

    Sisters (1991)

    Quantum Leap (1991)

    Knots Landing (1991)

    Homefront (1991)

    Quantum Leap (1992)

    Homefront (1992)

    Sirens (1993)

    The Great Defender (1995)

    ER (1995)

    EZ Streets (1997)

Allen, Debbie

    Fame (1983)

    The Bronx Zoo (1987)

    Family Ties (1987)

    Family Ties (1988)

    A Different World (1988)

    The Debbie Allen Special (1989)

    A Different World (1989)

    The Fresh Prince of Bel Air (1990)

    The Debbie Allen Special (1990)

    Quantum Leap (1990)

    A Different World (1990)

    The Fresh Prince of Bel Air (1991)

    A Different World (1991)

    Quantum Leap (1991)

    A Different World (1992)

    The Sinbad Show (1993)

    A Different World (1993)

Amato, Barbara

    Equal Justice (1990)

    I'll Fly Away (1991)

    Equal Justice (1991)

    Sisters (1992)

    I'll Fly Away (1992)

    The Commish (1993)

    Sisters (1993)

    Melrose Place (1993)

    The Commish (1994)

    Melrose Place (1994)

Anderson, Sarah Pia

    The Profiler (1997)

Ark, Joan Van

    Knots Landing (1990)

    Knots Landing (1991)

    Knots Landing (1992)

    Knots Landing (1993)

    Boys Will Be Boys (1994)

Arner, Gwen

    Paper Chase (1979)

    Family (1980)

    Nurse (1981)

    The Waltons (1982)

Falcon Crest (1982)
King's Crossing (1982)
Falcon Crest (1983)
Fame (1984)
Dynasty (1985)
The Colbys (1986)
Dynasty (1986)
Dynasty (1987)
Hotel (1988)
Heartbeat (1988)
Blue Skies (1988)
Tattingers (1989)
Island Son (1989)
Alien Nation (1989)
The Trials of Rosie O'Neill (1990)
The Outsiders (1990)
Island Son (1990)
Alien Nation (1990)
The Commish (1991)
Sisters (1991)
The Commish (1992)
Sisters (1992)
The Commish (1993)
Sisters (1993)
Beverly Hills 90210 (1993)
The Cosby Mysteries (1994)
Dr. Quinn, Medicine Woman (1994)
Sisters (1994)
Dr. Quinn, Medicine Woman (1995)
Homicide: Life on the Streets (1996)
Dr. Quinn, Medicine Woman (1996)

Arthur, Karen

Hart to Hart (1980)
Boone (1983)
Remington Steele (1984)
Emerald Point, NAS (1984)
Shadow of a Doubt (1991)
The Secret (1992)
Journey of the Heart (1997)

Askins, Judy (aka Judy Pioli)

Perfect Strangers (1989)
The Hogan Family (1989)
The Family Man (1990)

The Golden Girls (1991)
Step by Step (1992)
Wings (1993)
Getting By (1993)
First Time Out (1995)

Ballard, Christine

It's a Living (1985)
Charles in Charge (1985)
Alice (1985)
Night Court (1990)
Night Court (1991)

Bearse, Amanda

Simon (1996)
Married . . . with Children (1996)
Malcolm and Eddie (1996)
Pauly (1997)
Married . . . with Children (1997)

Beaumont, Gabrielle

Greatest American Hero (1982)
Private Benjamin (1982)
M*A*S*H (1982)
Flamingo Road (1982)
Archie Bunker's Place (1982)
Zorro and Son (1983)
Trauma Center (1983)
Secrets of a Mother and Daughter (1983)
M*A*S*H (1983)
The Corvini Inheritance (1984)
Gone Are the Days (1984)
Glitter (1984)
Remington Steele (1985)
Hotel (1985)
Hill Street Blues (1985)
Dynasty (1985)
The Colbys (1986)
Hotel (1986)
Hill Street Blues (1986)
Dynasty (1986)
Miami Vice (1987)
Beauty and the Beast (1987)
Beverly Hills Buntz (1988)
A Year in the Life (1988)

Studio 5B (1989)

Star Trek: The Next Generation
    (1989)

Doogie Howser, M.D. (1989)

A Fine Romance (1989)

Star Trek: The Next Generation
    (1990)

Doogie Howser, M.D. (1990)

Star Trek: The Next Generation
    (1991)

Doogie Howser, M.D. (1991)

Doogie Howser, M.D. (1992)

seaQuest DSV (1993)

Law & Order (1993)

seaQuest DSV (1994)

Moment of Truth: Cradle of
    Conspiracy (1994)

Law & Order (1994)

Vanishing Son (1995)

Dr. Quinn, Medicine Woman (1996)

Belli, Mary Lou

Charles in Charge (1985)

Major Dad (1992)

Bergmann, Gail

Who's the Boss (1986)

Who's the Boss (1987)

Blye, Rita Rogers

The Fresh Prince of Bel Air (1990)

The Fresh Prince of Bel Air (1991)

The Fresh Prince of Bel Air (1992)

Brown, Charlotte

Rhoda (1978)

The Associates (1979)

Between the Lines (1980)

Archie Bunker's Place (1980)

Archie Bunker's Place (1981)

It's Not Easy (1983)

Goodbye Girl (1984)

Second Edition (1984)

Cagney and Lacey (1985)

Real Life (1988)

The Tortellis (1988)

Capparelli, Mikki

227 (1988)

227 (1989)

227 (1990)

Chopra, Joyce

Confessions (1985)

Smooth Talk (1985)

The Lemon Sisters (1989)

The Widow Claire (1991)

The Danger of Love (1992)

Murder in New Hampshire: The
    Pamela Smart Story (1992)

The Baby Snatchers (1992)

The Disappearance of Nora (1993)

Angel Falls (1993)

The Corpse Had a Familiar Face
    (1994)

Deadline for Murder: From the Files
    of Edna Buchanan (1995)

My Very Best Friend (1996)

Coolidge, Martha

Twilight Zone (1985)

Sledge Hammer (1986)

Twilight Zone (1986)

Twilight Zone (1987)

Rough House (1988)

Trenchcoat in Paradise (1990)

Bare Essentials (1991)

Crazy in Love (1992)

Cooperstein, Nancy

Over the Limit (1990)

The Wonder Years (1991)

The Wonder Years (1992)

Cox, Nell

Liza's Pioneer Diary (1976)

The Waltons (1979)

9 to 5 (1982)

M*A*S*H (1983)

The Love Boat (1985)

Konrad (1985)

Hometown (1985)

L.A. Law (1987)

Read between the Lines (1988)

Traitor in My House (1990)

Cripe, Madeline

My Two Dads (1989)

It's Garry Shandling's Show (1989)

It's Garry Shandling's Show (1990)

The Fresh Prince of Bel Air (1993)

The Fresh Prince of Bel Air (1994)

The Fresh Prince of Bel Air (1995)

The Fresh Prince of Bel Air (1996)

In the House (1996)

In the House (1997)

Darling, Joan

The Mary Tyler Moore Show (1975)

M*A*S*H (1975)

Phyllis (1975)

Phyllis (1976)

Doc (1976)

Rhoda (1977)

Phyllis (1977)

Rhoda (1978)

Willa (1979)

Stockard Channing in Just Friends (1979)

Hizzoner (1979)

The Family Tree (1983)

A.K.A. Pablo (1983)

A.K.A. Pablo (1984)

Amazing Stories (1986)

Supermom's Daughter (1987)

Nothing Is Easy (1987)

Magnum P.I. (1987)

Hiroshima Maiden (1988)

Doogie Howser, M.D. (1990)

Civil Wars (1991)

Doogie Howser, M.D. (1991)

Jack's Place (1992)

Doogie Howser, M.D. (1992)

Civil Wars (1992)

Davidson, Janet

Earth 2 (1995)

Day, Linda

The Crew (1979)

Alice (1979)

WKRP in Cincinnati (1980)

Archie Bunker's Place (1980)

Alice (1980)

WKRP in Cincinnati (1981)

Too Close for Comfort (1981)

Archie Bunker's Place (1981)

Alice (1981)

WKRP in Cincinnati (1982)

Teachers Only (1982)

Star in the Family (1982)

I'd Rather Be Calm (1982)

Gimme a Break (1982)

Archie Bunker's Place (1982)

WKRP in Cincinnati (1983)

Star in the Family (1983)

Gimme a Break (1983)

Benson (1983)

Archie Bunker's Place (1983)

After George (1983)

Who's the Boss (1984)

The Facts of Life (1984)

It's Your Move (1984)

Gimme a Break (1984)

Diff'rent Strokes (1984)

Who's the Boss (1985)

Knots Landing (1985)

It's Your Move (1985)

Gimme a Break (1985)

Double Trouble (1985)

Dallas (1985)

Berrengers (1985)

Throb (1986)

Sweet Surrender (1986)

Knots Landing (1986)

Gimme a Break (1986)

Dallas (1986)

Harry (1987)

Gimme a Break (1987)

Changing Patterns (1987)

Mutts (1988)

Kate and Allie (1988)

Morton's by the Bay (1989)

Major Dad (1989)

Homeroom (1989)

Married . . . with Children (1990)

Beanpole (1990)

Top of the Heap (1991)

Married . . . with Children (1991)

Baby Talk (1991)

Baby Talk (1992)

Thea (1993)

Models, Inc. (1993)

The Nanny (1993)

Tall Hopes (1993)

Mad about You (1993)

Daddy Dearest (1993)

Almost Home (1993)

The Nanny (1994)

The 5 Mrs. Buchanans (1994)

Unhappily Ever After (1995)

The Parent'Hood (1995)

The 5 Mrs. Buchanans (1995)

Cleghorne! (1995)

Unhappily Ever After (1996)

Jeff Foxworthy (1996)

The Crew (1996)

Simon (1996)

Dave's World (1996)

Clueless (1997)

Unhappily Ever After (1997)

Deaton, Marion

Facts of Life (1986)

Facts of Life (1987)

Carol & Company (1990)

Martin (1997)

Deitch, Donna

Morning Glory (1985)

The Women of Brewster Place (1989)

Women in Prison (1990)

WIOU (1990)

Sexual Advances (1992)

A Change of Place (1994)

Robin's Hoods (1995)

NYPD Blue (1995)

Murder One (1995)

ER (1995)

Second Noah (1996)

NYPD Blue (1996)

Murder One (1996)

Moloney (1996)

Murder One (1997)

EZ Streets (1997)

Dugan, Iris

Designing Women (1989)

Sydney (1990)

Designing Women (1990)

Growing Pains (1991)

Growing Pains (1992)

High Society (1995)

Elzy-Jones, Erma

Moesha (1997)

Feldman, Rachel

True Confessions (1989)

Doogie Howser, M.D. (1992)

The Commish (1993)

Sisters (1994)

The Commish (1994)

Picket Fences (1994)

Dr. Quinn, Medicine Woman (1994)

Sisters (1995)

University Hospital (1995)

Sisters (1996)

Ferrara, Lorraine

Falcon Crest (1985)

Emerald Point (1985)

Dynasty (1985)

Trapper John, M.D. (1985)

Knots Landing (1985)

Berrengers (1985)

Knots Landing (1986)

Kay O'Brien (1986)

Knots Landing (1987)

Knots Landing (1988)

Knots Landing (1989)

Knots Landing (1990)

Sisters (1991)

Knots Landing (1991)
Homefront (1991)
Sisters (1992)
Picket Fences (1992)
Knots Landing (1992)
Homefront (1992)
Picket Fences (1993)
Northern Exposure (1993)
Moon over Miami (1993)
Dr. Quinn, Medicine Woman (1993)
Northern Exposure (1994)
Hotel Malibu (1994)
Dr. Quinn, Medicine Woman (1994)
Babylon 5 (1994)
VR5 (1995)
Second Noah (1996)

Ferraro, Delores

WKRP in Cincinnati (1981)
WKRP in Cincinnati (1982)
Facts of Life (1982)
Diff'rent Strokes (1983)
Mary (1986)
Newhart (1986)
Ellen Burstyn Show (1987)
Knots Landing (1988)

Fogle, JoeAnn

Doogie Howser, M.D. (1991)
Civil Wars (1991)
Doogie Howser, M.D. (1992)
Civil Wars (1992)
Doogie Howser, M.D. (1993)
The Byrds of Paradise (1994)
Sweet Justice (1994)
NYPD Blue (1995)
Murder One (1995)
Earth 2 (1995)
Murder One (1996)

Friedman, Kim

L.A. Law (1979)
Family (1979)
Square Pegs (1982)
Nurse (1982)
Knots Landing (1982)

Goodnight, Beantown (1983)
Square Pegs (1983)
Knots Landing (1983)
For Members Only (1983)
Alice (1984)
The Love Boat (1985)
Hotel (1985)
Hometown (1985)
Dynasty (1985)
The Love Boat (1986)
The Colbys (1986)
Jack and Mike (1986)
Head of the Class (1986)
Dynasty (1986)
The Colbys (1987)
Rags to Riches (1987)
Hooperman (1987)
A Different World (1987)
Hooperman (1988)
A Year in the Life (1988)
A Different World (1988)
Life Goes On (1989)
Just Temporary (1989)
Life Goes On (1990)
Life Goes On (1991)
Life Goes On (1992)
StarTrek: Deep Space Nine (1993)
Sweet Justice (1994)
StarTrek: Deep Space Nine (1994)
The Pursuit of Happiness (1995)
Sweet Justice (1995)
StarTrek: Voyager (1995)
Pig Sty (1995)
Almost Perfect (1995)
In the House (1996)
The Single Guy (1996)

Fryman, Pamela

Cafe Americain (1993)
Muddling Through (1994)
Friends (1994)
Cafe Americain (1994)
The Naked Truth (1995)
The Boys Are Back (1995)
Dweebs (1995)

Bringing Up Jack (1995)
Bless This House (1995)
Townies (1996)
The Naked Truth (1996)
Ned and Stacey (1996)
Good Company (1996)
Cybill (1996)
Caroline in the City (1996)
Bless This House (1996)
The Single Guy (1997)
Suddenly Susan (1997)
Frasier (1997)
Cybill (1997)

Garrett, Lila

Terraces (1977)
Archie Bunker's Place (1980)
Baby Makes Five (1983)
Spencer (1984)
Under One Roof (1985)
Spencer (1985)
Who Gets the Friends (1986)
Bridesmaids (1989)

Glatter, Leslie Linka

Tales of Meeting and Parting (1985)
Amazing Stories (1986)
Into the Homeland (1987)
Amazing Stories (1987)
War Story–Vietnam (1988)
Twin Peaks (1990)
Brewster Place (1990)
Twin Peaks (1991)
Smoldering Lust (1992)
On the Air (1992)
Slow Breed (1993)
Black Tie Affair (1993)
State of Emergency (1994)
NYPD Blue (1994)
Chicago Hope (1994)
Birdland (1994)
ER (1995)
Murder One (1996)
ER (1996)

Greek, Janet C.

St. Elsewhere (1985)
Max Headroom (1987)
L.A. Law (1987)
The Outsiders (1990)
Over My Dead Body (1990)
Going to Extremes (1992)
Going to Extremes (1993)
Babylon 5 (1994)
Northern Exposure (1995)
Babylon 5 (1995)
Melrose Place (1996)
Hypernauts (1996)
The Burning Zone (1997)
Melrose Place (1997)

Hamilton, Anne Lewis

thirtysomething (1990)
thirtysomething (1991)
Sirens (1993)

Hamrick, Lynn

This Is the Life (1986)
Family Ties (1986)
Family Ties (1987)
Testing Dirty (1991)
Growing Up Together (1992)
Babysitter's Club (1993)
Silk Stalkings (1993)
Silk Stalkings (1994)

Head, Helaine

St. Elsewhere (1986)
Sidekicks (1986)
Cagney and Lacey (1986)
St. Elsewhere (1987)
L.A. Law (1987)
Frank's Place (1987)
Cagney and Lacey (1987)
A Year in the Life (1987)
L.A. Law (1988)
Annie McGuire (1988)
A Year in the Life (1988)
Wiseguy (1989)
Tour of Duty (1989)

Top of the Hill (1989)
Snoops (1989)
Island Son (1989)
Brewster Place (1990)
Danger Team (1991)
You Must Remember This (1992)
Simple Justice (1993)
seaQuest DSV (1993)
Jack's Place (1993)
Harts of the West (1993)
Class of '96 (1993)
Sweet Justice (1994)
Sisters (1994)
seaQuest DSV (1994)
New York Undercover (1994)
Law & Order (1994)
Harts of the West (1994)
Touched by an Angel (1995)
The Client (1995)
New York Undercover (1996)
The Client (1996)

Heydon, Nancy
Too Close for Comfort (1984)
Alf (1986)
Alf (1987)
Growing Pains (1991)
Growing Pains (1992)

Hillshafer, Beth
St. Elsewhere (1985)
St. Elsewhere (1986)
The Slap Maxwell Show (1987)
St. Elsewhere (1987)
The Slap Maxwell Show (1988)
St. Elsewhere (1988)
Eisenhower & Lutz (1988)
Dear John (1988)
China Beach (1988)
TV 101 (1989)
The Wonder Years (1989)
Peaceable Kingdom (1989)
Hooperman (1989)
Beauty and the Beast (1989)

American Nuclear (1989)
WIOU (1990)
Ferris Bueller (1990)
Elvis (1990)
Beverly Hills 90210 (1990)
Ferris Bueller (1991)
Beverly Hills 90210 (1991)

Hochberg, Victoria G.
Jacob Have I Loved (1989)
Sweet 15 (1990)
Doogie Howser, M.D. (1990)
The Trials of Rosie O'Neill (1991)
Doogie Howser, M.D. (1991)
The Trials of Rose O'Neill (1992)
Melrose Place (1992)
Melrose Place (1993)
Models, Inc. (1994)
Melrose Place (1994)
Dr. Quinn, Medicine Woman (1994)
Touched by an Angel (1995)
Models, Inc. (1995)
Melrose Place (1995)
Central Park West (1995)
Touched by an Angel (1996)
Melrose Place (1996)

Hussein, Waris
Three Weeks (1977)
And Baby Makes Six (1979)
The Henderson Monster (1980)
Death Penalty (1980)
Baby Comes Home (1980)
Callie & Son (1981)
Little Gloria . . . Happy at Last (1982)
Come Out of the Ice (1982)
The Winter of Our Discontent
    (1983)
Princess Daisy (1983)
Surviving (1985)
Copacabana (1985)
Arch of Triumph (1985)
When the Bough Breaks (1986)
Maggie (1986)

Downpayment on Murder (1987)

*The Richest Man in the World:
    Aristotle Onassis* (1988)

Killer Instinct (1988)

Those She Left Behind (1989)

The Shell Seekers (1989)

Forbidden Nights (1990)

Switched at Birth (1991)

She Woke Up (1991)

*For the Love of a Child: The Anissia
    Ayala Story* (1993)

Murder between Friends (1994)

Fortitude (1994)

Fall from Grace (1994)

The Face on the Milk Carton (1995)

A Child's Wish (1997)

Jensen, Shelley

Webster (1985)

Brothers (1986)

Amen (1989)

Amen (1990)

The Royal Family (1991)

The Fresh Prince of Bel Air (1991)

The Royal Family (1992)

The Fresh Prince of Bel Air (1992)

Shaky Ground (1993)

The Fresh Prince of Bel Air (1993)

Hangin' with Mr. Cooper (1993)

The Fresh Prince of Bel Air (1994)

Hangin' with Mr. Cooper (1994)

The Fresh Prince of Bel Air (1995)

The Wayans Bros. (1995)

Hope & Gloria (1995)

Bless This House (1995)

The Naked Truth (1996)

The Jamie Foxx Show (1996)

The Fresh Prince of Bel Air (1996)

Suddenly Susan (1996)

Party Girl (1996)

Nick Freno (1996)

Bless This House (1996)

The Jamie Foxx Show (1997)

Life with Roger (1997)

Kapture, Mitzi

Silk Stalkings (1993)

Silk Stalkings (1994)

Keaton, Diane (aka Diane Hall)

Twin Peaks (1990)

China Beach (1990)

Twin Peaks (1991)

China Beach (1991)

Wild Flower (1991)

Northern Exposure (1997)

Keene, Elodie

L.A. Law (1990)

L.A. Law (1991)

L.A. Law (1992)

Civil Wars (1992)

L.A. Law (1993)

NYPD Blue (1994)

L.A. Law (1994)

ER (1994)

Strange Luck (1995)

NYPD Blue (1995)

My So-Called Life (1995)

Medicine Ball (1995)

American Gothic (1995)

The Deliverance of Elaine (1996)

Relativity (1996)

NYPD Blue (1996)

Murder One (1996)

American Gothic (1996)

Spy Game (1997)

Kerns, Joanna

Growing Pains (1993)

The Mommies (1995)

Hope & Gloria (1995)

Laird, Marlena

Double Trouble (1984)

Silver Spoons (1985)

Leder, MiMi

L.A. Law (1987)

Nightingales (1988)

Midnight Caller (1988)
Just in Time (1988)
Crime Story (1988)
China Beach (1988)
Buck James (1988)
A Year in the Life (1988)
China Beach (1989)
Sisters (1990)
China Beach (1990)
China Beach (1991)
There Was a Little Boy (1993)
The Sandman (1993)
Rio Shannon (1993)
Marked for Murder (1993)
House of Secrets (1993)
ER (1994)
Baby Brokers (1994)
ER (1995)
ER (1996)

Levinson, Shelley

Twilight Zone (1985)
Twilight Zone (1986)
Twilight Zone (1987)
L.A. Law (1987)
Falcon Crest (1989)

Lindo, Eleanore

Savannah (1996)
Savannah (1997)

Lyman, Dorothy

The Nanny (1995)
The Nanny (1996)
The Nanny (1997)
The Nanny (1998)

McCoy, Terri

In Living Color (1991)
In Living Color (1992)
Tall Hopes (1993)
In Living Color (1993)
South Central (1994)
Sister, Sister (1994)
The Apollo Theatre Hall of Fame
  (1994)

In Living Color (1994)
Sister, Sister (1995)
Ned and Stacey (1995)
In the House (1995)
Sister, Sister (1996)
Moesha (1996)
The Wayans Bros. (1997)
Pauly (1997)

Malone, Nancy

The Colbys (1985)
Dynasty (1985)
Hotel (1986)
Dynasty (1986)
There Were Times, Dear (1987)
Hotel (1987)
Dynasty (1987)
Hotel (1988)
Dynasty (1988)
Cagney and Lacey (1988)
Dynasty (1989)
The Bradys (1990)
The Trials of Rosie O'Neill (1991)
Sisters (1991)
Knots Landing (1991)
Beverly Hills 90210 (1991)
The Trials of Rosie O'Neill (1992)
Sisters (1992)
Melrose Place (1992)
Knots Landing (1992)
Melrose Place (1993)
Key West (1993)
Melrose Place (1994)
Vanishing Son (1995)
Touched by an Angel (1995)
Picket Fences (1995)
Bob Hope: Memories of World
  War II (1995)
LaVyrle Spencer's Home Song (1996)
Star Trek: Voyager (1997)

Mancuso, Gail

Camp Wilder (1992)
The Nanny (1993)
Roseanne (1993)

Joe's Life (1993)
Herman's Head (1993)
Camp Wilder (1993)
The Nanny (1994)
Roseanne (1994)
Monty (1994)
Herman's Head (1994)
Roseanne (1995)
Friends (1995)
Almost Perfect (1995)
Roseanne (1996)
Hudson Street (1996)
Friends (1996)
The Naked Truth (1997)
Suddenly Susan (1997)

Marshall, Penny

Working Stiffs (1979)
Booker (1990)
A League of Their Own (1993)

Mayron, Melanie

thirtysomething (1990)
thirtysomething (1991)
Tribeca Stories (1992)
Civil Wars (1992)
Tribeca Stories (1993)
Sirens (1993)
Moon over Miami (1993)
Winnetka Road (1994)
New York Undercover (1995)
Freaky Friday (1995)
Nash Bridges (1996)
New York Undercover (1996)

Miller, Sharron

The Life and Times of Grizzly Adams (1977)
The Woman Who Willed a Miracle (1982)
Paper Chase (1984)
Maximum Security (1984)
Cagney and Lacey (1984)
Cagney and Lacey (1985)
Pleasures (1986)

Cagney and Lacey (1986)
Bridges to Cross (1986)
L.A. Law (1987)
Cagney and Lacey (1987)
Pigeon Feathers (1988)
Little Girl Lost (1988)
Knightwatch (1988)
China Beach (1988)
The Outsiders (1990)
Father Dowling Mysteries (1990)
The Trials of Rosie O'Neill (1991)
Father Dowling Mysteries (1991)
Homefront (1992)
The Trials of Rosie O'Neill (1992)
Sisters (1993)
Second Chances (1993)
Homefront (1993)
Sisters (1994)
Second Chances (1994)
Hotel Malibu (1994)
Christy (1995)
Mr. & Mrs. Smith (1996)
The Client (1996)

Mitchell, Martha

Law & Order (1994)
The Wright Verdicts (1995)
Strange Luck (1995)
Live Shot (1995)
Law & Order (1995)
Courthouse (1995)
New York Undercover (1996)
Moloney (1996)
Malibu Shores (1996)
Law & Order (1996)
Chicago Hope (1996)
New York Undercover (1997)

Morse, Holly

Mulligan's Stew (1977)
Lucan (1977)
The Skatebirds (1977)
The New Operation Petticoat (1978)
The Skatebirds (1978)
The New Operation Petticoat (1979)

Fall Guy (1985)

Fall Guy (1986)

Patterson, Laura

Unsolved Mysteries (1993)

Unsolved Mysteries (1994)

Pelletier, Gabrille

Sirens (1994)

Sirens (1995)

Peters, Barbara

Boone (1983)

The Power of Matthew Star (1983)

The Renegades (1983)

Lottery! (1984)

Matt Houston (1984)

Remington Steele (1984)

Shadow Chasers (1985)

Finder of Lost Loves (1985)

Falcon Crest (1985)

Shadow Chasers (1986)

Piolo, Judy

The Hogan Family (1989)

The Hogan Family (1990)

The Golden Girls (1990)

The Family Man (1990)

Perfect Strangers (1990)

The Hogan Family (1991)

The Golden Girls (1991)

Perfect Strangers (1991)

The Family Man (1991)

Perfect Strangers (1992)

Place, MaryKay

Dream On (1993)

Dream On (1994)

Friends (1995)

Plonka, Liz

Clarissa Explains It All (1991)

Late Night with Conan O'Brien (1993)

Sabrina, the Teenage Witch (1997)

Pressman, Ellen

thirtysomething (1990)

thirtysomething (1991)

Sirens (1993)

Missing Persons (1993)

My So-Called Life (1994)

Party of Five (1995)

Medicine Ball (1995)

Party of Five (1996)

Reinisch, Deborah

Ask Me Again (1989)

thirtysomething (1990)

Andre's Mother (1990)

thirtysomething (1991)

The Antagonists (1991)

Sisters (1991)

Going to Extremes (1992)

Sisters (1992)

Missing Persons (1993)

Caught in the Act (1993)

Missing Persons (1994)

Earth 2 (1994)

VR5 (1995)

The Marshal (1995)

A Step toward Tomorrow (1996)

Rogers-Blye, Rita

Family Ties (1989)

The Fresh Prince of Bel Air (1991)

Hangin' with Mr. Cooper (1993)

Hangin' with Mr. Cooper (1994)

Rohrer, Susan

Sexual Considerations (1988)

Terrible Things Mother Told Me (1988)

Never Say Goodbye (1988)

For Jenny with Love (1989)

Mother's Day (1990)

If I Die before I Wake (1993)

Rooney, Bethany

Picket Fences (1988)

Danielle Steel's Mixed Blessings (1988)

The Slap Maxwell Story (1988)
St. Elsewhere (1988)
Elvis (1990)
The Wonder Years (1991)
Locked Up: A Mother's Rage (1991)
Dream On (1991)
Beverly Hills 90210 (1991)
Melrose Place (1992)
Home Fires (1992)
Beverly Hills 90210 (1992)
Class of '96 (1993)
Beverly Hills 90210 (1993)
Sister, Sister (1994)
Beverly Hills 90210 (1994)
The Other Mother (1995)
Beverly Hills 90210 (1995)
Touched by an Angel (1996)
She Cried No (1996)
Dr. Quinn, Medicine Woman (1996)
Danielle Steel's Remembrance (1996)
Danielle Steel's Full Circle (1996)
Beverly Hills 90210 (1997)

Rose, Sara Jane
The Commish (1993)
The Commish (1994)
Marker (1995)

Sanford, Arlene
The Ellen Burstyn Show (1987)
The Days and Nights of Molly Dodd (1987)
Duet (1987)
Designing Women (1987)
The Wonder Years (1988)
The Days and Nights of Molly Dodd (1988)
Dear John (1988)
Newhart (1989)
Hooperman (1989)
Coach (1989)
True Colors (1990)
Sisters (1990)
Open House (1990)
Elvis (1990)

Ferris Bueller (1990)
Cop Rock (1990)
True Colors (1991)
The Torkelsons (1991)
Sisters (1991)
Ferris Bueller (1991)
Dream On (1991)
The Torkelsons (1992)
Camp Wilder (1992)
The Second Half (1993)
Almost Home (1993)
Sweet Justice (1994)
The Second Half (1994)
Friends (1994)
Babymaker: The Cecil Jacobson Story (1994)
The Naked Truth (1995)
The Great Defender (1995)
Simon (1995)
Pride & Joy (1995)
Pig Sty (1995)
Dream On (1995)
All-American Girl (1995)
The Last Frontier (1996)
The Naked Truth (1997)
Temporarily Yours (1997)

Sargenti, Marina
Child of Darkness, Child of Light (1991)
Models, Inc. (1994)
Models, Inc. (1995)
Malibu Shores (1996)
Lying Eyes (1996)

Savoca, Nancy
Murder One (1995)
Dark Eyes (1995)
If These Walls Could Talk (1996)

Schneider, Sascha
Scarecrow & Mrs. King (1987)
Hill Street Blues (1988)

Schultz, Barbara

You Again? (1985)

Family Ties (1985)

Diff'rent Strokes (1986)

Family Ties (1986)

Webster (1987)

Family Ties (1987)

Scott, Carol

Day by Day (1989)

True Colors (1990)

True Colors (1991)

True Colors (1992)

Senna, Lorraine

Our Son, the Matchmaker (1996)

Feds (1997)

Sherry-Scelza, Roberta

Designing Women (1990)

Designing Women (1991)

Designing Women (1992)

Silver, Joan Micklin

*How to Be a Perfect Person in Just
    Three Days* (1984)

Finnegan Begin Again (1985)

A Private Matter (1992)

Sisters (1995)

Matt Waters (1995)

Mine Enemies (1996)

Matt Waters (1996)

Tewkesbury, Joan

The Tenth Month (1979)

The Acorn People (1980)

Alfred Hitchcock Presents (1986)

Elysian Fields (1989)

Cold Sassy Tree (1989)

Shannon's Deal (1990)

Wild Texas Wind (1991)

Shannon's Deal (1991)

The Stranger (1992)

Picket Fences (1992)

Northern Exposure (1992)

Promised Land (1994)

Thomas, Betty

Dream On (1988)

Hooperman (1988)

Peaceable Kingdom (1989)

Hooperman (1989)

Doogie Howser, M.D. (1989)

Shannon's Deal (1990)

Parent'Hood (1990)

Midnight Caller (1990)

Dream On (1990)

Sons and Daughters (1991)

Shannon's Deal (1991)

Midnight Caller (1991)

Arresting Behavior (1992)

Moon over Miami (1993)

Johnny Bago (1993)

Dream On (1993)

My Breast (1994)

The Late Shift (1996)

Tilley, Kate

Knots Landing (1985)

Knots Landing (1986)

Knots Landing (1987)

Falcon Crest (1988)

Knots Landing (1988)

Paradise (1988)

Dynasty (1989)

Weill, Claudia

The Twilight Zone (1986)

Johnny Bull (1986)

Fast Times (1986)

thirtysomething (1987)

Once a Hero (1987)

Cagney and Lacey (1987)

thirtysomething (1988)

thirtysomething (1989)

WIOU (1990)

Face of a Stranger (1991)

A Child Lost Forever (1992)

Birdland (1994)

Chicago Hope (1995)

Critical Choices (1996)

Writers

Note: This information consists of credits for works that appeared on television through 1996 and produced, but unaired, pilots.

Abbott, Jane
Evening Shade (1990)

Abner, Allison
Amen (1990)

Abrahamson, Terry
The Trials of Rosie O'Neill (1991)

Abramhoff, Sharyn
Trapper John, M.D. (1992)

Abrams, Gayle
The Fresh Prince of Bel Air (1994)

Adams, Claudia
Knots Landing (1979)
Cagney and Lacey (1982)

Adelman, Sybil
Lily (1975)
Charo (1976)
Magnum, P.I. (1985)
Growing Pains (1985–1987)
9 to 5 (1987)
Roomies (1987)
Anything but Love (1989)
Northern Exposure (1991)
Johnny Bago (1993)

Ader, Tammy
Quantum Leap (1989)
The Wonder Years (1990)
The Outsiders (1990)
WIOU (1991)
The Commish (1991–1992)
Going to Extremes (1992–1993)
Sisters (1994)

Adler, Allison
Beverly Hills 90210 (1991)
Murder, She Wrote (1992)

Adler, Alyson
Sirens (1995)

Ahern, Valerie
Parent'Hood (1995)

Ahlert, Eve
The Nanny (1993)
Someone Like Me (1994)
The Nanny (1994)

Albert, Lisa
My Sister Sam (1986–1987)
Mr. Belvedere (1987)
Annie McGuire (1988)
Major Dad (1989–1992)
The Cosby Show (1990–1991)

Delta (1992–1993)
Murphy Brown (1994)

Aldredge, Dawn P.
The Rowan & Martin Report (1975)
Sugar Time (1977–1978)
Handle with Care (1977)
The Love Boat (1978)
Flying High (1978)
Alice (1979)
Diff'rent Strokes (1979)
Diff'rent Strokes (1981–1984)
Who's the Boss (1984–1991)

Aldredge, Virginia F.
Dallas (1978)
The Bionic Woman (1979)
Fantasy Island (1979)
Buck Rogers in the 25th Century
   (1979)
Hart to Hart (1979)
Nurse (1981)
Fame (1982–1983)
Knight Rider (1983–1984)
The Twilight Zone (1987)
Beauty and the Beast (1988–1989)

Alexander, Marie
Diff'rent Strokes (1984)

Allen, Andrea
704 Hauser (1994)
The Fresh Prince of Bel Air (1994)

Allen, Jayne Meadows
Fantasy Island (1982)

Allen, Sheila R.
Hotel (1983)
Fantasy Island (1984)

Allen, Valerie
Vega$ (1979)
Fantasy Island (1980)

Allison, Judith
Makin' It (1979)
Private Benjamin (1981)

Wizards and Warriors (1982–1983)
Double Trouble (1984–1985)
Heartland (1989)
Blossom (1990–1994)
The John Larroquette Show (1993–
   1995)

Alu, Cheryl
Joanie Loves Chachi (1982)
Laverne and Shirley (1980)
Laverne and Shirley (1982–1983)
Silver Spoons (1984)
Perfect Strangers (1989–1993)
Getting By (1993–1994)

Anderson, Jane A.
Raising Miranda (1988)
The Wonder Years (1989)
The Positively True Adventures of the
   Alleged Texas Cheerleading–
   Murdering Mom (1992)

Anderson, Kathleen M.
Little House on the Prairie (1984)
Webster (1985)
Gimme a Break (1987)
227 (1988)
Amen (1988–1989)
The Cosby Show (1991)
South Central (1994)

Anderson, Lauren Eve
Roseanne (1988–1989)
Carol & Company (1990–1991)
Home Improvement (1992)

Anderson, Marilyn
The Facts of Life (1987)
Murphy Brown (1990)
Carol & Company (1991)

Anderson, Sheri
Falcon Crest (1989)

Anderson, Sheryl J.
Parker Lewis Can't Lose! (1991–
   1993)

Home Free (1993)
Dave's World (1994–1995)

Angelou, Maya
The Secrets of Sisters (1978)
I Know Why the Caged Bird Sings (1979)
Sister, Sister (1982)

Anthony, Sheila
Family Matters (1993–1994)

Anthony, Susan M.
Home Improvement (1992)

Appet, Leah
Mirror, Mirror (1979)
For Love and Honor (1983)

Arakelian, Deborah
Cagney and Lacey (1984–1985)
Houston Knights (1987)
Midnight Caller (1988)
Quantum Leap (1989)
Wolf (1989)

Arata, Elaine
The Cosby Show (1990–1991)
The Building (1993)

Arbus, Loreen J.
Angie (1980)
The Baxters (1980)

Archer, Beverly A.
A.L.F. (1988–1990)

Archibald, Dottie
Tony Orlando's First Special (1979)
The Shape of Things (1982)
Laverne and Shirley (1982)

Armen, Margaret A.
Wonder Woman (1976)
Young Daniel Boone (1977)
The Incredible Hulk (1979)
Fantasy Island (1980)
B.A.D. Cats (1980)

Flamingo Road (1980–1981)
Emerald Point, N.A.S. (1984)

Armor, Joyce
The Tony Randall Show (1977)
The Love Boat (1978–1979)
WKRP in Cincinnati (1978/1981)
Emerald Point, N.A.S. (1984)
Remington Steele (1984)

Armstrong, Adrienne
A.L.F. (1987)
Full House (1992–1993)

Arner, Gwen
Tattingers (1989)

Aronsohn, Lee
House Calls (1979)
The Love Boat (1979–1980)
Everything's Relative (1987)
Charles in Charge (1987–1988)
Who's the Boss (1987–1988)
The People Next Door (1989)
The Marshall Chronicles (1990)
Laughs! (1990)
Scorch (1992)
Just One of the Girls (1992)
Murphy Brown (1992–1993)
Joe's Life (1993)
Grace under Fire (1994)
Me and the Boys (1994)

Aronson, Elaine
Night Court (1990–1992)
Doogie Howser, M.D. (1992–1993)
Good Advice (1994)
The Byrds of Paradise (1994)
Roseanne (1994)
Cybill (1995)

Ashford, Michelle
Cagney and Lacey (1988)
21 Jump Street (1990)
WIOU (1991)

Asimov, Dyann
Complex of Fear (1993)

Audley, Nancy
  Lily Tomlin: Sold Out (1981)
  Miss All–American Beauty (1982)
  Crime Story (1988)

Austin, Bethe
  Matlock (1989)

Avedon, Barbara
  Fish (1978)
  Grandpa Goes to Washington (1978)
  Trapper John, M.D. (1980)
  Harper Valley P.T.A. (1981)
  Cagney and Lacey (1981–1982)
  This Girl for Hire (1983)
  Cagney and Lacey: The Return
    (1994)

Ayers, Diana M.
  9 to 5 (1983)
  Webster (1984)
  Living Dolls (1989)
  Dear John (1990–1991)
  The Family Man (1990–1991)
  The Torkelsons (1991)
  Full House (1992)
  Frannie's Return (1992)
  Delta (1992–1993)

Ayers, Vicky
  Growing Pains (1988–1989)

Ayres, Jenny
  Who's the Boss (1988)

Bader, Hilary
  Star Trek: The Next Generation
    (1992)
  Star Trek: Deep Space Nine (1993–
    1994)
  Lois & Clark: The New Adventures
    of Superman (1995)

Baer, Jill
  The Love Boat (1980–1984)
  Too Close for Comfort (1981)
  Finder of Lost Loves (1984–1985)

Baerwald, Susan
  Jackie Collins' Lucky/Chances (1990)

Bagni–Dubov, Gwen
  Wonder Woman (1976)
  Backstairs at the White House
    (1976)
  Young Pioneers (1976)
  Shirley (1976)
  Thursday's Child (1983)
  Eight Is Enough: A Family Reunion
    (1987)

Bailey, Anne Howard
  Robert Montgomery Presents: U.S.
    Steel Hour
  Armstrong Circle Theatre
  Kraft Television Theatre (1950s)
  Beacon Hill (1975)
  Halfway Home (1981)

Baker, Deborah
  Portrait of a Teenage Shoplifter
    (1981)

Baker, Kathryn
  Murphy Brown (1989)
  Coach (1990)
  Sons and Daughters (1991)
  Wings (1991)
  Key West (1993)
  The Adventures of Brisco County, Jr.
    (1994)
  Hawkeye (1995)

Bannick, Lisa
  The Love Boat (1984)
  Domestic Life (1984)
  Oh, Madeline (1984)
  Family Ties (1984)
  Alice (1984)
  Mr. Belvedere (1985)
  Alice (1985)
  Our Time (1985)
  9 to 5 (1986–1987)
  A.L.F. (1987–1989)

The Royal Family (1991)
Almost Home (1993)
The Mommies (1993–1994)
Love & War (1994)

Banta, Gloria
Lily (1975)
Rhoda (1975–1976)
Cousins (1976)
Angie (1980)
Making a Living (1980–1981)
Cagney and Lacey (1982)

Barchilon, Jeri
The Facts of Life (1987)

Barish, Leora
The Hitchhiker (1985–1986)

Barker, Lynn
The Powers of Matthew Star (1983)
Whiz Kids (1984)
The Twilight Zone (1985)

Barnes, Joanne
Buck Rogers (1979)
Terror among Us (1981)
T. J. Hooker (1982)
Hunter (1985)

Barnes, Margaret Anne
Murder in Coweta County (1983)

Barnett, Gina
In the Heat of the Night (1994)

Baron, Deborah
Rags to Riches (1987)
Leg Work (1987)
Major Dad (1990)
Hunter (1990–1991)

Barr, Nancy
The Hidden Room (1993)

Barrett, Gina
In the Heat of the Night (1993)

Barrett, Helen
Kate and Allie (1989)

Barris, Kate
Top Cops (1992–1993)

Barthel, Joan
A Death in California (1985)

Bartlett, Juanita
The New Maverick (1978)
The Rockford Files (1979)
Young Maverick (1979)
Stone (1980)
Tenspeed & Brownshoe (1980)
Burnt Offerings (1981)
The Greatest American Hero (1981–1982)
The Quest (1982)
Scarecrow & Mrs. King (1984)
No Man's Land (1984)
Maggie (1986)
Spenser: For Hire (1986–1987)
The Rockford Files: I Still Love L.A. (1994)

Baruch, Jeanne
His & Hers (1990)

Bascom, Cheryl
Designing Women (1990)

Baskin, Susan
Loving Friends and Perfect Couples (1983)
Remington Steele (1983–1984)
Dynasty (1984–1985)
Berrengers (1985)
Born Too Soon (1993)
Labor of Love: The Arlette Schweitzer Story (1993)

Bass, Kim
Not Necessarily the News (1990)
In Living Color (1990–1992)
Sister, Sister (1994)

Batchler, Janet Scott
The Equalizer (1988)

Baxter, Elizabeth
Highlander (1992–1994)

Baxter, Lucretia
*A Mother's Right: The Elizabeth
Morgan Story* (1992)

Beatts, Anne
Saturday Night Live (1977–1979)
The Best of Saturday Night Live
(1979)
Square Pegs (1982–1983)
Faerie Tale Theatre (1984)
Julia Brown: The Show (1989)
A Comedy Salute to Michael Jordan
(1991)
Murphy Brown (1991)

Beaupre, Theresa
Top Cops (1992–1993)

Beavers, Susan
Newhart (1985)
My Sister Sam (1986–1987)
Growing Pains (1987)
Empty Nest (1990–1991)
Nurses (1991–1993)
Dudley (1993)
Empty Nest (1993)

Beber, Neena
Doctor, Doctor (1990–1991)

Beckett, Ann
Sara (1976)
Love's Dark Side (1979)
The Gymnast (1980)
Portrait of an Escort (1980)
The Oklahoma City Dolls (1981)
Dial 911 (1981)
The Adventures of Pollyanna (1982)
Having It All (1982)
Midas Valley (1985)
Little Girl Lost (1988)
The Broken Cord (1992)

Begel, Cindy
The Bad News Bears (1980)
Laverne and Shirley (1980–1981)
Happy Days (1981)
Mork and Mindy (1981)
Too Close for Comfort (1981)
Checking In (1981)
The Jeffersons (1981)
Joanie Loves Chachi (1982)
Star of the Family (1982)
Gimme a Break (1983)
Alice (1984)
Oh, Madeline (1984)
Still the Beaver (1984)
The New Leave It to Beaver (1985–
1986)
Together We Stand (1987)
13 East (1989)
Head of the Class (1990)
Babes (1991)
The Martin Short Show (1994)

Behar, Esther
Top Cops (1992–1993)

Bender, Kay
The Paper Chase (1978)
Trapper John, M.D. (1982–1983)

Benedek, Barbara
I'm a Big Girl Now (1980–1981)
Making a Living (1981)
Laverne and Shirley (1982)
Condo (1983)
The Big Chill (1983)
The Line (1987)

Benjamin, Cynthia
Beauty and the Beast (1988)

Benjamin, Lisa
The Cosby Show (1982)

Bennett, Meg
You Are the Jury (1987)

Bennett, Ruth

    Laverne and Shirley (1980–1981)

    The Facts of Life (1982)

    Family Ties (1982–1983)

    Sara (1985)

    Duet (1987)

    Family Ties (1989)

    Someone Like Me (1994)

    Something Wilder (1995)

Bennett, Susan

    All the Way Home (1986)

Berardo, Christine

    Overexposed (1992)

    Because Mommy Works (1994)

Bergesen, Doreen

    Blue Thunder (1984)

Bergman, Linda

    Just Tipsy, Honey (1989)

    The Lookalike (1990)

    Rio Shannon (1993)

    Against Their Will: Women in Prison (1994)

Berk, Michele Rogers

    Baywatch (1992–1993)

    Baywatch (1995)

Bernheim, Robin

    Remington Steele (1984–1987)

    MacGyver (1986)

    Matlock (1987)

    Beauty and the Beast (1988)

    Houston Knights (1988)

    Over My Dead Body (1990–1991)

    Tequila and Bonetti (1992)

    Quantum Leap (1992–1993)

    Diagnosis Murder (1994)

Bernstein, Eve

    ER (1984)

Betancourt, Jeanne

    I Want to Go Home (1984)

    Don't Touch (1985)

    Teen Father (1986)

    Supermom's Daughter (1987)

    The Babysitters Club (1991–1992)

Beverly, Nancy

    Blossom (1990–1991)

Bicks, Jenny

    It Had to Be You (1993)

    The 5 Mrs. Buchanans (1994)

Biderman, Ann

    NYPD Blue (1994)

Bingham, Charlotte

    Oh, Madeline (1983)

    Love with the Perfect Stranger (1985)

Black, Carol

    Oh, Madeline (1983)

    Amanda's (1983)

    Newhart (1984)

    Three's Company (1984)

    Growing Pains (1985)

    The Wonder Years (1987–1988)

    Laurie Hill (1992)

    These Friends of Mine (1994)

Black, Susan

    State of Emergency (1994)

Blackton, Jenny

    On Our Own (1977–1978)

    Mother and Me, M.D. (1979)

    Me and Mrs. C (1987)

    Heartbeat (1989)

Blake, Jean

    Mike Hammer (1984)

Bloodworth–Thomason, Linda

    Over and Out (1976)

    Rhoda (1977–1978)

    Dribble (1980)

    Filthy Rich (1981–1982)

London and Davis in New York
(1984)
Lime Street (1985)
Designing Women (1986–1993)
Evening Shade (1990–1993)
Hearts Afire (1992–1994)
Woman in the House (1995)

Bloomberg, Beverly
Ladies Man (1980)
Happy Days (1980–1983)
CHiPs (1982)

Bolton, Martha
Bob Hope Lampoons the New TV
Scene (1986)
Bob Hope's Christmas Show (1987)
NBC Investigates Bob Hope (1987)
Bob Hope's High Flying Birthday
Extravaganza (1987)
Bob Hope with His Beautiful Easter
Bunnies and Other Friends (1987)
From Tahiti, Bob Hope's Tropical
Comedy Special (1987)
Hope News Network (1988)
Bob Hope's Jolly Christmas Show
with All–American Champs (1989)
Bob Hope's Easter Vacation in the
Bahamas (1989)
Bob Hope's Super Bowl Party (1989)
Ooh–La–La, It's Bob Hope's Fun
Birthday Spectacular from Paris'
Bicentennial (1989)
Bob's Love Affair with Lucy (1989)
The Bob Hope Christmas Special
(1989)
Ole! It's Bob Hope's Acapulco Spring
Fling of Comedy and Music
(1989)
Bob Hope's Winter Special (1990)
Bob Hope's Cross-Country
Christmas (1991)
Bob Hope and Other Young

Comedians: The World Laughs,
Young and Old (1992)
Bob Hope's America: Red, White and
Beautiful—The Swimsuit
Edition (1992)
Bob Hope's Bag Full of Christmas
Memories (1994)
Bob Hope's Young Comedians
Making America Laugh (1994)

Bombeck, Erma
Maggie's Way (1981)

Bonaduce, Celia
Hello, Larry (1979)
Good Times (1979)
The Jeffersons (1980)
One Day at a Time (1981)

Bond, Nancy
Trapper John, M.D. (1982–1985)
Simon & Simon (1988)
In the Heat of the Night (1988–
1989)
Mann & Machine (1992)
Dr. Quinn, Medicine Woman (1994)
Sweet Justice (1995)

Bonniere, Nancy
Night Heat (1987)

Boone, Eunetta T.
Roc (1991–1993)
The Fresh Prince of Bel Air (1992)
Getting By (1993–1994)
Living Single (1994–1995)

Boorstin, Sharon
Grandpa Goes to Washington (1978)
Ripley's Believe It or Not (1982)
Hart to Hart (1982)
Fame (1983)
Hotel (1988)
Falcon Crest (1989)
Angel of Death (1990)
Dark Shadows (1991)

Boosler, Elayne

    The Rodney Dangerfield Show
      (1981)

    The Shape of Things (1982)

    Rodney Dangerfield: It's Not Easy
      Being Me (1984)

    Disney Goes to the Academy Awards
      (1985)

    Mable and Max (1987)

Borns, Betsy

    Roseanne (1993–1994)

Borowitz, Susan

    Amanda's (1983)

    Webster (1983)

    Family Ties (1983–1984)

    Joanie (1984)

    Dreams (1984)

    ER (1984–1985)

    Family Ties (1987–1989)

    Day by Day (1988)

    The Fresh Prince of Bel Air (1990–
      1991)

    Out All Night (1992–1993)

Botkin, Nancy Trites

    Race to Freedom: The Underground
      Railroad (1994)

Botsford, Diana Dru

    Star Trek: The Next Generation
      (1992–1993)

Boutlier, Kate

    Growing Pains (1987–1988)

    Just the Ten of Us (1988–1989)

    Baywatch (1990)

    Northern Exposure (1992)

    Growing Pains (1992)

    Freshman Dorm (1992)

    Lois & Clark: The New Adventures
      of Superman (1994)

Bowser, Yvette Lee

    Living Single (1994)

Bradford, Barbara Taylor

    Hold That Dream (1986)

Bradley, J. Elizabeth

    Happy Days (1980)

Braff, Wendy

    Growing Pains (1992)

    Empty Nest (1992–1993)

    The Good Life (1994)

Braithwaite, Diana

    Race to Freedom: The Underground
      Railroad (1994)

Brattlestreet, Caliope K.

    Poisoned by Love: Kern County
      Murders (1993)

    While Justice Sleeps (1994)

Braunstein, Laura

    Highway to Heaven (1987)

Breslin, Rosemary

    NYPD Blue (1995)

Brez, Ethel

    Roxy Page (1976)

    The Triangle Factory Fire Scandal
      (1978)

    The Miracle of Kathy Miller (1981)

    Goldie and the Boxer Go to
      Hollywood (1981)

Bridges, Beverly

    Quantum Leap (1990–1992)

    Tequila and Bonetti (1992)

    Covington Cross (1992)

Brin, Susan Hamilton

    Baywatch (1993–1995)

Brittany, Anne

    Held Hostage: The Sis and Jerry
      Levin Story (1991)

Brock, Trisha

    Twin Peaks (1990–1991)

Bromfield, Lois
   Roseanne (1992–1994)

Bromfield, Valri
   Head of the Class (1987/1989)
   Inside America's Totally Unsolved
     Lifestyles (1992)
   She TV (1994)

Brooker, Joan
   Harper Valley P.T.A. (1981)
   Joanie Loves Chachi (1983)
   Benson (1984)
   Scarecrow & Mrs. King (1984)
   The Love Boat (1984–1985)
   Full House (1987)
   Gimme a Break (1987)

Brooks, Hindi
   Eight Is Enough (1978)
   Family (1978)
   The Flame Is Love (1979)
   Before and After (1979)
   Skag (1979)
   Eight Is Enough (1980)
   The Long Days of Summer (1980)
   Nurse (1981–1982)
   Fame (1982)
   Lottery! (1983–1984)
   Jesse (1984)

Brooks, Holly Holmberg
   Taxi (1982–1983)

Broussellet, Marie
   Highlander (1992–1994)

Brown, Charlotte
   The Partridge Family (1972–1974)
   The Bob Newhart Show (1972–
     1978)
   Really Raquel (1974)
   Rhoda (1974–1978)
   Bumpers (1977)
   Letting Go (1985)
   Real Life (1988)
   The Powers That Be (1992)

Brown, Julie
   Quantum Leap (1990)
   The Edge (1992–1993)

Brown, Maria A.
   Davis Rules (1992)
   Woops! (1992)
   Step by Step (1993–1995)

Brown, Rita Mae
   I Love Liberty (1982)
   The Long Hot Summer (1986)
   The Woman Who Loved Elvis (1993)

Browne, L. Virginia
   Knots Landing (1980/1982)
   Dirty Dancing (1988)
   Danielle Steel's "Daddy" (1991)
   Deadly Medicine (1991)

Brownell, Janet
   Sweet Revenge (1990)
   Backfield in Motion (1991)
   Christmas in Connecticut (1992)
   The Amy Fisher Story (1993)
   Judith Krantz's "Torch Song" (1993)
   Children of the Dark (1994)

Bryant, Louise
   Happy Days (1981)

Bustany, Judith
   Who's the Boss (1984–1987)
   Diff'rent Strokes (1985)

Byrne, Erica
   Matt Houston (1982)
   Strike Force (1982)
   Hardcastle & McCormick (1982)

Byron, Ellen
   Flying Blind (1992–1993)
   Joe's Life (1993)
   Wings (1994–1995)

Caldwell, Cecila Hoagland
   That's Incredible (1980–1981)
   Those Incredible Kids (1981)

Cameron, Julia
  Elvis & the Beauty Queen (1981)

Campanelli, Linda
  Remington Steele (1985)
  Newhart (1986–1987)
  Beauty and the Beast (1989)
  Dark Shadows (1991)

Campany, Rebecca
  America's Most Wanted (1992–1993)

Caraway, Louella Lee
  Dallas (1987–1991)

Carr, Camilla
  Escape from Terror: The Teresa Stamper Story (1995)

Carrigan–Fauci, Jeanne
  Star Trek: Deep Space Nine (1993)

Carrington, Jane–Howard
  The Hostage Tower (1980)

Carroll, Colleen
  Falcon Crest (1989)

Caruso, Dee
  A Special Oliva Newton–John (1976)
  What's Happening (1978)
  Going Bananas (1984)
  America Censored (1985)

Cash, Rita A.
  Motown Merry Christmas (1987)
  The Essence Awards (1992)
  The Essence Awards (1994)

Castle, Sue
  Our Kids and the Best of Everything (1987)

Catz, Sarit
  Full House (1992)
  Cafe Americain (1993–1994)

Caves, Sally
  Star Trek: Deep Space Nine (1993)

Chaidez, Natalie
  New York Undercover (1994–1995)

Chancellor, Mary
  That's Incredible (1982)

Chandler, Elizabeth
  Afterburn (1992)

Chapman, Lori
  Mark Twain's America (1978)

Charis, Pamela Herbert
  Phyllis (1977)
  Rhoda (1977–1978)
  Having Babies III (1978)
  Starting Fresh (1979)
  Love, Sidney (1982–1983)
  Under One Roof (1985)
  Scarecrow & Mrs. King (1986)

Charno, Sara B.
  The X-Files (1995)

Chatman, Delle
  The Righteous Apples (1980)
  The Yellow Rose (1983)
  Snoops (1989)
  The Young Riders (1991)

Cherbak, Cynthia
  Switch (1976)
  Welcome Home, Jellybean (1984)
  Broken Angel (1988)
  American Eyes (1990)
  Kissing Place (1990)
  Lucy & Desi: Before the Laughter (1991)
  The Secret (1992)

Chernin, Lisa
  Murphy Brown (1990–1991)
  Married . . . with Children (1992)

Cherry, Carole S.
   Illusions (1983)
   Cowboys (1983)
   Carpool (1983)

Childs, Suzanne
   Knots Landing (1992)

Chrane, Susan Howard
   Dallas (1987)

Churin, Nancy
   Joanie Loves Chachi (1982)

Cidre, Cynthia
   I Saw What You Did (1988)

Cioffi, Rebecca Parr
   Cheers (1993)
   Hearts Afire (1994–1995)

Clark, Cassandra
   227 (1989)
   Designing Women (1989–1991)
   Sugar and Spice (1990)
   13 East (1990)
   Nurses (1991)
   Delta (1992–1993)

Clark, Elizabeth
   Having Babies III (1978)
   Secrets of Midland Heights (1980)
   Seven Brides for Seven Brothers
     (1982)
   Dad's Out of a Job (1982)

Clark, Karen
   Trauma Center (1983)
   The Long Journey Home (1988)
   Midnight Caller (1990–1991)
   For the Very First Time (1991)
   Beyond Suspicion (1993)

Clark, Mary Higgins
   The Cradle Will Fall (1983)
   A Man Called Hawk (1989)

Clarke, Jean
   Hotel (1988)
   Nightingales (1989)

Clarkson, Marianne
   Hardcastle & McCormick (1985)
   Hunter (1987)
   MacGyver (1989)

Clauser, Suzanne
   Home to Stay (1978)
   Little Women (1979)
   The Pride of Jesse Halam (1981)
   Country Western Anthology (1982)
   Calamity Jane (1984)
   The Californians (1985)
   Christmas Snow (1986)
   Danielle Steel's "Message from
     Nam" (1993)
   John Jakes' "Heaven and Hell: North
     and South," Part II (1994)

Clay, Charlotte
   Hunter (1987–1988)
   A Man Called Hawk (1989)

Cline, Rachel
   Knots Landing (1991–1992)
   Class of '96 (1993)

Coben, Sherry
   Oh Boy! Babies! (1982)
   Kate and Allie (1983–1985)

Coe, Liz
   Miss Winslow and Son (1978)
   Married: The First Year (1978)
   In the Beginning (1978)
   Me and My Maniac Mom (1978)
   Family (1979)
   Friends (1979)
   Skag (1980)
   When the Whistle Blows (1980)
   The Day the Loving Stopped (1981)
   Games Mother Never Taught You
     (1982)

The Off Season (1982)
Finder of Lost Loves (1984–1985)
Cagney and Lacey (1986–1987)
Life Goes On (1990–1991)
*Moment of Truth: Why My
   Daughter?* (1993)
Mad about You (1994)

Coen, Dana
Carol & Company (1990–1991)
Room for Two (1992)

Coker, Katherine E.
Kate Loves a Mystery (1979)
The Incredible Hulk (1979–1980)
Quincy (1979–1981)
Sheriff Lobo (1979/1981)
Buck Rogers (1980)
Code Red (1981)
Magnum, P.I. (1981)
Gavilan (1982)
The Master (1984)
The A–Team (1984)
Jessie (1984)
Hunter (1984)
MacGruder and Loud (1985)

Collins, Anna C.
Wonder Woman (1978–1979)
Buck Rogers in the 25th Century
   (1979)
The Curse of King Tut's Tomb (1980)
Vega$ (1980–1981)
The Devlin Connection (1981)
King's Crossing (1982)
Fantasy Island (1982–1984)
Glitter (1984)
Cover Up (1984)
Me & Mom (1985)
*Perry Mason: The Case of the
   Shooting Star* (1986)
*Perry Mason: The Case of the Lost
   Love* (1987)
*Perry Mason: The Case of the
   Sinister Spirit* (1987)

Matlock (1987–1995)
*Perry Mason: The Case of the
   Defiant Daughter* (1990)

Collins, Jackie
Hollywood Wives (1985)
Lady Boss (1992)

Collins, Jeanette
In Living Color (1990)
A Different World (1990–1993)
Good Advice (1994)

Collins, Suzanne
Hi Honey, I'm Home (1991)

Collins, Terrie
Chicken Soup (1989)
Carol & Company (1990–1991)
Daddy Dearest (1993)

Colquhoun, Judy
Snowy River: The McGregor Saga
   (1993)

Combs, Nina
The Cosby Show (1992)

Comici, Liz
Silk Stalkings (1993–1994)

Compton, Juleen
Women at West Point (1979)

Condon, Jill
The Cosby Show (1992)
The Boys Are Back (1994)

Conley, Mary
Ferris Bueller (1990–1991)

Conn, Eileen
Get a Life! (1991)
Dream On (1992–1993)
Mad about You (1993–1995)

Conrad, Christine
Love Thy Neighbor (1984)

Conran, Shirley
Lace (1985)

Constanza, Joyce
Carol & Company (1990–1991)

Convy, Anne
One Day at a Time (1978–1979)
13 Queen's Blvd (1979)
The Stockard Channing Show
(1979)
Eight Is Enough (1979)
Ladies' Man (1980–1981)
It's Not Easy (1983)
Small Wonder (1985)
Me and Mrs. C (1987)
The Tortellis (1987)
A.L.F. (1987)
Annie McGuire (1989)
True Colors (1990–1991)
The Powers That Be (1992)

Cook, Martie
Full House (1990–1993)

Cooke–Leonard, Janice
Fantasy Island (1984)

Cooper, Ilene
The Jeffersons (1983)

Cooper, Susan
The Dollmaker (1984)
Foxfire (1987)
A Promise to Keep (1990)
To Dance with the White Dog (1993)

Corday, Barbara
Fish (1977–1978)
Grandpa Goes to Washington (1978)
Turnabout (1979–1981)
An American Dream (1981)
Cagney and Lacey (1981–1982)
This Girl for Hire (1983)
Cagney and Lacey: The Return
(1994)

Corder, Sharon
Top Cops (1992)

Corigliano, Theresa G.
Guns of Paradise (1990–1991)

Corwen, Carol
Head of the Class (1990–1991)

Costello, Kimberley
Picket Fences (1992–1993)
Sisters (1992–1993)
Melrose Place (1993–1995)

Couture, Suzette
Conspiracy of Silence (1992)
Child of Rage (1992)
Betrayal of Trust (1993)
Million Dollar Babies (1994)

Covino, Christina L.
The Commish (1992–1993)

Cowgill, Linda J.
Quincy (1981–1982)
Life Goes On (1989)
The Young Riders (1991)

Cozen, Wendy
Miami Vice (1984)

Craviotto, Darlene
Married: The First Year (1978)
Dallas (1978)
Angel Dusted (1981)
Sentimental Journey (1985)
Love Is Never Silent (1985)

Crawford, Joanna
Forever (1978)
Betrayal (1978)
Friendships, Secrets, and Lies (1979)
Sophia Loren: Her Own Story
(1980)
Her Life as a Man (1984)

Crawford, Nell McCue
  Star Trek: Deep Space Nine (1993)

Crawford, Rebecca
  The Roots of Country (1994)

Cridland, Susan
  My Two Dads (1989)

Croner, Karen
  TV 101 (1989)
  *Scattered Dreams: The Kathryn
    Messenger Story* (1993)

Cross, Alison
  Anatomy of a Seduction (1979)
  The Hearst and Davies Affair (1985)
  Roe vs. Wade (1989)
  With Hostile Intent (1993)
  *Serving in Silence: The Margarethe
    Cammermeyer Story* (1995)

Cruise, Mary
  Highway to Heaven (1987)

Culver, Carmen
  The Fitzpatricks (1977–1978)
  Family (1977–1978)
  First You Cry (1977–1978)
  Mary and Joseph (1979)
  When She Was Bad (1979)
  Willa (1979)
  To Race the Wind (1980)
  Inmates: A Love Story (1981)
  The Thorn Birds (1982)
  Murder Is Easy (1982)
  The Last Days of Pompeii (1984)
  The Last Prostitute (1991)

Cumerbatch, Ingrid
  Top Cops (1992–1993)

Currier, Lauren
  Those Secrets (1992)

Curtin, Susan Connaugh
  Kate and Allie (1987)

Curtin, Valerie
  Good & Evil (1991)

Cusuna, Susan
  Joshua's Heart (1990)

Cutler, Devorah
  T. J. Hooker (1982)

Dailey, Diane P.
  Angie (1980)

Daley, Madelyn
  Phyl & Mikhy (1979)

Dalton, Deborah
  Precious Victims (1993)
  A Kiss to Die For (1993)

D'Amore, Dorie
  Blossom (1995)

Daniels, Dari
  Taxi (1983)
  Mr. Smith (1984)

Darby, Diana
  Full House (1995)

Darland, Dottie
  Frannie's Turn (1992)
  Grace under Fire (1993–1994)
  Cybill (1995)
  Caroline in the City (1996–1999)

Darnell, Cynthia
  St. Elsewhere (1984–1985)
  Cagney and Lacey (1985)
  Spenser: For Hire (1986–1987)
  Amazing Stories (1987)
  Falcon Crest (1987–1989)
  Tour of Duty (1989)

David, Madeline
  Valentine Magic on Love Island
    (1980)

David, Marjorie S.
> *Hill Street Blues* (1986–1987)
> *Lifestories* (1990)
> *I'll Fly Away* (1992–1993)
> *Into the Badlands* (1992)
> *With Hostile Intent* (1993)
> *Under Suspicion* (1995)

Davidson, Sara
> *Jessie* (1984)
> *Our Kind of Town* (1986)
> *Jack and Mike* (1986–1987)
> *Heartbeat* (1988)
> *Bloodlines: Murder in the Family*
> (1993)
> *Dr. Quinn, Medicine Woman*
> (1993–1995)

Davilman, Barbara
> *Amen* (1988)

Davis, Barbara
> *Husbands, Wives & Lovers* (1978)
> *Honeymoon Hotel* (1979)
> *The Incredible Hulk* (1979/1981)
> *Fantasy Island* (1980–1981)
> *The Fall Guy* (1983–1984)
> *Streethawk* (1984)
> *Knight Rider* (1984)
> *Codename: Foxfire* (1985)
> *She Led Two Lives* (1994)

Davis, Geena
> *Buffalo Bill* (1984)

Davis, Jeanne
> *Dr. Quinn, Medicine Woman* (1994)

Davis, Jill
> *Late Night with David Letterman*
> (1992–1994)

Davis, Madelyn
> *I Love Lucy* (1952–1957)
> *Here's Lucy* (1968–1974)
> *The Lucille Ball Special* (1977)
> *Dorothy* (1979)
> *Life with Lucy* (1986)

Davison, Kathryn
> *Mama's Family* (1984)
> *Major Dad* (1992–1993)

Dawson, Christy
> *Quantum Leap* (1990–1991)

Dawson, Deborah Zoe
> *The Waverly Wonders* (1978)
> *Flying High* (1979)
> *Trapper John, M.D.* (1979–1984)
> *The Wizard* (1987)
> *Bring Me the Head of Dobie Gillis*
> (1988)
> *Nightingales* (1989)

Deats, Paula
> *Those Incredible Kids* (1980)
> *Those Amazing Animals* (1980–
> 1981)
> *The Future: What's Next?* (1981)
> *That's Incredible* (1981–1982)

De Benedictis, Lisa
> *Kate and Allie* (1989)
> *Mad about You* (1992–1993)
> *Dream On* (1993–1994)

DeClue, Denise
> *Missing Persons* (1993–1994)

DeCrane, Linda
> *The Young Riders* (1991)

DeGarmo, Denise
> *Kate's Secret* (1986)
> *Terror in the Night* (1994)

DeKeyser, Dawn
> *All–American Girl* (1994–1995)

Demberg, Lisa
> *In Search Of. . .* (1980)

Deming, Cynthia
> *In the Heat of the Night* (1990–
> 1994)

DePriest, Margaret
    Behind the Screen (1981–1982)

Desberg–Greenburg, Joan
    On Our Own (1977–1978)
    Me and Mrs. C (1987)
    Heartbeat (1989)

Desmarais, Alison R.
    Victims of Love (1991)
    Night Court (1991–1992)
    Madman of the People (1994)

Despres, Loraine
    Family (1978)
    The Waltons (1979)
    The Love Boat (1979)
    Dallas (1979–1980)
    Knots Landing (1980)
    The Baxters (1980)
    Romance Theater (1982)
    Dynasty (1982)
    CHiPs (1983)
    Highlander (1992–1993)

Diamond, Janis
    Law & Order (1995)

Dick, Peggy Chantler
    The Partridge Family (1972)
    Little Women (1979)
    Leave 'em Laughing (1981)

Dickey, Harriet
    Sirens (1983)

Dixon, Dianne
    A Different Twist (1984)
    Family Ties (1988)
    First Impressions (1988)
    Nurses (1991)

Dobbs, Charlotte M.
    Doctors Private Lives (1979)
    Paris (1979)

    The Boy Who Drank Too Much (1980)
    Dynasty (1981)
    Happy Days (1981)
    Laverne and Shirley (1981)
    Down to Earth (1985)

Dobbs, Denise
    Northern Exposure (1992–1993)

Donahue, Ann
    China Beach (1988)
    Sharing Richard (1988)
    Nightingales (1989)
    Mancuso, FBI (1990)
    The Round Table (1992)
    Beverly Hills 90210 (1992–1993)
    Picket Fences (1993–1995)

Donnell, Kathy
    The Tony Randall Show (1977)
    Lacy and the Mississippi Queen (1978)
    Three's Company (1978)
    Eight Is Enough (1979)
    Fantasy Island (1981)

Donner, Jill Sherman
    Jessica Novak (1981)
    The Incredible Hulk (1982)
    Cutter to Houston (1983)
    The Voyagers (1983)
    Magnum, P.I. (1984)
    Codename: Foxfire (1985)
    The Magical World of Disney (1988)
    Baywatch (1989)
    Star Trek: Deep Space Nine (1993)

Donofrio, Beverly
    Phenom (1994)

Donoghue, Mary Agnes
    Beggerman, Thief (1979)

Dougherty, Pat
    Empty Nest (1990–1993)
    Coach (1992)

Phenom (1993)
All–American Girl (1994)
Muscle (1995)

Douglas, Pamela
Mike Hammer (1981)
Palmerstown (1981)
Insight (1983)
Trapper John, M.D. (1984)
TV 101 (1989)
Paradise (1989)
Different Worlds: A Story of Interracial Love (1992)

Down, Rena
Dallas (1978–1981)
Knots Landing (1979–1980)
King's Crossing (1981)
Nurse (1981–1982)
Summer Fantasies (1984)
Hotel (1988)
Falcon Crest (1989)

Downer, Leilani
A Different World (1990)
Growing Pains (1990–1992)
Hangin' with Mr. Cooper (1992–1994)

Doyle, Carol
Sirens (1994)

Doyle, Danna
The Trials of Rosie O'Neill (1991)
Murder, She Wrote (1993)

Doyle, Sharon E.
Cagney and Lacey (1988)
Peaceable Kingdom (1989)
Top of the Hill (1989)
Reasonable Doubts (1992–1993)
Gregory K (1993)
Stolen Babies (1993)
Baby Maker: The Dr. Cecil Jacobsen Story (1994)

Doyne, Nancy
Tales from the Crypt (1994)

Drennan, Kathryn M.
Babylon 5 (1994)

Drescher, Fran
The Nanny (1993–1995)

Droney, Marie–Chantal
Highlander (1992–1993)

Duarte, Eva
Billy (1992)

Ducky, Princess
That's TV (1982)

Duclon, Deborah J.
Silver Spoons (1984)

Dunkleberger, Amy
Other Mothers (1993)

Dunn–Dern, Lisa
Roc (1992–1993)

DuPont, Pennie
Torn between Two Fathers (1989)

Durham, Holly
Trapper John, M.D. (1984–1985)

Dworkin, Susan
Dirty Dancing (1988)

Dysinger, Carol L.
The Christmas Star (1986)

Earle, Anitra
The Love Boat (1979)
Sweepstakes (1979)
Aloha Paradise (1981)

Easton, Charleen
All–American Girl (1995)

Eddo, Nancy
> *Benson* (1982–1983)
> *The Love Boat* (1984)
> *Full House* (1987)
> *Gimme a Break* (1987)

Edelman, Rosemary
> *Side by Side* (1988)

Edmonds, Jacque
> *Martin* (1993–1995)

Eells, Pamela
> *Starting Now* (1989)
> *Family Matters* (1990–1991)
> *Princesses* (1991)
> *Step by Step* (1992)
> *Mad about You* (1992–1993)
> *The Nanny* (1993–1994)
> *Madman of the People* (1994)

Ehrin, Kerri
> *Moonlighting* (1984)
> *Newhart* (1986–1987)
> *Shell Game* (1987)
> *Moonlighting* (1987–1988)
> *The Wonder Years* (1990)

Eisner, Jane Breckenridge
> *A New Kind of Family* (1979)

Elder, Ann W.
> *The Flip Wilson Special* (1974)
> *The Paul Lynde Comedy Hour* (1975)
> *The Lily Tomlin Special* (1975)
> *The Flip Wilson Special* (1976)
> *The Marilyn McCoo and Billy Davis Jr. Show* (1977)
> *Four Specials for the Price of One* (1978)
> *The Big Hex of Little Lulu* (1979)
> *Playboy Roller Disco Pajama Party* (1979)
> *Carol Burnett & Co.* (1979)
> *Zack and the Magic Factory* (1980)

NBC Family Christmas (1981)
> *Lily Tomlin: Sold Out* (1981)
> *Lily for President* (1982)
> *Madame's Place* (1982)
> *Texaco Star Theater—Opening Night* (1982)
> *This Is Your Life* (1987)
> *Superstars and Their Moms* (1987)
> *Live! Dick Clark Presents* (1988)
> *The 1989 Miss USA Pageant* (1989)
> *The 1989 Miss Universe Pageant* (1989)
> *Miss Teen USA Pageant* (1989)
> *This Is Your Life* (1993)

Elias, Caroline
> *Breaking Away* (1980)
> *Secrets of Midland Heights* (1980)
> *Magnum, P.I.* (1981)

Elias, Cindy
> *Baby Talk* (1991–1992)
> *Dudley* (1993)
> *The Mommies* (1993–1995)
> *Empty Nest* (1994)
> *A Whole New Ballgame* (1995)

Elias, Jeannie
> *Catwalk* (1992–1993)
> *Designing Women* (1993)

Eliasberg, Jan
> *Sisters* (1995)

Eliason, Joyce
> *A Matter of Sex* (1984)
> *Wet Gold* (1984)
> *Right to Kill?* (1985)
> *Surviving* (1985)
> *Babycakes* (1989)
> *In Sickness and in Health* (1992)

Elstad, Linda
> *Quincy* (1979)
> *Eight Is Enough* (1979)
> *Secrets of Midland Heights* (1980)

Dallas (1980–1983)
Divorce Wars (1981)
Fantasy Island (1981)
American Dream (1981)
Fame (1982)
The Second Family Tree (1982–1983)
Ryan's Four (1983)
Lottery (1983–1984)
One Day at a Time (1984)
Call to Glory (1984)
Two Marriages (1984)
A Desperate Exit (1986)
Falcon Crest (1989)
Island Son (1990)
Civil Wars (1992)
Hawkeye (1994)

Emerson, Joanna
Love Tapes (1980)
Dynasty (1987)

Endo–Dizon, Ellen
The Love Boat (1984–1985)

Engles, Judy
The Hand–Me–Down Kid (1983)
It's No Crush, I'm in Love (1983)
Mom's on Strike (1985)

English, Diane
The Lathe of Heaven (1980)
Her Life as a Man (1984)
Call to Glory (1984)
Foley Square (1985)
One Hogan Place (1985)
My Sister Sam (1987–1988)
Murphy Brown (1988–1992)
Love & War (1992–1994)
Double Rush (1995)

English, Priscilla A.
Fallen Angel (1980)
Country Gold (1982)
Forbidden Love (1983)

Dynasty (1984)
Desperate Rescue: The Cathy Mahone Story (1993)
Moment of Truth: Stalking Back (1993)

Epstein, Deborah
Catwalk (1992–1993)

Ervin, Judith Raye
Blansky's Beauties (1977)
Laverne and Shirley (1979)

Esensten, Barbara
Dynasty (1987–1989)
Rich Men, Single Women (1990)
The Love Boat: A Valentine Voyage (1990)
Father Dowling Mysteries (1990–1991)

Espenson, Jane
Monty (1994)
Dinosaurs (1994)
Me and the Boys (1994–1995)

Estabrook, Susana
Falcon Crest (1988)

Evans, Shelley
Beyond Betrayal (1994)

Eyre, Bett
Bridesmaids (1989)

Faciano, Debra
Married People (1990)
Saved by the Bell: The College Years (1993)

Fales, Susan
A Different World (1987–1993)

Falkenstein, Beth Fieger
Mad about You (1994)

Farr, Amie
The Love Boat (1978–1979)

Farr, Lynne

> *The Bob Newhart Show* (1972–1978)
> *Bobbie Gentry's Happiness Hour* (1974)
> *The Love Boat* (1978–1979)
> *We've Got It Made* (1983)
> *2½ Dads* (1986)
> *Baghdad Cafe* (1990)

Farrell, Judy

> *The Kid from Nowhere* (1982)
> *Fame* (1983)

Faulkerner, Nancy

> *The Incredible Hulk* (1981)

Fay, Deirdre

> *Ladies' Man* (1981)
> *The Facts of Life Goes to Paris* (1982)
> *The Facts of Life* (1982–1983)
> *Double Trouble* (1984)
> *One Day at a Time* (1984)
> *All Together Now* (1984)
> *The Facts of Life* (1985)
> *Sweet Surrender* (1986–1987)
> *Ann Jillian* (1989)
> *Madman of the People* (1994)

Feather, Jacqueline

> *Little Women* (1979)
> *Elena* (1985)
> *The Richest Man in the World: The Story of Aristotle Onassis* (1988)
> *Whose Child Is This? The War for Baby Jessica* (1993)

Fein, Judith

> *Life Goes On* (1990)

Feldman, Judith

> *L.A. Law* (1991–1992)

Ferguson, Kathleen

> *New Adventures of Wonder Woman* (1978)
> *Buck Rogers in the 25th Century* (1979)

Ferrer, Sasha

> *In Defense of a Married Man* (1990)

Fine, Sylvia

> *Musical Comedy Tonight* (1979)

Finestra, Carmen

> *Johnny Cash and Friends* (1976)
> *Mel and Susan Together* (1978)
> *Joe and Valerie* (1978)
> *The Harvey Korman Show* (1978)
> *The Love Boat* (1978–1979)
> *Highcliff Manor* (1979)
> *The Johnny Cash Spring Fever* (1979)
> *Good Times* (1979)
> *Angie* (1979)
> *The Johnny Cash Christmas Special* (1979)
> *Jake's Way* (1980)
> *Insight* (1980)
> *Capital Cities Family Theater* (1980)
> *The Baxters* (1980)
> *All Commercials: A Steve Martin Special* (1980)
> *Steve Martin: Comedy Is Not Pretty* (1980)
> *Ladies Man* (1981)
> *Twilight Theater II* (1982)
> *It's Not Easy* (1983)
> *The Best Times* (1983)
> *Punky Brewster* (1984)
> *The Goodbye Girl* (1984)
> *The Cosby Show* (1984–1990)
> *Home Improvement* (1991–1993)
> *Thunder Alley* (1994)

Finney, Sara A.

> *The Jeffersons* (1981)
> *Full House* (1983)

The Jeffersons (1983)
Silver Spoons (1983)
227 (1985–1986)
The Facts of Life (1987)
Family Matters (1990–1995)

Fisch, Julia
Step by Step (1992–1993)

Fischer, Janice
I Married Dora (1987)
The Golden Girls (1987)

Fisher, Carrie
The Young Indiana Jones Chronicles (1992–1993)

Fisher, Terry Louise
Cutter to Houston (1983)
The Mississippi (1983)
Your Place or Mine (1983)
This Girl for Hire (1983)
Cagney and Lacey (1983–1985)
L.A. Law (1986–1988)
Sister Margaret and the Saturday Night Ladies (1987)
Hooperman (1987)
Blue Bayou (1990)
2000 Malibu Road (1992)
Cagney and Lacey: The Return (1994)

Flackett, Jennifer
L.A. Law (1992–1993)
Civil War (1993)
Beverly Hills 90210 (1993)
Earth 2 (1994)

Flacks, Diane
The Kids in the Hall (1992–1994)

Flaherty, Joy
Limited Partners (1988)

Flavin, Courtney
Annie McGuire (1988)
Torn between Two Fathers (1989)
The Cosby Show (1991–1992)

Fleet–Giordana, Anne
Kate and Allie (1986–1989)
Working It Out (1991)
Baby Talk (1991–1992)
Frasier (1993–1995)

Flint, Carol
China Beach (1989–1991)
L. A. Law (1991–1992)
Crime & Punishment (1993)
Earth 2 (1994–1995)

Flynn, Miriam
The Tim Conway Show (1980)

Fogle, Ellen L.
Saturday Night Live (1982)
Facts of Life (1987)
Married . . . with Children (1988–1993)
Vinny & Bobby (1992)
Rachel Gunn, R.N. (1992)
Parent'Hood (1995)

Foley, Jane
It's No Crush, I'm in Love (1983)

Fontana, D. C.
Star Trek: The Next Generation (1993)
Star Trek: Deep Space Nine (1993)
Babylon 5 (1994)

Forbes, Maya
The Larry Sanders Show (1992–1994)

Ford, Diane
Home Improvement (1994)

Ford, Jean
The Love Boat (1980)
The Love Boat (1982)
The Love Boat (1984)

Ford, Kathryn
Cagney and Lacey (1986–1988)
Family Ties (1987–1989)
Day by Day (1988)

Equal Justice (1990)
WIOU (1991)
Monty (1994)
Christy (1994)
Dr. Quinn, Medicine Woman
   (1994–1995)

Forrester, Patricia
   Boy Meets World (1993)

Foster, Christine
   Top Cops (1992–1993)

Fowler, Marjorie
   The Waltons (1981)
   A Wedding on Walton's Mountain
      (1982)

Fox, J. Rae
   Pros & Cons (1991)

Fox, Terry Curtis
   Hill Street Blues (1986–1987)
   Men (1989)
   The Perfect Witness (1989)
   Sweet Justice (1995)

Frank, Debra
   Diff'rent Strokes (1980–1982)
   One in a Million (1981)
   9 to 5 (1981)
   House Calls (1981–1982)
   Benson (1984)
   Cagney and Lacey (1985)
   Me and Mom (1985)
   Remington Steele (1985)
   MacGyver (1985)
   Moonlighting (1986)
   The Wonder Years (1989)

Frank, Katherine Sheldon
   Here's Boomer (1980)

Fraser, Prudence
   Alice (1981)
   It's Not Easy (1983)
   Three's Company (1984)

Oh, Madeline (1984)
Who's the Boss (1984–1985)
The Charmings (1986–1987)
Married People (1990)
The Nanny (1993)

Freeman, Marion C.
   The Rowan & Martin Report (1975)
   Handle with Care (1977)
   Baby I'm Back (1978)
   Alice (1978–1979)

Friedgen, Julie
   House Calls (1980)
   Magnum, P.I. (1983)
   Too Close for Comfort (1983)
   Knight Rider (1984)
   Crazy Like a Fox (1985)
   Eye to Eye (1985)
   In the Heat of the Night (1990–
      1991)
   Walker, Texas Ranger (1994)

Friedman, Iris
   Obsessive Love (1984)
   Nobody's Children (1993)

Friedman, MiMi
   In Living Color (1990)
   A Different World (1990–1993)
   Good Advice (1994)

Friedman, Racelle
   Silver Spoons (1986–1987)
   TV 101 (1989)

Friedman, Tracey
   The Antagonists (1990)
   Murder, She Wrote (1992)
   Reasonable Doubts (1992)
   TimeTrax (1993–1994)
   The Adventures of Brisco County, Jr.
      (1994)

Friese, Kim C.
   Our House (1987–1988)
   In the Heat of the Night (1990)

Davis Rules (1991–1992)
The Wonder Years (1992–1993)
Evening Shade (1993–1994)
Me and the Boys (1994–1995)

Frohman, Star
Life Goes On (1990–1991)
Beverly Hills 90210 (1990–1993)

Frolov, Diane
Magnum, P.I. (1981)
The Incredible Hulk (1981–1982)
Hot Pursuit (1984)
V (1984)
Rags to Riches (1987)
Northern Exposure (1990–1995)
Alien Nation: Dark Horizon (1994)

Fruedberg, Judy
The Dick Cavett Show (1975)
Cos: The Bill Cosby Special (1975)
ABC vs. Cos (1976)
Sesame Street . . . 20 Years and Still Counting (1989)

Fuller, Kim
The Tracey Ullman Show (1987)

Gabriel, Judith
Harper Valley P.T.A. (1981)

Gallagher, Mary B.
Nobody's Child (1986)
Bonds of Love (1993)

Gallagher, Michelle
Against the Law (1990–1991)

Gallagher, Sarah Woodside
L.A. Law (1990–1992)

Gallen, Barbara
Top of the Pops: A Very Special Christmas (1987)

Gallery, Michele
Lou Grant (1978–1982)
High School Confidential (1984)

Things Are Looking Up (1984)
Making Out (1984)
The Best Times (1985)
Old Dogs (1987)
L.A. Law (1988–1989)
Daughters of Privilege (1991)
Sexual Advances (1992)

Gamble, Tracy J.
Newhart (1985)
227 (1986–1987)
My Two Dads (1988)
The Golden Girls (1989–1992)
Here and Now (1992)
Daddy Dearest (1993)
The 5 Mrs. Buchanans (1994–1995)

Gansberg, Judith M.
The Love Boat (1984)

Gard, Cheryl
The Ellen Burstyn Show (1987)
A Different World (1988–1990)
Designing Women (1989)
The Fresh Prince of Bel Air (1990–1992)
Hangin' with Mr. Cooper (1993)

Gardenia, Gabrielle
The Cosby Show (1992)

Gardner, Sibyl
Law & Order (1992–1993)

Garland, Trish
Baywatch (1992–1993)

Garman, Stephanie
Happy Days (1979–1981)
Mr. Merlin (1981)
Eight Is Enough (1981)
One Day at a Time (1982)
Private Benjamin (1982–1983)
Fantasy Island (1982–1983)
At Ease (1983)

The Love Boat (1984)

Down to Earth (1984)

Our Time (1985)

Dallas (1986)

Hunter (1987)

The Love Boat: A Valentine Voyage (1990)

Garrett, Lila F.

This Better Be It (1976)

Newman's Drugstore (1976)

Baby, I'm Back (1978)

Getting There (1980)

The Trouble with Celia (1980)

The Other Woman (1983)

Who Gets the Friends (1988)

The Nanny (1994)

Gary, Carol D.

The Mary Tyler Moore Show (1978)

Barney Miller (1979)

Irene (1981)

Open All Night (1981)

Buffalo Bill (1983)

Fame (1984)

Second Stage (1988)

Grand (1990)

Dave's World (1994)

Gaughan, Shannon

Family Ties (1988–1989)

Saturday Night Live (1989)

The Fresh Prince of Bel Air (1990–1991)

Down the Shore (1992–1993)

Love & War (1992–1994)

Gaver, Eleanor E.

Dead in the Water (1991)

Gayle, Nancy

Jayne Mansfield: A Symbol of the Fifties (1980)

Gaylor, Mary Lee

Magnum, P.I. (1984–1985)

Gelman, Laurie S.

Please Stand By (1978)

The Waverley Wonders (1978)

Brothers & Sisters (1979)

Out of the Blue (1979)

The Goodtime Girls (1980)

House Calls (1980–1981)

Too Close for Comfort (1982–1983)

Oh, Madeline (1983)

Condo (1983)

The Love Boat (1984)

Laverne and Shirley (1985)

The Days and Nights of Molly Dodd (1986)

A.L.F. (1987)

Roseanne (1988–1989)

Gendelman, Michele

Newhart (1989–1990)

Gennis, Jean

L.A. Law (1994)

Sweet Justice (1995)

Gerard, Anne

The Rape of Dr. Willis (1991)

A Town Apart (1992)

Gibbs, Ann L.

A Year at the Top (1977)

The Love Boat (1977–1980)

Chico and the Man (1978)

Carter Country (1978–1979)

The Baxters (1979–1980)

Joe's World (1980)

The Facts of Life (1980–1981)

Joanie Loves Chachi (1982–1983)

Teachers Only (1983)

The Jeffersons (1984)

Throb (1986–1987)

Gibbs, Marla

The Jeffersons (1984)

Gibson, Allison

Parent'Hood (1990–1991)

Home Improvement (1991)

Gill, Elizabeth P.

Having It All (1982)

Sins of the Father (1985)

Convicted: A Mother's Story (1987)

Roxanne: The Prize Pulitzer (1989)

My So–Called Life (1994)

Gilliland, Deborah A.

Trapper John, M.D. (1982–1983)

Trapper John, M.D. (1985)

The Magical World of Disney (1989)

Gioffre, Marisa

A Very Delicate Matter (1981)

It's a Fact of Life (1981)

Star Struck (1981)

Gittlin, Joyce R.

Marie (1980)

Three's Company (1980)

The Jeffersons (1981–1984)

Brothers (1985)

Wings (1994)

Glazer, Mindy

Kate and Allie (1985)

Who's the Boss (1987)

My Two Dads (1988)

Live–In (1989)

Glenmore, Molly

Acapulco H.E.A.T. (1993–1994)

Glickman, Jennifer

Something Wilder (1994–1995)

Gold, Loree

The Country Music Hall of Fame 25 (1992)

Goldberg, Betty

Trapper John, M.D. (1980–1981)

Benson (1983)

Diff'rent Strokes (1983)

A Little Piece of Heaven (1991)

One Special Victory (1991)

Leave of Absence (1994)

Goldberg, Susan C.

Cutter to Houston (1983)

Knots Landing (1984)

Misfits of Science (1985)

Shadow Chasers (1985)

Fame (1987)

Goldemberg, Rose Leiman

Land of Hope (1976)

Mother and Daughter: The Loving War (1980)

Born Beautiful (1982)

The Burning Bed (1984)

The Nightingale Saga (1984)

Stone Pillow (1985)

Dark Holiday (1989)

Goldman, Gina Fredrica

Family (1979)

Joe and Valerie (1979)

Good Time Harry (1980)

Marie (1980)

King's Crossing (1982)

Condo (1983)

The Facts of Life (1983)

Simon & Simon (1983)

Scarecrow & Mrs. King (1983)

Gimme a Break (1983)

Partners in Crime (1984)

Codename: Foxfire (1985)

The Cosby Show (1985)

Jack and Mike (1987)

Hooperman (1988)

Eisenhower & Lutz (1988)

Dear John (1988–1989)

Hot Prospects (1989)

Baghdad Cafe (1990)

The Wonder Years (1992)

Goldman, Peggy

Forever Fernwood (1977–1978)

Mary Hartman, Mary Hartman (1978)

Cliffhangers (1979)

Madame's Place (1981)

Remington Steele (1982–1983)

Lottery! (1983)

Hot Pursuit (1984)

V (1985)

Starman (1987)

Goldman, Wendy

Just in Time (1988)

Room for Two (1992–1993)

Goldsmith, Gloria

The Streets of San Francisco (1976)

Goldstein, Shelly

Laverne and Shirley (1980)

Facts of Life (1984)

Head of the Class (1990)

Goldstone, Deena

Family (1978)

Love Child (1982)

When She Says No (1984)

A Bunny's Tale (1985)

Gonzales, Gloria

The Day the Women Got Even (1980)

The Cosby Show (1984)

Goodrich, Frances

The Diary of Anne Frank (1980)

Goodrich, Taenha

Airwolf (1984)

Gordon, Billi

227 (1987)

Gordon, Jill

Archie Bunker's Place (1982)

One Day at a Time (1982)

Diff'rent Strokes (1982)

Laverne and Shirley (1982–1983)

Whiz Kids (1984)

Double Trouble (1984)

Paper Dolls (1984)

Benson (1984)

Silver Spoons (1984–1995)

MacGruder and Loud (1985)

Hooperman (1988–1989)

Doogie Howser, M.D. (1989–1990)

thirtysomething (1989–1991)

The Wonder Years (1990–1991)

Harts of the West (1993)

Graham (1994)

My So–Called Life (1994–1995)

Gordon, Margie

A New Kind of Family (1979)

Matt Houston (1984)

Gore, Chris

Faeries (1980)

Fame (1981)

Gorman, Sharee Anne

A Little Bit Strange (1989)

Gould, Diana

Family (1977–1978)

The Rock Rainbow (1978)

Knots Landing (1980–1981)

Knots Landing (1983)

Berrengers (1984)

Dynasty (1984)

I'll Take Manhattan (1987)

Sisters (1990–1991)

A House of Secrets and Lies (1992)

Gould, Jane

Webster (1987)

Graf, Wendy

A.L.F. (1987–1988)

Murder, She Wrote (1989)

Grafton, Sue

Rhoda (1976–1977)

Walking through Fire (1979)

Sex and the Single Parent (1979)

Mark, I Love You (1980)

Nurse (1980)

Seven Brides for Seven Brothers (1982)

A Killer in the Family (1983)

A Caribbean Mystery (1983)

The Love Boat (1983)

Love on the Run (1985)

Tonight's the Night (1987)

Grant, Barra

Mabel and Max (1987)

Dirty Dancing (1988–1989)

Living Single (1994)

Grant, Susannah

Party of Five (1995)

Graphia, Toni

China Beach (1989–1990)

Cop Rock (1990)

Quantum Leap (1991)

Life Goes On (1991–1993)

Melrose Place (1992–1993)

Grassle, Karen

Battered (1978)

Greek, Janet C.

Passions (1984)

Green, Katherine D.

Bob Hope's World of Comedy (1976)

Bob Hope's Bicentennial Star Spangled Spectacular (1976)

Alice (1979)

That's TV (1979)

The Ropers (1980)

Taxi (1980–1983)

The Two of Us (1981)

Cheers (1982)

Newhart (1982/1986)

Mama's Family (1983–1984)

The Duck Factory (1984)

It's Your Move (1984)

Royal Match (1985)

Brothers (1986–1987)

Married . . . with Children (1991–1994)

Rachel Gunn, R.N. (1992)

Dave's World (1995–1996)

Green, Patricia M.

Shirley (1979)

Better Late Than Never (1979)

I'll Love You When You're More Like Me (1979)

King's Crossing (1979)

Eight Is Enough (1979–1981)

American Dream (1981)

Knots Landing (1982)

The Mississippi (1983)

Two Marriages (1984)

Cagney and Lacey (1984–1985)

North and South (1985)

Scarecrow & Mrs. King (1986)

Perry Mason: The Case of the Murdered Madam (1987)

Hope Division (1987)

China Beach (1989)

L.A. Law (1990–1992)

Christy (1994)

Green, Robin

A Year in the Life (1987–1988)

Almost Grown (1989)

Capital News (1990)

Northern Exposure (1990–1995)

Greenwald, Nancy

Sharon: Portrait of a Mistress (1977)

Greyhosky, Babs

Father Dowling Mysteries (1989)

The Trials of Rosie O'Neill (1991)

TimeTrax (1993–1994)

Walker, Texas Ranger (1994)

Griffin, Wanda

Amen (1989)

Grippo, Joelyn

The Pursuit of Happiness (1987)

Met Life Presents The Apollo Theatre (1987)

Hall of Fame (1994)

Grodin, Marion

Princess (1991)

Gross, Marjorie

A.L.F. (1988)

Newhart (1988)

Get a Life! (1991)
Anything but Love (1991–1992)
Vinnie & Bobby (1992)
The Larry Sanders Show (1992–1993)
Seinfeld (1994)

Gross, Mary
Saturday Night Live (1983)

Grossman, Terry
Angie (1979)
Benson (1980–1984)
Condo (1983)
The Lucie Arnaz Show (1984)
Hail to the Chief (1985)
The Golden Girls (1985–1990)
The Fanelli Boys (1990–1991)
Pacific Station (1991)
The Mommies (1993)

Guitar, Sheree
The Days and Nights of Molly Dodd (1986)
Duet (1987)
Anything but Love (1989)
Roseanne (1990)

Guppy, Nancy
Julie (1992)

Guthrie, Lee
A Place for Annie (1993)

Guy, Jasmine
A Different World (1990–1993)

Guylas, Ellen
The Charmings (1987)
Who's the Boss (1987)
Live–In (1989)
Newhart (1989)
Free Spirit (1990)
Full House (1990–1995)

Hague, Renee Orin
Fame (1982–1983)

Hailey, Elizabeth F.
Love, Sidney (1981)
Isabel's Choice (1981)
The Cosby Show (1987)

Hall, Barbara E.
Double Trouble (1981)
Family Ties (1983)
Condo (1983)
It Takes Two (1983)
Newhart (1983–1984)
The Duck Factory (1983–1984)
Dreams (1984)
We Got It Made (1984)
Young Again (1986)
Moonlighting (1988)
A Year in the Life (1988)
Anything but Love (1989)
Ann Jillian (1990)
I'll Fly Away (1991–1993)
Northern Exposure (1993–1994)

Hall, Karen L.
Eight Is Enough (1980–1981)
M*A*S*H (1980–1983)
Hiil Street Blues (1982–1984)
Maximum Security (1984)
Tough Love (1985)
The Betty Ford Story (1987)
Moonlighting (1987)
The Women of Brewster Place (1989)
Quantum Leap (1990–1991)
I'll Fly Away (1992)
Darkness before Dawn (1993)

Hamil, Jayne
The Nanny (1994)

Hamilton, Anne Lewis
Matt Houston (1984)
The Equalizer (1987)
Hard Copy (1987)
Blue Skies (1988)
thirtysomething (1989–1991)
Sirens (1993)
Party of Five (1994–1995)

Hammerstein, Jane Howard
Summer of My German Soldier
(1979)
Long Road Home (1981)

Hammond, Diana
Princess Daisy (1983)

Hampton, Brenda
Sister Kate (1989)
Blossom (1990–1994)
Lenny (1991)
The John Larroquette Show (1993)
Daddy's Girls (1994)

Hampton, Elin
The Jackie Thomas Show (1992–
1993)
Dream On (1993–1994)
House of Buggin' (1995)

Hannaway, Dorian R.
Madame's Place (1982)

Hansen, Elizabeth
American Eyes (1990)

Harris, Karen
The Incredible Hulk (1979–1980)
Simon & Simon (1981)
Born to Be Sold (1981)
Knight Rider (1982)
Scene of the Crime (1984)
Streethawk (1985)
Deadline (1988)
Studio 5B (1989)
Peaceable Kingdom (1989)
The Human Factor (1992)
Renegade (1992)
*Roseanne: An Unauthorized
Biography* (1994)

Harris, Susan
The Partridge Family (1970)
Maude (1972)
Fay (1976–1977)

Daughters (1977)
Benson (1979)
Soap (1979–1981)
I'm a Big Girl Now (1980–1981)
It Takes Two (1982)
The Golden Girls (1984–1989)
Hail to the Chief (1985)
Empty Nest (1988)
Good & Evil (1991)
Nurses (1991)
The Golden Palace (1992–1993)

Harrison, Lindsay
Too Close for Comfort (1982)
One Day at a Time (1983)
Alice (1983)
The Four Seasons (1984)
Dads (1986)
Take My Daughters, Please (1988)
Turn Back the Clock (1989)
My Boyfriend's Back (1989)
Coins in the Fountain (1990)
*White Hot: The Mysterious Murder
of Thelma Todd* (1991)
Cutters (1993)
It Had to Be You (1993)
Sisters (1995)

Hart, Carole
The Dick Cavett Show (1975)
Oh Boy! Babies! (1981)

Hartman, Becky
In Living Color (1990–1991)
Room for Two (1992–1993)
Living Single (1993–1995)

Hartman, Jan A.
*The Late Great Me: Story of a
Teenage Alcoholic* (1979)
Family Reunion (1979)

Hatfield, Carol A.
*The Sensational, Shocking, Wild, and
Crazy 70s* (1980)

I've Had It Up to Here (1981)
Book of Lists (1982)

Hayward, Lillie
The Shaggy Dog (1994)

Heaney, Janet
Mrs. Lambert Remembers Love
(1991)
Lies and Lullabies (1993)

Hearn, Shari
Valerie's Family (1987)
The Hogan Family (1988)
The Hogan Family (1990–1991)
Going Places (1991)
Shaky Ground (1992–1993)
Perfect Strangers (1993)
Joe's Life (1993)

Heath, Jennifer
Roseanne (1990–1992)
Dave's World (1993–1994)

Hecht, Sylvia
Turnabout (1979)
The Love Boat (1980)

Hegge, Virginia
Man of the People (1991–1992)
The Torkelsons (1992)
Shaky Ground (1992–1993)

Heimel, Cynthia
Dear John (1991)

Heisler, Eileen
Doogie Howser, M.D. (1991–1992)
Down the Shore (1992)
Roseanne (1992–1993)
Murphy Brown (1993–1995)

Helberg, Sandy and Harriet
The Golden Girls (1989)
Perfect Strangers (1990–1991)

Heline, De Ann
Doogie Howser, M.D. (1991–1992)
Down the Shore (1992)
Roseanne (1992–1993)
Murphy Brown (1993–1995)

Helm, Merry
Following Her Heart (1994)

Henderson, Felicia D.
Family Matters (1994)

Hendler, Janis B.
The Fall Guy (1981)
Matt Houston (1982)
Farrell for the People (1982)
Knight Rider (1983–1984)
T. J. Hooker (1984)
Partners in Crime (1984)
Half Nelson (1985)

Henjum-Williams, Colleen
Mystery Science Theater 3000
(1994–1995)

Hensley, Terry
Three's Company (1982)

Herman, Ellen
Newhart (1989–1990)
Gabriel's Fire (1990–1991)
Northern Exposure (1990–1991)
Doogie Howser, M.D. (1991–1992)
Melrose Place (1992–1993)
Moon over Miami (1993)
My So-Called Life (1994–1995)

Herman, Maxine
9 to 5 (1982)
Highway to Heaven (1983)
Trapper John, M.D. (1984)
Hotel (1985)

Herman, Thelma
Love, Sidney (1982)

Herndon, Barbara J.
Throb (1986–1987)

Herrera, Suzanne M.
Falcon Crest (1983)
International Airport (1985)

Herring, Susan
Throb (1986–1987)
The Tracey Ullman Show (1987)
Cheers (1988)
Cheers (1990–1991)
Cheers (1993)

Hervey, Winifred C.
Laverne and Shirley (1981)
Mork and Mindy (1982)
The New Odd Couple (1983)
Benson (1983–1984)
The Golden Girls (1984–1988)
The Cosby Show (1986)
Baby Boom (1989)
The Fresh Prince of Bel Air (1991–1993)

Hester, Holly
The Good Life (1994)
Someone Like Me (1994)
Ellen (1994)

Hickey, Janice
Her Wicked Ways (1991)

Hickey, Pamela
Robocop (1994)

Hickman, Gail Morgan
Crime Story (1987–1988)
The Equalizer (1988–1989)
Mancuso, FBI (1989–1990)
The Flash (1990–1991)
P.S. I Luv U (1991–1992)
Drug Wars: The Cocaine Cartel (1992)
One West Waikiki (1994)

Hicks, Regina Y.
True Colors (1990–1992)

Hicks, Terri Schaffer
Thea (1993–1994)
Martin (1994)

Hildebrand, Kari
Hostage for a Day (1994)

Hill, Danielle
Love, Lies, and Murder (1991)
Armed and Innocent (1994)
Fatal Vows: The Alexandra O'Hara Story (1994)

Hill, Fern
Against the Law (1990–1991)

Hill, Kimberly H.
One Day at a Time (1980)
It's a Living (1981)
The Facts of Life (1982–1983)
Double Trouble (1984)
ER (1984)
Family Ties (1985)
The Tortellis (1987)
Cheers (1987)
Empty Nest (1989)

Himelstein, Janet
The Young Riders (1989)
Sisters (1992–1993)

Hire, Lois
Young Maverick (1979)
The Millionaire (1979)
Hello Larry (1979–1980)

Hirsch, Janis E.
Square Pegs (1982–1983)
One Day at a Time (1983)
The Facts of Life (1983)
Double Trouble (1983–1984)
Aftermash (1984)
Dreams (1984)
Rags to Riches (1986)
Easy Street (1986)
Stranded (1986)
Act II (1987)
Day by Day (1988)
Anything but Love (1989)
Little White Lies (1989)

Anything but Love (1990–1991)
L.A. Law (1992–1993)
The Nanny (1994)

Hite, Kathleen
    The Waltons (1978–1981)
    Falcon Crest (1982)

Hobson, Laura Z.
    Consenting Adults (1985)

Hochberg, Victoria G.
    I Married a Centerfold (1984)
    Final Jeopardy (1986)
    Just a Regular Kid: An AIDS Story (1987)
    Me and Mrs. G (1987)

Hock, Allison
    Quincy (1982–1983)
    T. J. Hooker (1983)
    The Master (1984)
    Hotel (1984)
    Blue Thunder (1984)
    Knots Landing (1984)
    Miami Vice (1985)
    Cagney and Lacey (1987–1988)
    Star Trek: The Next Generation (1992–1993)
    Sirens (1994)
    Sisters (1994)

Hoeffner, Karol Ann
    Working Stiffs (1979)
    The Baxters (1979)
    Eight Is Enough (1980)
    One in a Million (1980)
    It's a Living (1981)
    Too Close for Comfort (1981)
    Alice (1981–1983)
    The Facts of Life (1984)
    Newhart (1984)
    Burning Rage (1984)
    Scorned and Swindled (1984)
    Sara (1985)
    Danielle Steel's Kaleidoscope (1991)

Danielle Steel's Palomino (1991)
Miss America: Behind the Crown (1992)
Voices from Within (1994)
Danielle Steel's Family Album (1994)

Hoelscher, Jean
    This Girl for Hire (1983)

Hogle, Cynthia
    Roseanne (1994)

Holden, Amy
    Jack's Place (1992)

Holliday, Cheryl
    Herman's Head (1991)
    Empty Nest (1992–1993)
    Camp Wilder (1993)
    Martin (1993–1994)

Holzman, Winnie
    thirtysomething (1990–1991)
    My So–Called Life (1994–1995)

Honigberg, Gail
    Out of This World (1991)
    Something Wilder (1994)

Honigblum, Carrie E.
    The Charmings (1987–1988)
    Baby Boom (1989)
    Major Dad (1990–1993)
    Sister, Sister (1994–1995)

Horvath, Gillian
    Beverly Hills 90210 (1992–1993)

Horwits, Vicki
    Baghdad Cafe (1990–1991)

Hosbach, Gretchen
    America's Most Wanted (1992–1993)

Houghton, Mona
    Knots Landing (1981–1982)

Houston, Christine
  Punky Brewster (1985)
  227 (1986–1987)

Houston, Dianne
  Brewster Place (1990)

Hsiao, Rita
  Thunder Alley (1994)

Hunt, Bonnie
  The Building (1993)

Iacobuzio, Janet
  Another World: Summer Desire
    (1992)

Irving, Patricia
  Baby Boom (1989)

Ison, Tara
  Doogie Howser, M.D. (1990–1991)

Iverson, Portia
  Blossom (1991–1992)

J., Myra
  Hangin' with Mr. Cooper (1993–
    1994)

Jacker, Corinne
  Loose Change (1978)

Jackson, Janet Lynn
  Family Matters (1990–1991)
  704 Hauser (1994)

Jackson, Tracey
  Babes (1991)

Jaffe, Jewel
  Guide for the Married Woman
    (1978)

James, Judith Rutherford
  Funny, You Don't Look 200 (1987)

James, Syrie Astrahan
  Buck James (1987)
  Starman (1987)
  Danielle Steel's Once in a Lifetime
    (1994)

Jansen, Susan Estelle
  Home Improvement (1991–1993)
  Boy Meets World (1993–1995)
  *ABC Saturday Morning Preview
    Special* (1994)

Janzen, Naomi
  The Hidden Room (1993)
  Highlander (1993–1994)
  Treacherous Beauties (1994)

Jeffries, Georgia
  Cagney and Lacey (1984–1987)
  China Beach (1989–1990)
  Sisters (1993)

Jennings, Sandra
  The Summer My Father Grew Up
    (1991)
  Desperate Choices: To Save My Child
    (1992)
  Moment of Truth: Broken Pledges
    (1994)

Jett, Sue
  Infidelity (1987)
  Christine Cromwell: In Vino Veritas
    (1990)

Johns, Victoria
  Flying High (1979)
  Trapper John, M.D. (1979–1984)
  The Wizard (1987)
  Bring Me the Head of Dobie Gillis
    (1988)
  Nightingales (1989)

Johnson, Connie
  Tales from the Crypt (1994)

Johnson, Dee
> *I'll Fly Away* (1992–1993)
> *Melrose Place* (1993–1995)

Johnson, Monica
> *Good Sports* (1991)

Johnson, Sharon D.
> *The Sinbad Show* (1993–1994)

Jones, Amy
> *Indecency* (1990)

Jones, Bridget
> *Mystery Science Theater 3000*
> (1994–1995)

Jones, Claylene
> *Who's the Boss* (1989)

Jones, Jacque
> *Entertainment Tonight* (1982)

Jones, Michelle
> *Out All Night* (1992–1993)
> *Thea* (1993–1994)
> *Parent'Hood* (1995)

Jones, Patricia
> *The Bob Newhart Show* (1972–
> 1978)
> *Mary* (1978)
> *The Last Resort* (1979)
> *The Mary Tyler Moore Hour* (1979)
> *Report to Murphy* (1982)
> *Fame* (1982)
> *Packin' It In* (1983)
> *The Bronx Zoo* (1988)
> *The Debbie Allen Special* (1989)
> *His & Hers* (1990)
> *Brooklyn Bridge* (1993)

Jordan, Delia
> *Inmates: A Love Story* (1981)

Jordan, Janice
> *Roseanne* (1992–1993)

Joseph, Jackie
> *Family* (1978)
> *Barnaby Jones* (1979)

Joseph, Kathy
> *Gimme a Break* (1981)

Joyce, Patricia
> *Shannon* (1981)

Joyner, C. Courtney
> *Distant Cousins* (1993)

Julian, Mady
> *Gimme a Break* (1984–1987)
> *Empty Nest* (1989)
> *A Family Named Joe* (1990)
> *The Powers That Be* (1992–1993)

Jung, Cathy
> *Head of the Class* (1989)
> *Growing Pains* (1991–1992)
> *Full House* (1992–1994)

Junge, Alexa
> *Danger Theatre* (1993)
> *The Second Half* (1993)
> *Friends* (1994–1995)

Junkermann, Kelly
> *A Day in the Life of Country Music*
> (1993)

Kadish, Lynne
> *Married People* (1990)

Kahan, Judy
> *Love, Natalie* (1980)
> *How to Eat Like a Child* (1981)
> *St. Elsewhere* (1985–1986)
> *The Days and Nights of Molly Dodd*
> (1987)
> *Dolphin Cove* (1989)

Kalish, Irma
> *Good Times* (1974–1978)
> *Love Nest* (1975)
> *Supercops* (1975)

Good Heavens (1976)

Mason (1977)

Wilder and Wilder (1978)

Carter Country (1978)

Rendezvous Hotel (1978)

Out of the Blue (1979)

Ghost of a Chance (1980)

Too Close for Comfort (1980–1982)

Foot in the Door (1983)

Oh, Madeline (1983–1984)

Lottery! (1984)

Finder of Lost Loves (1984)

The Facts of Life (1988)

227 (1989)

Kander, Susan

St. Elsewhere (1986–1987)

Kane, Kristi

Double Your Pleasure (1989)

Kane, Patricia

Diff'rent Strokes (1980)

Kanin, Fay

Hustling (1974)

Friendly Fire (1978)

Heartsounds (1984)

Kanter, Donna

FBI: The Untold Story (1991–1992)

The Flood: Who Will Save Our Children? (1993)

Kaplan, Janice

Our Kids and the Best of Everything (1988)

Kapsin, Janet

The Yellow Rose (1984)

Kapstrom, Lissa

Flying Blind (1992–1993)

Joe's Life (1993)

Wings (1994–1995)

Karol, Shelley

Blossom (1992–1993)

Karpf, Elinor

Kung Fu (1972–1975)

Letters from Frank (1978)

Devil Dog—Hound of Hell (1978)

Having Babies: Julie Farr, M.D. (1978)

Jayne Mansfield: A Symbol of the 50s (1979)

Dynasty (1984)

Kasica, Maryanne E.

Topper (1979)

Kate Loves a Mystery (1979)

Hart to Hart (1980–1981)

Darkroom (1981)

Tales of the Gold Monkey (1982)

Tucker's Witch (1982)

Falcon Crest (1982)

Hotel (1983/1985)

Highway to Heaven (1985)

The Wizard (1986)

Moonlighting (1986)

Spies (1987)

Murder, She Wrote (1987–1994)

Matlock (1988)

TimeTrax (1993)

Silk Stalkings (1993–1994)

Katz, Gloria

A Father's Homecoming (1988)

Mothers, Daughters, and Lovers (1989)

Katz, Shelly

A Vacation in Hell (1979)

Kauffman, Marta

Dream On (1990–1995)

Sunday Dinner (1991)

The Powers That Be (1992)

Family Album (1993)

Couples (1994)

Friends (1994)

Kaufman, Margo

A Different World (1989)

Kaufman, Suzi
  Son–Rise: A Miracle of Love (1979)

Kavner, Karen
  Lois & Clark: The New Adventures of Superman (1994)

Kay, Suzanne
  Babes (1991)

Kay, Terry
  In the Heat of the Night (1993)

Keel, Charlene
  Fantasy Island (1981–1984)
  Romance Theater (1982)

Keener, Joyce
  Loving Friends/Perfect Couples (1982–1983)
  Emerald Point, N.A.S. (1983)
  Knots Landing (1983–1985)
  Hometown (1985)

Keilstrup, Margaret K.
  The Equalizer (1988)

Kelley, Margaret
  Dolphin Cove (1989)

Kelly, April
  John Denver Rocky Mountain Christmas (1975)
  The Jim Stafford Show (1975)
  The Carpenters (1976)
  The Jacksons (1976–1977)
  The Captain and Tennille (1976–1977)
  Szysznyk (1977)
  The Starland Vocal Band (1977)
  The Paul Lynde Comedy Hour (1977)
  Goober and the Trucker's Paradise (1978)
  Baby I'm Back (1978)
  John Denver in Australia (1978)
  How to Survive the 70s (1978)

Happy Days (1979)
  Mork & Mindy (1979–1981)
  Golden Glove Awards (1980)
  You Asked for It (1981–1982)
  Love, Sidney (1982)
  Teachers Only (1983)
  9 to 5 (1983)
  Partners in Crime (1984)
  Legmen (1984)
  Webster (1985–1986)
  Your Mother Wears Combat Boots (1989)
  Free Spirit (1989)
  I Still Dream of Jeannie (1991)
  Billy (1992)
  Where I Live (1993)
  Boys Meets World (1993–1994)

Kelsey, Lynne
  Private Benjamin (1982)
  Scarecrow & Mrs. King (1987)
  Murder, She Wrote (1989–1991)

Kennedy, Karen
  A Different World (1993)

Kennedy, Mimi
  Knots Landing (1990–1991)

Kenney, Anne
  The Pursuit of Happiness (1987)
  L.A. Law (1992–1994)
  Civil Wars (1993)
  Sweet Justice (1994–1995)
  Under Suspicion (1995)

Kerns, Joanna
  Growing Pains (1988)

Kerwin–Tree, Jeannine
  The 1995 Miss USA Pageant (1995)

Kesend, Ellen
  Convicted: A Mother's Story (1987)

Kessler, Susan
  Diff'rent Strokes (1984)

Ketterer, Gloria
Full House (1992–1993)
Cafe Americain (1993–1994)

Kettner, Carla
Dolphin Cove (1989)
Due South (1995)

Kidwell, Pamela
Mr. Belvedere (1989)

Kimbrough, Lore
The Cosby Show (1990–1991)
Hangin' with Mr. Cooper (1992–1993)
Where I Live (1993)
Living Single (1993–1994)
On Our Own (1994)

King, Janna
The Heights (1992)

Kirgo, Dinah
One Day at a Time (1979–1981)
One of the Boys (1981–1982)
Fantasy Island (1982)
Mr. Merlin (1982)
Teachers Only (1982–1983)
Reggie (1983)
Hometown (1985)
Baby Talk (1991)
Sibs (1991)
Murphy Brown (1992–1993)
Madman of the People (1995)

Kirgo, Julie
One Day at a Time (1979–1981)
One of the Boys (1981–1982)
Fantasy Island (1982)
Mr. Merlin (1982)
Teachers Only (1982–1983)
Reggie (1983)
Hometown (1985)

Kirkland, Lori
Blue Skies (1994)

Kite, Lesa
Happy Days (1980–1981)
Laverne and Shirley (1980–1981)
Too Close for Comfort (1981)
Checking In (1981)
The Jeffersons (1981)
Mork & Mindy (1981–1982)
Star of the Family (1982)
Joanie Loves Chachi (1982)
Gimme a Break (1982–1983)
Oh, Madeline (1984)
Alice (1984–1985)
Still the Beaver (1985)
13 East (1989)
Head of the Class (1990)
Babes (1991)

Klein, Jessica
Mancuso, FBI (1990)
The Antagonists (1990)
Beverly Hills 90210 (1991–1995)

Klein, Norma
Mom, the Wolfman, and Me (1980)

Kleinman, Maggie
Desperate Choices: To Save My Child (1992)

Kletter, Lenore
Tribeca (1993)

Klugman, Deborah
Quincy (1979/1983)

Knapton, Robyn E.
The Facts of Life (1981)

Kohan, Jenji
The Fresh Prince of Bel Air (1994)

Kohan, Rhea
Funny Women of Television: A Museum of Television & Radio Tribute (1991)

Kout, Wendy
Mork & Mindy (1980–1982)
9 to 5 (1982–1983)

The Days and Nights of Molly Dodd
(1987)
Anything but Love (1989)

Kovalcik, Janet
Maybe Baby (1988)
The World's Oldest Living Brides–
maid (1990)
Freshman Dorm (1992)

Kramer, Stepfanie
Hunter (1989)

Krantz, Judith
Princess Daisy (1983)
Mistral's Daughter (1984)

Kravit, Mardee
Class Act: A Teacher's Story (1987)

Krinski, Sandy
The Donny and Marie Osmond
Show (1975)
Newman's Drug Store (1976)
Donny and Marie (1976–1979)
The Paul Lynde Comedy Hour
(1977)
Busting Loose (1977–1978)
Baby I'm Back (1978)
Komedy Tonight (1978)
Getting There (1980)
The Trouble with Celia (1980)
Alice (1981–1982)
Gimme a Break (1982–1983)
We Got It Made (1984)
Three's Company (1984)
Spencer (1984)
Throb (1986–1987)
Who Gets the Friends (1988)
Empty Nest (1992)
The Nanny (1994)

Kroll, Gerry
Eight Is Enough (1981)
The Love Boat (1983)

Krzemien, Dee K.
The Incredible Hulk (1979)
Big Shamus, Little Shamus (1979)

Kurtz, Jennifer Burton
Diff'rent Strokes (1983)

Kuti, Linda Dew
Evening Shade (1990–1991)

Labine, Claire
The Bride in Black (1990)
She Woke Up (1992)
Danielle Steel's Star (1993)

LaBrown, Linda Jean
Designing Women (1993)

Lacusta, Deb
The Tracey Ullman Show (1990)

LaDuke, Dee
Island Son (1990)
Sugar and Spice (1990)
Designing Women (1990–1993)
George (1994)

Lakin, Rita
Makin' It (1978)
Torn between Two Lovers (1979)
A Shining Moment (1980)
The Home Front (1980)
Flamingo Road (1980–1981)
Emerald Point, N.A.S. (1984)
Her Life as a Man (1984)
Peyton Place: The Next Generation
(1986)

LaMond, Jo
Hart to Hart (1979–1983)
The Fall Guy (1982)
Hotel (1983–1985)
Finder of Lost Loves (1984)
American Werewolf (1984)
Mr. & Mrs. Ryan (1986)
Crossings (1986)
Lady Scarface (1989)

Lampert, Jodi
> *Day by Day* (1989)

Landau, Shelley
> *Webster* (1987)
> *Growing Pains* (1989–1991)
> *Wings* (1994)

Lane, Linda
> *Full House* (1994)

Lane, Nancy
> *Taxi* (1981)

Lapiduss, Maxine
> *Charles in Charge* (1988)
> *Dear John* (1989)
> *Roseanne* (1990–1992)
> *Baby Talk* (1991)
> *Home Improvement* (1992–1993)

Lapiduss, Sally
> *Starting Now* (1989)
> *Family Matters* (1989–1991)
> *Princesses* (1991)
> *Step by Step* (1992)
> *Mad about You* (1992–1993)
> *The Nanny* (1993–1994)
> *Madman of the People* (1994)

LaPlante, Lynda
> *Prime Suspect 3* (1994)

Larsen, Regina Stuart
> *Family Matters* (1991–1993)
> *Empty Nest* (1993–1995)

Lasko, Laurie
> *Charlie's Angels* (1979–1981)

Latham, Lynn Marie
> *Delta House* (1979)
> *Fantasy Island* (1980)
> *Mama Malone* (1982)
> *Berrengers* (1984–1985)
> *Knots Landing* (1985–1991)

> *Homefront* (1991–1993)
> *Second Chance* (1993–1994)
> *Hotel Malibu* (1994)

Lauro, Shirley M.
> *Open Admissions* (1988)

Lawrence, Lynn
> *Unsolved Mysteries* (1989–1992)
> *Final Appeal: From the Files of*
> *Unsolved Mysteries* (1992)

Lawrence, Nancy
> *Swiss Family Robinson* (1975)
> *On Trial: A Case of Teenage*
> *Pregnancy* (1978)
> *The Phoenix* (1980–1982)
> *Jesse* (1984)
> *The Twilight Zone* (1987)

Lawrence, Nancy Gail
> *Bob Hope's Comedy Christmas*
> *Special* (1980)

Layman, Ramona K.
> *My Sister Sam* (1987)

Leahy, Janet M.
> *Newhart* (1985–1986)
> *Cheers* (1986)
> *The Cosby Show* (1987–1988)
> *Major Dad* (1989–1991)
> *The Cosby Show* (1990–1992)
> *Wings* (1992–1993)
> *Love & War* (1994–1995)

LeBlanc, Deirdre
> *The Young Riders* (1990–1991)

Lee, Donna R.
> *Fantasy Island* (1979)
> *Fame* (1983)

Lee, Joanna
> *Babe* (1976)
> *Mulligan's Stew* (1977)
> *Like Normal People* (1979)

Mirror, Mirror (1979)
The Love Tapes (1980)
Juvi (1987)
The Kid Who Wouldn't Quit: The Brad Silverman Story (1987)
15 and Getting Straight (1989)
My Dad Can't Be Crazy . . . Can He? (1989)

Lee, Susan H.
We Got It Made (1984)
Webster (1987)

Lee, Yvette Denise
A Different World (1989–1992)
Hangin' with Mr. Cooper (1992–1993)
Living Single (1993–1994)

Lee–Goss, Laurie
Married . . . with Children (1994)

Leifer, Carol
The Sinbad Show (1993)
Seinfeld (1994–1995)

Leiken, Molly–Ann
Rags to Riches (1987)

Lerman, Rhoda
Eleanor, First Lady of the World (1982)

Leschin, Deborah J.
Rhoda (1975–1976)
Busting Loose (1977)
Laverne and Shirley (1978–1979)
Makin' It (1979)
I'm a Big Girl Now (1980–1981)
Making a Living (1981)
Condo (1983)
Suzanne Pleshette Is Maggie Briggs (1984)
Open House (1990)
Who's the Boss (1990–1991)
The Royal Family (1992)

Leslie, Bethel
Matt Helm (1975)
The Rookies (1976)
Here's Boomer (1979)
Falcon Crest (1982)

Leslie, Marcia
You Take the Kids (1991)
The Cosby Show (1992)

Lesser, Elana
Sheriff Lobo (1981)
Code Red (1982)

Lette, Kathy M.
The Facts of Life (1988)

Levangie, Gigi
In the Heat of the Night (1992–1993)

Levin, Audrey Davis
Heart in Hiding (1974)
First Lady's Diaries: Edith Wilson (1975)
The Long Journey (1978)
Washington Mistress (1981)
Shattered Vows (1984)
Stranger in My Bed (1987)
The Ann Jillian Story (1988)
The Face of Love (1990)
Reason for Living: The Jill Ireland Story (1991)
Fatal Memories (1992)

Levin, Lissa A.
WKRP in Cincinnati (1980–1982)
Gloria (1982–1983)
Cheers (1984)
Three's a Crowd (1984)
Off the Rack (1984)
Family Ties (1984)
Brothers (1984)
Double Trouble (1984–1985)
Who's the Boss (1985)

Newhart (1986)
A Different World (1987)
Married People (1990)
Home Free (1993)
Thunder Alley (1994)

Levine, Deborah Joy
Equal Justice (1990–1991)
Something to Live For: The Alison Gertz Story (1992)
Lois & Clark: The New Adventures of Superman (1993–1994)
Sweet Justice (1994)

Levine, Emily B.
Husbands, Wives, and Lovers (1978)
Angie (1979)
Grandpa Goes to Washington (1979)
All in the Family (1981)
The Alan King Show (1986)
Room for Two (1992–1993)
Designing Women (1993)
Love & War (1994–1995)

Levine, Laura S.
The Bob Newhart Show (1972–1978)
The Paul Lynde Comedy Hour (1975)
The Flip Wilson Comedy Special (1975)
Joe and Valerie (1979)
Hizzoner (1979)
Who's On Call (1979)
Lewis & Clark (1981)
Three's Company (1981)
Private Benjamin (1982)
We Got It Made (1983)
Throb (1986–1987)
Out of This World (1990–1991)
Harry and the Hendersons (1991)

Levitt, Beverly D.
Miles to Go (1986)

Lewis, Jodie
Highway to Heaven (1989)

Lichterman, Victoria
Kate and Allie (1984)

Lideks, Mara
Forever Fernwood (1978)
Joe and Valerie (1978)
Top Ten (1979)
Diff'rent Strokes (1981)
The Brady Bunch (1981)
One Day at a Time (1982)
Private Benjamin (1982)
Archie Bunker's Place (1982–1983)
Head of the Class (1988)

Lilly, Brenda
Parker Lewis Can't Lose! (1991–1992)

Lindner, Susan Jane
Laverne and Shirley (1982–1983)
Taxi (1983)
St. Elsewhere (1984)
Double Trouble (1984)

Lintz, Paula
Mr. Merlin (1981)

Lipp, Stacie
Married . . . with Children (1991–1994)

Lippman, Amy
L.A. Law (1989)
Christine Cromwell: Only the Good (1989)
Die Young (1990)
Equal Justice (1990)
Eddie Dodd (1991)
Sisters (1991–1994)
Party of Five (1994–1995)

Lisanti, Michelle Poteet
Hotel (1988)
MacGyver (1988)

Liss, Stephanie A.
Julie Farr, M.D. (1978)
Desperate Lives (1982)
David (1988)
Runaway Father (1991)
A Child Lost Forever (1992)
Shameful Secrets (1993)

List, Shelley
And Baby Comes Home (1980)
Something So Right (1982)
Between Friends (1983)
Cagney and Lacey (1986–1988)
Barbara Taylor Bradford's Remember
(1993)

Lizer, Kari
Empty Nest (1994)
Weird Science (1994)

London, Barbara
Romance Theater (1982)

Long, Pamela K.
Christy (1994)

Longstreet, Renee
Julie Farr, M.D. (1978)
The Gathering II (1979)
Cliffhangers (1979)
The Promise of Love (1980)
Father Murphy (1982)
Voyagers (1983)
Trauma Center (1983)
The Sky's No Limit (1984)
Hot Pursuit (1985)
Power's Play (1986)
Rags to Riches (1987)
Frog Girl: The Jennifer Graham
Story (1989)
With a Vengeance (1993)
Gunsmoke: One Man's Justice (1994)

Loomer, Lisa
Studio 5B (1989)
Room for Two (1992)
Hearts Afire (1992–1994)

Lowell, Janna
Webster (1987)

Lucas, Caryn
Uncle Buck (1991)
Out All Night (1992–1993)
Monty (1994)

Luckett, Bernadette
Living Single (1993–1994)
Sister, Sister (1994–1995)

Lukinson, Sara
The Kennedy Center Honors (1987)
Carnegie Hall: The Grand
Reopening (1987)
The 43rd Annual Tony Awards
(1989)
The Kennedy Center Honors (1993)
GM Mark of Excellence: The
Kennedy Center Honors (1994)

Lyden, Mona
Nothing in Common (1987)

Lynch, Christina
Unhappily Ever After (1995)

McCall, Cheryl
Hard Copy (1987)

McCall, Mitzi
The Stockard Channing Show
(1979)
Eight Is Enough (1979)
13 Queens Blvd (1979)
One Day at a Time (1979)
Ladies Man (1980–1981)
It's Not Easy (1983)
Small Wonder (1985)
A.L.F. (1987)
The Tortellis (1987)

McCarn, Louise
Walker, Texas Ranger (1993)

MacCarthy, Eve
  House Calls (1980)

McCarty, Vicky
  Fantasy Island (1984)

McClurg, Edith
  The David Letterman Show (1980)

McCormick, Kathy
  Hill Street Blues (1987)
  The Bronz Zoo (1987)
  In the Heat of the Night (1988)
  Falcon Crest (1988)
  Hunter (1990–1991)
  Shannon's Deal (1990–1991)
  The Trials of Rosie O'Neill (1991)
  Law & Order (1991)
  Reasonable Doubts (1991–1993)
  Lois & Clark: The New Adventures of Superman (1994–1995)

McCreery, GiGi
  Hangin' with Mr. Cooper (1993)

McCullough, Colleen
  The Thorn Birds (1983)

McFadden, Cyra
  13 Queens Blvd (1979)

McGibbon, Josann
  Sirens (1987)

MacGillivray, Heather
  Sisters (1993)

McKeand, Carol Evan
  Family (1978–1979)
  Norma Rae (1981)
  Insight (1981)
  Cassie & Company (1981–1982)
  Second Family Tree (1982–1983)
  Ryan's Four (1983)
  Alex: The Life of a Child (1986)
  Blue Skies (1986)
  For the Love of Nancy (1994)

McKearny, Grace J.
  The Slap Maxwell Story (1987–1988)
  St. Elsewhere (1988)
  Roseanne (1988–1989)
  Grand (1990)
  The Byrds of Paradise (1994)
  The Client (1995)

McKenzie, Madora
  The Baxters (1979)
  The Love Boat (1980)

MacLachlan, Patricia
  Skylark (1993)

MacLaine, Shirley
  Out on a Limb (1987)

McMahon, Jenna
  The Carol Burnett Show (1977)
  The Grass Is Always Greener over the Septic Tank (1978)
  Carol Burnett & Company (1979)
  The Facts of Life (1979)
  A New Kind of Family (1979)
  Diff'rent Strokes (1979)
  It's a Living (1980)
  Flo (1980)
  Soap (1980–1981)
  Eunice (1981)
  Mama's Family (1982–1983)
  A Carol Burnett Special (1987)
  Julie (1992)
  Men, Movies, & Carol (1994)

Madduz, Rachell
  Who'll Save Our Children? (1978)

Mamet, Lynn
  Under Suspicion (1994)

Mann, Abby
  The Family Holvak (1974)
  The First 50 Years (1976)
  King (1978)

Skag (1979)

The Atlanta Child Murders (1985)

Kojak: The Price of Justice (1987)

Murderers among Us: The Simon Wiesenthal Story (1989)

Indictment: The McMartin Trial (1995)

Mann, Myra

Indictment: The McMartin Trial (1995)

Manning, Paula Mitchell

Where I Live (1993)

Marchetta, Camille

Lucan (1977–1978)

Dallas (1979)

Scruples (1981)

Nurse (1981)

Dynasty (1984–1985)

Marcus, Ann

Women at West Point (1979)

Flamingo Road (1980)

Knots Landing (1981–1982)

Falcon Crest (1984)

The Hogan Family (1990)

Knots Landing (1992–1993)

Marcus, Cindy

Star Trek: Deep Space Nine (1994)

Marcus, Diana Kopald

The Angie Dickinson Show (1981)

King's Crossing (1982)

Quincy (1982)

Emerald Point, N.A.S. (1984)

Knots Landing (1984–1986)

Falcon Crest (1987–1988)

Matlock (1988–1991)

Father Dowling Mysteries (1989)

Marcus, Ellyn

Alan King's Thanksgiving Special (1980)

Marienberg, Evelyn S.

The Love Boat (1980–1981)

Mark, Bonnie

Homicide: Life on the Streets (1994)

Markoe–Klein, Deborah

Murphy Brown (1990)

Baby Talk (1991)

Markowitz, Peachy

Challenge of a Lifetime (1985)

A Fine Romance (1989)

Marks, Dara

A Different World (1992)

Marks, Joan

The Violation of Sarah McDavid (1981)

Laverne and Shirley (1983)

Markus, Leah

Family (1978)

Dallas (1980–1981)

Paper Dolls (1982)

Falcon Crest (1982)

Dynasty (1982)

Fame (1982–1983)

Paper Dolls (1984)

Dallas (1987–1988)

Marr, Linda

The Mommies (1993–1994)

Marsh, Linda

Five Women (1979)

13 Queens Blvd (1979)

The Love Boat (1979)

One Day at a Time (1979–1980)

The Facts of Life (1980–1985)

The Facts of Life Goes to Paris (1982)

No Complaints (1985)

Marshall, Emily Prudum

The Bob Newhart Show (1972–1978)

Angie (1979–1980)
Newhart (1982–1985)
Mary (1985–1989)
Coming of Age (1988–1989)

Marshall, Mona
Who's the Boss (1990–1991)

Martin, Andrea
SCTV Network (1981–1983)

Martin, Ann
Crystal (1980)
Teachers Only (1982–1983)

Martin, Jayne
Woman with a Past (1992)
Moment of Truth: A Child Too Many (1993)
Moment of Truth: Cradle of Conspiracy (1994)

Martin, Julie
Home Fires (1992)
L.A. Law (1992–1994)
Homicide: Life on the Streets (1994–1995)

Martin, Suzanne
The Good Life (1994)
These Friends of Mine (1994)
Ellen (1994–1995)

Marvin, Mitzi
King's Crossing (1981)
Secrets of Midland Heights (1981)
Seven Brides for Seven Brothers (1982)

Marx, Christy
Babylon 5 (1994)

Mason, Bertha
Sisters (1995)

Mason, Judi Ann
A Different World (1990–1991)
Beverly Hills 90210 (1991)
I'll Fly Away (1991–1992)

Massock, Dianne
Avonlea (1993–1994)

Matheson, Ali Marie
Fame (1983)
Moonlighting (1984–1985)
Growing Pains (1985)
Amazing Stories (1987)
Big Brother Jake (1990–1994)

Mathews, Temple
Eden (1993)

Mathious, Linda
Sisters (1993)

Mathison, Melissa
Son of the Morning Star (1991)

Matthias, Jean Louise
Star Trek: The Next Generation (1992–1993)

Maxwell, Robin
Passions (1984)

Maynard, Joyce
Brooklyn Bridge (1993)

Mayron, Melanie
Tribeca (1993)

Meara, Anne
The Other Woman (1983)

Mecchi, Irene
Lily Tomlin: Sold Out (1981)
The Popcorn Kid (1987)

Medway, Lisa A.
The Barbara Mandrell Show (1980)
Barbara Mandrell & the Mandrell Sisters (1980–1981)
Blondes vs. Brunettes (1984)
Baby Talk (1991–1992)
The Nanny (1994)

Melamed, Lisa
    Brooklyn Bridge (1992)
    Summer Stories: The Mall (1992)
    "First Impressions" (1992)
    Sisters (1992–1995)
    Party of Five (1995–1997)

Melloan, Maryanne
    McKenna (1994)

Melman, Lana Freistat
    Beverly Hills 90210 (1992–1995)

Melnyk, Debra
    Top Cops (1992)

Mendelsohn, Carol S.
    Stingray (1987–1988)
    J. J. Starbuck (1987–1988)
    Wiseguy (1988)
    Midnight Caller (1989)
    Heartbeat (1989)
    Tour of Duty (1989–1990)
    The Trials of Rosie O'Neill (1991–1992)
    Northern Exposure (1992)
    Crossroads (1993)
    Melrose Place (1994–1995)

Merl, Judy
    Trapper John, M.D. (1980)
    King's Crossing (1981)
    Flamingo Road (1981)
    Falcon Crest (1981)
    Night Partners (1983)
    The Paper Chase: The Second Year (1985)
    Detective in the House (1985)
    A Fight for Jenny (1986)
    Shootdown (1988)
    The Trials of Rosie O'Neill (1990)

Meyer, Marlane X.
    Prison Stories: Women on the Inside (1991)

Sirens (1993)
    Better Off Dead (1993)

Meyers, Nancy J.
    Private Benjamin (1981)
    Baby Boom (1988)

Meyers, Susan
    Free Spirit (1989)

Michael, Jo Lynne
    Quincy (1981)
    Baby Sister (1983)

Michael, Judith
    Deceptions (1985)

Michaels, Andrea Carla
    Designing Women (1991)

Michaels, Susan
    Fantastic Facts (1990)

Michon, Cathryn
    China Beach (1990–1991)
    Sisters (1991)
    Designing Women (1991–1993)
    George (1993)

Middleton, Vanessa
    Saturday Night Live (1992)
    Sister, Sister (1994)
    Hangin' with Mr. Cooper (1994)

Midkiff, Marcia
    Jailbirds (1990)

Milburn, Sue
    Rafferty (1977)
    The Child Stealer (1979)
    Reunion (1980)
    Johnny Belinda (1982)
    Partners in Crime (1984)

Miller, Carolyn Handler
    Here's Boomer (1980)
    Mystery at Fire Island (1981)

Sometimes I Don't Love My Mother
(1982)

Miller, Chris

Delta House (1979)

Square Pegs (1982)

Another Jerk (1983)

Side Kicks (1986)

The New Gidget (1987)

Miller, Jennifer A.

Testimony of Two Men (1977)

Loose Change (1978)

The Babysitter (1980)

In Custody of Strangers (1982)

Forty Days for Danny (1982)

Deadly Lessons (1983)

Paper Dolls (1984)

A Deadly Silence (1989)

Family Pictures (1992)

Telling Secrets (1993)

Miller, Karyl Geld

Diff'rent Strokes (1979)

First Time, Second Time (1980)

Maggie's Way (1981)

Love, Sidney (1982)

Three's a Crowd (1984)

The Cosby Show (1985)

Kate and Allie (1985)

My Sister Sam (1987–1988)

Davis Rules (1992)

Miller, Marilyn Suzanne

Lily (1975)

Rhoda (1977)

NBC Saturday Night Live (1977–
1979)

Barney Miller (1980)

The Tracey Ullman Show (1989)

Miller, Marsha

Me and Mom (1985)

Miller, Mary

When the Whistle Blows (1980)

Miller, Nancy Ann

The Secrets of Midland Heights
(1981)

The Renegades (1983)

Houston Knights (1987)

Law & Order (1991)

Mann & Machine (1992)

Bodies of Evidence (1992)

The Round Table (1992)

Against the Grain (1993)

Cosby Mysteries (1994)

The Marshal (1995)

Miller, Susan

Knots Landing (1981)

Second Sight: A Love Story (1984)

Dynasty (1984)

Me and Mom (1985)

The Paper Chase: The Third Year
(1985)

Dirty Dancing (1985)

The Trials of Rosie O'Neill (1991–
1992)

Miller–Smith, Alice

L.A. Law (1994)

Milmore, Jane

Newhart (1989)

Anything but Love (1989–1991)

I Love Lucy: The Very First Show
(1990)

Nurses (1991)

Martin (1992–1993)

Daddy Dearest (1993)

The Wayans Bros. (1995)

Milstein, Beth

Down Home (1990–1991)

Mimieux, Yvette

Obsessive Love (1984)

Minsky, Terri

Doctor, Doctor (1989–1991)

Teech (1991)

Down the Shore (1992–1993)
Flying Blind (1992–1993)

Mintz, Melanie I.
Loving Friends and Perfect Couples
(1983)
Knots Landing (1984)

Mishkin, Julie
Laverne and Shirley (1979)

Mitchell, Cathy
Attack of Fear (1984)

Mitchell, Esther
Swiss Family Robinson (1975)
Charlie's Angels (1979)
Hawaii Five–O (1979)
Buck Rogers (1980–1981)
CHiPs (1982)

Mitchell, Judith Paige
Club Med (1986)
American Geisha (1986)
Roses Are for the Rich (1987)
Desperate for Love (1989)
Burning Bridges (1990)
Crossroads (1993)
*Black Widow Murders: The Blanche
Taylor Moore Story* (1993)
Bloodlines: Murder in the Family
(1993)
*Lies of the Heart: The Story of Laurie
Kellogg* (1994)

Mitchell, Shelly
Hawaii Five–O (1979)

Monahan, Dara
Hearts Afire (1994–1995)

Monpere, Carol
Pink Lightning (1991)
French Silk (1994)
Someone She Knows (1994)

Montgomery, Jo
Hunter (1988)

Montgomery, Kathryn J.
High Midnight (1979)
Babies Having Babies (1985)
Firefighter: A Greater Alarm (1986)

Montgomery, Lynn
Carol & Company (1990–1991)
The Torkelsons (1991–1992)

Moore, Rosalind
Home Improvement (1992–1995)

Moran, Patricia Rae
Simon & Simon (1983)

Morgan, Tracy
Gus Brown and Midnight Brewster
(1985)
Me and Mrs. C (1987)

Morland, Amy
Tom (1994)

Morris, Linda
Dorothy (1979)
Welcome Back Kotter (1979)
Private Benjamin (1981–1982)
Just Our Luck (1983–1984)
Alice (1984–1985)
Our Time (1985)
Roomies (1987)
I Married Dora (1988)
Hooperman (1989)
Doogie Howser, M.D. (1989–1993)
Frasier (1994)

Morrison, Pam
Angie (1980)

Moskowitz, Julie
Falcon Crest (1988–1989)
Visions of Murder (1993)
Hush Little Baby (1994)

Moss, Denise
  Nearly Departed (1989)
  Head of the Class (1989)
  Murphy Brown (1989–1991)
  The Wonder Years (1991–1992)
  Roseanne (1992–1993)
  Frasier (1993–1994)

Mozilo, Lori
  The Road Home (1994)

Mueller, Elaine
  An Invasion of Privacy (1983)

Murphy, Maureen
  The Shape of Things (1982)

Murphy, Phyllis
  L.A. Law (1994)
  Sweet Justice (1995)

Myatt, Nancylee
  Night Court (1990–1992)
  The Powers That Be (1992–1993)
  Muddling Through (1994)
  The 5 Mrs. Buchanans (1994–
    1995)

Myers, Cindy
  *Forgotten Prisoners: The Amnesty
    File* (1990)
  When No One Would Listen (1993)
  Incident in a Small Town (1994)
  Someone Else's Child (1994)
  A Woman of Independent Means
    (1995)

Nanus, Susan
  Go Toward the Light (1988)
  Danielle Steel's Changes (1991)
  *Shattered Trust: The Shari Karney
    Story* (1993)
  Baby Brokers (1994)
  Heart of a Child (1994)

Nardo, Patricia R.
  Lily (1975)
  Rhoda (1976)
  Cousins (1976)
  Clapper (1978)
  The Goodbye Girl (1981)
  It's Not Easy Stepping (1982–1983)
  Goodbye Charlie (1985)
  Civil Wars (1992)
  Almost Home (1993)

Nathan, Deborah
  Top Cops (1993)
  Avonlea (1993–1994)

Nedler, Barrie
  Camp Wilder (1993)
  Home Improvement (1994)

Needleman, Eve
  Blossom (1992–1993)
  The John Larroquette Show (1993–
    1994)

Nelson, Eva
  9 to 5 (1986)

Nemeth, Sally
  The Trials of Rosie O'Neill (1992)
  Law & Order (1992–1993)
  Crime & Punishment (1993)
  *Rise and Walk: The Dennis Byrd
    Story* (1995)

Nepus, Ria
  Happy Days (1979–1980)
  Laverne and Shirley (1979–1981)
  Happy Days (1982)
  Just Our Luck (1983)

Neufeld, Nancy
  The Edge (1992–1993)
  In Living Color (1992–1993)
  Married . . . with Children (1994)

Newbound, Laurie
  House Calls (1981)
  One of the Boys (1981)

Starman (1987)
Kate and Allie (1989)
Down Home (1990)

Newman, Elaine
The Baxters (1979)
Diff'rent Strokes (1980)
Hello, Larry (1980)
Trapper John, M.D. (1982–1983)
Mama's Family (1984)
The Jeffersons (1984)
Hart to Hart (1985)
Highway to Heaven (1987)
The Young Riders (1991)
The Fresh Prince of Bel Air (1991)
Dr. Quinn, Medicine Woman (1993)

Newman, Molly
The Larry Sanders Show (1993–
1994)
Frasier (1994)
Murphy Brown (1994)

Newman, Tracy
Cheers (1991–1992)
Bob (1992–1993)
The Nanny (1994)
Hardball (1994)
Ellen (1995)

Newton, Julia
Raising Miranda (1988)
Heartland (1989)
Doctor, Doctor (1990)
The Family Man (1990–1991)
Step by Step (1991–1995)

Nicholas, Denise
In the Heat of the Night (1992–
1993)

Niedzialek, Patricia
A.L.F. (1990)

Nielsen, Judith Anne
Barney Miller (1979)
A Christmas without Snow (1980)

Nigro–Chacon, Giovanna
Romance Theater (1982)

Norman, Marsha W.
Skag (1980)
The Laundromat (1985)

Norris, Pamela R.
Saturday Night Live (1980–1984)
The News Is News (1983)
Joe Piscopo Special (1983)
It's Your Move (1984–1985)
Remington Steele (1985)
Gimme a Break (1985)
Misfits of Science (1985)
The Equalizer (1986)
The Ellen Burstyn Show (1986)
Designing Women (1989–1992)
Hearts Afire (1995)

North, Sheryl
Me and the Boys (1994–1995)

Noxon, Marti M.
Life Goes On (1990–1991)

Numeroff, Laura
Mr. Belvedere (1989)

Oberman, Margaret G.
Saturday Night Live (1981–1987)
Square Pegs (1982)
A Girl's Life (1989)

O'Connor, Elyse
In the Heat of the Night (1993–
1994)

O'Hara, Catherine
SCTV Network (1981–1983)

O'Hare, Eileen
The Nanny (1994–1995)

O'Hare, Laura
Empty Nest (1990–1991)

O'Kelly, Barbara
    African Skies (1993–1994)

Olin, Marilyn
    I Got through and So Can You
      (1980)
    How to Be Your Own Best Friend
      (1982)

Oliver, Lyla
    All–Star Salute to Mother's Day
      (1981)
    Coach (1990–1991)
    Empty Nest (1992)
    Julie (1992)

Olsen, Dana R.
    Laverne and Shirley (1980–1981)
    Joanie Loves Chachi (1982)

Omine, Carolyn
    Home Free (1993)
    Full House (1993–1994)

O'Neill, Teresa
    Night Court (1986–1987)
    My Two Dads (1988)
    Down the Shore (1992–1993)
    Coach (1993)

Orin, Renee
    The Facts of Life (1987)

Osborn, Marilyn
    The Commish (1992–1993)
    The X–Files (1994)
    Touched by an Angel (1994)

Oshry, Suzanne
    Wiseguy (1989)

Packer, Juliet
    Hizzoner (1978)
    Another Day (1978)
    Eight Is Enough (1979)
    The Waltons (1979–1981)

    Palmerstown (1980–1981)
    Family (1980)
    Bring 'em Back Alive (1982)
    Falcon Crest (1985)

Pagliaro, Joanne M.
    The Archie Situation Comedy
      Musical Show (1978)
    The Last Resort (1979)
    WKRP in Cincinnati (1979)
    The Jeffersons (1979)
    Lou Grant (1979)
    What's Happening (1979)
    Laverne and Shirley (1980–1981)
    Report to Murphy (1981)
    The White Shadow (1981)
    Family Ties (1982)
    Cagney and Lacey (1982)
    Fantasy Island (1984)
    Boone (1984)
    Fame (1984)
    Cheers (1987)
    The Bronx Zoo (1988)
    His & Hers (1990)

Palermo, Michelle
    Boy Meets World (1994)

Paley, Sarah C.
    Saturday Night Live (1979)
    Steve Martin's Best Show Ever
      (1981)
    The New Show (1984)

Palyo, Renee
    Parker Lewis Can't Lose! (1991–
      1993)
    Saved by the Bell: The College Years
      (1993–1994)

Parent, Gail
    Sons and Daughters (1974)
    The Smothers Brothers Show (1975)
    Sills and Burnett at the Met (1976)
    Three Girls Three (1977)
    Sheila (1977)

Rhoda (1977)
Finder of Lost Loves (1984)
Amazing Stories (1986)
The Golden Girls (1989–1992)
Platypus Man (1995)

Parker, Bonnie
Simon & Simon (1988)

Parker, Hildy
Night of 100 Stars (1982)
Parade of Stars (1983)
The Best of Everything (1983)
Night of 100 Stars II (1984)
The Tony Awards (1984)
The Emmy Awards (1986)
*Placido Domingo Steppin' Out with
    the Ladies* (1986)
Happy Birthday, Hollywood (1987)
The Magical World of Disney (1989)
61st Annual Academy Awards (1989)

Parker, Joan
A Man Called Hawk (1989)
B. L. Stryker: High Rise (1989)
Spencer: Ceremony (1994)
Spencer: Pale Kings and Princes
    (1994)

Parker, Judith E.
First Affair (1983)
The Seduction of Gina (1984)
The Other Lover (1985)
L.A. Law (1989)
Studio 5B (1989)
A Child Lost Forever (1992)

Parker, Monica S.
Who's the Boss (1984)

Parr, Rebecca
Max Headroom (1987)
Simon & Simon (1988)
Roseanne (1989)
Free Spirit (1989)
Baghdad Cafe (1990–1991)

The Fanelli Boys (1990–1991)
Billy (1992)

Parrent, Joanne
Dr. Quinn, Medicine Woman (1994)

Parres, Laurie
Full House (1995)

Parriott, Sara
Voyagers! (1983)
Sirens (1987)

Pascal, Francine P.
The Hand–Me–Down Kid (1983)

Patik, Vickie
Do You Remember Love (1985)
Children of the Night (1985)
Trapped in Silence (1987)
Silent Cries (1993)
Broken Promises: Taking Emily Back
    (1993)

Patrick, Lougenia
The Love Boat (1980–1981)

Pearl, Debbie
227 (1989)
Designing Women (1989–1991)
Sugar and Spice (1990)
13 East (1990)
Nurses (1991)
Delta (1992–1993)

Pehl, Mary Jo
Mystery Science Theater 3000
    (1994–1995)

Pekkonen, Donna
Hart to Hart (1982)
Hotel (1983)

Penders, Maura
Days of Our Lives: Winter Heat
    (1994)

Perlman, Heide
> *Cheers* (1982–1983)
> *Cheers* (1985)
> *The Tracey Ullman Show* (1987–1990)
> *Sibs* (1991–1992)
> *Cheers* (1993)
> *The George Carlin Show* (1994)
> *Related by Birth* (1994)

Perry, Jo
> *Snoops* (1989)

Perry, Joyce
> *Having Babies* (1978)
> *The Waltons* (1978)
> *Flamingo Road* (1981)
> *Nurse* (1982)
> *Romance Theater* (1982)
> *Fantasy Island* (1983)

Perry, Marlene
> *The Love Boat* (1981)

Pershing, Diane
> *The Love Boat* (1984)
> *What's Happening Now* (1985)

Persky, Dana
> *Kate and Allie* (1989)

Peters, Marjorie J.
> *13 Queens Blvd* (1979)
> *The Love Boat* (1979)
> *Five Women* (1979)
> *One Day at a Time* (1979–1980)
> *The Facts of Life* (1980–1985)
> *The Facts of Life Goes to Paris* (1982)
> *No Complaints* (1985)
> *A Different World* (1988–1989)

Peterson, Bonnie K.
> *That's Hollywood* (1981)

Petrie, Dorothea
> *Orphan Train* (1979)

Petteway, Jane
> *A Fine Romance* (1989)

Pettit, Christine
> *Beverly Hills 90210* (1994)

Pettler, Pamela
> *Charles in Charge* (1984–1985)
> *George Burns Comedy Week* (1985)
> *The Incredible Ida Early* (1987)
> *Shelley Duvall's Tall Tales* (1987)
> *Shivers* (1989)

Philipp, Jo William
> *In the Heat of the Night* (1989)
> *Jake and the Fatman* (1990)
> *Murder, She Wrote* (1991)

Phillips, Gael
> *Jake and the Fatman* (1989)

Phillips, Laura
> *The Christmas Toy* (1986)

Phillips, Renee
> *The Charmings* (1987–1988)
> *Baby Boom* (1989)
> *Major Dad* (1990–1993)
> *Sister, Sister* (1994–1995)

Phillips, Stephanie
> *America's Funniest People* (1990)

Pierson, Dori D.
> *The Great Imposter* (1984)
> *Obsessed with a Married Woman* (1985)

Pioli, Judy R.
> *Laverne and Shirley* (1977–1979)
> *Goodtime Girls* (1980)
> *I'm a Big Girl Now* (1980–1981)
> *Laverne and Shirley* (1981–1983)
> *Too Good to Be True* (1983)
> *Webster* (1984)
> *Charles in Charge* (1985)
> *Valerie* (1986–1987)

Valerie's Family (1987–1988)
The Hogan Family (1988–1989)

Piper, Monica
Roseanne (1992–1993)

Pizer, Elizabeth
Knots Landing (1984)

Plain, Belva
Evergreen (1985)

Podkin, Leslie Ann
A.L.F (1990)

Pollack, Eileen P.
Dynasty (1981–1983)
The Colbys (1985–1986)
Dynasty: The Reunion (1991)

Pollon, Daphne
Laugh Trax (1982)
Valerie's Family (1987)
Married People (1990)
Jack's Place (1992)
Rachel Gunn, R.N.

Polon, Vicki
Deadly Medicine (1991)

Polson, Beth
Go toward the Light (1988)

Pond, Mimi
Designing Women (1993)

Poole, Victoria
Thursday's Child (1983)

Pope, Elaine
Lily Tomlin: Sold Out (1981)
Fridays (1981–1982)
Lily for President (1982)
Seinfeld (1991–1993)
Love & War (1992–1994)

Potter, Emily
Double Trouble (1984)

Povare, Ruth
Down the Long Hills (1987)

Powell, Ann
Mariah (1987)
Crime Story (1987)
Dream Street (1989)
Mancuso, FBI (1989)
Drug Wars: The Camarena Story (1990)
DEA (1990–1991)
Night Owl (1993)
Birdland (1994)
Under Suspicion (1995)

Powers, Katharyn Michaelian
Kung Fu (1972–1975)
Khan! (1975)
Sara (1976)
The Fantastic Journey (1977)
Logan's Run (1977–1978)
The Fitzpatricks (1977–1978)
I Married Wyatt Earp (1978)
Flying High (1978)
The New Adventures of Wonder Woman (1978)
The Young Pioneers (1978)
The Kid from Left Field (1979)
The Dukes of Hazzard (1979)
Charlie's Angels (1979–1980)
Rodeo Girl (1980)
Toni's Boys (1980)
Falcon Crest (1982–1983)
Fantasy Island (1982–1983)
The Tom Swift and Linda Craig Mystery Hour: The Treasure of Rancho del Sol (1983)
Star Trek: Deep Space Nine (1993)

Powers, Stephanie
Family Secrets (1984)

Pratt, Deborah M.
Airwolf (1984)
Magnum, P.I. (1984)
Quantum Leap (1989–1993)

Pratt, Kathryn
WIOU (1991)
Sisters (1993–1994)

Prestwich, Dawn
The Trials of Rosie O'Neill (1990–1992)
Melrose Place (1992–1993)
Birdland (1994)
Touched by an Angel (1994)

Prince, Gina
A Different World (1993)
South Central (1994)
Sweet Justice (1994)
What about Your Friends? (1995)

Pullbrook, Violet
Over My Dead Body (1990–1991)

Quayton, Zora
seaQuest DSV (1994)

Radkoff, Vivienne
Always Remember I Love You (1990)
The Commish (1992)
Street Justice (1992–1993)
Cobra (1993–1994)

Raffaghello, Andrea
Top Cops (1992–1993)

Randall, Alice
XXX's and OOO's (1994)

Ranney, Jody Ann
Trapper John, M.D. (1981)

Raper, P. Karen
Roc (1991–1993)
The Fresh Prince of Bel Air (1992)
Getting By (1993)

Raschella, Carole
The Waltons (1977)
Friends (1978)
California Fever (1979)
The Waltons (1979)

The Buffalo Soldiers (1979)
Little House on the Prairie (1979–1981)
Here's Boomer (1980)
Code Red (1982)
Girls of the White Orchid (1983)
The Secret World of the Very Young (1985)

Raskin, Carolyn
Hart to Hart (1982)
Laugh Trax (1982)

Ray, Leslie
Free Spirit (1989)
My Two Dads (1990)
Full House (1990–1991)
The Royal Family (1991)
The Fresh Prince of Bel Air (1992–1994)
Hearts Afire (1994)

Raznick, Deborah J.
Laverne and Shirley (1980–1981)
Mork & Mindy (1980–1982)

Reback, Katherine J.
Husbands, Wives, and Lovers (1978)
Joe and Valerie (1979)
One Day at a Time (1979)
The Line (1987)

Reback, Theresa
American Dreamer (1990)
Brooklyn Bridge (1991–1992)
Here and Now (1992)
L.A. Law (1992–1994)
NYPD Blue (1995)

Reckling, Ann C.
St. Elsewhere (1986–1988)
Dolphin Cove (1989)

Regel, Cindy
Married . . . with Children (1994)

Reo, Dorothy
The John Larroquette Show (1994)

Resnick, Patricia
Cher (1978)
Cher . . . and Other Fantasies (1979)
9 to 5 (1981)

Rester–Zodrow, Gina L.
The Wonderful World of Disney (1980)

Reston, Dana
The Good Life (1994)
Monty (1994–1995)
The Nanny (1994–1995)

Rhinehart, Susan M.
China Beach (1988–1991)
Baby Snatcher (1992)
Memphis (1992)

Rhodes, Vivian
You Again? (1985)

Rhomberg, Rachelle
Just the Ten of Us (1989)

Rice, Susan C.
Something in Common (1986)
Opposites Attract (1990)
Tears and Laughter: The Joan and Melissa Rivers Story (1994)

Rich, Lisa
Star Trek: Deep Space Nine (1993)

Richmond, Jane
On Our Own (1977–1978)
Aloha Paradise (1981)
Kate and Allie (1984)

Rickett, Frances
Romance Theater (1982)

Rieder–Rasmussen, Leslie
Major Dad (1990–1991)
Roseanne (1992–1993)
The Good Life (1994)
Evening Shade (1994)

Ritchie, Dawn
The Hitchhiker (1989)
E.N.G. (1989)
Fly by Night (1990)
My Secret Identity (1990)
The Adventures of the Black Stallion (1991)
Top Cops (1992–1993)
Secret Service (1992–1993)
Sweet Valley High (1994)
Fast Forward (1995)

Rivers, Caryl
The Cheats (1989)

Robbins, Allison
Reasonable Doubts (1992–1993)
South Beach (1993)
Melrose Place (1993–1995)

Robertson, Lanie
Diana Ross . . . Red Hot Rhythm & Blues (1987)

Robinson, Barbara
The Best Christmas Pageant Ever (1983)

Robinson, Dorothy
Airwolf (1984)

Robinson, Mitzi
King's Crossing (1982)

Robinson, Sally
Freestyle (1978)
Family (1979)
Lou Grant (1979)
When the Whistle Blows (1980)
The Secrets of Midland Heights (1980)
King's Crossing (1982)
Second Family Tree (1982)
When Your Lover Leaves (1982)
Two Marriages (1983)
The Family Tree (1983)

A Letter to Three Wives (1985)
Indiscreet (1988)

Rock, Gail
Night Court (1990)
The 1990 Miss USA Pageant (1990)
The 1990 Miss Universe Pageant (1990)
The 1995 Miss USA Pageant (1995)

Rogerton, Theresa
Big Dreams & Broken Hearts: The Dottie West Story (1995)

Rohrer, Susan
If I Die before I Wake (1993)

Rollins, Darice
Amen (1990–1991)
Martin (1993/1995)

Romano, Jeanne
Flesh 'n Blood (1991)

Roper, Carol
Knots Landing (1981)
Hometown (1985)

Rosen, Marjorie
The Alfred G. Graebner Memorial High School Handbook, Rules and Regulations (1985)
Read between the Lines (1987)

Rosenberg, Lorna
Happy Days (1983)

Rosenberg, Melissa
Class of '96 (1993)

Rosenfeld–Demarais, Alison
Night Court (1988/1991)

Rosenthal, Lisa J.
Head of the Class (1987–1990)
The Fresh Prince of Bel Air (1990–1992)
Martin (1992–1993)

Rosin, Karen
Beverly Hills 90210 (1991–1994)

Ross, Shelley Z.
Show Business (1981)
On Stage America (1984)
Getting the Last Laugh (1984)
Our Time (1986)

Ross–Leming, Eugenie
Highcliff Manor (1978–1979)
On Ice (1979)
Why Us (1981)
Fit for a King (1982)
Scarecrow & Mrs. King (1982–1983)
The Cartier Affair (1984)
Suburban Beat (1985)
Further Adventures (1988)
Sons and Daughters (1991)
Yesterday/Today (1992)
Roseanne and Tom: Behind the Scenes (1994)

Roth, Deanne
Designing Women (1990–1991)

Roth, Lynn
Joe and Sons (1975–1976)
This Better Be It (1976)
A Lucille Ball Special (1976)
Happily Ever After (1981)
The Paper Chase: The Third Year (1984)
A Bunny's Tale (1985)
Babies (1990)
Chance of a Lifetime (1991)
Just My Imagination (1992)

Roth, Paula A.
Makin' It (1979)
Laverne and Shirley (1979)
Goodtime Girls (1979–1980)
It's a Living (1980)
I'm a Big Girl Now (1980–1981)
Laverne and Shirley (1981)

Joanie Loves Chachi (1983)
Happy Days (1983)
The Love Boat (1984–1985)
Perfect Strangers (1986–1993)

Rothe, Jodi
A Different Affair (1986)

Roum, Christine
Law & Order (1991–1993)

Rowell, Kathleen Knutson
She Says She's Innocent (1991)
She Led Two Lives (1994)

Rowland, Melody A.
Gloria (1983)

Ryan, Pamela
CHiPs (1982)
Happy Days (1982–1983)

Sacco, Jill M.
Throb (1986–1987)

Sackett, Nancy
Growing Pains (1978)
Family (1979)
Skyward (1980)
Lou Grant (1982)
Glitter (1984)
Bridge to Terabithia (1985)
When Will I Be Loved? (1990)
Charles & Diana: Unhappily Ever After (1993)

Sage, Liz
The Carol Burnett Show (1977)
The Trucker's Paradise (1978)
Welcome Back Kotter (1978–1979)
Dorothy (1979)
Starting Fresh (1979)
Mama's Family (1982–1983)
Rodney Dangerfield: I Can't Take It Any More (1983)
Punky Brewster (1984)

Heart's Island (1985)
Fenster Hall (1985)
Rodney Dangerfield Exposed (1985)
Chapter One (1985)
Mr. Belvedere (1988–1989)
Growing Pains (1991–1992)
Stand by Your Man (1992)
Major Dad (1992–1993)

St. John, Thania
Midnight Caller (1989)
Booker (1990)
Under Cover (1991)
Spy Game (Part II) (1991)
Life Goes On (1991–1993)
Human Target (1992)
Lois & Clark: The New Adventures of Superman (1993–1994)

Salzman, Linda
Blue Skies (1988)
Island Son (1989)
Jack's Place (1992–1993)

Samuel, Lillian
Secret Sins of the Father (1994)

Samuels, Barbara
The Jim Henson Hour (1989)

Sandercock, Leonie
Captive (1991)

Sandler, Ellen
Taxi (1981)
The White Shadow (1981)
Open All Night (1982)
After George (1982)
Kate and Allie (1984)
Empire (1984)
My Sister Sam (1987)
Baby Talk (1991–1992)
Dudley (1993)
The Mommies (1993–1995)
Empty Nest (1994)
A Whole New Ballgame (1995)

Sandor, Anna
Tarzan in Manhattan (1989)
Stolen: One Husband (1990)
Miss Rose White (1992)
A Family of Strangers (1993)
For the Love of My Child: The Anissa Ayala Story (1993)

Sanford, Arlene
On Our Own (1977–1978)
Diff'rent Strokes (1980)

Sanford, Lana
Hart to Hart (1982)

Saraceno, Carol
Quincey (1979)
Vega$ (1979)
The Promise of Love (1980)
Shannon (1981)
Hart to Hart (1982–1984)
Fantasy Island (1984)
Paper Dolls (1984)
Hotel (1984)
The Colbys (1987)
In the Heat of the Night (1989)
Jake and the Fatman (1990–1991)

Sarasohn, Carol
Whatever Became Of . . . (1981)
The Best of Times (1981)
To the Max (1981)

Sardi, Jan
Mission: Impossible (1990)

Satrina, Carole
Tales from the Dark Side (1984–1985)

Saunders, Cynthia
thirtysomething (1989)
L.A. Law (1990)
Sisters (1991)

Savel, Dava
Eisenhower & Lutz (1988)
Babes (1991)
Dinosaurs (1992)
Grace under Fire (1993–1994)
Dream On (1995)

Sawyer, Beverly M.
Heart and Soul (1989)
Stompin' at the Savoy (1992)

Sayres, Julie
Knots Landing (1988)
Midnight Caller (1989)
Heartbeat (1989)
Crossroads (1993)

Schacht, Rose A.
Crime Story (1987)
Mariah (1987)
Dream Street (1989)
Mancuso, FBI (1989)
Drug Wars: The Camarena Story (1990)
DEA (1990–1991)
Night Owl (1993)
Birdland (1994)
Under Suspicion (1995)

Schaeffer, Racelle Rossett
Blossom (1990–1991)
Lenny (1991)
thirtysomething (1991)

Schapiro, Mimi Rothman
Drop Dead Gorgeous (1991)
In My Daughter's Name (1992)
Exclusive (1993)
A Promise Kept: The Oksana Baiul Story (1994)

Scharfer, Shari
Full House (1990)

Schechter, Marlene
Archie Bunker's Place (1982–1983)

Schibi, Margaret J.
Family (1979)
Secrets of Midland Heights (1980)
Behind the Screen (1981)
King's Crossing (1982)
Romance Theater (1982)

Schiff, Robin L.
Aloha Paradise (1981)
Rags to Riches (1988)
Just Temporary (1989)
Working Girl (1990)
Princesses (1991)
Delta (1992–1993)

Schiffman, Barbara
The Trials of Rosie O'Neill (1990)

Schneider, Carol Starr
Who's the Boss (1990–1991)
Two Teens and a Baby (1992)

Schneider, Mindy
Who's the Boss (1989)
Growing Pains (1989)
Dream On (1992–1993)

Schor, Amy
Jack's Place (1992)

Schreder, Carol
Call to Glory (1984–1985)
In Love and War (1987)

Schreyer, Linda
A Place at the Table (1988)
A House of Secrets and Lies (1992)

Schrock, Laura
Valerie (1987)

Schroder, Diane
Diff'rent Strokes (1983)

Schroeder, Nita
Scene of the Crime (1984)

Schudt, Alicia Marie
A.L.F. (1988–1989)
The Hogan Family (1990)

Schuler, Annie Caroline
One Day at a Time (1981)
Trapper John, M.D. (1982)

Schwartz, Deborah Bonann
Baywatch (1992–1994)
Thunder in Paradise (1994)

Scott, Ann
Ebony, Ivory, and Jade (1979)
The Two Lives of Carol Letner (1981)

Scott, Sheila
Diff'rent Strokes (1983)

Scovell, Nell
The Smothers Brothers Comedy Hour (1988)
Newhart (1990)
Coach (1991–1993)
Murphy Brown (1993–1994)

Sebastian, Susan E.
9 to 5 (1983)
Webster (1985)
Who's the Boss (1988)
Living Dolls (1989)
Dear John (1990–1991)
Family Man (1990–1991)
The Torkelsons (1991)
Full House (1992)
Frannie's Turn (1992)
Delta (1992–1993)

Seeger, Charlene
Mr. & Mrs. Dracula (1980)
Duet (1987)
Open House (1990)
Family Matters (1990–1991)
Hangin' with Mr. Cooper (1994)

Seeger, Susan

Laverne and Shirley (1979)

Working Stiffs (1979)

I'm a Big Girl Now (1980)

In Trouble (1980)

The James Boys (1982)

9 to 5 (1982–1983)

A Girl's Life (1983)

The Lucie Arnaz Show (1984)

Cheers (1985)

Hardesty House (1986)

Kate's Secret (1986)

Duet (1987)

American Dreamer (1990)

Hangin' with Mr. Cooper (1993–1994)

Blossom (1994–1995)

Seibel, Deborah Starr

Sons and Daughter (1991)

Seidman, Lisa

Cagney and Lacey (1984)

Scarecrow & Mrs. King (1984)

Whiz Kids (1984)

Falcon Crest (1987–1988)

Dallas (1989–1991)

Knots Landing (1992–1993)

Murder, She Wrote (1994)

Selbo, Juel

Raising Miranda (1988)

Annie McGuire (1988)

Life Goes On (1989–1991)

The Flash (1990–1991)

Prison Stories: Women on the Inside (1991)

The Young Indiana Jones Chronicles (1992–1993)

Johnny Bago (1993)

Young Indiana Jones and the Mystery of the Blues (1993)

Models, Inc. (1994–1995)

Semple, Maria

Beverly Hills 90210 (1992–1993)

The George Carlin Show (1994)

Ellen (1994)

Serra, Deborah

Punky Brewster (1985)

Second Chance (1988)

Highway Heartbreaker (1992)

The Man with Three Wives (1993)

Shah, Diane K.

Robocop (1994)

Shank, Linda

Murder, She Wrote (1984)

Shankar, Naren

Star Trek: Deep Space Nine (1993)

Star Trek: The Next Generation (1993)

Shapiro, Esther

Dynasty (1980–1981)

Emerald Point, N.A.S. (1983)

Dynasty II: The Colbys (1985)

When We Were Young (1989)

Dynasty: The Reunion (1991)

Shapiro, Ruth

Shannon's Deal (1990–1991)

Getting Out (1994)

Sharp, Saundra

Palmerstown (1980)

Shea, Patt

All in the Family (1979)

Archie Bunker's Place (1979–1982)

Sanford (1980)

Happy Days (1980)

Lou Grant (1980–1981)

Gloria (1982)

Cagney and Lacey (1982)

Mama Malone (1982)

Baby Makes Five (1983)

It Takes Two (1983)

Scarecrow & Mrs. King (1984)
The Golden Girls (1987)
Valerie (1987)
In the Heat of the Night (1992)

Shearer, Hannah L.
Knight Rider (1982)
Streethawk (1984)
Island Son (1990)
Star Trek: Deep Space Nine (1993)

Sheiner, Mary–David
Happy Days (1979)
Shirley (1979)
The Jeffersons (1979)
The Mary Tyler Moore Hour (1979)
The Love Boat (1985)

Shelby, Carolyn J.
Growing Pains (1987)
Once a Hero (1987)
The Charmings (1987)
Dirty Dancing (1989)
The Antagonists (1990)
Civil Wars (1992)

Shelley, Kathleen A.
Flamingo Road (1981)
Romance Theater (1982)
Bare Essence (1983)
Falcon Crest (1983)
The Yellow Rose (1983)
Emerald Point, N.A.S. (1983)
Knots Landing (1983–1984)
North and South (Episode 3)
  (1985)
Scarecrow & Mrs. King (1985)

Shengold, Nina
Hothouse (1988)
Working It Out (1991)
Earth Angel (1991)
Blind Spot (1993)

Shepherd, Sandra
The Baxters (1979–1980)

Sherman, Amy
Roseanne (1990–1994)

Sherman, Jill C.
The Incredible Hulk (1979–1980)
Voyagers! (1982–1983)
Cutter to Houston (1983)

Shilliday, Susan A.
thirtysomething (1988–1991)

Shipley, Jolene
Second Start (1988)

Shoemaker, Emily
Family (1979–1983)
The Second Family Tree (1982)

Shuster, Rosie
Saturday Night Live (1979–1987)
Square Pegs (1982)
The Larry Sanders Show (1992–
  1993)

Shyer, Marlene Fanta
Welcome Home, Jellybean (1984)

Siamis, Korby L.
Diff'rent Strokes (1979)
First Time, Second Time (1980)
Maggie's Way (1981)
Love, Sidney (1982)
Three's a Crowd (1984)
The Cosby Show (1985)
Kate and Allie (1985)
My Sister Sam (1987)
Murphy Brown (1988–1993)

Sidaris, Arlene T.
Obsessed with a Married Woman
  (1985)

Siddall, Teddi
Midnight Caller (1990–1991)

Siefert, Lynn
I'll Fly Away (1992–1993)

Siegel, Sandra Kay

Laverne and Shirley (1978)
Wonderland Cove (1979)
Friends (1979)
Shirley (1979)
California Fever (1979–1980)
Eight Is Enough (1979–1981)
Fantasy Island (1980)
The Stockard Channing Show (1980)
The Brady Brides (1981)
Falcon Crest (1981)
The Love Boat (1981–1982)
Fame (1982)
Private Benjamin (1982)
The Facts of Life (1982–1983)
Teenage Beauty (1983)
The Mississippi (1983)
Boone (1983)
Finder of Lost Loves (1984)
Knight Rider (1984)
Berrengers (1984)
Safe at Home (1985)
Morning Star, Evening Star (1986)
Hotel (1987)
The Bradys (1990)

Siler, Meredith

Dear John (1990–1991)
Empty Nest (1990–1991)
Step by Step (1991–1994)

Sillman, Deanne

Square Pegs (1983)
A Different World (1988)

Silver, Franelle

Donny and Marie (1976–1979)
The Carol Burnett Show (1977)
Three's Company (1979)
The Steve Landesburg Television Show (1983)
The Jerk, Too (1984)

Silver, Susan A.

The Bob Newhart Show (1972–1978)
Square Pegs (1982–1983)
Herndon (1983)
Glitter (1984)

Silverman, Treva

The Mary Tyler Moore Show (1970–1977)
Just in Time (1988)
The Fanelli Boys (1990–1991)

Silvers, Nancy

Battling for Baby (1992)

Silverton, Doris

Torn between Two Lovers (1979)
The Hamptons (1983)
The Colbys (1985–1987)
Hotel (1987)
A Year in the Life (1988)

Simon, Ronni S.

Addicted to Love (1988)

Simonds, P. K.

Eddie Dodd (1991)
Doogie Howser, M.D. (1992–1993)
Earth 2 (1994)
Dead at 21 (1994)

Singer, Eugenia Bostwick

Beyond Obsession (1994)

Singer, Rachel

Microcops (1989)

Sisko, Susan

Strike Force (1981)
Quincy (1983)
The Renegades (1983)
The Fall Guy (1984)
Hart to Hart (1985)
Cagney and Lacey (1985/1987)
Almost Grown (1989)

Island Son (1989)
The Antagonists (1990)
The Marshal (1995)

Sisson, Rosemary Ann
A Town Like Alice (1981)
The Manions of America (1981)
Mistral's Daughter (1984)
The Young Indiana Jones Chronicles
(1992–1993)
A Change of Place (1994)

Slevin, Kathy
City (1990)
Ferris Bueller (1990–1991)
You Take the Kids (1991)
Room for Two (1992–1993)
Due South (1994–1996)

Sloan, Holly Goldberg
Indecency (1992)

Small, Emilie R.
Trapper John, M.D. (1982/1984)
St. Elsewhere (1984)

Smith, April
Friends (1979)
Family (1979–1980)
Lou Grant (1979–1982)
Knots Landing (1980)
Cagney and Lacey (1982)
Best Kept Secrets (1984)
Ernie Kovacs: Between the Laughter
(1984)
Love Lives On (1987)
Taking Back My Life (1992)

Smith, Debbie
The Trials of Rosie O'Neill (1990)
Murder, She Wrote (1993)

Smith, Kat
Lifestories (1990)
Summer Stories (1992)

Smith, Patricia Falken
Bare Essence (1983)

Snodgrass, Melinda
The Antagonists (1990)
L.A. Law (1990–1991)
Reasonable Doubts (1992–1993)
seaQuest DSV (1993)

Snyder, Anne
She Drinks a Little (1981)

Snyder, K.
The Fresh Prince of Bel Air (1992–
1994)

Soladay, Rebecca
Empty Cradle (1993)

Soodik, Trish B.
The Cavanaughs (1986–1988)
Live–In (1989)
Homeroom (1989)
Johnny Bago (1993)
Harts of the West (1994)

Sorkin, Arlene
Down Home (1990–1991)

Spears, Vida
Full House (1983)
Silver Spoons (1993)
The Jeffersons (1984–1985)
227 (1985–1986)
The Facts of Life (1987)
Family Matters (1990–1995)

Specktor, Katherine
Convicted: A Mother's Story (1987)

Speer, Kathy
Angie (1979)
Benson (1980–1984)
Condo (1983)
The Lucie Arnaz Show (1984)
Hail to the Chief (1985)

The Golden Girls (1985–1989)
The Fanelli Boys (1990–1991)
Pacific Station (1991)
The Mommies (1993)

Spelman, Sharon
Rags to Riches (1987)

Spheeris, Penelope
Roseanne (1990)
Danger Theater (1993)

Spicer, Doreen
Martin (1995)

Spies, Amy
The Ordeal of Patty Hearst (1979)
Hanging by a Thread (1979)
T. J. Hooker (1985)
Beverly Hills 90210 (1991)
Melrose Place (1992–1993)

Sprung, Sandy
The Jeffersons (1983)
It's Your Move (1984–1985)
Married . . . with Children (1987)
Cagney and Lacey (1987)
Unhappily Ever After (1995)

Squerciati, Marie
Empty Nest (1989)
Sunday Dinner (1991)

Staahl, Meg
Wyatt Earp: Walk with a Legend (1994)

Stagner, Rama Laurie
Ohara (1988)
Other Women's Children (1993)
And Then There Was One (1994)
A Passion for Justice: The Hazel Brannon Smith Story (1994)

Stallings, Penny
Hi Honey, I'm Home (1991)

Stanley, Dianne Messina
House Calls (1979–1981)
Harper Valley P.T.A. (1982)
The Jeffersons (1982)
Archie Bunker's Place (1982)
The Facts of Life (1982–1983)
Webster (1984)
The Love Boat (1984)
Knots Landing (1987)
Knots Landing (1990–1991)
Homefront (1991–1993)
Hotel Malibu (1994)

Steen, Nancy
Buckshot (1980)
Happy Days (1981–1983)
The Love Boat (1982)
Police Squad (1982)
Dreams (1984)
Mr. Belvedere (1985)
Webster (1987)
Night Court (1988–1990)
Stand by Your Man (1992)
Married . . . with Children (1994)

Stein, Robin
Amen (1990–1991)

Steinberg, Ellen
Our Kids and the Best of Everything (1987)

Steinkellner, Cheri L.
The Facts of Life (1984)
The Jeffersons (1984–1985)
Benson (1985)
Who's the Boss (1985–1986)
Cheers (1986–1992)
The Tortellis (1987)
Bob (1992–1993)

Sternwood, Carmen
Beverly Hills 90210 (1991)

Stevens, Judith
Maggie's Secrets (1990)
Catwalk (1992–1993)

Stevens, Laurie
TimeTrax (1993–1994)

Stevens, Leslie C.
The Gemini Man (1976)
Stonestreet: Who Killed the Centerfold Model? (1977)
Jacqueline Susann's Valley of the Dolls (1981)

Stewart, Heather
Newhart (1989)

Stewart, Susan Misty
Julie Farr, M.D. (1979)
Harper Valley P.T.A. (1981)
Knots Landing (1981)
Romance Theater (1982)
Fantasy Island (1984)

Stiehm, Meredith
Northern Exposure (1994)
Beverly Hills 90210 (1994–1995)

Stivers, Bunny
A Tribute to the Juke Box Award Winners (1980)
Annual Circus of the Stars (1981–1987)
Celebrity Daredevils (1983)
Fourteenth Annual Circus of the Stars (1989)
All New Circus of the Stars and Side Show (1991)
Circus of the Stars Goes to Disneyland (1994)

Stoddard, Sylvia
Simon & Simon (1988)
Over My Dead Body (1990–1991)

Stoddart, Alexandra
Harper Valley P.T.A. (1981)
The Love Boat (1984)

Stone, Noreen
The Paper Chase (1979)
Palmerstown (1980–1981)

Nurse (1981)
Dynasty (1984)
Power's Play (1986)
Tricks of the Trade (1988)

Stotsky, Lisa B.
A.L.F. (1987–1988)

Strain, Leslie
The Cosby Show (1992)

Strassman, Julie
Full House (1990)

Strauss, Susan
First Impressions (1988)
Day by Day (1989)

Stumpe, Karen Ann
Cheers (1992–1993)
Phenom (1993–1994)
Grace under Fire (1994)

Styler, Adele
Joe and Sons (1975–1976)
Doc (1976)
The Carol Burnett Show (1978)
Joe's World (1979–1980)
Too Close for Comfort (1981)

Sullivan, Beth
His Mistress (1984)
A Cry for Help: The Tracey Thurman Story (1989)
When He's Not a Stranger (1989)
The Trials of Rosie O'Neill (1990)
Dr. Quinn, Medicine Woman (1993)
For the Love of My Child: The Anissa Ayala Story (1993)

Sunshine, Madeline
Open All Night (1981–1982)
Star of the Family (1982)
The New Odd Couple (1983)
Webster (1983–1985)

Almost Home (1986)
The People Next Door (1989)
Julie (1992)

Sussman, Sally
The Facts of Life (1980–1981)
Too Close for Comfort (1983)
Freshman Dorm (1992)

Svaco, Ellen
Murphy Brown (1993)
Living Single (1994)

Taber, Colleen
Murphy Brown (1993)
Living Single (1994)

Taggart, Millee
The New Odd Couple (1983)
Joanie Loves Chachi (1983)
Dynasty (1984)
Nothing in Common (1987)

Tait, Jennifer
Dr. Quinn, Medicine Woman (1995)

Tarnofsky, Dawn
Trapper John, M.D. (1985)

Tatham, Jamie
Davis Rules (1992)
Full House (1992–1995)

Taylor, Alison
Roc (1993–1994)

Taylor, Jeri C.
California Fever (1979)
Salvage (1979)
Cliffhangers (1979)
The Incredible Hulk (1981)
Please Don't Hit Me, Mom (1981)
Little House on the Prairie (1981)
Quincy (1982–1983)
Blue Thunder (1984)
A Place to Call Home (1987)

In the Heat of the Night (1988)
Jake and the Fatman (1989–1990)
Father Dowling Mysteries (1990–1991)
Star Trek: The Next Generation (1992–1994)
Star Trek: Voyager (1995)

Taylor, Renee
Paradise (1974)
A Lucille Ball Special (1975)
Bedtime Story (1978)
A Cry for Love (1978)
Going Up (1980)
Lovers and Other Strangers (1982)
Bedrooms (1984)

Tebo, Amy
Falcon Crest (1988)
Dallas (1990)

Teigh, Judith
Funny, You Don't Look 200 (1987)

Tenney, Susan
Blossom (1993)

Tewkesbury, Joan
The Tenth Month (1978)
The Acorn People (1980)
Elysian Fields (1989)
Shannon's Deal (1990–1991)

Thacker, Julie
The Golden Palace (1992–1993)
The Powers That Be (1992–1993)
The Trouble with Larry (1993)

Thomas, Betsy
My So–Called Life (1994)

Thompson, Cynthia L.
The Love Boat (1982)
The Love Boat (1984–1985)
Head of the Class (1987–1989)

Thompson, Selma R.
> *Charles and Diana: A Royal Love Story* (1982)
> *Locked Up: A Mother's Rage* (1991)
> *Woman with a Past* (1992)
> *Men Don't Tell* (1993)
> *No Child of Mine* (1993)

Thuna, Leonora
> *The Natural Look* (1977)
> *Lou Grant* (1977)
> *In the Beginning* (1978)
> *Grandpa Goes to Washington* (1978)
> *Lou Grant* (1979)
> *Angie* (1979)
> *Starting Fresh* (1979)
> *I Know Why the Caged Bird Sings* (1979)
> *Goodtime Girls* (1980)
> *Broadway* (1982)
> *Family Secrets* (1984)
> *Judith Krantz's Torch Song* (1993)

Tibbles, Barbara
> *Hello, Larry* (1980)

Tilly, Jennifer
> *Mary* (1986)

Tilly, Meg
> *Winnetka Road* (1994)

Timberman, Sarah
> *Catwalk* (1992–1993)

Title, Susan L.
> *Baby Sister* (1983)
> *The Other Lover* (1985)

Tobin, Noreen
> *Backfield in Motion* (1991)

Tokatyan, Diana Bell
> *Here's Boomer* (1980)
> *Bravo Bridge* (1982)
> *For Love and Honor* (1983)

Toll, Judy
> *Just in Time* (1988)

Toomin, Amy
> *The Boys Are Back* (1994)

Topping, Gabrielle
> *Married . . . with Children* (1991–1993)

Torme, Tracy
> *Saturday Night Live* (1982–1983)
> *Intruders* (1992)

Towbin, Freddi
> *One in a Million* (1980)
> *Here's Boomer* (1980)
> *Harper Valley P.T.A.* (1982)
> *Love, Sidney* (1982)
> *The Love Boat* (1982–1983)
> *9 to 5* (1983)
> *Webster* (1983)
> *Throb* (1985–1987)
> *The Facts of Life* (1986)
> *Davis Rules* (1991)

Tracy, Emily
> *Miss All–American Beauty* (1982)
> *Too Good to Be True* (1983)
> *The Parade* (1984)
> *The Cosby Show* (1985)
> *Whattley by the Bay* (1988)
> *Doodles* (1988)
> *Missing Persons* (1993)

Treas, Terri
> *Cobra* (1993–1994)
> *Silk Stalkings* (1993–1994)

Trigiani, Adriana
> *Practically Sixteen* (1989)
> *A Different World* (1989–1990)
> *Blue Ridge* (1990)
> *Working It Out* (1991)
> *The Cosby Show* (1991–1992)

Trogdon, Miriam
  Newhart (1983–1987)
  Family Ties (1985)
  Major Dad (1989–1991)
  Empty Nest (1990–1991)
  Coach (1991–1992)
  Delta (1992–1993)
  Roseanne (1993–1994)

Trump, Jill
  *My Wicked, Wicked Ways: The
    Legend of Errol Flynn* (1985)

Tully, Elizabeth
  Hart to Hart (1983)

Turner, Barbara
  The War between the Tates (1978)
  The Robber Baroness (1979)
  Freedom (1980)
  Sessions (1984)
  Eye of the Sparrow (1987)
  Somebody's Daughter (1992)
  Out of Darkness (1994)

Turner, Bonnie
  Saturday Night Live (1987–1989)
  Saturday Night Live (1992)
  She TV (1994)
  3rd Rock from the Sun (1996)

Turner, Constance
  Szysznyk (1977)
  Steve Martin: Comedy Is Not Pretty
    (1980)

Turner, Francesca
  Battlestar Galactica (1979)

Turner, Kriss
  Sister, Sister (1994–1995)

Tyson, Nona
  Cliffhangers (1979)

Ullman, Tracey
  The Tracey Ullman Show (1987)
  Tracey Ullman: Takes on New York
    (1994)
  Tracey Takes on . . . (1995–1996)

Valentine, Karen
  Jane Doe (1983)

Val Jean, Michele
  Jake and the Fatman (1990–1991)

Vallely, Jean
  Heartbeat (1988)

Van, Dorothy
  Mama's Family (1983)
  Silver Spoons (1984–1985)
  Punky Brewster (1985)
  Major Dad (1992)

Van der Velde, Nadine
  Catwalk (1992–1993)

Van Gores, Alida
  He's Not Your Son (1984)

Varela, Migdia
  Brothers & Sisters (1979)
  The Facts of Life (1980/1982)

Va Salle, Linda
  Who's the Boss (1990–1992)
  Getting By (1983)
  Roc (1993)

Veasey, Pam
  Gimme a Break (1987)
  The Robert Guillaume Show (1989)
  In Living Color (1992–1993)

Vela, Norma S.
  St. Elsewhere (1985–1987)
  Spenser: For Hire (1986–1987)
  The Slap Maxwell Story (1988)
  Studio 3B (1989)

Roseanne (1989–1990)
Davis Rules (1991)
The Torkelsons (1991)
Designing Women (1992–1993)
Good Advice (1993)
George (1993)

Ventresca, Angela
China Beach (1990–1991)

Vince, Nancy
The Jeffersons (1979/1981)

Vorgan, GiGi
Full House (1990)

Vosburgh, Marcy
The Jeffersons (1982–1983)
It's Your Move (1984–1985)
Married . . . with Children (1986–1987)
Cagney and Lacey (1987)
Unhappily Ever After (1995)

Vosper, Margery
Alfred Hitchcock Presents (1985)

Vote, Robin
Blinded by the Light (1980)
Murderers among Us: The Simon Wiesenthal Story (1989)

Vradenburg, Trish
Everything's Relative (1987)

Wade, Gloria
Please Stand By (1979)
One in a Million (1980)

Wade, Sally
One in a Million (1980)
ER (1985)

Wagner, Carla Jean
Shell Game (1987)
Her Secret Life (1987)
Fort Figueroa (1988)

Agatha Christie's The Man in the Brown Suit (1989)
Murder by Moonlight (1989)

Wagner, Jane
Lily (1975)
The Lily Tomlin Special (1975)
Lily Tomlin: Sold Out (1981)
Lily for President (1982)

Wagner, Madeline D.
The Tony Randall Show (1977)
Lacy and the Mississippi Queen (1978)
Three's Company (1978)
Eight Is Enough (1979)
Fantasy Island (1981)

Wald, Susan
Life Goes On (1990–1991)

Walden, Lois A.
Debby Boone: One Step Closer (1982)

Walder, Joyce
My Breast (1994)

Walker, Susan F.
That's Incredible (1981)
Prime Times (1983)
Season's Greetings from The Honeymooners (1985)
The Honeymooners' Anniversary (1985)
Jackie Gleason's Second Honeymoon (1985)

Wallace, Barbara
Murphy Brown (1992–1993)
Nurses (1993–1994)
Wild Oats (1994)

Wallace, Mary
The Museum of Television & Radio Presents: Science Fiction, a Journey into the Unknown (1994)

Wallace, Pamela
  *A Murderous Affair: The Carolyn
    Warmus Story* (1992)

Wallem, Linda
  She TV (1994)
  Cybill (1995)

Wapner, Phyllis
  Trapper John, M.D. (1982–1983)

Wasserstein, Wendy J.
  The Comedy Zone (1984)
  Liza Minnelli in Sam Found Out
    (1988)

Webb, Amy
  Harper Valley P.T.A. (1981)

Webb, Chris
  Weird Science (1994)

Webber, Marilyn
  Montana Crossroads (1993)

Webster, Diana
  In Search of. . . (1979–1981)
  Ripley's Believe It or Not (1982)
  Manbeast! (1983)

Wegher, Barbara
  In Search of . . . (1979–1981)

Weingartner, Martha
  Robin Cook's Harmful Intent (1993)

Weisberg, Barbara M.
  Charles in Charge (1985)

Weiskopf, Kim R.
  Good Times (1978–1979)
  Carter Country (1979)
  Three's Company (1979–1981)
  9 to 5 (1981)
  We Got It Made (1984)
  Gatlin (1984)
  Automan (1984)

What's Happening Now (1985)
She's with Me (1985)
Full House (1988–1990)
Dear John (1992)
Vinnie & Bobby (1992)
Rachel Gunn, R.N. (1992)
Married . . . with Children (1993–
  1994)

Weisman, Margaret A.
  One Day at a Time (1983)
  We Got It Made (1984)

Weiss, Harriett
  In the Beginning (1978)
  All in the Family (1978)
  Archie Bunker's Place (1979–1982)
  Sanford (1980)
  Happy Days (1980)
  Lou Grant (1980–1981)
  Gloria (1982)
  Mama Malone (1982)
  Cagney and Lacey (1982)
  Baby Makes Five (1983)
  It Takes Two (1983)
  Scarecrow & Mrs. King (1984)
  Kate and Allie (1984)
  Spenser: For Hire (1985)
  Valerie (1987)
  The Golden Girls (1987–1988)

Weissman, Ginny
  Highway to Heaven (1987)

Welch, Mitzie
  Bing Crosby and His Friends (1974)
  Sills and Burnett at the Met (1976)
  Ben Vereen: His Roots (1978)
  Dolly & Carol in Nashville (1979)
  Linda in Wonderland (1980)
  Hope, Women, and Song (1980)
  Hal Linden's Big Apple (1980)
  Walt Disney—One Man's Dream
    (1981)
  Bonnie and the Franklins (1981)

*Life of the Party: The Story of
    Beatrice* (1982)
Burnett Discovers Domingo (1984)
Barbara Mandrell's Christmas
    (1986)
Walt Disney World's 15th Birthday
    (1986)
A Carol Burnett Special (1987)
*America's All–Star Tribute to
    Elizabeth Taylor* (1989)
AT&T Presents: Julie and Carol
    (1989)
Carol & Company (1990–1991)
Carol Burnett: The Special Years
    (1994)
Men, Movies, & Carol (1994)

Welch, Raquel
    From Raquel with Love (1980)

Welch, Roseanne
    Beverly Hills 90210 (1994)

Wells, Kimberly
    Kate and Allie (1989)
    Harts of the West (1994)

Wendkos, Gina
    Private Eye (1987)
    My Two Dads (1988)
    Hooperman (1988)
    Wiseguy (1988)
    One of the Boys (1989)
    Sugar and Spice (1990)
    Married People (1990)
    The Man in the Family (1991)
    Good Advice (1993)
    Darling (1995)
    Can't Hurry Love (1995)

Wengrod, Karen L.
    Who's the Boss (1985–1989)
    Cheers (1986)
    Getting By (1993)
    George (1994)

West, Valerie D.
    Houston Knights (1987)
    Blue Skies (1988)
    One of Her Own (1994)

Weston, Ann H.
    Getting Physical (1984)
    The Disappearance of Vinnie (1994)

Weston, Ellen
    Fear Stalk (1989)
    Lies before Kisses (1991)
    Sin and Redemption (1994)
    See Jane Run (1995)

Westphal, Chris R.
    Murphy Brown (1990)
    Baby Talk (1991)

Whitaker, Claire
    Eight Is Enough (1979)
    The Waltons (1979–1980)
    Falcon Crest (1984–1985)
    Our House (1988)
    Baywatch (1990)
    A Walton Thanksgiving Reunion
        (1993)
    A Walton Wedding (1995)

Whitcomb, Cynthia
    Eleanor: First Lady of the World
        (1981)
    Leave 'em Laughing (1981)
    Not in Front of the Children (1982)
    Grace Kelly (1983)
    Jane Doe (1983)
    One Terrific Guy (1985)
    I Know My First Name Is Steven
        (1989)
    Follow Your Heart (1990)
    When You Remember Me (1990)
    Guilty until Proven Innocent (1991)
    Mark Twain and Me (1991)

White, Ethel Lina
    Alfred Hitchcock Presents (1985)

Whitelaw, Debbie
 Fantasy Island (1984)

Wick, Pamela
 My Two Dads (1989)
 The Family Man (1990–1991)

Wick, Susan Cridland
 My Two Dads (1989)
 The Family Man (1990–1991)
 Evening Shade (1993–1994)
 Models, Inc (1994)

Wilk, Babette
 Three's Company (1983)

Wilk, Diane E.
 It Takes Two (1982–1983)
 Amanda's (1983)
 9 to 5 (1983)
 Emily (1985)
 Herman's Head (1991)
 Billy (1992)
 The Nanny (1993–1994)

Wilkinson, Deborah M.
 227 (1988)

Willens, Michele
 9 to 5 (1982)
 Jesse (1984)

Willhardt, E. Gail
 Against the Law (1990–1991)

Williams, Lona
 Someone Like Me (1994)
 Hardball (1994)

Williams, Maiya
 The Robert Guillaume Show (1989)
 Going Places (1991)
 Roc (1992–1993)
 The Fresh Prince of Bel Air (1993–1995)

Williamson, Martha A.
 The Homemade Comedy Special (1984)
 Joan Rivers and Friends Salute (1984)
 Heidi Abromowitz (1985)
 The Facts of Life (1987–1988)
 Raising Amanda (1988)
 Living Dolls (1989)
 The Family Man (1990–1991)
 Jack's Place (1992–1993)
 Touched by an Angel (1994–1995)

Willis, Mary P.
 Some Kind of Miracle (1979)
 Seizure: The Story of Kathy Morris (1980)
 Wanted: The Perfect Guy (1986)
 The Babysitters Club (1991–1992)

Wilson, Brenda
 Dirkham Detective Agency (1983)
 Private Affairs (1989)

Wilson, Elizabeth V.
 Fun and Games (1980)
 Dynasty (1981)

Wilson, Sheree J.
 Walker, Texas Ranger (1994)

Wilson–Klein, Nita
 Kate and Allie (1987)

Wittman, Ellen
 Fantasy Island (1980)

Wolff, Michele
 Who's the Boss (1990–1992)
 The Golden Girls (1991)
 Rachel Gunn, R.N. (1992)

Wolff, Ruth
 Sisters (1992–1993)

Wolitzer, Hilma
 Single Women, Married Men (1989)

Wollens, Susan
    Matlock (1990)

Wong, Elizabeth
    All–American Girl (1994–1995)

Wood, Norma Jean
    B. L. Stryker: Die Laughing (1989)

Woodall, Ann
    Mr. Merlin (1981)

Woods, Mae
    Tales from the Crypt (1994)

Woodward, Lydia
    St. Elsewhere (1987)
    China Beach (1989–1991)
    Angel Street (1992)
    ER (1994–1995)

Woollen, Susan L.
    The Incredible Hulk (1978)
    B.J. & the Bear (1979)
    The Master (1984)
    Remington Steele (1985)
    Alfred Hitchcock Presents (1986)
    The Equalizer (1988)

Wooten, Jamie
    Homeroom (1989)
    The Golden Girls (1990–1992)
    The Golden Palace (1992–1993)
    The 5 Mrs. Buchanans

Worcester, Marjorie
    Quincy (1980)

Worrell, Mary
    The Waltons (1981)

Worth, Jody T.
    Hill Street Blues (1987)
    NYPD Blue (1994)

Worthington, Janet W.
    Policewoman Centerfold (1983)
    Romance on the Orient Express
        (1985)

Lady in Blue (1985)
I Had Three Wives (1985)
Dirty Dancing (1988)
Freshman Dorm (1992)
Danielle Steel's Heartbeat (1993)
Danielle Steel's A Perfect Stranger
    (1994)

Wunsch, Toni
    Diff'rent Strokes (1984)

Wynn, Tracy Keenan
    The Quest (1976)
    In the Line of Duty: The FBI
        Murders (1988)
    The Revenge of Al Capone (1989)
    Carolina Skeletons (1991)

Yahr, Betty
    Alice (1982)
    The Love Boat (1984)

Yale, Kathleen
    Johnny Bull (1985)

Yearwood, Linda M.
    True Colors (1992)
    The Fresh Prince of Bel Air (1992–
        1993)

Yellin, Linda
    Charles and Diana: A Royal Love
        Story (1982)
    Jacobo Timerman: Prisoner without
        a Name, Cell without a Number
        (1983)

Yorkin, Nicole
    The Trials of Rosie O'Neill (1990–
        1992)
    Melrose Place (1992–1993)
    Birdland (1994)
    Touched by an Angel (1994)

Young, Cathleen
    MacGyver (1991)
    Posing: Inspired by Three Real
        Stories (1992)

Dr. Quinn, Medicine Woman (1993)
A Time to Heal (1994)
A Place for Annie (1994)

Young, Dalene A.

Dead Man's Curve (1978)
Can You Hear the Laughter? (1978)
The Freddie Prinze Story (1979)
The Plutonium Incident (1980)
Will There Really Be a Morning?
  (1983)
Hot Stuff (1984)
Heartbeat: The Dreamers (1984)
Why Me! (1985)
I Love You Perfect (1989)
Living a Lie (1991)
A Message from Holly (1992)
Jonathan: The Boy Nobody Wanted
  (1992)
The Yarn Princess (1994)
Is There Life Out There? (1994)

Young–Silver, Kimberly

Top of the Heap (1991)
Unhappily Ever After (1995)

Zabel, Jackie

Dallas (1990)

Zambrano, Jacqueline

The Equalizer (1989)
The Young Riders (1989)
Gabriel's Fire (1990)
Going to Extremes (1992–1993)
Under Suspicion (1994)

Zander, Christine

Saturday Night Live (1987–1989)
Saturday Night Live (1992)
Nurses (1994)
She TV (1994)

Zellman, Shelly F.

Donny and Marie (1976–1979)
Baby I'm Back (1978)

Barney Miller (1978)
James at 16 (1978)
Semi–Tough (1980)
When the Whistle Blows (1980)
Nobody's Perfect (1980)
Benson (1980)
It's a Living (1980–1981)
Three's Company (1981/1983)
Newhart (1983–1989)
Charles in Charge (1984)
Spencer (1984)
Mary (1985)
Eisenhower & Lutz (1988)
Dear John (1991)

Ziegler, Ursula

Head of the Class (1990–1991)
Empty Nest (1992–1994)

Ziff, Sherri

Baywatch (1993–1994)

Zola, Marion J.

Sharing Richard (1988)

Emmy Winners

This listing gives only the names of female recipients; the notation "other" or "others" refers to the male corecipient(s) of a given award. The chronological list of winners is followed by names of women who have won the most Emmy awards.

1948–1949
Most Outstanding Personality   Shirley Dinsdale

1949–1950
No female winners

1950–1951
Best Actress   Gertrude Berg

1951–1952
Best Actress   Imogene Coca

1952–1953
Best Situation Comedy   *I Love Lucy*
Best Actress   Helen Hayes
Best Comedienne   Lucille Ball

1953–1954
Best Situation Comedy   *I Love Lucy*
Best Children's Program   *Kukla, Fran & Ollie*
Best Female Star   Eve Arden
Best Supporting Actress   Vivian Vance

1954–1955
Best Actress
  Series   Loretta Young
  Single Performance   Judith Anderson
Best Supporting Actress   Audrey Meadows
Best Female Singer   Dinah Shore
Best Choreographer   June Taylor

1955–1956

Best Single Program	*Peter Pan*
Best Actress	
Series	Lucille Ball
Single Performance	Mary Martin
Best Supporting Actress	Nanette Fabray
Best Comedienne	Nanette Fabray

1956–1957

Best Female Singer	Dinah Shore
Best Actress	
Series	Loretta Young
Single Performance	Claire Trevor
Best Comedienne	Nanette Fabray
Best Supporting Actress	Pat Carroll
Best Female Personality	Dinah Shore

1957–1958

Best Variety Show	*Dinah Shore Chevy Show*
Best Performance in a Series	Dinah Shore
Best Actress	
Series	Jane Wyatt
Single Performance	Polly Bergen
Best Supporting Actress	Ann B. Davis

1958–1959

Best Variety Show	*Dinah Shore Chevy Show*
Best Actress	
Drama Series	Loretta Young
Comedy Series	Jane Wyatt
Single Performance	Julie Harris
Variety	Dinah Shore
Best Supporting Actress	
Drama	Barbara Hale
Comedy	Ann B. Davis

1959–1960

Outstanding Actress	
Series	Jane Wyatt
Single Performance	Ingrid Bergman

1960–1961

Outstanding Actress	
Series	Barbara Stanwyck
Single Performance	Judith Anderson

1961–1962

Program of the Year	*Victoria Regina*
Outstanding Daytime Program	*Purex Specials for Women*

Outstanding Actress
    Series   Shirley Booth
    Single Performance   Julie Harris
Outstanding Performance (Variety)   Carol Burnett
Outstanding Supporting Actress   Pamela Brown

1962–1963

Outstanding Music Program   *Julie and Carol at Carnegie Hall*
Outstanding Actress
    Series   Shirley Booth
    Single Performance   Kim Stanley
Outstanding Supporting Actress   Glenda Farrell
Outstanding Performance (Variety)   Carol Burnett

1963–1964

Outstanding Actress
    Series   Mary Tyler Moore
    Single Performance   Shelley Winters
Outstanding Supporting Actress   Ruth White

1964–1965

Outstanding Entertainment Program   *My Name Is Barbra*
Outstanding Achievement in Entertainment   Lynn Fontanne, Barbra Streisand

1965–1966

Outstanding Actress
    Drama Series   Barbara Stanwyck
    Comedy Series   Mary Tyler Moore
    Single Performance   Simone Signoret
Outstanding Supporting Actress
    Drama   Lee Grant
    Comedy   Alice Pearce
Outstanding Achievement in
Educational Programming   Julia Child

1966–1967

Outstanding Variety Special   *The Sid Caesar, Imogene Coca, Carl Reiner, Howard*
                                               Morris Special

Outstanding Actress
    Drama Series   Barbara Bain
    Single Performance   Geraldine Page
    Comedy Series   Lucille Ball
Outstanding Supporting Actress
    Drama   Agnes Moorehead
    Comedy   Frances Bavier
Outstanding Achievement (Special Class)   Eleanor Perry for adaptation of *A Christmas Memory*

1967–1968

Outstanding Dramatic Program	*Elizabeth the Queen*
Outstanding Actress	
Drama Series	Barbara Bain
Drama Special	Maureen Stapleton
Comedy Series	Lucille Ball
Outstanding Supporting Actress	
Drama	Barbara Anderson
Comedy	Marion Lorne
Best Female Singer	Dinah Shore

1968–1969

Outstanding Actress	
Drama Special	Geraldine Page
Comedy Series	Hope Lange
Drama Series	Barbara Bain
Special	Ana Calder–Marshall
Outstanding Supporting Actress (Series)	Susan Saint James

1969–1970

Outstanding Actress	
Drama Special	Patty Duke
Drama Series	Susan Hampshire
Comedy Series	Hope Lange
Outstanding Supporting Actress	
Drama	Gail Fisher
Comedy	Karen Valentine

1970–1971

Outstanding Actress	
Drama Special	Lee Grant
Drama Series	Susan Hampshire
Comedy Series	Jean Stapleton
Outstanding Supporting Actress	
Drama	Margaret Leighton
Comedy	Valerie Harper

1971–1972

Outstanding New Series	*Elizabeth R*
Outstanding Drama Series	*Elizabeth R*
Outstanding Musical Series	*The Carol Burnett Show*
Outstanding Actress	
Single Performance	Glenda Jackson
Drama Series	Glenda Jackson
Comedy Series	Jean Stapleton
Outstanding Supporting Actress	
Drama	Jenny Agutter
Comedy	Valerie Harper, Sally Struthers

Outstanding Writing (Special)	Anne Howard Bailey
Outstanding Costume Design	Elizabeth Waller

1972–1973

Outstanding Variety Series	Julie Andrews Hour
Outstanding Variety Progam	*Singer Presents, Liza with a "Z"*
Outstanding Daytime Program	*Dinah's Place*
Outstanding Actress	
Drama Series	Michael Learned
Special	Susan Hampshire
Comedy Series	Mary Tyler Moore
Single Performance	Cloris Leachman
Outstanding Supporting Actress	
Drama	Ellen Corby
Comedy	Valerie Harper
Outstanding Writing (Drama Special)	Abby Mann
Outstanding Adaptation	Eleanor Perry
Outstanding Writing	
Variety Series	Gail Parent & others
Variety Special	Renee Taylor & others
Outstanding Achievement	
Daytime Drama	Mary Fickett
Nondramatic Series	Dinah Shore
Children's Programming	Shari Lewis

1973–1974

Outstanding Special	*The Autobiography of Miss Jane Pittman*
Outstanding Variety Series	*Carol Burnett Show*
Outstanding Variety Special	Lily Tomlin
Outstanding Children's Special	*Marlo Thomas and Friends in Free to Be You and Me*
Outstanding Actress	
Drama	Michael Learned
Comedy	Mary Tyler Moore
Limited Series	Mildred Natwick
Special	Cicely Tyson
Actress of the Year	
Series	Mary Tyler Moore
Special	Cicely Tyson
Outstanding Supporting Actress	
Drama Series	Joanna Miles
Comedy Series	Cloris Leachman
Supporting Actress of the Year	Joanna Miles
Outstanding Supporting Actress (Variety)	Brenda Vaccaro
Outstanding Writing	
Drama	Joanna Lee
Original Teleplay	Fay Kanin
Adaptation	Tracy Keenan Wynn
Comedy	Treva Silverman

Outstanding Technical Crafts	Lynda Gurasich
Outstanding Actress	
Daytime	Elizabeth Hubbard
Daytime Special	Cathleen Nesbit
Outstanding Writing (Daytime)	Lila Garrett
Daytime Writer of the Year	Lila Garrett
Outstanding Host (Variety or Talk)	Dinah Shore
Outstanding Directing (News)	Pamela Hill
Outstanding Film Editing	Ann Chegwidden

1974–1975

Outstanding Comedy Series	*The Mary Tyler Moore Show*
Outstanding Variety Series	*The Carol Burnett Show*
Outstanding Classical Music Program	*Profile in Music: Beverly Sills*
Outstanding Actress	
Drama	Jean Marsh
Comedy	Valerie Harper
Limited Series	Jessica Walter
Special	Katharine Hepburn
Outstanding Supporting Actress	
Drama	Ellen Corby
Comedy	Betty White
Single Performance	Cloris Leachman, Zohra Lambert
Special	Juliet Mills
Variety	Cloris Leachman
Outstanding Choreography	Marge Champion
Outstanding Art Direction (Drama Feature/Film)	Carmen Dillion, Tessa Davies
Outstanding Costume Design	Margaret Furse
Outstanding Technical Craft	Edie Panda
Outstanding Actress	
Daytime	Susan Flannery
Special	Kay Lenz
Outstanding Writing (Special)	Audrey Davis Levin
Outstanding Variety Series	*Dinah!*
Outstanding Host (Variety or Talk)	Barbara Walters
Outstanding Achievement in Children's Programming	Elinor Bunin

1975–1976

Outstanding Comedy Series	*The Mary Tyler Moore Show*
Outstanding Actress	
Drama	Michael Learned
Comedy	Mary Tyler Moore
Single Performance	Kathryn Walker
Limited Series	Rosemary Harris
Special	Susan Clark
Outstanding Supporting Actress	
Drama	Ellen Corby
Comedy	Betty White

Single Performance   Fionnula Flanagan
Special   Rosemary Murphy
Variety   Vicki Lawrence
Outstanding Costume Design   Jane Robinson
Outstanding Daytime Drama Special *First Ladies' Diaries: Edith Wilson*
Outstanding Actress
 Daytime Drama   Helen Gallagher
 Daytime Drama Special   Elizabeth Hubbard
Outstanding Series (Variety or Talk) *Dinah!*
Outstanding Host (Variety or Talk) Dinah Shore
Outstanding Writing (Special)   Audrey Davis Levin

1976–1977
Outstanding Comedy Series   *The Mary Tyler Moore Show*
Outstanding Special (tie)   *Sybil,* and *Eleanor and Franklin: The White House Years*
Outstanding Actress
 Drama   Lindsay Wagner
 Comedy   Beatrice Arthur
 Single Performance   Beulah Bondi
 Limited Series   Patty Duke
 Special   Sally Field
Outstanding Supporting Actress
 Drama   Kristy McNichol
 Comedy   Mary Kay Place
 Single Performance   Olivia Cole
 Special   Diana Hyland
 Variety   Rita Moreno
Outstanding Art Direction   Jan Scott, Anne D. McCulley
Outstanding Film Editing   Rita Roland
Outstanding Technical Crafts   Emma di Vittorio, Vivienne Walker
Outstanding Achievement (Children's Programming) Jean De Joux, Elizabeth Savel
Outstanding Actress (Daytime Drama) Helen Gallagher
Outstanding Directing (Daytime Drama) Lela Swift
Outstanding Writing (Daytime Drama) Claire Labine, Mary Munisteri
Outstanding Drama Special   *The American Woman: Portraits in Courage*
Achievement in Broadcast Journalism League of Women Voters
NATAS Community Service   *Rape: A Woman's Special*

1977–1978
Outstanding Actress
 Drama   Sada Thompson
 Comedy   Jean Stapleton
 Limited Series   Meryl Streep
 Single Performance   Rita Moreno
 Special   Joanne Woodward
Outstanding Supporting Actress
 Drama   Nancy Marchand
 Comedy   Julie Kavner

Single Performance	Blanche Baker
Special	Eva Le Gallienne
Variety	Gilda Radner
Outstanding Variety Special	*Bette Midler–Ol' Red Hair Is Back*
Outstanding Writing	
Special	Caryl Ledner
Variety	Liz Sage, Franelle Silver, Jenna McMahan & others
Outstanding Actress (Daytime Drama)	Laurie Heinemann
Outstanding Writing (Daytime Drama)	Claire Labine, Mary Munisteri, Judith Pinsker & others
Outstanding Achievement (Children's Programming)	
Film Editing	Bonnie Karrin
Cinematographer	Brianne Murphy
Daytime Programming	
Costume Design	Connie Wexter
Videotape Editing	Joyce Tamara Grossman
Outstanding Religious Program	*Woman of Valor*
Outstanding Performer (Religious Programming)	Carolee Campbell

1978–1979

Outstanding Actress	
Drama	Mariette Hartley
Comedy	Ruth Gordon
Limited Series	Bette Davis
Outstanding Variety Special	*Steve & Eydie Celebrate Irving Berlin*
Outstanding Supporting Actress	
Drama	Kristy McNichol
Comedy	Sally Struthers
Special	Esther Rolle
Outstanding Writing (Drama)	Michele Gallery
Outstanding Costume Design	Ann Hollowood, Sue Le Cash, Christine Wison
Outstanding Hairstyling	Janice D. Brandow
Outstanding Actress (Daytime Drama)	Irene Dailey
Outstanding Supporting Actress	
(Daytime Drama)	Suzanne Rogers
Outstanding Directing (Daytime Drama)	Lela Swift
Outstanding Writing (Daytime Drama)	Claire Labine, Mary Munisteri, Judith Pinsker & others
Outstanding Achievement (Children's Programming)	
Actress	Geraldine Fitzgerald
Costume Design	Dorothy Weaver

1979–1980

Outstanding Special	*The Miracle Worker*
Outstanding Actress	
Drama	Barbara Bel Geddes
Comedy	Catherine Damon
Limited Series	Patty Duke Astin
Outstanding Supporting Actress	
Drama	Nancy Marchand

Comedy	Loretta Swit
Special	Mare Winningham
Outstanding Actress (Daytime Drama)	Judith Light
Outstanding Supporting Actress (Daytime Drama)	Francesca James
Outstanding Directing (Daytime)	Lela Swift
Outstanding Writing (Daytime Drama)	Claire Labine, Mary Munisteri, Judith Pinsker & others
Outstanding Achievement (Children's Programming)	
Performer	Melissa Sue Anderson, Maia Danziger, Butterfly McQueen
Writing	Sherry Cohen, Carole Hart, Marianne Meyer & others
News Writing	Marlene Sanders, Judy Towers Reemtsma

1980–1981

Outstanding Variety Program	*Lily: Sold Out*
Outstanding Actress	
Drama	Barbara Babcock
Comedy	Isabel Sanford
Limited Series	Vanessa Redgrave
Outstanding Supporting Actress	
Drama	Nancy Marchand
Comedy	Eileen Brennan
Limited Series	Jane Alexander
Outstanding Hairstyling	Shirley Padgett
Outstanding Film Sound Editing	Denise Horta, Eileen Horta & others
Outstanding Individual Achievement	Sarah Vaughan
Outstanding Actress (Daytime Drama)	Judith Light
Outstanding Supporting Actress (Daytime Drama)	Jane Elliot
Outstanding Directing (Daytime)	Marlena Laird & others
Outstanding Writing (Daytime)	Nancy Franklin & others
Outstanding Achievement (Children's Programming)	
Performer	Marlo Thomas
Writers	Blossom Elfman, Mary Munisteri
Costume Design	Dorothy Weaver
Puppet Design/Costuming	Caroly Wilcox, Cheryl Blalock & others
News	
Writers	Judy Crichton, Marlene Sanders, Judy Tower Reemtsma
Film Editing	Mili Bonsignori
Founder's Award	Shaun Sutton
Trustees Award	Agnes E. Nixon

1981–1982

Outstanding Drama Special	*A Woman Called Golda*
Outstanding Actress	
Drama	Michael Learned
Comedy	Carol Kane
Outstanding Supporting Actress	
Drama	Nancy Marchand

Comedy	Loretta Swit
Limited Series	Ingrid Bergman
Special	Penny Fuller
Outstanding Choreography	Debbie Allen
Outstanding Hairstyling	Hazel Catmull
Outstanding Individual Achievement (Special)	Nell Carter
Outstanding Actress (Daytime Drama)	Robin Strasser
Outstanding Supporting Actress (Daytime Drama)	Dorothy Lyman
Outstanding Directing (Daytime)	Marlena Laird & others
Outstanding Writing (Daytime)	Patricia Mulcahey & others
Outstanding Technical Achievement (Daytime Drama)	Diana Wenman, Jean Dedario, Barbara Martin Simmons, Barbara Wood & others
Outstanding Design Achievement (Daytime Drama)	Vicki McCarter, Diane Lewis, Katherine Kotarakos, Debbie Holmes, Jill Farren Phelps & others
Outstanding Achievement	
Writing	Elaine Meryl Brown, Betty Cornfield, Mary Ann Donahue, Robin Weston
Costume Design	Nancy Simmons
Makeup & Hair Design	Judi Cooper Sealy
Outstanding Interviewer	Barbara Walters

1982–1983

Outstanding Informational Series	*Barbara Walters Specials*
Outstanding Actress	
Drama	Tyne Daly
Comedy	Shelley Long
Limited Series	Barbara Stanwyck
Outstanding Supporting Actress	
Drama	Doris Roberts
Comedy	Carol Kane
Limited Series	Jean Simmons
Outstanding Writing (Variety)	Andrea Martin, Mary Charlotte Wilcox & others
Outstanding Choreography	Debbie Allen
Outstanding Costume Design	
Series	Theadora Van Runkle
Special	Phyllis Dalton
Outstanding Hairstyling	Edie Panda
Outstanding Film Sound Editing	Eileen Horta, Constance A. Kazmer & others
Outstanding Actress (Daytime Drama)	Dorothy Lyman
Outstanding Supporting Actress (Daytime Drama)	Louise Shaffer
Outstanding Writing (Daytime)	Claire Labine, Mary Ryan Munisteri, Judith Pinsker, Nancy Ford & others
Outstanding Host	
Game Show	Betty White
Variety	Leslie Uggams
Outstanding Children's Special	*The Woman Who Willed a Miracle*
Outstanding Performer (Children's Special)	Cloris Leachman
Outstanding Directing (Children's Special)	Sharon Miller

Outstanding Technical Achievement (Drama)	Diana Wenman, Jean Dadario, Fran Gertler, Kathryn Tucker-Bacheider, Barbara Woods & others
Outstanding Design Achievement (Drama)	Donna Larson, Carol Luikan, Sylvia Lawrence, Teri Smith & others
Outstanding Achievement (Religious)	
Performer	Lois Nettleton

1983–1984

Outstanding Drama Special	*Something About Amelia*
Outstanding Actress	
Drama	Tyne Daly
Comedy	Jane Curtin
Special	Jane Fonda
Outstanding Supporting Actress	
Drama	Alfre Woodard
Comedy	Rhea Perlman
Special	Roxana Zal
Outstanding Performance (Variety)	Cloris Leachman
Outstanding Costume Design (Special)	Julie Weiss
Outstanding Film Sound Editing (Limited Series)	Catherine Shorr, Jill Taggert & others
Outstanding Videotape Editing (Special)	Catherine Shields
Outstanding Special Visual Effects	Nancy Rushlow & others
Outstanding Actress (Daytime Drama)	Erika Slezak
Outstanding Supporting Actress (Daytime Drama)	Judi Evans
Outstanding Writing (Daytime)	Claire Labine, Mary Ryan Munisteri, Judith Pinsker, Nancy Ford
Outstanding Talk Series	*Woman to Woman*
Outstanding Writing (Children's Programming)	Sara Compton, Judy Freudberg, Emily P. Kingsley, Sonia Manzano & others
Outstanding Technical Achievement	Marianne Malitz, Susan Pomerantz, Leona K. Zeira & others
Outstanding Design Achievement	Susan Saccavino, Linda Williams, Barbara Miller, Alba Samperisi
Outstanding Host (Special)	Dorothy Hamill
Outstanding News Story	Jessica Savitch
Outstanding Writing (Special)	Judy Crichton, Pamela Hill

1984–1985

Outstanding Series (Drama)	*Cagney and Lacey*
Outstanding Actress	
Drama	Tyne Daly
Comedy	Jane Curtin
Special	Joanne Woodward
Outstanding Supporting Actress	
Drama	Betty Thomas
Comedy	Rhea Perlman
Special	Kim Stanley
Outstanding Directing (Drama)	Karen Arthur

Outstanding Writing
  Drama   Patricia Green
  Special   Vickie Patik

Outstanding Choreography   Twyla Tharp
Outstanding Costume Design (Special)   Barbara Lane
Outstanding Actress (Daytime)   Kim Zimmer
Outstanding Supporting Actress (Daytime)   Beth Maitland
Outstanding Directing (Daytime)   Irene M. Pace, Joanne Rivituso, Joanne Sedwick,
Outstanding Writing (Daytime)   Agnes Nixon, Lorraine Broderick, Mary K. Wells, Clarice Blackburn, Susan Kirshenbaum, Elizabeth Wallace, Elizabeth Page, Carlina Della Pietra & others

Outstanding Ingenue (Daytime)   Tracey E. Bergman
Outstanding Directing (Children)   Joan Darling
Outstanding Music Composition   Susan Markowitz & other
Outstanding Costume Design   Madeline Graneto
Outstanding Hairstyling   Deborah Holmes, Katherine Kotarakos, Mary Guerrero, Catherine Marcatto

Outstanding Videotape Editing   Evamarie Keller & others
Outstanding Graphic Design   Wendy Vanguard & other
Outstanding News
  Segment   Charlayne Hunter-Gault, Lesley Stahl
  Investigative   Karen Ranucci & other, Rita Braver
Outstanding Writing (Special)   Judy Crichton, Kathy Slobogin & others
Outstanding Film Editing   Alison Ellwood

1985–1986

Outstanding Drama   *Cagney and Lacey*
Outstanding Comedy   *The Golden Girls*
Outstanding Children's Program   *Anne of Green Gables*
Outstanding Actress
  Drama   Sharon Gless
  Comedy   Betty White
  Special   Marlo Thomas
Outstanding Supporting Actress
  Drama   Bonnie Bartlett
  Comedy   Rhea Perlman
  Special   Colleen Dewhurst
Outstanding Musical Performance   Whitney Houston
Outstanding Costume Design (Miniseries or Special)   Ella Maklakova, Sibylle Ulsamer
Outstanding Costuming
  Series   Susan Smith-Nashold, Ann Winsor, Kathy O'Rear & others
  Miniseries   Joie Hutchinson, Vicki Sanchez
Outstanding Hairstyling   Bernadette "Bunny" Parker
Outstanding Art Direction (Series)   Jacqueline Webber
Outstanding Editing (Multicamera)   Pam Marshall
Outstanding Sound Editing (Series)   Lettie Odney, Denise Whiting & others

Outstanding Graphics (Series)	Betty Green
Outstanding Actress (Daytime)	Erika Slezak
Outstanding Supporting Actress (Daytime)	Leann Hunley
Outstanding Directing (Daytime)	Betty Rothenberg & others
Outstanding Writing (Daytime)	Pam Long Hammer, Addie Walsh, Megan McTavish, Mary Pat Gleason, Gail N. Lawrence, Nancy Curlee
Outstanding Ingenue	Ellen Wheeler
Outstanding Performer (Children's Program)	Pearl Bailey
Outstanding Writing	
Children's Series	Sara Compton, Judy Freudberg, Emily Kingsley, Sonia Manzano, Cathi Rosenberg-Turow, Nancy Sans & others
Children's Special	Kathryn Montgomery
Special Class	Catherine Faulkner
Outstanding Music (Daytime)	Patricia Stotter, Jill Diamond & others
Outstanding Costume Design (Daytime)	Nanzi Adzima & others
Outstanding Makeup (Daytime)	Pam P. K. Cole, Diane Lewis, Donna Messina, Catherine McCann Davison, Sundi Martino, Becky Bowen
Outstanding Hairstyling	
Special	Sherry Baker
Series	Linda Librizzi Williams
Outstanding Film Editing (Daytime)	Janice Bendiksen & others
Outstanding Film Sound Editing	Laura Civiello & others
Special Recognition	Pamela Iliott
News	
Outstanding Single Segment	Jane Bryant Quinn
Outstanding Analysis	
Program	Bobbie Birieffi
Segment	Marie MacLean
Outstanding Continuing Story	Karen Barnes
Outstanding Historical Program	Gail Harris
Outstanding Individual Achievement	
Writer	Elana Mannes, Judy Crichton
Director	Elena Mannes
Cinematography	Belinda Wright
Videography	Isadore Bleckman
Sound	Joan Franklin, Belinda Wright
Film Editing	Annamaria Szanto, Deborah Hoffman

1986–1987

Outstanding Comedy Series	*The Golden Girls*
Outstanding Animated Program	*Cathy*
Outstanding Actress	
Drama	Sharon Gless
Comedy	Rue McClanahan
Special or Miniseries	Gena Rowlands

Outstanding Supporting Actress
    Drama   Bonnie Bartlett
    Comedy   Jackee Harry
    Special or Miniseries   Piper Laurie
Outstanding Guest Performance (Drama)   Alfre Woodard
Outstanding Writing (Drama)   Terry Louise Fisher
Outstanding Choreography   Dee Dee Wood & other
Outstanding Costume Design (Miniseries or Special)   Jane Robinson
Outstanding Costuming
    Series   Nanrose Buchman
    Miniseries   Frances Hays
Outstanding Hairstyling
    Series   Kathryn Blondell, Josee Normand
    Miniseries   Marsha Lewis & others
Outstanding Graphics   Sandy Dvore
Outstanding Actress (Daytime)   Kim Zimmer
Outstanding Supporting Actress (Daytime)   Kathleen Noone
Outstanding Ingenue   Martha Byrne
Outstanding Directing (Daytime)   Betty Rothenberg & others
Outstanding Writing (Daytime)   Peggy O'Shea, Lanie Bertram, Ethel M. Brez & others
Outstanding Talk Show   *The Oprah Winfrey Show*
Outstanding Talk Show Host   Oprah Winfrey
Outstanding Performer (Children's)   Madeline Kahn
Outstanding Writing (Children's)   Cathi Rosenberg-Turow, Sonia Manzano, Belinda
                                        Ward, Sara Compton, Emily Perl Kingsley, Judy
                                        Freudberg, Nancy Sans & others
                                        Andrea Joel & others

Outstanding Art Direction
Outstanding Costume Design
    Children's   Victoria deKaye Bodwell
    Series   Kathi Nishimoto
Outstanding Makeup
    Children's   Sharon Ilson Reed
    Series   Sue Saccavino & other
Outstanding Hairstyling
    Children's   Sally Hershberger & other
    Series   Linda Williams & other
Outstanding Cinematography   Dyanna Taylor & others
Outstanding Lighting Direction   Candice Dunn & other
Outstanding Graphics   Prudence Fenton & other
News & Documentary
    Outstanding Program (Special Class)   *Children of Ellis Island with Jane Pauley*
Outstanding Individual Achievement
    Writers   Mary Lou Teel, Linda Ellerbee
    Researcher   Andrea Weiss
    Tape Editor   Tressa Anna Verna

1987–1988

Outstanding Actress (Drama)   Tyne Daly

Comedy	Bea Arthur
Special	Jessica Tandy
Outstanding Supporting Actress	
Drama	Patricia Wettig
Comedy	Estelle Getty
Miniseries or Special	Jane Seymour
Outstanding Guest Performance	
Drama	Shirley Knight
Comedy	Beah Richards
Outstanding Director (Music Program)	Patricia Birch & other
Outstanding Costume Design	
(Miniseries or Special)	Jane Robinson
Outstanding Costuming	
Series	Paula Kaatz & other
Special	Deborah Hopper & other
Outstanding Makeup (Miniseries or Special)	Linda De Vetta, Pauline Heys & other
Outstanding Hairstyling	
Series	Judy Crown, Monique De Sart
Miniseries	Claudia Thompson, Jan Archibald & others
Outstanding Graphic Design	Liz Friedman
Outstanding Editing (Series)	Elodie Keene
Outstanding Sound Mixing	
Comedy	Lenora Peterson & others
Drama	Susan Chong & others
Outstanding Actress (Daytime)	Helen Gallagher
Outstanding Supporting Actress (Daytime)	Ellen Wheeler
Outstanding Ingenue	Julianne Moore
Outstanding Directing (Daytime)	Betty Rothenberg, Heather Hill & others
Outstanding Writing (Daytime)	Agnes Nixon, Clarice Blackburn, Lorraine Broderick, Susan Kirshenbaum, Kathleen Klein, Karen L. Lewis, Megan McTavish, Elizabeth Page, Peggy Sloan, Gillian Spencer, Elizabeth Wallace, Mary K. Wells & others
Outstanding Talk Show	*The Oprah Winfrey Show*
Outstanding Writing	
Children's Series	Sara Compton, Judy Freudberg, Emily Kingsley, Sonia Manzano, Cathi Rosenberg-Turow, Nancy Sans, Jocelyn Stevenson, Belinda Ward & others
Children's Special	Victoria Hochberg
Outstanding Music (Daytime)	Liz Lachman & others
Outstanding Makeup (Daytime)	Carol Brown, Gail Hopkins, Lucia Bianca & others
Outstanding Hairstyling (Daytime)	Zora Sloan, Pauletta Lewis
News and Documentary	
Outstanding Individual Achievement	
Interview Segment	Barbara Walters
Writer	Callie Crossley
Directors	Ann Petrie, Jeanette Petrie
Researcher	Teresa Koenig

Tape Editor
NATAS Trustees Award

Ruth Iwano
Peggy Charren

1988–1989

Outstanding Variety Show	*The Tracey Ullman Show*
Outstanding Informational Special	*Lillian Gish: The Actor's Life for Me*
Outstanding Actress	
Drama	Dana Delaney
Comedy	Candice Bergen
Miniseries or Special	Holly Hunter
Outstanding Supporting Actress	
Drama	Melanie Mayron
Comedy	Rhea Perlman
Miniseries or Special	Colleen Dewhurst
Outstanding Musical Performance	Linda Ronstadt
Outstanding Guest Actress	
Drama	Kay Lenz
Comedy	Colleen Dewhurst
Outstanding Writing	
Comedy	Diane English
Variety	Shannon Gaughan, Bonnie Turner, Christine Zander & others
Miniseries or Special	Abby Mann & others
Outstanding Casting	
Miniseries or Special	Lynn Kressel
Outstanding Costume Design (Series)	Judy Evans
Outstanding Costuming	
Series	Julie Glick & others
Miniseries or Special	Paula Kaatz, Andrea Weaver, Janice Lawler Dallas
Outstanding Makeup (Miniseries or Special)	Carla Palmer, Jean Black & other
Outstanding Hairstyling	
Series	Virginia Kearns
Special	Betty Glasow, Stevie Hall, Elaine Bowerbank
Outstanding Art Direction (Variety)	Portia Iversen
Outstanding Actress (Daytime)	Marcy Walker
Outstanding Supporting Actress (Daytime)	Debbi Morgan
Outstanding Juvenile Female	Kimberley McCullough
Outstanding Directing (Daytime)	Heather Hill, Betty Rothenberg, Kathryn Foster & others
Outstanding Writing (Daytime)	Anne Howard Bailey, Courtney Simon, Lynda Myles, Jane Atkins & others
Outstanding Talk Show	*The Oprah Winfrey Show*
Outstanding Talk Show Host	Sally Jesse Raphael
Outstanding Writing (Children's)	Sara Compton, Judy Freudberg, Emily Perl Kingsley Sonia Manzano, Cathi Rosenberg-Turow, Nancy Sans, Belinda Ward & others
Outstanding Costume Design	
Special	Calista Hendrickson

Series	Margarita Delgado & other
Outstanding Makeup (Daytime)	Dawn Marando & others
Outstanding Hairstyling	Yolanda Toussieng & other
Children's Daytime	Janet Medford, Valerie Scott
Outstanding Cinematography (Children's)	Dyanna Taylor, Jeri Sopanen & others
Outstanding Sound Mixing (Children's)	Pam Bartella, Ferne Friedman & others
Outstanding Lighting (Daytime)	Donna Larson
Outstanding Graphics (Children's)	Barbara Laszewski & others
Lifetime Achievement Award	Joan Ganz Cooney
News and Documentary	
Outstanding Investigative Segment	Meredith Vieira
Outstanding Coverage	
Continuing Segment	Meredith Vieira
Continuing Story	Laural Barclay, Suki Cheong & others, Victoria Corderi & others, Meredith Vieira
Outstanding Informational Segment	Meredith Vieira
Outstanding Film Editing	Holly K. Fine, Margot Francis, Joan Morris
NATAS Governors Award	Lucille Ball

1989–1990

Outstanding Comedy Series	*Murphy Brown*
Outstanding Children's Program	*A Mother's Courage: The Mary Thomas Story*
Outstanding Actress	
Drama	Patricia Wettig
Comedy	Candice Bergen
Miniseries or Special	Barbara Hershey
Outstanding Supporting Actress	
Drama	Marg Helgenberger
Comedy	Bebe Neuwirth
Miniseries or Special	Eva Marie Saint
Outstanding Variety Performance	Tracey Ullman
Outstanding Dance Performance	Katarina Witt & others
Outstanding Guest Actress	
Drama	Viveca Lindfors
Comedy	Swoosie Kurtz
Outstanding Writing (Variety)	Tracey Ullman, Heide Perlman, Marilyn Suzanne Millier, Dinah Kirgo & others
Outstanding Choreography	Paula Abdul & others
Outstanding Costume Design	
Series	Patricia Norris
Special	Shelley Komarov
Outstanding Costuming	Frances H. Hays
Outstanding Makeup (Series)	Michelle Burke, Katalin Elek & others, Bari Dreiband-Burman
Outstanding Hairstyling	
Series	Linle White, Peggy Shannon
Special	Janice Alexander

Outstanding Actress (Daytime) — Kim Zimmer

Outstanding Supporting Actress (Daytime) — Julia Barr

Outstanding Female Juvenile — Cady McClain

Outstanding Directing (Daytime) — Jeanine Guarneri-Frons, Pamela Fryman & others

Outstanding Writing (Daytime) — Pamela K. Long, Nancy Curlee, Nancy Williams, Patty Gideon Sloan, Gail Lawrence, Melissa Salmons & others

Outstanding Talk Show — *Sally Jesse Raphael*

Outstanding Talk Show Host — Joan Rivers

Outstanding Writing (Children's) — Sara Compton, Judy Freudberg, Emily Perl Kingsley, Sonia Manzano, Cathi Rosenberg-Turow, Nancy Sans, Belinda Ward & others

Outstanding Music Direction
   Daytime — Amy Burkhard & others
   Children's — Sarah Durkee, Cheryl Hardwick & others

Outstanding Hairstyling (Drama) — Angel De Angelis, Annette Bianco, Joyce Sica & others

Outstanding Graphics — Penelope Gottlieb

Outstanding Directing Special Class — Victoria Hochberg

Outstanding Costume Design
   Children's — Caroly Wilcox, Connie Peterson & others
   Drama (tie) — Carol Luiken & other, Margarita Delgado & other

Outstanding Direction/Camerawork — Janice Bendiksen & others

News and Documentary
   Outstanding Breaking News
      Program — Kathleen Sullivan & others
      Segments — Mary Alice Williams, Deborah Norville, Katherine Couric & others

Outstanding Instant Coverage (Program) — Jeanne Moss & others

Outstanding Background (Segment) — Betty Rollin

Outstanding Investigative Report (Program) — Diane Sawyer & others

Outstanding Interview (Segment) — Lesley Stahl, Connie Chung

Outstanding Coverage of Continuing News Story (Program) — Victoria Corderi, Faith Daniels, Erin Moriarty & others

Outstanding Individual Achievement (Program) — Judy Irving, Ruth Landy & other

Outstanding Researching — Marjorie M. Mooney

Outstanding Film Editing — Sara Fishko, Mary Alfieri

Outstanding Graphics — Katherine Dillion, Victoria Hunter, Barbara Gill & others

Founder's Award — Joan Ganz Cooney

1990–1991

Outstanding Actress
   Drama — Patricia Wettig
   Comedy — Kirstie Alley
   Miniseries or Special — Lynn Whitfield

Outstanding Supporting Actress
   Drama — Madge Sinclair

Comedy	Bebe Neuwirth
Miniseries or Special	Ruby Dee
Outstanding Guest Actress	
Drama	Peggy McCay
Comedy	Colleen Dewhurst
Outstanding Choreography	Debbie Allen
Outstanding Costuming	
Series	Linda Serijan-Fasmer
Special	Cathy A. Smith & others
Outstanding Costume Design (Miniseries or Special)	Maria Hruby & other
Outstanding Hairstyling	
Series	Dee Dee Petty, Jan Van Uchelen, Susan Boyd
Miniseries or Special	Katklin Kajtar & other
Outstanding Editing (Single Camera)	Joe Ann Fogle
Outstanding Actress (Daytime)	Finola Hughes
Outstanding Supporting Actress (Daytime)	Jess Walton
Outstanding Young Actress	Anne Heche
Outstanding Directing	
Daytime	Jeanine Guarneri-Frons, Pamela Fryman, Robin Raphaelian & others
Outstanding Writing	
Daytime	Sheri Anderson, Maralyn Thoma, Linda Hamner, Lynda Myles & others
Children's	Sara Compton, Judy Freudberg, Emily Perl Kingsley, Sonia Manzano, Cathi Rosenberg-Turow, Nancy Sans, Belinda Ward & others
Children's Special	Courtney Flavin, Tracey Thompson, Beth Thompson
Outstanding Performer (Children's)	Joanne Vannicola
Outstanding Talk Show	*The Oprah Winfrey Show*
Outstanding Talk Show Host	Oprah Winfrey
Outstanding Writing (Special Class)	Kathy Easterling, Debbie Griffin, Michele Johnson, Carol Campbell & others
Outstanding Music Direction	Barbara Miller-Gidaly & others
Outstanding Makeup (Daytime)	Carol Brown, Lucia Bianca, Gail Hopkins & others
Outstanding Hairstyling	
Syndicated Series	Jody Ann Lawrence
Daytime	Janet Medford, Valerie Scott
Outstanding Costume Design (Children's)	Jacqueline Mills, Jill Thraves
Daytime	Sandra Bojin-Sedlik
Outstanding Art Direction (Children's)	Debbie Madalena & others
Outstanding Cinematography	Hanania Baer
Outstanding Film Editing	Barbara Pokras
Outstanding Technical Direction	Janice L. Bendiksen & others
News and Documentary	
Outstanding Coverage	
Single Breaking Story	Jacqueline Adams, Erin Moriarty & other
Instant Coverage	Jackie Judd & others
Interview	Connie Chung

Continuing Story
    Program   Carole Simpson & others
    Segment   Diane Sawyer
Outstanding Informational Segment   JoAnna Simon, Meredith Vieira
Outstanding Directors   Elena Mannes
Outstanding Researcher   Kristin Schneeman, Elizabeth Sams & others
Outstanding Video Editor   Betty Ciccarelli
Outstanding Film Editor   Connie Rinehart
Outstanding Graphics   Angela Fernan, Laura Vaccaro-Seeger
Outstanding Sound   Beverly Joubert & others

1991–1992

Outstanding Comedy Series   *Murphy Brown*
Outstanding Miniseries   *A Woman Named Jackie*
Outstanding Made-for-TV Movie   *Miss Rose White*
Outstanding Informational Special   *Abortion: Desperate Choices*
Outstanding Actress
    Drama   Dana Delaney
    Comedy   Candice Bergen
    Miniseries or Special   Gena Rowlands
Outstanding Supporting Actress
    Drama   Valerie Mahaffey
    Comedy   Laurie Metcalf
    Miniseries or Special   Amanda Plummer
Outstanding Directing (Variety or Music)   Patricia Birch
Outstanding Writing
    Drama   Diane Frolov & other
    Comedy   Elaine Pope & other
Outstanding Music Performance   Bette Midler
Outstanding Costume Design
    (Miniseries or Special)   Charlotte Holdich
Outstanding Costuming
    (Miniseries or Special)   Molly Harris Campbell, Bridget Ostersehlte & other
Outstanding Makeup (Series)   June Haymore, Karen J. Westerfield, Tania McComas
                                        & others
Outstanding Multicamera Editing   Janet Ashikaga
Outstanding Sound Editing   Barbara Schechter, Barbara Issak & others
Outstanding Voice-Over Performance   Nancy Cartwright, Julie Kavner, Marcia Wallace
                                        & others
Outstanding Classical Performance   Kathleen Battle
Outstanding Actress (Daytime)   Erika Slezak
Outstanding Supporting Actress (Daytime)   Maeve Kinkead
Outstanding Younger Actress (Daytime)   Tricia Cast
Outstanding Daytime Directing   Susan Strickler, Carol Sedwick, Mary Madeiras, Janet
                                        Andrews & others
Outstanding Daytime Writing   Kay Alden, Janice Ferri & others
Outstanding Children's Performer   Shari Lewis
Outstanding Children's Writing   Sara Compton, Judy Freudberg, Emily Perl Kingsley,

Sonia Manzano, Cathi Rosenberg-Turow, Nancy
Sans, Belinda Ward, Molly Boylan & others

Outstanding Talk Show	*The Oprah Winfrey Show*
Outstanding Talk Show Host	Oprah Winfrey
Outstanding Daytime Hairstyling	Angel De Angelis, Annette Bianco, Joyce Sica
Outstanding Costume Design	Jacqueline Saint Anne
Daytime	Sandra Bojin-Sedlik
Outstanding Lighting (Daytime)	Lauri Moorman & other
News and Documentary	
Outstanding Interview	Beverly Schuch
Outstanding Coverage (Continuing Story)	Diane Sawyer
Outstanding Writers	Sherry Jones
Outstanding Researcher	Jane Goddall
Outstanding Film Editor	Lisa Fredrickson
Outstanding Sound	Grace Niska Atkins & others

1992–1993

Outstanding Minseries	*Prime Suspect 2*
Outstanding Actress	
Drama	Kathy Baker
Comedy	Roseanne Arnold
Miniseries or Special	Holly Hunter
Outstanding Supporting Actress	
Drama	Mary Alice
Comedy	Laurie Metcalf
Miniseries or Special	Mary Tyler Moore
Outstanding Guest Actress	
Drama	Elaine Stritch
Comedy	Tracey Ullman
Outstanding Directing (Comedy)	Betty Thomas
Outstanding Writing (Miniseries or Special)	Jane Anderson
Outstanding Costume Design	
Series	Peggy Farrell
Miniseries or Special Variety or Music Program	Shelley Komarov, Emi Wada, Julie Taymor
Outstanding Makeup	
Series	Karen J. Westerfield, Jill Rockow & others
Miniseries or Special	Deborah La Mia Denaver, Lynne Eagan & others
Outstanding Hairstyling	
Series	Joy Zapata, Candy Neal, Patty Miller, Laura Connolly, Josee Normand, Julia Walker & others
Miniseries or Special	Linda De Andrea
Outstanding Classical Performance	Catherine Malfitano
Outstanding Achievement in	
Informational Programming	Audrey Hepburn
Outstanding Actress (Daytime)	Linda Dano
Outstanding Supporting Actress (Daytime)	Ellen Parker
Outstanding Younger Actress (Daytime)	Heather Tom
Outstanding Writing (Daytime)	Nancy Curlee, Lorraine Broderick, Nancy Williams

Watt, Barbara Esensten, N. Gail Lawrence, Sally
Mandel, Dorothy Ann Purser, Peggy Schibi,
Courtney Simon & others

Outstanding Children's Performer	Shari Lewis
Outstanding Writing (Children's)	Shari Lewis & others
Outstanding Talk Show	*The Oprah Winfrey Show*
Outstanding Talk Show Host	Oprah Winfrey
Outstanding Writing (Special Class)	Victoria Costello
Outstanding Makeup (Daytime)	Christine G. Lai, Donna Moss-Guilbeau
Outstanding Hairstyling (Daytime)	Angel DeAngelis, Joyce Sica, Annette Bianco & other
Outstanding Costume Design	Sandra Bojin-Sedlik
Outstanding Lighting Direction	Lauri Moorman

News and Documentary
  Outstanding Coverage

Single Breaking Story (Program)	Gayle Young, Christiane Amanpour
Outstanding Background Analysis	
Program	Natalie Bizic
Segment	Diane Sawyer, Lesley Stahl
Outstanding Investigative Journalism	
Program	Erin Moriarty, Regina Blakely, Edie Magnus
Segment	Natalie Bizic, Penny Marshall
Outstanding Interview (Segment)	Barbara Walters, Diane Sawyer
Outstanding Informational Programming (Segment)	Diane Sawyer
Outstanding Program (Special Class)	Natalie Bizic
Individual Achievement (Special Class)	Natalie Bizic
Outstanding Writers	Marilyn Meadows & others
Outstanding Researchers	Maia Harris & other
Outstanding Sound/Audio	Jeanne Rawlings, Edna Snow & others

1993–1994

Outstanding Miniseries	*Prime Suspect 3*
Outstanding Actress	
Drama	Sela Ward
Comedy	Candice Bergen
Miniseries or Special	Kirstie Alley
Outstanding Supporting Actress	
Drama	Leigh Taylor-Young
Comedy	Laurie Metcalf
Miniseries or Special	Cicely Tyson
Outstanding Guest Actress	
Drama	Faye Dunaway
Comedy	Eileen Hackart
Outstanding Writing (Drama)	Ann Biderman
Outstanding Variety Performance	Tracey Ullman
Outstanding Choreography	Linda Talcott
Outstanding Art Direction	
Series	Mary Ann Biddle & other
Miniseries or Special	Amy McGary & other

Outstanding Costume Design
  Series   Joan Wadge
  Variety Program   Jane Ruhm

Outstanding Costuming
  Series   Shelly Levine, Loree Parral
  Miniseries or Special   Nicoletta Massone

Outstanding Makeup
  Series   MaryKay Morse & others
  Miniseries or Special   Ashlee Peterson, Camille Calvert & others

Outstanding Hairstyling
  Series   Laura Lee Grubich, Cheri Huffman, Shirley Dolle,
                                              Virginia Grobeson, Barbara Minster, Rebecca
                                              De Morrio
  Miniseries or Special   Linda De Andrea, Darlene Brumfield & other

Outstanding Editing
  Single Camera (Special)   Lois Freeman-Fox

Oustanding Sound Editing
  Series   Kimberley Lambert, Patty Von Arx, Alicia Stevenson
                                              & others
  Miniseries or Special   Kristi Johns, Jill Schachne & others

Outstanding Personal Achievement
  Informational Programming
    Editor   Catherine Shields
    Rerecording Mixer   Beverly Joubert
  Cultural Programming
    Writer   Nuala O'Conner

Outstanding Actress (Daytime)   Hillary B. Smith
Outstanding Supporting Actress (Daytime)   Susan Haskell
Outstanding Younger Actress (Daytime)   Melissa Hayden
Outstanding Directing (Daytime)   JoAnne Sedwick, Irene Pace, Lisa Connor & others
Outstanding Writing (Daytime)   Jean Passanante, Susan Bedsow-Horgan, Becky Cole
                                              & others

Outstanding Children's Performer   Shari Lewis
Outstanding Children's Writing   Sara Compton, Judy Freudberg, Emily Kingsley, Sonia
                                              Manzano, Cathi R. Turow, Nancy Sans, Belinda
                                              Ward, Molly Boylan & others

Outstanding Writing (Children's Special)   Amy Dunkleberger
Outstanding Talk Show   *The Oprah Winfrey Show*
Outstanding Talk Show Host   Oprah Winfrey
Outstanding Achievement
  (Writing; Special Class)   Kathy Easterling, Debbie Griffin & others
Outstanding Music Direction (Daytime)   Barbara Miller-Gidaly & others
Outstanding Makeup (Daytime)   Eva Polywka, Gloria Grant, Diane Ford
Outstanding Hairstyling (Drama)   Annette Bianco, Joyce Sica
Outstanding Costume Design (Drama)   Margarita Delgado & other
Outstanding Lighting Direction (Daytime)   Lauri Moorman
Sports
  Outstanding Graphic Design (tie)   Paula Goldstein, Sue Bennett, Jana Fetner, Michelle

Green, Karen Perrine & others, Terri Finaro, Ann
Smith, Marcia Bujold & others

Outstanding Music
Vanessa Williams, Amy Grant, Donna Summer,
Salt 'n Pepa

News and Documentary
Outstanding Coverage
Breaking Story
Program
Erin Moriarty, Deborah Norville, Sharon Collins,
Peggy Knapp

Segments
Sheila MacVicar
Outstanding Background Segment
Diane Sawyer
Outstanding Investigative Segment
Diane Sawyer
Outstanding Coverage Continuing Story (Program)
Paula Zahn
Outstanding Personal Achievement (Special Class)
Reporter
Christiane Amanpour
Executive Producer
Sheila Nevins
Outstanding Director
Allison Argo
Outstanding Film Editor
Lisa Fredrickson
Outstanding Music
Jennie Muskett

1994–1995

Outstanding Music Special
Barbra Streisand
Outstanding Actress
Drama
Kathy Bates
Comedy
Candice Bergen
Miniseries or Special
Glenn Close
Outstanding Supporting Actress
Drama
Julianna Margulies
Comedy
Christine Baranski
Miniseries or Special (tie)
Judy Davis, Shirley Knight
Outstanding Guest Actress
Drama
Shirley Knight
Comedy
Cyndi Lauper
Outstanding Director (Drama)
Mimi Leder
Outstanding Writing
Comedy
Anne Flett-Giordano
Miniseries or Special
Alison Cross
Outstanding Performance (Special)
Barbra Streisand
Outstanding Art Direction (Variety)
Kathleen Ankers
Outstanding Costume Design
Series
Madeleine Stewart
Miniseries
Julie Weiss
Outstanding Costuming (tie)
Brenda Cooper, Shelly Levine, Loree Paul
Outstanding Makeup
Camille Calvet, Karen Westerfield, Karen Iverson
& others

Outstanding Hairstyling
Series
Kelly Klein, Deborah Holmes Dobson, Virginia

Outstanding Hairstyling	Grobeson, Leslie Anne Anderson, Laura Connolly,
Series, *continued*	Caryl Codon, Carol Pershing
Miniseries or Special	Linda De Andrea, Tricia Cameron
Outstanding Editing	Janet Ashikaga
Outstanding Sound Editing	
Series	Catherine Flynn, Susan Mick & others
Miniseries or Special	Patricia Von Arx, Jill Schachne & others
Outstanding Actress (Daytime)	Erika Slezak
Outstanding Supporting Actress (Daytime)	Rena Sofer
Outstanding Young Actress (Daytime)	Sarah Michelle Gellar
Outstanding Directing (Daytime)	Barbara Martin Simmons, Shirley Simmons, Robin Maizes, Sybil Costello & others
Outstanding Writing (Daytime)	Claire Labine, Eleanor Mancusi, Meg Bennett, Michele Val Jean, Stephanie Braxton, Karen Harris, Judith Pinsker & others
Outstanding Children's Performer	Shari Lewis
Outstanding Directing (Children's Series)	Lisa Simon, Emily Squires & other
Outstanding Children's Writing	Sara Compton, Judy Freudberg, Emily P. Kingsley, Sonia Manzano, Cathi R. Turow, Nancy Sans, Belinda Ward, Christine Ferraro, Molly Boylan & others
Outstanding Performance (Animated Program)	Lili Tomlin
Outstanding Talk Show	*The Oprah Winfrey Show*
Outstanding Service Show	*Martha Stewart Living*
Outstanding Talk Show Host	Oprah Winfrey
Outstanding Service Show Host	Martha Stewart
Outstanding Original Song	Gloria Sklerov & other
Outstanding Music Direction	Carole Severson-Weiss, Susan-Beth Markowitz & others
Outstanding Hairstyling (Daytime)	Zora Sloan, Terrie Velazquez
Outstanding Costume Design	Lois De Armond
Outstanding Art Direction	Laura Brock & other
Outstanding Sound Editing	Melissa Gentry-Ellis, Phyllis Ginter, Jenifer Mertens & others
Outstanding Sound Mixing	Melissa Gentry-Ellis, Deborah Adair & others
Special Lifetime Achievement Award	Ted & Betty Corday
News and Documentary	
Outstanding Investigative Segment	Diane Sawyer
Outstanding Interview Segment	Renee Poussaint
Outstanding Writer	Melissa Peltier
Outstanding Director	Leanne Klein
Outstanding Researchers	Denise Greene, Meredith Woods, Michele McKenzie
Outstanding Graphic Designers	Bettina Ewing, Paula Goldstein, Norma Benitez, Mary Devitt, Jana Fetner, Joann Flaherty, Susan Nalle, Karen Perrine & others
Outstanding Title Sequence	Susan Pomerantz & others
Outstanding Art Directors	Bettina Ewing, Rene Lagler & others
Outstanding Music	Jennie Muskett
Outstanding Sound	Suzanne Tygielski & other

1995–1996

Outstanding Actress
  Drama   Kathy Baker
  Comedy   Helen Hunt
  Miniseries or Special   Helen Mirren
Outstanding Supporting Actress
  Drama   Tyne Daly
  Comedy   Julia Louis–Dreyfus
  Miniseries or Special   Greta Scacchi
Outstanding Guest Actress
  Drama   Amanda Plummer
  Comedy   Betty White
Outstanding Writing (Comedy)   Anne Flett–Giordano, Linda Morris & others
Outstanding Choreography   Anita Mann, Charonne Mose
Outstanding Art Direction
  Series   Mindy Roffman, Mary Ann Biddle
  Miniseries or Special   Rosalind Shingleton & others
  Variety   Jane Ruhm
Outstanding Costuming
  Series   Leslie Simmons Potts, Marion Kirk & other
  Miniseries or Special   Jean Rosone
Outstanding Makeup
  Series   Tina Kalliongis-Hoffman & others
  Miniseries or Special   Patricia Green & other
Outstanding Hairstyling   Kelly Kline, Deborah Dobson, Laura Lee Grubich, Virginia Grobeson, Christine Lee & other

Outstanding Sound Editing
  Series   Debby Ruby-Winberg, Susan Welsh, Kitty Malone & others
  Miniseries or Special   Kristi Johns, Jill Schachne & others
Outstanding Graphic Design   Carol Johnsen & others
Outstanding Animation   Natasha Dabizha
Outstanding Actress (Daytime)   Erika Slezak
Outstanding Supporting Actress (Daytime)   Anna Holbrook
Outstanding Young Actress (Daytime)   Kimberly McCullough
Outstanding Directing (Daytime)   Heather Hill, Kathryn Foster, Betty Rothenberg, Sally McDonald & others
Outstanding Writing (Daytime)   Agnes Nixon, Lorraine Broderick, Megan McTavish, Gail Lawrence, Karen L. Lewis, Elizabeth Smith, Michelle Patrick, Bettina F. Bradbury, Judith Donato, Kathleen Klein & others
Outstanding Children's Performer   Shari Lewis
Outstanding Performer (Special)   Kate Burton
Outstanding Directing of Children's Series   Shelley R. Jensen & others
Outstanding Achievement in Animation
  Directors   Liz Holzman, Andrea Romano
  Artists   Norma Rivera & others
Outstanding Talk Show   *The Oprah Winfrey Show*

Outstanding Service Show
   Outstanding Service Show Host
   Outstanding Makeup
Outstanding Hairstyling (Daytime)
Outstanding Single Camera Editing
Outstanding Sound Editing
News and Documentary
   Outstanding Coverage
      Single Breaking Story
         Program
         Segment
         Instant Coverage
         Continuing Story
   Outstanding Background Analysis
   Outstanding Investigative Segment
   Outstanding Interview (tie)
   Outstanding Historical Program
   Outstanding Researcher
   Outstanding Lighting Directors
   Outstanding Graphic Designers

In Julia's Kitchen with Master Chefs
Julia Child
Helen M. Gallagher, Josephine Rosa & others
Kathy Weltman & other
Nina Gilberti
Ella Bracket & others

Erin Moriarty, Susan Spencer
Jane Pauley
Rita Braver, Nanette Hansen, Jane Robelot & others
Martha Teichner
Meredith Vieira
Catherine Crier
Diane Sawyer, Renee Poussaint
Renee Poussaint
Geraldine Moriba-Meadows
Carole Farneti Foster
Alisa Robbins

1996–1997

Outstanding Miniseries
Outstanding Variety Program
Outstanding Actress
   Drama
   Comedy
   Miniseries or Special
Outstanding Supporting Actress
   Drama
   Comedy
   Miniseries or Special
Outstanding Guest Actress
   Drama
   Comedy
Outstanding Writing (Comedy)
Outstanding Music Performance
Outstanding Choreography (tie)
Outstanding Costume Design
   Series
   Miniseries or Special (tie)
   Variety or Music Program
Outstanding Makeup
   Series
   Miniseries or Special
Outstanding Hairstyling
   Series

Prime Suspect 5
Tracey Takes On...

Gillian Anderson
Helen Hunt
Alfre Woodard

Kim Delaney
Kristen Johnston
Diana Rigg

Dianne Wiest
Carol Burnett
Ellen DeGeneres, Tracy Newman & others
Bette Midler
Sarah Kawahara, Marguerite Derricks

Melina Root
Mary Malin, Jenny Beaven
Jane Ruhm

Bari Dreiband-Burman, Kathy Berekely & others
Tracy Levy, Ashlee Peterson, Jill Rockow

Susan Bagdadi, Karen Asanao Myers, Monique De
    Sartre, Charlotte Gravenor, Diane Pepper & others

Miniseries or Special

Outstanding Technical Direction
  Miniseries or Special

Outstanding Sound Editing
  Series

Miniseries or Special

Outstanding Animation

Outstanding Actress (Daytime)

Outstanding Supporting Actress (Daytime)

Outstanding Young Actress (Daytime)

Outstanding Directing (Daytime)

Outstanding Writing (Daytime)

Gloria M. Montemayor, Lola McNalley, Dorothy Andre

Donna Stock & others

Debby Ruby-Winberg, Susan Welsh & others

Linda Keim, Barbara Issak, Alysin Dee Moore, Ginger
    Geary & others

Lorraine Marshall

Jess Walton

Michelle Stafford

Sarah Brown

Heather Hill, Kathryn Foster, Betty Rothberg & others

Agnes Nixon, Lorraine Broderick, Millee Taggart,
    Christina Covino, Courtney Simon, Karen L.
    Lewis, Elizabeth Smith, Michelle Patrick, Bettina
    F. Bradbury, Judith Donato, Jane Owen Murphy,
    Kathleen Donato & others

Outstanding Talk Show

Outstanding Talk Show Host

Outstanding Service Show

Outstanding Service Show Host

Outstanding Writing (Special Class)

Outstanding Makeup

The Oprah Winfrey Show

Rosie O'Donnell

Baking with Julia

Martha Stewart

Kathy Easterling, Debbie Griffin & others

Anna Lujan, Judith Silverman-Orr, Gail J. Hopkins,
    Nina Wells, Corina C. Duran, Joleen Rizzo, Gail
    Brubaker

Outstanding Hairstyling

Outstanding Costume Design

Outstanding Art Direction

Outstanding Scenic Design (tie)

Outstanding Graphic Design

Outstanding Technical Direction

Terri Velazquez, Natascha Ladek

Durinda Wood

Laura Brock & others

Sheree Miller & others, Andrea Joel & others

Thalia Kalodimos, Harriet Seitler, Suzanne Kiley

Janice Bendiksen, Donna Stock, Sandra Harris, Tracy
    Lawrence & others

Outstanding Single Camera Editing

Outstanding Sound Editing (Special Class)

Felicity Oram & others

Melissa Gentry-Ellis, Jennifer E. Mertens, Phyllis
    Ginter & others

Outstanding Sound Mixing (Special Class)

Outstanding Direct to Tape Sound Mixing

Outstanding Individual Achievement Sports
  (Special Class)

News and Documentary
  Outstanding Coverage
    Single Breaking Story
      Program
      Newscasts
    Instant Coverage
      Program

      Newscasts

Melissa Gentry-Ellis, Deb Adair & others

Denise Palm-Stones, Maryann Jorgenson & others

Lisa Lax

Erin Moriarty
Vicki Mabrey & others

Judy Woodruff, Joie Chen, Bonnie Anderson, Donna
    Kelley, Jeanne Meserve & others
Rita Braver, Vicky Mabrey, Diana Olick & others

Outstanding Background Analysis (Segment)	Lesley R. Stahl (two different segments)
Outstanding Scenic Designers	Katherine Henry & others
Outstanding Graphic Designers	Cathy Krebs & others, Jill Taffet, Helene Plotkin & others
Outstanding Producer	Nicole Betancourt
Outstanding Researchers	Allyson Luchak, Amanda Pollack, Diane Hamilton & others

1997–1998

Outstanding Actress	
Drama	Christine Lahti
Comedy	Helen Hunt
Miniseries or Special	Ellen Barkin
Outstanding Supporting Actress	
Drama	Camryn Manheim
Comedy	Lisa Kudrow
Miniseries or Special	Mare Winningham
Outstanding Guest Actress	
Drama	Cloris Leachman
Comedy	Emma Thompson
Outstanding Writing (Variety)	Leah Krinsky & others
Outstanding Choreography	Marguerite Derricks, Peggy Holmes
Outstanding Makeup	
Series	Margie Latinopoulous, Brigette Myre-Ellis, Robin Beauchesne, Dayne Johnson & others
Miniseries or Special	Aileen Seaton & others
Outstanding Hairstyling	
Miniseries or Special	Vicki Phillips, Lynda Gurasich
Outstanding Costume Design	Ann Hollowood
Outstanding Costuming	Amy Stofsky
Outstanding Sound Editing	
Miniseries or Special	Kristi Johns, Suzanne Angel, Adriane Marfiak, Jill Schachne & others
Outstanding Art Direction	
Series	Shirley Inget
Miniseries or Special	Karen Brookes & others
Oustanding Costuming (Series)	Luellyn Harper, Karen Lupo
Outstanding Single Camera Editing	Heather MacDougall
Outstanding Sound Editing	Lisa Hannan & others
Outstanding Costume Design	Jane Ruhm
Outstanding Actress (Daytime)	Cynthia Watros
Outstanding Supporting Actress (Daytime)	Julia Barr
Outstanding Young Actress (Daytime)	Sarah Brown
Outstanding Talk Show	*The Rosie O'Donnell Show*
Outstanding Service Show	*The Pet Department*
Outstanding Talk Show Host (tie)	Oprah Winfrey, Rosie O'Donnell

Outstanding Directing (Daytime)	Heather Hill, Kathryn Foster, Sally McDonald, Betty Rothenberg & others
Children's	Lisa Simon, Emily Squires & others
Outstanding Writing (Daytime)	Agnes Nixon, Lorraine Broderick, Christina Covino, Peggy Sloane, Karen L. Lewis, Michelle Patrick, Bettina F. Bradbury, Judith Donato, Kathleen Klein, Caroline Franz, Jane Owen Murphy, Charlotte Gibson & others
Outstanding Children's Writing	Sara Compton, Judy Freudberg, Emily P. Kingsley, Sonia Manzano, Cathi R. Turow, Nancy Sans, Belinda Ward, Christine Ferraro, Molly Boylan, Annie Evans & others
Outstanding Art Direction (Daytime)	Gretchen Goelz & others
Outstanding Makeup	
Drama	Marianne Skiba, Leslie Shreve, Robin Kaiser, Jane Di Persio
Nondrama	Mariella Smith-Masters, Cindy Gardner, Cindy Mudd Lindberg
Outstanding Hairstyling (tie)	Deidre Flaharty & other, Kathy Weltman & other
Outstanding Graphic & Title Design	Caris Palm Turpen

Women Who Have Won the Most Emmy Awards

Shari Lewis	12
Sesame Street Writing Team	10
(consisting of, at various times, Sara Compton, Judy Freudberg, Emily P. Kingsley, Sonia Manzano, Cathi R. Turow, Nancy Sans, Belinda Ward, Christine Ferraro, Molly Boylan, Annie Evans, and others)	
Diane Sawyer	8
Dinah Shore	8
Mary Tyler Moore	7
Oprah Winfrey	7
Carol Burnett	6
Tracey Ullman	6
Lily Tomlin	6
Cloris Leachman	6
Candice Bergen	5
(but removed her name from consideration in 1996)	
Tyne Daly	5
Erika Slezak	5
Agnes Nixon (and writing team)	5

Television Hall of Fame

The following is a list of women—and one program—in the Television Hall of Fame.

Gracie Allen (with George Burns)
Lucille Ball
Carol Burnett
Marcy Carsey
Joan Ganz Cooney
*I Love Lucy**
Angela Lansbury
Mary Tyler Moore
Agnes Nixon
Dinah Shore
Barbara Walters
Betty White
Oprah Winfrey

*In 1991, this became the first program to be inducted into the Hall of Fame.

Bibliography

Adler, Richard P., ed. *Understanding Television: Essays on Television as a Social and Cultural Force.* New York: Praeger Publishers, 1981.

————. *Channels of Discourse, Reassembled: Television and Contemporary Criticism.* Chapel Hill: University of North Carolina Press, (1987) 1992.

Adler, Richard P., and Douglass Cater. *Television as a Cultural Force.* New York: Praeger Publishers, 1976.

————. *Television as a Social Force.* New York: Praeger Publishers, 1976.

Alley, Robert S., and Irby B. Brown. *Love Is All Around: The Making of* The Mary Tyler Moore Show. New York: Delta Press, 1989.

————. Murphy Brown: *Anatomy of a Sitcom.* New York: Dell Publishing, 1990.

Altschyler, Glenn C., and David I. Grossvogel. *Changing Channels: America in* TV Guide. Chicago: University of Illinois Press, 1992.

Andersen, Robin. *Consumer Culture and TV Programming.* Boulder, CO: Westview Press, 1995.

Applebaum, Irwyn. *The World according to Beaver.* New York: Bantam Books, 1984.

Baehr, Helen, and Gillian Dyer, eds. *Boxed In: Women and Television.* London: Pandora Press, 1987.

Ball-Rokeach, Sandra J., and Muriel G. Cantor, eds. *Media Audience and Social Structure.* Beverly Hills: Sage Publications, 1986.

Banks, Jack. *Monopoly TV: MTV's Quest to Control Music.* Boulder, CO: Westview Press, 1996.

Barnouw, Erik. *Tube of Plenty.* New York: Oxford University Press, (1975) 1990.

Basow, Susan A. *Gender Stereotypes and Roles.* Pacific Grove, CA: Brooks-Cole Publishing Co., 1992.

Berger, Arthur Asa. *TV Guided American.* New York: Walker & Co., 1976.

Bianculli, David. *Dictionary of Teleliteracy: Television's 500 Biggest Hits, Misses, and Events.* Syracuse, NY: Syracuse University Press, 1996.

———. *Teleliteracy: Taking Television Seriously.* New York: Continuum Publishing Co., 1994.

Boddy, William. *Fifties Television: The Industry and Its Critics.* Chicago: University of Illinois Press, 1993.

Bogle, Donald. *Blacks in American Films and Television: An Illustrated Encyclopedia.* New York: Garland Publishing, 1988.

Brown, Mary Ellen, ed. *Television and Women's Culture: The Politics of the Popular.* Newbury Park, CA: Sage Publications, 1990.

Brunsdon, Charlotte, Julie D'Acci, and Lynn Spiegel, eds. *Feminist Television Criticism.* New York: Oxford University Press, 1997.

Bryars, Chris. *The Real Mary Tyler Moore.* New York: Pinnacle Books, 1976.

Burnett, Carol. *One More Time.* New York: Random House, 1986.

Butler, Jeremy G. *Television: Critical Methods and Applications.* Belmont, CA: Wadsworth Publishing Co., 1994.

Butler, Matilda, and William Paisley. *Women and the Mass Media.* New York: Human Sciences Press, 1980.

Cader, Michael, ed. Saturday Night Live: *Twentieth Anniversary Book.* New York: Houghton Mifflin, 1994.

Carey, James W., ed. *Media, Myths, and Narratives: Television and the Press.* Newbury Park, CA: Sage Publications, 1988.

Carroll, Diahann, with Ross Firestone. *Diahann: An Autobiography.* Boston: Little, Brown and Co., 1986.

Castleman, Harry, and Walter J. Podrazik. *Watching TV: Four Decades of American Television.* New York: McGraw-Hill, 1982.

Caute, David. *The Great Fear: The Anti-Communist Purge under Truman and Eisenhower*. New York: Simon & Schuster, 1979.

Ceplair, Larry, and Steven Englund. *The Inquisition in Hollywood: Politics in the Film Community, 1930–1960*. Garden City, NY: Anchor Press, 1980.

Cole, Barry, ed. *Television Today: A Close-up View*. New York: Oxford University Press, 1981.

Cross, Donna Woolfolk. *Mediaspeak: How Television Makes Up Your Mind*. New York: New American Library, 1984.

D'Acci, Julie. *Defining Women: Television and the Case of* Cagney & Lacey. Chapel Hill: University of North Carolina Press, 1994.

Davis, Donald C. "Portrayal of Women in Prime Time Network Television: Some Demographic Characteristics." *Sex Roles* (September 1990): 325–332.

Davis, Jeffrey. *Children's Television 1947–1990*. Jefferson, NC: McFarland & Co., 1995.

Dintrone, Charles V. *Television Program Master Index*. Jefferson, NC: McFarland & Co., 1997.

Dominick, Joseph R. "The Portrayal of Women in Prime Time, 1953–1977." *Sex Roles* (August 1979): 405–411.

Donati, William. *Ida Lupino: A Biography*. Lexington: University of Kentucky Press, 1996.

Dow, Bonnie J. "Hegemony, Feminist Criticism, and *The Mary Tyler Moore Show*." *Critical Studies in Mass Communications* (September 1990): 261–274.

———. *Prime-Time Feminism: Television, Media Culture, and the Women's Movement since 1970*. Philadelphia: University of Pennsylvania Press, 1996.

Edelman, Rob, and Audrey E. Kupferberg. *Angela Lansbury: A Life on Stage and Screen*. New York: Carol Publishing, 1996.

Eisner, Joel, and David Krinsky. *Television Comedy Series: An Episode Guide to 153 TV Sitcoms in Syndication*. Jefferson, NC: McFarland & Co., 1984.

Ellerbee, Linda. *And So It Goes*. New York: G. P. Putnam's Sons, 1986.

———. *Moving On: Adventures in the Real World*. New York: G. P. Putnam's Sons, 1991.

Esslin, Martin. *The Age of Television*. New York: W. H. Freeman & Co., 1981.

Faludi, Susan. *Backlash: The Undeclared War against American Women.* New York: Crown, 1991.

Fariello, Griffin. *Red Scare: Memories of the American Inquisition.* New York: Avon Books, 1995.

Felder, Deborah G. *The 100 Most Influential Women of All Time.* New York: Citadel Press, 1996.

Feuer, Jane. "Genre Study and Television." In *Channels of Discourse, Reassembled: Television and Contemporary Criticism,* edited by Robert C. Allen. 138–160. Chapel Hill: University of North Carolina Press, (1987) 1992.

———. "Narrative Form in American Network Television." In *High Theory/Low Culture: Analyzing Popular Television and Film,* edited by Colin MacCabe, 101–114. New York: St. Martin's Press, 1986.

Feuer, Jane, Paul Kerr, and Tise Vahimagi, eds. *MTM "Quality Television."* London: British Film Institute, 1984.

Fishman, Katherine. *Women in Popular Culture: A Reference Guide.* Westport, CT: Greenwood Press, 1982.

Fiske, John. *Television Culture.* New York: Routledge, 1990.

Fitch, Noel Riley. *Appetite for Life: The Biography of Julia Child.* New York: Doubleday, 1997.

Funicello, Annette. *A Dream Is a Wish Your Heart Makes: My Story.* New York: Hyperion, 1994.

Gilbert, Annie. *All My Afternoons.* New York: A&W Visual Library, 1979.

Gitlin, Todd, ed. *Inside Prime Time.* New York: Pantheon Books, 1983.

———. *Watching Television.* New York: Pantheon Books, 1986.

Gregg, Rodman, ed. *Who's Who in Television.* Beverly Hills: Packard House, 1987.

Grote, David. *The End of Comedy: The Sitcom and the Comedic Tradition.* Hamden, CT: Archon Books, 1983.

Gunter, Barrie. *Television and Sex Role Stereotyping.* London: John Libbey & Co., 1986.

Gwinn, Alison, ed. *The 100 Greatest TV Shows of All Time.* New York: Time Inc. Home Entertainment, 1998.

Haskell, Deborah. "The Depiction of Women in Prime Time Television." *Journal of Broadcasting* (Spring 1979): 191–196.

Hayes, Helen. *My Life in Three Acts*. New York: Harcourt Brace Jovanovich, 1989.

Hill, George H., ed. *Ebony Images: Black Americans and Television*. Los Angeles: Daystar Publishing Co., 1986.

Hill, George, Lorraine Raglin, and Chas Floyd Johnson. *Black Women in Television: An Illustrated History and Bibliography*. New York: Garland Publishing, 1990.

Hill, Tom, ed. *Nick at Nite's Classic TV*. New York: Fireside Books, 1996.

Himmelstein, Hal. *TV Myth and the American Mind*. New York: Praeger Publishers, 1984.

Holmes, John P., and Ernest Wood. *The TV Game Show Almanac*. Radnor, PA: Chilton Book Co., 1995.

Hunter College Women's Studies Collective. *Women's Realities, Women's Choices*. New York: Oxford University Press, 1983.

Jarvis, Robert M., and Paul R. Joseph, eds. *Prime Time Law: Fictional Television as Legal Narrative*. Durham, NC: Carolina Academic Press, 1998.

Javna, John. *The Best of TV Sitcoms: The Critics' Choice: Burns and Allen to the Cosby Show, the Munsters to Mary Tyler Moore*. New York: Harmony Books, 1988.

Johnson, Nicholas. *How to Talk Back to Your Television Set*. Boston: Little, Brown & Co., 1970.

Jones, Gerald. *Honey, I'm Home! Sitcoms: Selling the American Dream*. New York: Grove Weidenfeld, 1992.

Jones, Jenny. *My Story*. Kansas City, MO: Andrews & McMeel Publishing, 1997.

Kaminsky, Stuart M., with Jeffrey H. Mahan. *American Television Genres*. Chicago: Nelson-Hall, 1988.

Kellner, Douglas. "TV, Ideology, and Emancipatory Popular Culture." In *Television: The Critical View*, edited by Horace Newcomb, 471–503. New York: Oxford University Press, (1976) 1989.

Kessler, Judy. *Inside* Today: *The Battle for the Morning*. New York: Villard Books, 1992.

Kisselhoff, Jeff. *The Box: An Oral History of Television 1920–1961*. New York: Viking Press, 1995.

Kuhns, William. *Why We Watch Them: Interpreting TV Shows*. New York: Benziger, 1970.

Kurtz, Howard. *Hot Air: All Talk All the Time*. New York: Basic Books, 1997.

Lauzen, Martha M. "Making a Difference: The Role of Women on Screen and behind the Scenes in the 1995–96 Prime-Time Season." Unpublished paper, August 1996.

Lazere, Donald. *American Media and Mass Culture: Left Perspectives.* Berkeley: University of California Press, 1987.

Leibman, Nina C. *Living Room Lectures: The Fifties Family in Film and Television.* Austin: University of Texas Press, 1995.

Lenberg, Jeff. *The Encyclopedia of Animated Cartoons.* New York: Facts on File, 1991.

Lichter, S. Robert, Linda S. Lichter, and Stanley Rothman. *Watching America.* New York: Prentice Hall Press, 1991.

MacCabe, Colin, ed. *High Theory/Low Culture: Analyzing Popular Television and Film.* New York: St. Martin's Press, 1986.

MacDonald, J. Fred. *Blacks and White TV: African Americans in Television since 1940.* Chicago: Nelson-Hall Publishers, 1992.

McGrath, Tom. *The Making of a Revolution: MTV.* Philadelphia: Running Press, 1996.

McHenry, Robert, ed. *Famous American Women.* New York: Dover Publications, 1980.

McNeil, Jean C. "Feminism, Femininity, and the Television Series: A Content Analysis." *Journal of Broadcasting* (Summer 1975): 259–271.

McWilliams, Michael. *TV Sirens: A Tantalizing Look at Prime Time's Fabulous Females.* New York: Perigee Books, 1987.

Mair, George. *Oprah Winfrey: The Real Story.* New York: Carol Publishing Group, 1994.

Marc, David. *Comic Visions: Television Comedy and American Culture.* Boston: Unwin Hyman, 1989.

———. *Demographic Vistas: Television in American Culture.* Philadelphia: University of Pennsylvania Press, 1996.

Marschall, Rick. *The Golden Age of Television.* New York: Exter Books, 1987.

Martin, Jean, ed. *Who's Who of American Women in the Twentieth Century.* New York: Crescent Books, 1995.

Matelski, Marilyn J. *The Soap Opera Evolution: America's Enduring Romance with Daytime Drama.* Jefferson, NC: McFarland & Co., 1988.

Meadows, Audrey. *Love, Alice: My Life as a Honeymooner.* New York: Crown, 1994.

Meehan, Diane M. *Ladies of the Evening: Women Characters of Prime Time Television.* Metuchen, NJ: Scarecrow Press, 1964.

Meyrowitz, Joshua. *No Sense of Place: The Impact of Electronic Media on Social Behavior.* New York: Oxford University Press, 1985.

Miller, Mark Crispin. *Boxed In: The Culture of TV.* Evanston, IL: Northwestern University Press, 1988.

————. "Deride and Conquer." In *Watching Television,* edited by Todd Gitlin, 183–229. New York: Pantheon Books, 1986.

Mintz, Lawrence E. "Situation Comedy." In *TV Genres: A Handbook and Reference Guide,* edited by Brian C. Rose, 107–122. Westport, CT: Greenwood Press, 1985.

Mitz, Rick. *The Great TV Sitcom Book.* New York: Richard Marek, 1980.

Modleski, Tania, ed. *Studies in Entertainment: Critical Approaches to Mass Culture.* Indianapolis: Indiana University Press, 1986.

Moore, F. Michael. *Drag! Male and Female Impersonators on Stage, Screen, and Television.* Jefferson, NC: McFarland & Co., 1994.

Moore, Mary Tyler. *After All.* New York: G. P. Putnam's Sons, 1995.

Morley, David. *Family Television: Cultural Power and Domestic Leisure.* London: Comedia Publishing Group, 1986.

Munson, Wayne. *All Talk: The Talkshow in Media Culture.* Philadelphia: Temple University Press, 1993.

Museum of Television & Radio. *Worlds without End: The Art and History of the Soap Opera.* New York: Harry N. Abrams, 1997.

Nash, Alana. *Golden Girl: The Story of Jessica Savitch.* New York: Harper Paperbacks, 1988.

Neale, Steve, and Frank Krutnik. *Popular Film and Television Comedy.* New York: Routledge, 1990.

Newcomb, Horace, Ed. "American Television Criticism, 1970–1985." *Critical Studies in Mass Communication* (June 1986): 217–228.

————. *Television: The Critical View.* New York: Oxford University Press, (1976) 1989.

————. *TV: The Most Popular Art.* New York: Anchor Books, 1974.

Nichols, Nichelle. *Beyond Uhura.* New York: G. P. Putnam's Sons, 1994.

O'Connor, John E. *American History/American Television: Interpreting the Video Past.* New York: Frederick Ungar Publishing Co., 1983.

O'Dell, Cary. *Women Pioneers in Television.* Jefferson, NC: McFarland & Co., 1997.

Owen, Rob. *Gen-X TV.* Syracuse, NY: Syracuse University Press, 1997.

Paisner, Daniel. *The Imperfect Mirror: Inside Stories of Television Newswomen.* New York: William Morrow, 1989.

Parenti, Michael. *Make Believe Media.* New York: St. Martin's Press, 1991.

Parish, James Robert. *The Unofficial* Murder, She Wrote *Casebook.* New York: Kensington Books, 1997.

Parish, James Robert, and Vincent Terrace. *The Complete Actor's Television Credits (1948–1988).* Metuchen, NJ: Scarecrow Press, 1990.

Phillips, Louis, and Burnham Holmes. *The TV Almanac.* New York: Macmillan, 1994.

Pilato, Herbie J. *The* Bewitched *Book.* New York: Delta Press, 1992.

Press, Andrea L. *Women Watching Television: Gender, Class, and Generation in the American Television Experience.* Philadelphia: University of Pennsylvania Press, 1991.

Primeau, Ronald. *The Rhetoric of Television.* New York: Longman, 1979.

Rapping, Elayne. *Media-Tions: Forays into the Culture and Gender Wars.* Boston: South End Press, 1994.

Read, Phyllis J., and Bernard L. Witlieb. *The Book of Women's Firsts.* New York: Random House, 1992.

Reyes, Luis, and Peter Rubie. *Hispanics in Hollywood.* New York: Garland Publishing, 1994.

Rose, Brian G., ed. *TV Genres: A Handbook and Reference Guide.* Westport, CT: Greenwood Press, 1985.

Rowland, Willard D., Jr., and Bruce Watkins, eds. *Interpreting Television: Current Research Perspectives.* Beverly Hills: Sage Publications, 1984.

RuPaul. *Lettin' It All Hang Out.* New York: Hyperion, 1995.

Sackett, Susan. *Prime Time Hits: Television's Most Popular Network Programs (1950 to the Present).* New York: Billboard Books, 1993.

Sanders, Coyne Steven, and Tom Gilbert. *Desilu: The Story of Lucille Ball and Desi Arnaz.* New York: William Morrow, 1993.

Sanders, Marlene, and Marcia Rock. *Waiting for Prime Time: The Women of Television News.* New York: Harper & Row, 1988.

Seger, Linda. *When Women Call the Shots: The Developing Power and Influence of Women in Television and Film.* New York: Henry Holt, 1996.

Smith, Betsy Covington. *Breakthrough: Women in Television.* New York: Walker & Co., 1989.

Sochen, June. *Enduring Values: Women in Popular Culture.* New York: Praeger Publishers, 1987.

Spigel, Lynn. *Make Room for TV: Television and the Family Ideal in Postwar America.* Chicago: University of Chicago Press, 1992.

Spigel, Lynn, and Denise Mann, eds. *Private Screenings: Television and the Female Consumer.* Minneapolis: University of Minnesota Press, 1992.

Sprafkin, Joyce, Carol Swift, and Robert Hess, eds. *Rx Television: Enhancing the Preventive Impact of TV.* New York: Hawthorne Press, 1983.

Spurlock, Jeanne, and Carolyn B. Robinowitz. *Women's Progress: Promises and Problems.* New York: Plenum Press, 1990.

Stark, Steven D. *Glued to the Set: The 60 Television Shows and Events That Made Us Who We Are Today.* New York: Free Press, 1997.

Stempel, Tom. *Storytellers to the Nation: A History of American Television Writing.* New York: Continuum Publishing Co., 1992.

Streenland, Sally. "Prime Time Women: An Analysis of Older Women on Entertainment Television." Report sponsored by the National Commission on Working Women, 1986.

———. "Unequal Picture: Black, Hispanic, Asian and Native American Characters on Television." Report sponsored by the National Commission on Working Women, 1989.

————. "What's Wrong with This Picture: The Status of Women on Screen and behind the Camera in Entertainment Television." Report sponsored by the National Commission on Working Women, 1990.

Tannenbaum, Percy H., ed. *The Entertainment Functions of Television.* Hillsdale, NJ: Lawrence Erlbaum Associates, 1980.

Taylor, Ella. *Prime Time Families: Television Culture in Postwar America.* Berkeley: University of California Press, 1989.

Tedesco, Nancy S. "Patterns in Prime Time." *Journal of Communications* (Spring 1974): 119–124.

Thompson, Robert J. *Television's Second Golden Age: From* Hill Street Blues *to* ER. New York: Continuum Publishing Co., 1996.

Tichi, Cecelia. *Electronic Hearth: Creating an American Television Culture.* New York: Oxford University Press, 1991.

Trotta, Liz. *Fighting for Air: In the Trenches with Television News.* New York: Simon & Schuster, 1991.

Tuchman, Gaye, ed. *The TV Establishment: Programming for Power and Profit.* Englewood Cliffs, NJ: Prentice-Hall, 1974.

Tuchman, Gaye, Arlene Kaplan Daniels, and James Benet, eds. *Hearth and Home: Images of Women in the Mass Media.* New York: Oxford University Press, 1978.

TV Guide editors. *The* TV Guide *Book of Lists.* New York: Harper Paperbacks, 1998.

Ullman, Tracey. *Tracey Takes on …* New York: Hyperion, 1998.

Waggett, Gerald J. *The Soap Opera Book of Lists.* New York: Harper Paperbacks, 1996.

Weibel, Kathryn. *Mirror, Mirror: Images of Women Reflected in Popular Culture.* Garden City, NY: Anchor Books, 1977.

Weinert, Ed, and the editors of *TV Guide. The* TV Guide *TV Book.* New York: Harper Perennial, 1992.

Weisbrot, Robert. *Xena, Warrior Princess.* New York: Main Street Books, 1998.

Weissman, Ginny, and Coyne Steven Sanders. The Dick Van Dyke Show: *Anatomy of a Classic.* New York: St. Martin's Press, 1983.

White, Betty. *Here We Go Again: My Life in Television.* New York: Scribner, 1995.

White, Mimi. *Tele-Advertising: Therapeutic Discourse in American Television.* Chapel Hill: University of North Carolina Press, 1992.

White, Vanna. *Vanna Speaks.* New York: Warner Books, 1987.

Zenda, Thomas H. "*The Mary Tyler Moore Show* and the Transformation of Situation Comedy." In *Media, Myths, and Narratives: Television and the Press,* edited by James W. Carey, 126–145. Newbury Park, CA: Sage Publications, 1988.

Zenka, Lorraine. Days of Our Lives: *The Complete Family Album.* New York: HarperCollins, 1995.

Index

Note: **boldface** page numbers following a heading refer to encyclopedia entries devoted to that topic.